POR QUE SÉ

POR QUE NO

Nuevos Rumbos

Nuevos Rumbos

*A Short Course
for Elementary Spanish*

Ronni L. Gordon
Harvard University Extension

David M. Stillman
Harvard University Extension

With the assistance of
Juan Alberto Méndez-Herrera, Suffolk University

D. C. HEATH AND COMPANY
Lexington, Massachusetts   Toronto

Illustration Credits

Cover painting by Raúl Rodríguez Camacho, in the collection of architects Raúl and Rosa Castillo.

Photographs:

Owen Franken: pp. 1, 43, 45, 223, 245, 259

Bohdan Hrynewych: pp. 143, 187, 190, 241

Terry McCoy: p. 193

Peter Menzel: pp. 17, 29, 57, 73, 91, 93, 109, 141, 157, 173, 207, 273, 288

Spanish National Tourist Office, New York: p. 123

Para nuestros padres

Preface ♣

Nuevos Rumbos: A Short Course for Elementary Spanish has been written for those introductory courses where Spanish is taught in a limited number of class periods. This book is also designed for the student who wishes to acquire a practical command of the language for use with native speakers in everyday situations. *Nuevos Rumbos* covers the fundamentals of Spanish thoroughly enough, however, to enable the student to go on to more advanced work.

In order to achieve our goals we have used an active vocabulary of fewer than 1,200 words and have presented for active control only those grammatical patterns that are essential for basic communication. Structures of lower frequency are provided for recognition only, and the student does not need to master any of them actively in order to proceed successfully through the text. To encourage the use of Spanish as early as possible, we have presented a number of classroom expressions in a section entitled *To the Student* before the regular chapters. These expressions should be used whenever possible so that students will quickly become accustomed to hearing and understanding spoken Spanish without translating it. A section on pronunciation is also included in Appendix C, and the workbook has a complete set of pronunciation practice sections.

Each of the eighteen lessons begins with a list of objectives for student achievement and an outline of the grammatical topics to be studied. New vocabulary and structures are introduced in context by means of short dialogues, letters, and brief narratives that are lively, authentic, and interesting, and that represent different areas of the Spanish-speaking world. New vocabulary, together with further examples of key structural points, is also given in the section entitled *Ampliación*. Comprehension on the initial reading is tested by the *Preguntas sobre la Presentación*. These questions are followed by the *Estructuras*, where the essential structural patterns of Spanish are presented and practiced. Grammatical explanations have been made as clear and succinct as possible in order to facilitate student comprehension and to allow for individualized instruction. Concepts that the student may be unsure of are explained and illustrated with English examples, wherever necessary. We have also endeavored to make grammatical practice meaningful by devising exercises that form a connected narrative or by building exercises around themes that are of high interest to students. The *Estructuras* are followed by communication activities—personal questions, conversations (*Charlas*), and short reports (*Situación*)—that encourage free, spontaneous expression. Each lesson concludes with a variety of written exercises and sentences for translation that may be used for tests or for homework assignments. A review lesson with a cultural reading appears after every third lesson.

Even a cursory perusal of *Nuevos Rumbos* will reveal our firm belief that language and culture are inseparable. We have thus ensured that every element of the text—illustrations, dialogues, readings, examples, and exercises—integrate Hispanic cultural patterns and values, since only by assimilating them will the student be able to make effective use of the Spanish language. We have also stressed the concerns and aspirations of Hispanic minorities in the United States, because many students looking for a practical command of basic Spanish are planning to use the language in work situations involving Hispanics living in this country.

Verb tables, two vocabularies (Spanish-English and English-Spanish), and an Index are also provided. The Spanish-English vocabulary indicates the lesson in which each word or expression first appears, in order to aid teachers in developing supplementary materials and tests.

The *Workbook / Laboratory Manual* for *Nuevos Rumbos* provides extensive writing practice, leading to written self-expression in short paragraphs and compositions. The language laboratory worksheets are to be used in conjunction with the tape program. The ten hours of recorded material provide the student with valuable exercises in grammar and pronunciation as well as numerous opportunities for listening comprehension practice.

Individual lessons of *Nuevos Rumbos* were tested in manuscript form by Dr. Gordon in first-year Spanish classes at the Harvard University Extension. These lessons were successful in awakening interest for further study and in motivating students to communicate in Spanish.

Ronni L. Gordon

David M. Stillman

Acknowledgments

We would like to thank the following friends and acquaintances who gave so unselfishly of their time to serve as linguistic and cultural informants for *Nuevos Rumbos*. Their careful work with the book in manuscript form has immeasurably enhanced the quality and authenticity of our book.

Eduardo Andere   (Mexico)
Celeste and Arturo Díaz   (Puerto Rico)
Hugo Díaz   (Venezuela)
Mario Hurtado   (Cuba)
Dr. Armando Lares   (Venezuela)
Professor Juan Alberto Méndez-Herrera   (Chile)
Gustavo Ochoa   (Ecuador)
Adriana Ospina Lara   (Colombia)
Elena Otamendi de Lares   (Venezuela)
Manuel Rubio Requena   (Spain)

We are also grateful for the valuable insights and constructive criticism of *Nuevos Rumbos* found in the reviews done by Professor Armando Armengol, University of Texas at El Paso, Dr. David Hill, University of South Carolina, Columbia, S.C., and Professor Denise Thompson of the University of Illinois at Chicago Circle.

Special thanks also go to the Modern Language staff of D. C. Heath and Company. Their support and hard work helped in every stage of the preparation of this manuscript.

Contents ❧

10   Cubans in the United States (A Mother and Daughter Speak)   143

11   Banking in Caracas, Venezuela   157

12   Medicine: Bogotá, Colombia (Diary of a Colombian Doctor)   173

13   The Immigration Office, New York City (An Illegal Alien)   193

Appendices 291

Additional Materials

Workbook/Laboratory Manual
Audio Program
  Number of reels: 9 7″ dual track
  Speed: 3-3/4 ips
  Running time: 9 hours (approximately)

Also available in 9 cassettes.

To the Student

The goal of *Nuevos Rumbos* is to give you a practical command of basic Spanish in as short a time as possible. Your teacher will practice the following classroom expressions with you so that you can begin using Spanish as a medium of communication from the first day of class.

Abran los libros.	Open your books.
Cierren los libros.	Close your books.
Escuchen ustedes.	Listen.
Repita usted.	Repeat (*to one person*).
Repitan Uds. or **Repitan todos.**	Everyone repeat.
Todos juntos.	Everyone together.
Conteste.	Answer.
Contesten todos.	Answer, class.
Dígalo en español.	Say it in Spanish.
Hable más fuerte.	Speak louder.
No entiendo.	I don't understand.
Más despacio, por favor.	Slower, please.
Otra vez, por favor.	Again, please.
Siéntese Ud.	Please sit down.
Escriba usted.	Write (*to one person*).
Escriban ustedes.	Write (*to more than one person*).
—¿Cómo se llama usted?	What's your name?
—Me llamo ____.	My name is ____.
—¿Cómo se llama él?	What's his name?
—Se llama ____.	His name is ____.
—¿Cómo se llama ella?	What's her name?
—Se llama ____.	Her name is ____.
—¿Cuál es tu dirección?	What's your address?
—¿Cuál es tu teléfono?	What's your phone number?

(*Student introduces herself.*)

—Claudia Ochoa, para servirle.	I'm Claudia Ochoa.
—Mucho gusto.	Pleased to meet you.

lección 1

Objectives

Structure You will learn the subject pronouns, the present tense of regular verbs of the **-a-** class (1st conjugation), how Spanish nouns differ from English nouns, and how to form questions.

Vocabulary You will learn the days of the week and the names of some important languages.

Conversation By the end of the lesson, you will be able to name the languages you study and tell where and when you work.

Culture You will learn where Spanish is spoken and how it compares with English as a major world language.

Outline

Estructura 1 Subject pronouns / Formal and informal forms of address
Estructura 2 Present tense of **-a-** class (**-ar**) verbs
Estructura 3 *Verb + infinitive* constructions
Estructura 4 Negative sentences
Estructura 5 Question formation
Estructura 6 Gender and number of nouns / Definite and indefinite articles

1. Do You Speak English?

John Reynolds is visiting Spain. He studies Spanish, but he doesn't speak much.

  J.: Excuse me, sir. Do you speak English?
Man: No, I'm sorry. But it seems that you speak Spanish.
  J.: Well, I want to speak Spanish well.
Man: But you already speak Spanish quite well.

2. Antonio Has to Work

Pablo is talking with Antonio. Pablo wants to visit the museum.

P.: Who wants to visit the museum on Tuesday?
A.: Not me. Tuesday I'm working in the store.
P.: What a bore! Do you work all day?
A.: Yes, unfortunately I have to work a lot.
P.: Do they pay well?
A.: Are you kidding? I don't earn much. (= I earn little.)

Presentación

1. ¿Habla usted inglés?

John Reynolds visita España. Él estudia español, pero no habla mucho.

John	—Perdone, señor. ¿Habla usted inglés?
Señor	—No, lo siento. Pero parece que usted habla español.
John	—Bueno, deseo hablar bien el español.
Señor	—Pero Ud. ya habla bastante bien el español.

2. Antonio necesita trabajar

Pablo habla con Antonio. Pablo desea visitar el museo.

Pablo	—¿Quién desea visitar el museo el martes?
Antonio	—Yo no. El martes trabajo en la tienda.
Pablo	—¡Qué lata! ¿Trabajas todo el día?
Antonio	—Sí, por desgracia necesito trabajar mucho.
Pablo	—¿Pagan bien?
Antonio	—¡Qué va! Gano poco.

Ampliación

—Perdone, **señor.**
  (señora, señorita)
—¿Habla usted **inglés?**
  (francés, italiano, portugués,
  alemán, ruso)
—Parece que **usted** habla español.
  (el señor, la señora, la señorita, el
  muchacho, la muchacha.)[1]

*Excuse me, **sir.***
  (ma'am, miss)
*Do you speak **English?***
  *(French, Italian, Portuguese,
  German, Russian)*
*It seems that **you** speak Spanish.*
  *(the man, the woman, the young
  woman, the boy, the girl)*

---

[1] **El chico** and **la chica** are synonymous with **el muchacho** and **la muchacha,** respectively.

—¿Trabajas **hoy** también, Pablo?
  (mañana, pasado mañana, ahora)

*Do you work **today** too, Pablo?*
  (*tomorrow, the day after tomorrow, now*)

—Sí, trabajo todos los días.

Yes, I work every day.

Trabajan en **una tienda.**
  (una oficina, un banco, un café, un restaurante, un hotel, un supermercado)

*They work in **a store.***
  (*an office, a bank, a café, a restaurant, a hotel, a supermarket*)

Trabajamos **los lunes.**
  (los martes, los miércoles, los jueves, los viernes, los sábados, los domingos)

*We work on **Mondays.***
  (*on Tuesdays, on Wednesdays, on Thursdays, on Fridays, on Saturdays, on Sundays*)

¿Quién desea visitar el museo?
  (quiénes desean)

***Who** wants to visit the museum?*
  (*who [pl.] wants to*)

¿Cuándo trabajas?
  (dónde, qué día, con quién, con quiénes)[2]

***When** do you work?*
  (*where, what day, with whom, with whom [pl.]*)

¿Pagan bien o mal?

Do they pay well or badly?

Ganamos **poco.**
  (más, menos, bastante)

*We earn **little.***
  (*more, less, quite a bit*)

NOTAS CULTURALES

1. Cafés are an important institution in Spanish-speaking countries. They are places where people can spend hours over a cup of coffee with friends or play dominoes or cards. Cafés serve alcoholic and nonalcoholic beverages, snacks, and sometimes complete meals.

2. Spanish became a major world language through colonial expansion by Spain. It is the official language of eighteen countries in the Western Hemisphere as well as of Puerto Rico. It still retains a prestigious position in the Philippines and is easily understood by the more than 100 million speakers of Portuguese as well. Spanish is also the first or second language of some 15 million citizens of Hispanic descent in the United States.

3. While written Spanish is relatively uniform throughout the entire Spanish-speaking world, the spoken language shows regional differences in pronunciation, grammar, and vocabulary. These variations are relatively minor, however, as are the differences between American and British English, and pose no problem for mutual understanding among speakers of Spanish.

---

[2] Spanish has a form **quiénes,** *who,* which is the plural of **quién** and is used when the speaker is referring to more than one person.

Preguntas sobre la Presentación

Diálogo 1

1. ¿Qué estudia John Reynolds?
2. ¿Habla bien?
3. ¿Habla el señor inglés?

Diálogo 2

1. ¿Qué desea visitar Pablo?
2. ¿Qué día desea visitar el museo?
3. ¿Dónde trabaja Antonio?
4. ¿Antonio necesita trabajar todo el día?
5. ¿Antonio gana mucho?

Vocabulario activo

ahora   now
el **alemán**   German
el **banco**   bank
  bastante   quite a lot; enough; rather
  bien (*adv.*)   well
  bueno (*interj.*)   well
el **café**   café
la **chica**   girl
el **chico**   boy
  con   with
  ¿cuándo?   when?
  desear   to want
el **día**   day
el **domingo**   Sunday
  ¿dónde?   where?
  en   in
el **español**   Spanish
  estudiar   to study
el **francés**   French
  ganar   to earn; to win
  hablar   to speak, to talk
el **hotel**   hotel
  hoy   today
el **inglés**   English
el **italiano**   Italian
el **jueves**   Thursday
el **lunes**   Monday
  mal (*adv.*)   badly
  mañana   tomorrow
el **martes**   Tuesday
  más   more
  menos   less

el **miércoles**   Wednesday
la **muchacha**   girl
el **muchacho**   boy
  mucho   a lot, much
el **museo**   museum
  muy   very
  necesitar   to need; to have to
  no   no, not
  o   or
la **oficina**   office
  pagar   to pay
  pero   but
  poco   little
el **portugués**   Portuguese
  ¿qué?   what?
  ¿quién? (*pl.* ¿quiénes?)   who?
el **restaurante**   restaurant
el **ruso**   Russian
el **sábado**   Saturday
el **señor**   man, Mr., sir
la **señora**   woman, Mrs.
la **señorita**   young woman, Miss
  sí   yes
el **supermercado**   supermarket
  también   also
la **tienda**   store
  todo   all
  trabajar   to work
el **viernes**   Friday
  visitar   to visit
  y   and
  ya   already

EXPRESIONES

¿con quién, (-es)?   with whom?
lo siento   I'm sorry
parece que   it seems that
pasado mañana   day after tomorrow

perdone, señor   excuse me, sir
por desgracia   unfortunately
¡qué lata!   what a bore!
¡qué va!   are you kidding?, of course not!, nonsense!

Estructura 1

Subject pronouns / Formal and informal forms of address

Análisis

SUBJECT PRONOUNS

Singular		Plural	
yo	I	**nosotros**	we (*masc.*)
		nosotras	we (*fem.*)
tú	you	**vosotros**	you (*masc.*)
		vosotras	you (*fem.*)
él	he, it	**ellos**	they (*masc.*)
ella	she, it	**ellas**	they (*fem.*)
usted	you	**ustedes**	you

▸ **Usted** and **ustedes** may be abbreviated in writing to **Ud.** and **Uds.,** respectively. The full forms and the abbreviations are used interchangeably.

▸ **Tú, usted, vosotros (-as)** and **ustedes** are equivalent to English *you*. The speaker's choice of one of these forms reflects a particular social relationship involving politeness, formality, seniority, as well as number. (English *you* does not change to show any of these categories.)

▸ **Tú** is used in addressing a person with whom one has a relationship that Hispanic culture defines as *informal*: for example, a close friend, a fellow student, a member of one's family (especially someone of the same age or younger), and children.

▸ **Usted** is used to address a person with whom one has a relationship that Hispanic culture describes as *formal*. An older person, a teacher, or a stranger would be addressed in this way.

▸ **Ustedes** serves as the plural for both the informal **tú** and the formal **usted** in Spanish America.

▸ **Vosotros,** the plural of **tú,** is used only in Spain, not in Spanish America. The forms of the verbs used with **vosotros** will appear in verb tables (see Appendix B) but will not be practiced until Lesson 9, the first lesson that deals with Spain.

▸ The plural forms **nosotros, vosotros,** and **ellos** are used to refer to males or to males and females together.

Estructura 2

*Present tense of **-a-** class (**-ar**) verbs*

Análisis

▸ The present tense of verbs of the **-a-** class (**-ar** verbs) is formed in the following manner:

	Stem	Class-vowel	Person-ending	Full form
INFINITIVE				**hablar**
Singular				
1st person	habl-	—	**o**	**hablo**
2nd person	habl-	**a**	**s**	**hablas**
3rd person	habl-	**a**	—	**habla**
Plural				
1st person	habl-	**a**	**mos**	**hablamos**
2nd person	habl-	**á**	**is**	**habláis**
3rd person	habl-	**a**	**n**	**hablan**

▸ All Spanish verbs belong to one of three different classes. The **-a-, -e-,** or **-i-** classes are also known as **-ar, -er, -ir** verbs or first, second, and third conjugation verbs, respectively.

▸ Spanish verbs consist of at least three parts: (1) the stem—the part of the verb that carries the meaning; (2) the class-vowel—the **-a-, -e-,** or **-i-** that tells which class (conjugation) the verb belongs to; and (3) the person-ending that marks the person who performs the action.

▸ The verb forms ending in **-ar, -er, -ir** are known as infinitives. The infinitive is unmarked for person. (Verbs are listed in the infinitive form in the vocabulary lists of this book.)

▸ Spanish verb forms vary according to the subject and do not require the subject pronouns to show to whom the speaker is referring. Spanish speakers use the subject pronouns with verb forms only to highlight or emphasize the subject. In spoken English this is done by moving the principal stress of the sentence onto the subject pronoun. It is important to be aware of this property of English in order to understand the use of the subject pronouns in Spanish:

Trabajamos los jueves.　　　　*We work on Thursdays.*
Nosotros trabajamos los jueves,　*We work on Thursdays, but they*
　pero **ellos** trabajan los viernes.　　*work on Fridays.*

▸ **Usted** and **ustedes** may convey politeness as well as emphasis. They are used with the third person singular and plural forms of the verb, respectively.

▸ The present tense forms of a Spanish verb have several possible meanings in English.

Trabajo. $\begin{cases} \textit{I work.} \\ \textit{I am working.} \\ \textit{I do work.} \end{cases}$

Spanish present tense forms, like the *-ing* form in English, can refer to the future if another element of the sentence expresses future time.

Mañana trabajo.   *I'm working tomorrow.*

Práctica

A. Change the verb according to each new cue.

MODELO: Hablo español.   (tú)   *I speak Spanish.*   (*you*)
          → Hablas español.   *You speak Spanish.*

1. Ganamos mucho.
   (yo, tú, él, nosotros, ellos)

2. Trabajan bastante.
   (Ud., ellos, tú, yo, la chica, tú y yo)

3. Estudias con Antonio mañana.
   (yo, las muchachas, Ud., Ud. y yo, el señor, Uds.)

B. Change the verb according to each new cue. This time include the subjects in your response.

MODELO: Pablo habla español.   (tú)   *Pablo speaks Spanish.*   (*you*)
          → Tú hablas español.   ***You** speak Spanish.*

1. El señor estudia portugués.
   (los señores, yo, nosotros, la señorita, Uds.)

2. Tú y yo visitamos el museo.
   (ellos, la chica, nosotras, tú, Uds.)

3. Ellos pagan hoy.
   (Ud. y yo, las muchachas, Ud., tú, yo, la señora)

C. Change the personal name to **señor** or **señorita** and the verb form from informal to formal. Add **usted.**

MODELO: ¿Hablas español, María?   *Do you speak Spanish, María?*
        → ¿Habla Ud. español, señorita?   *Do you speak Spanish, Miss?*

1. ¿Estudias francés, Carlos?   4. ¿Hablas ruso, Pedro?
2. ¿Trabajas en un banco, Juan?   5. ¿Necesitas estudiar más, Anita?
3. ¿Deseas ganar mucho, Francisca?   6. ¿Visitas el hotel, Elena?

D. Change both the informal and formal singular forms to the plural.

MODELOS: ¿Estudias alemán? ⎫
        ¿Estudia Ud. alemán? ⎬   *Are you studying German?*
        → ¿Estudian Uds. alemán?   *Are you* (pl.) *studying German?*

1. ¿Trabaja Ud. los domingos?   4. ¿Paga Ud. los martes?
2. ¿Hablas francés y alemán?   5. ¿Necesitas ganar más?
3. ¿Estudia Ud. inglés también?   6. ¿Trabajas todos los días?

Estructura 3

Verb + infinitive constructions

Análisis

▸ The following sentences contain two verbs each, the second of which is an infinitive:

Deseo hablar español.   *I want to speak Spanish.*
Necesitamos trabajar.   *We have to work.*

▸ One of the important functions of an infinitive is to serve as a complement (completion form) in *verb + infinitive* constructions.

Práctica

A. Change the subject according to the cues. Do not add subject pronouns.

1. Desea trabajar en una oficina.
   (yo, ustedes, nosotros, ellos, ella)

2. Necesito pagar ahora.
   (Uds. y yo, usted, ellos, el señor, ustedes)

B. Change each verb to a *verb + infinitive* construction by adding the corresponding form of **necesitar.** Follow the model.

MODELO: La señora trabaja en un banco.   *The woman works in a bank.*
→ La señora necesita trabajar   *The woman has to work in a*
en un banco.   *bank.*

1. Hablamos italiano también.
2. Las chicas estudian todo el día.
3. Trabajo en el supermercado.

4. Trabajan los martes.
5. Estudias todos los días.
6. Pagan hoy.

Estructura 4

Negative sentences

Análisis

▸ Spanish sentences are made negative by placing the word **no** before the verb.

No hablamos español.   *We don't speak Spanish.*

▸ In *verb + infinitive* constructions, **no** is placed before the conjugated verb.

El muchacho **no necesita** estudiar.   *The boy **doesn't have** to study.*

Práctica

Answer the following questions in the negative, as in the model.

MODELO: ¿Ganan Uds. bastante?   *Do you earn enough?*
No, no ganamos bastante.   *No, we don't earn enough.*

1. ¿Estudian ellos ruso?
2. ¿Trabaja Ud. menos hoy?
3. ¿Necesitas hablar portugués?

4. ¿Paga Ud. todos los días?
5. ¿Desean Uds. hablar inglés?
6. ¿Habla él con la señorita?

Estructura 5

Question formation

Análisis

▸ In English we usually turn statements into questions by means of the auxiliary verb *do*. There is no equivalent for *do* in Spanish.

▸ Spanish speakers form questions from statements in the following ways:
  1. By changing the intonation of the statement to question intonation.

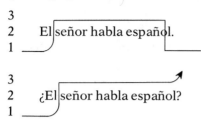

2. By moving the subject to a position after the verb or to the end of the sentence. The element that stands last in the sentence is usually the one the speaker wishes to focus on.

STATEMENT:
La señorita estudia francés.   *The young woman is studying French.*

QUESTION:
¿Estudia la señorita francés?   *Is the young woman studying **French?***

¿Estudia francés la señorita?   *Is **the young woman** studying French?*

NOTE: In addition to the question mark at the end of a sentence, all questions in written Spanish have an inverted question mark at the beginning.

Práctica

Change the following statements into questions. Give three possible answers for each.

1. Las chicas visitan el museo.   4. Los chicos necesitan trabajar.
2. El estudia francés.   5. Usted gana mucho.
3. Ella estudia todos los días.   6. Ella trabaja en el banco.

Estructura 6

Gender and number of nouns / Definite and indefinite articles

Análisis

▸ All Spanish nouns are either masculine or feminine, as indicated by the form of the definite article (English *the*) that precedes them.

▸ Nouns that take the definite article **el** are called masculine; those that take the definite article **la** are called feminine. Before a plural noun **el** changes to **los** and **la** changes to **las**.

> el muchacho   la muchacha
> los muchachos   las muchachas

▸ The Spanish indefinite article (English *a, an*) is **un** before masculine nouns and **una** before feminine nouns. **Un** and **una** have plural forms **unos, unas,** respectively, that mean *some, a couple of.*

> un museo   una oficina
> unos museos   unas oficinas

▸ Summary of the articles:

	Definite article (*the*)		**Indefinite article** (*a, an*)	
	Masculine	*Feminine*	*Masculine*	*Feminine*
Singular	**el**	**la**	**un**	**una**
Plural	**los**	**las**	**unos**	**unas**

▸ Most nouns that end in **-o** or that refer to males are masculine (**el banco, el señor**), while most nouns that end in **-a** or refer to females are feminine (**la oficina, la señora**).[3] Names of languages and the days of the week are masculine (**el francés, el jueves**).

▸ Nouns are made plural in Spanish by adding **-s** to nouns ending in a vowel and **-es** to nouns ending in a consonant.

> chico → chicos   hotel → hoteles

Práctica

A. Give the plural of the following noun phrases (article and noun).

1. el señor
2. el supermercado
3. el chico
4. la muchacha
5. la oficina

B. Change **el** to **un** and **la** to **una** in each of the above entries.

---

[3] Note, however, that **el día** is masculine.

C. Give the singular for each of the following noun phrases.

1. los días
2. los hoteles
3. las tiendas
4. los bancos
5. los restaurantes

Comunicando

Preguntas personales

A. These questions are all directed to **Ud.** Therefore, your answers will be given in the **yo**-form of the verb.

1. ¿Estudia Ud. español o ruso?
2. ¿Necesita Ud. estudiar mucho?
3. ¿Dónde trabaja Ud.?
4. ¿Trabaja Ud. todos los días?
5. ¿Gana Ud. mucho?
6. ¿Qué días estudia Ud. español?

B. These questions are all directed to **Uds.** Answer using the **nosotros**-form of the verb.

1. ¿Qué desean visitar Uds.?
2. ¿Cuándo desean visitar ____?
3. ¿Con quiénes desean visitar ____?
4. ¿Hablan Uds. italiano?

Charlas

The purpose of the **charlas** (*chats*) is to get you to converse in Spanish by providing a topic and questions. Each **charla** is meant to be done between two students or between a student and the instructor. The first student makes the statement appearing in boldface. The second student asks him the questions, one by one, while the first student answers them logically, in accordance with his original statement. For example:

1st Student:

Necesito trabajar hoy.

2nd Student:
¿Dónde trabajas?
¿Trabajas todo el día?
¿Trabajas poco?
¿Ganas bastante?

Possible answers:
Trabajo en un banco.
Sí, trabajo todo el día.
No, trabajo mucho.
¡Qué va! Gano muy poco.

1. —**El señor habla español.**
   ¿Habla español bien o mal?   ¿Hablas tú español?   ¿Necesitas hablar español donde trabajas?

2. —**Deseo visitar el museo.**
   ¿Cuándo deseas visitar el museo?   ¿Con quién deseas visitar el museo? ¿No deseas visitar los hoteles también?

3. —**Necesito trabajar.**
   ¿Dónde desea Ud. trabajar, señor(a), en un restaurante o en un banco? ¿Qué días desea trabajar?   ¿Necesita ganar mucho?

Situación

Report to the class about your studies and job. Tell what you study, where you work and on what days, how much you earn, etc.

Para escribir

A. Rewrite each sentence making the substitution indicated and all necessary changes.

> MODELO: La señorita estudia francés.   (muchachos)
>   → Los muchachos estudian francés.

1. Yo estudio y hablo español todos los días.
   (ella, los chicos, nosotros)

2. El muchacho desea visitar el museo.
   (señoras, chica, muchachos)

3. Los señores pagan mal.
   (ellos, nosotros, Juan Carlos)

4. ¿Trabajas los sábados?
   (Uds., ella, ellas)

5. Gano bastante en el restaurante.
   (nosotros, Uds., la señorita)

B. Write a sentence having the same structure as the original one by making the substitutions indicated.

> MODELO: Juan, ¿con quién estudias   en el museo?
>   (señor)   (trabajar)   (oficina)
>   → Señor, ¿con quién trabaja en la oficina?

1. Los chicos estudian francés los sábados.
   (tú)   (hablar) (inglés)   (domingo)

2. ¿Qué día   desean   ustedes   estudiar?
   (cuándo)   (necesitar)   (él)   (pagar)

3. Señor,   ¿cuándo   estudia usted   español?
   (María)   (con quiénes)   (visitar)   (el museo)

C. Rewrite each of the following sentences in the negative.

1. Las señoras estudian inglés.
2. El chico necesita trabajar hoy.
3. Estudiamos francés los miércoles.
4. Yo deseo visitar el museo.

D. Join each pair of sentences by means of **pero** (*but*). Add the appropriate subject pronoun to each verb, thus contrasting the subjects.

MODELO: Estudio español. / Estudian   *I study Spanish. / They*
          italiano. (*masc.*)   *study Italian.*
          → Yo estudio español,   *I study Spanish but*
          pero ellos estudian   *they study Italian.*
          italiano.

1. Estudiamos los jueves. / Estudias los lunes.
2. Visito las tiendas. / Visita el museo. (*she*)
3. Trabaja en un banco. (*he*) / Trabajas en un restaurante.
4. Pagamos bien. / Paga más. (*you, formal*)

E. Translate the following sentences into Spanish.

1. We don't work in an office on Thursdays.
2. You (*formal sing.*) want to visit some museums the day after tomorrow.
3. Unfortunately the girls need to study German all day. What a bore!
4. Who (*pl.*) do the men want to speak with?
5. Where do I earn more, in the restaurant or in the hotel?

lección 2

Objectives

Structure   You will learn how the present tense of other regular verbs is formed and what demonstratives and quantifying modifiers are. You will also learn how to count to 20.

Vocabulary   You will learn terms related to school and to the professions.

Conversation   By the end of the lesson you will be able to describe your own program in school and find out about the courses your friends are taking.

Culture   You will examine some of the differences between the systems of higher education in the United States and in Spanish-speaking countries.

Outline

Estructura 1   Present tense of **-e-** and **-i-** class (**-er** and **-ir**) verbs
Estructura 2   Demonstrative adjectives **este, ese, aquel**
Estructura 3   Cardinal numbers 1–20
Estructura 4   Quantifying modifiers

The University

Manolo and Joaquín are talking about the classes at the university.

J.: Hi, Manolo, how are things? Are you taking exams this week?
M.: Yes, I'm studying like a madman. I spend my (= the) life in the library.
J.: Are you taking the history exam on Thursday?
M.: Yes, and the economics exam next week.
J.: But what if you don't get a seven on those exams?
M.: Gosh, what a pessimist! I think I study enough.
J.: I also study a lot. I read a lot of books and write compositions.
M.: Are you learning a lot of chemistry and a lot of physics?
J.: Yes, but I'm learning more biology and math.

Presentación

La universidad

Manolo y Joaquín hablan de las clases en la universidad.

Joaquín —Hola, Manolo, ¿qué tal? ¿Tomas los exámenes[1] esta semana?
Manolo —Sí, estudio como un loco. Paso la vida en la biblioteca.
Joaquín —¿Tomas el examen de historia el jueves?
Manolo —Sí, y el examen de economía la semana que viene.
Joaquín —Pero si no sacas siete[2] en esos exámenes . . .
Manolo —Por Dios,[3] ¡qué pesimista! Creo que estudio bastante.
Joaquín —Yo también estudio mucho. Leo muchos libros y escribo composiciones.
Manolo —¿Aprendes mucha química y mucha física?
Joaquín —Sí, pero aprendo más biología y matemáticas.

Ampliación

Enseño en **una escuela.**	*I teach in **an elementary school.***
(un colegio)	(*high school*)
—¿Cuándo llegas al[4] colegio?	*When do you get to [high]school?*
—Llego **temprano.**	*I arrive **early.***
(tarde, a tiempo)	(*late, on time*)
—¿Qué estudias?	*What are you studying?*
—Estudio **medicina.**	*I'm studying **medicine.***
(derecho, ingeniería, literatura, idiomas, ciencias políticas)	(*law, engineering, literature, languages, political science*)

---

[1] **Exámenes** has a written accent mark on the plural form only.
[2] Seven is the passing grade on the scale of ten used in some Spanish-speaking countries.
[3] Literally *by God.* Such oaths are not considered offensive among Spanish-speakers and are used even by religious people.
[4] The preposition **a** (*to*), contracts with **el** (*the*) to form **al.** A does not form contractions with other forms of the definite article: **a la, a los, a las.**

Estudio para **médico.**
   (dentista, abogado, ingeniero,
   profesor, profesora, enfermera)

—¿Cuántas materias tomas este año?

—Debo tomar dos.
—¿Cuáles?
—Tomo sicología y sociología.

—Paso **la vida** en la biblioteca.
   (el fin de semana, mucho / poco /
   tanto / demasiado tiempo)
—¿Por qué estudias tanto?
—Porque deseo sacar buenas notas.

*I'm studying to be a **doctor.***
   (*dentist, lawyer, engineer, teacher*
   [*masc.*], *teacher* [*fem.*], *nurse*)

*How many subjects are you taking this
   year?*
I should take two.
Which ones?
I'm taking psychology and sociology.

*I spend **my life** in the library.*
   (*the weekend, a lot of / not much /
   so much / too much time*)
Why do you study so much?
Because I want to get good grades.

Preguntas sobre la Presentación

1. ¿De qué hablan Manolo y Joaquín?
2. ¿Cómo estudia Manolo?
3. ¿Estudia mucho en la biblioteca?
4. ¿Cuándo toma Manolo el examen de historia?
5. ¿Joaquín lee y escribe mucho?
6. ¿Qué materias toma Joaquín?

NOTA CULTURAL

Since high schools in Spanish-speaking countries are strong in areas such as
literature, philosophy, and history, the student's general education is considered
complete upon graduation from secondary school. Traditionally, universities are
groups of **facultades** or professional schools, such as law, medicine, engineering, arts
and letters, that prepare the student for his or her career. University students,
therefore, take courses only in their area of specialization. Their program usually
consists of from four to six subjects. Classes are mostly in the form of lectures, and
very few elective subjects are allowed.

Vocabulario activo

a   to
el **abogado**   lawyer
el **año**   year
  aprender   to learn
  aquel   that (over there)
  bastante   enough

la **biblioteca**   library
la **biología**   biology
la **ciencia**   science
las **ciencias políticas**   political science
la **clase**   class
el **colegio**   high school; school

como   like, as
¿cómo?   how?
la composición   composition
creer   to think, to believe
¿cuál? (*pl.* ¿cuáles?)   which one(s)?
¿cuánto,(-a)?   how much?
¿cuántos,(-as)?   how many?
de   of, from
deber   should; must; ought
demasiado   too much; (*pl.*) too many
el (la) dentista   dentist
el derecho   law (*subject*)
la economía   economics
la enfermera   nurse
enseñar   to teach
escribir   to write
la escuela   school; elementary school
ese   that
este   this
el examen   test, exam
el fin de semana   weekend
la física   physics
la historia   history
¡hola!   hi!, hello!
el idioma   language
la ingeniería   engineering
el ingeniero   engineer
leer   to read
el libro   book
la literatura   literature
el loco   madman, crazy person
llegar   to arrive
las matemáticas   mathematics
la materia   subject (*school*)

la medicina   medicine
el (la) médico   doctor
muchos,(-as)   many, a lot of
la nota   grade, mark
para   for, to
pasar   to spend (*time*); to happen
pocos,(-as)   few
¿por qué?   why
porque   because
el profesor,(-a)   teacher, professor
que   that, which
la química   chemistry
la semana   week
la sicología   psychology
tanto,(-a)   so much
tantos,(-as)   so many
tarde   late
temprano   early
el tiempo   time
tomar   take
la universidad   university
la vida   life

EXPRESIONES
a tiempo   on time
estudiar para (+ *name of a profession*)   to study to be a ____
pasar la vida   to spend one's life
¡por Dios!   gosh!, my goodness!
¡qué pesimista!   what a pessimist!
¿qué tal?   how are things?, how are you?
sacar buenas / malas notas   to get good / poor grades
la semana que viene   next week

Estructura 1

Present tense of -e- and -i- (-er and -ir) verbs

Análisis

▸ Verbs of the -e- class are conjugated exactly like verbs of the -a- class, except that the class vowel position is occupied by -e- instead of -a-.

	Stem	Class-vowel	Person-ending	Full form
INFINITIVE				**aprender**
Singular				
1st person	aprend-	—	o	**aprendo**
2nd person	aprend-	e	s	**aprendes**
3rd person	aprend-	e	—	**aprende**
Plural				
1st person	aprend-	e	mos	**aprendemos**
2nd person	aprend-	é	is	**aprendéis**
3rd person	aprend-	e	n	**aprenden**

▸ In verbs of the **-i-** class, the class vowel **-i-** appears only in the infinitive and in the **nosotros-** and **vosotros-**forms. It is replaced by **-e-** in the other persons.

	Stem	Class-vowel	Person-ending	Full form
INFINITIVE				**escribir**
Singular				
1st person	escrib-	—	o	**escribo**
2nd person	escrib-	e	s	**escribes**
3rd person	escrib-	e	—	**escribe**
Plural				
1st person	escrib-	i	mos	**escribimos**
2nd person	escrib-	í	s	**escribís**
3rd person	escrib-	e	n	**escriben**

Práctica

A. Change the verb to agree with each new cue.

1. Leemos poco para esta clase.
   (tú, usted, yo, ustedes, él, Ud. y yo)

2. Debemos llegar a tiempo.
   (él, yo, usted, tú, ellas, tú y yo)

3. Escribe tres composiciones.
   (los chicos, la profesora, yo, tú, nosotros, Uds.)

B. Reduce each *verb + infinitive* construction by removing the first verb. Use the original subject in the new sentence.

MODELO: Debemos leer más.   *We ought to read more.*
          → Leemos más.   *We read more.*

1. Deben aprender bastante.
2. No debo llegar tarde.
3. Desean escribir más.
4. Necesitamos escribir cuatro composiciones.
5. Debes leer todo el día.
6. Necesito tomar química.

Estructura 2

*Demonstrative adjectives **este, ese, aquel***

Análisis

➤ Spanish demonstratives, like the definite and indefinite articles, change in form to agree in gender and number with the nouns they modify.

➤ **Este** means *this,* that is, it refers to something associated with or near the speaker. **Ese** and **aquel** both mean *that.* **Ese** labels something associated with or near the person spoken to while **aquel** signals that the noun it modifies is removed from both the speaker and the person spoken to.

➤ The forms of the Spanish demonstrative adjectives:

	este	**ese**	**aquel**
masc. sing. *masc. pl.*	**este** libro **estos** libros	**ese** libro **esos** libros	**aquel** libro **aquellos** libros
fem. sing. *fem. pl.*	**esta** tienda **estas** tiendas	**esa** tienda **esas** tiendas	**aquella** tienda **aquellas** tiendas

NOTE: The demonstratives *this* and *that* are the only modifiers[5] remaining in the English language that show number agreement.

this / that book   these / those books

Práctica

A. Answer each of the following questions in the negative according to the model.

MODELO: ¿Necesitas este libro?   *Do you need this book?*
No, no necesito ese libro.   *No, I don't need that book.*

1. ¿Visitas estos museos?
2. ¿Tomas esta materia?
3. ¿Trabajas en esta oficina?
4. ¿Estudias con estas profesoras?
5. ¿Hablas este idioma?
6. ¿Lees estas composiciones?

---

[5] Words such as articles and demonstratives, which help limit or define a noun, are called *modifiers.*

B. Answer the questions of Exercise A according to the following model.

MODELO: ¿Necesitas ese libro?   *Do you need that book?*
                 No, no necesito este libro.   *No, I don't need this book.*

C. Now answer the questions of Exercise A using **aquel** in both question and answer.

MODELO: ¿Necesitas aquel libro?   *Do you need that book (over there)?*
                 No, no necesito aquel libro.   *No, I don't need that book.*

Estructura 3

Cardinal numbers 1–20

Análisis

▸ The numbers 1–20 in Spanish are:

1	**uno**	6	**seis**	11	**once**	16	**dieciséis**
2	**dos**	7	**siete**	12	**doce**	17	**diecisiete**
3	**tres**	8	**ocho**	13	**trece**	18	**dieciocho**
4	**cuatro**	9	**nueve**	14	**catorce**	19	**diecinueve**
5	**cinco**	10	**diez**	15	**quince**	20	**veinte**

▸ **Uno** is used in counting. It shortens to **un** directly before a masculine singular noun (**un libro**) and changes to **una** before a feminine noun (**una clase**). Its forms are identical to those of the indefinite article.

▸ The numbers 16–19 may also be written as three words each.

diez y seis   diez y siete   diez y ocho   diez y nueve

Práctica

A. Read the following phrases aloud.

1. 5 hoteles
2. 10 exámenes
3. 1 chico
4. 20 días
5. 9 materias
6. 18 profesoras
7. 14 abogados
8. 16 señoritas

B. Read each of the following numbers aloud. Then give the number that follows.

2   4   6   9   12   15   19

Estructura 4

Quantifying modifiers

Análisis

▶ Quantifying modifiers agree in gender and number with the noun they modify.

¿Cuántos idiomas habla usted?	***How many** languages do you speak?*
¿Cuántas materias toma usted?	***How many** subjects are you taking?*
Paso **muchos** días en la biblioteca.	*I'm spending **many** days in the library.*
(pocos, tantos, demasiados)	*(few, so many, too many)*
Estudio **muchas** materias.	*I'm studying **many** subjects.*
(pocas, tantas, demasiadas)	*(few, so many, too many)*

▶ When these quantifying modifiers function as adverbs (that is, as modifiers of verbs), they are invariable: they end in **-o** and do not change for gender and number.

¿Cuánto estudian?	***How much** do they study?*
Estudian **mucho.**	*They study **a lot.***
(poco, tanto, demasiado)	*(not much, so much, too much)*

NOTE: **Todo el, toda la** mean *the whole*: **todo el día,** *all day.*
Todos los, todas las mean *every*: **todos los días,** *every day.*

Práctica

A. Remove the numeral and turn the statement into a question beginning with **¿cuántos?** or **¿cuántas?**

MODELO:	Trece muchachas sacan siete en el examen.	*Thirteen girls get seven on the test.*
	→ ¿Cuántas muchachas sacan siete en el examen?	*How many girls get seven on the test?*

1. Tomo cuatro materias.
2. Quince señoritas toman francés.
3. Ocho profesores enseñan física.
4. Escribimos dos composiciones.
5. Debes aprender nueve idiomas.
6. Leen cinco libros.

B. Repeat Exercise A changing the statements into exclamations using **¡tantos!** or **¡tantas!** instead of the numerals.

MODELO: Trece muchachas sacan siete en el examen.
¡Tantas muchachas sacan siete en el examen!

Comunicando

Preguntas personales

1. ¿Tomas los exámenes ahora?
2. ¿Pasas mucho tiempo en la biblioteca?
3. ¿Llega Ud. temprano a la universidad?
4. ¿Qué materias toma Ud. este año?
5. ¿Lee usted mucho para la clase de sicología? (historia, inglés, literatura)
6. ¿Escribe usted muchas composiciones para la clase de inglés?
7. ¿Para qué clase estudia usted más?

Charlas

1. —**Mañana tomo el examen de química.**
   ¿Estudias mucho?   ¿Dónde estudias?   ¿Cuánto deseas sacar en ese examen?   ¿Qué día tomas el examen de biología?

2. —**Estudio para médico.**
   ¿En qué universidad estudias?   ¿Tomas biología?   ¿Sacas buenas notas en biología?   ¿Y en química?

Situación

Report to the class about your work at college. Tell what you are studying, which exams you are taking now, how your grades are, what you want to be, etc.

Para escribir

A. Rewrite each sentence substituting the verb in parentheses for the original verb. Do not change the subject.

1. **Leemos** la composición.   (escribir)
2. **Toma** historia.   (aprender)
3. **Necesitan** tomar inglés.   (deber)
4. **Hablan** mucho.   (leer)
5. **Deben** sacar buenas notas.   (desear)

B. Compositions. Develop the lead statement into a paragraph by answering the questions.

1. Carlos estudia para ingeniero.
   ¿En qué facultad estudia?
   ¿Qué toma, literatura o matemáticas?
   ¿Qué ciencias debe tomar?
   ¿Debe estudiar mucho?

2. Este año necesitamos estudiar mucho.
   ¿Por qué estudian tanto?
   ¿Qué materias toman?
   ¿Para qué trabajan más?
   ¿Escriben muchas composiciones? ¿En qué clase?
   ¿Pasan mucho tiempo en la biblioteca?

C. Add **todo, toda, todos, todas** to each sentence and make all necessary changes.

> MODELO:　Paso el día con el ingeniero.
> → Paso todo el día con el ingeniero.

1. Necesito escribir las composiciones.
2. Tomo los exámenes la semana que viene.
3. Pasan el fin de semana con Pilar.
4. Trabajamos los miércoles.
5. Hoy deseo visitar los colegios.

D. Translate the following sentences into Spanish. Omit the subject pronouns unless there is a contrast between subjects in a particular sentence.

1. Why are those (*over there*) girls taking sociology?
2. They're spending too much time in the library.
3. This teacher teaches in that high school.
4. I'm not studying to be an engineer.
5. He wants to get good marks in political science, but she wants to get good marks in physics.

lección 3

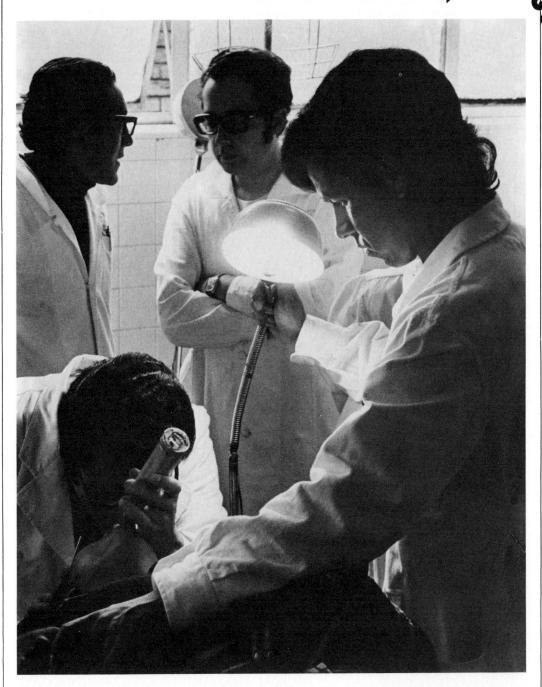

Objectives

Structure   You will learn the forms of **estar** (*to be*) and the irregular verb **tener** (*to have*). You will also practice using the various forms of adjectives.

Vocabulary   You will learn the terms for members of the family and adjectives that describe health and different mental states.

Conversation   By the end of the lesson you will be able to tell how you feel physically and mentally and to inquire about the health of your friends and their families.

Culture   You will learn about the divisions of the day in Hispanic countries, and you will see the contrast in attitudes toward time held by English and Spanish speakers.

Outline

Estructura 1   **Estar** (*to be*)
Estructura 2   Form and agreement of adjectives
Estructura 3   Possessive adjectives
Estructura 4   Use and omission of the definite article with titles
Estructura 5   **Tener; tener que** + *infinitive*

In the Hospital

Juanito Madero has an infection and is in the hospital. Dr. Vargas has just arrived.

Dr. V.: Good morning. How are you today?

   J.: Good morning, doctor. Well, a little better, thanks, but I'm still very tired.

Dr. V.: You have to stay in bed a few more days. Also, you should take two of these pills every four hours.

   J.: But doctor, I have a lot of work this week.

Dr. V.: Never mind. You have to rest. You're sick.

   J.: Gosh, I'm finished (= fried). I have to hand in two papers.

Dr. V.: I understand why you're worried. This afternoon I'll talk with your teachers and I'll explain to them that you're sick.

   J.: Thanks a lot, doctor.

Dr. V.: You're welcome. Goodbye.

Presentación

En el hospital

Juanito Madero tiene una infección y está en el hospital. La doctora Vargas acaba de[1] llegar.

Dra. Vargas	—Buenos días. ¿Cómo está Ud. hoy?
Juanito	—Buenos días, doctora. Pues un poco mejor, gracias, pero todavía estoy muy cansado.
Dra. Vargas	—Necesita guardar cama algunos días más. También, debe tomar dos de estas pastillas cada[2] cuatro horas.
Juanito	—Pero doctora, tengo mucho trabajo esta semana.
Dra. Vargas	—No importa. Ud. tiene que descansar. Está enfermo.
Juanito	—Caray, pues estoy frito. Tengo que entregar dos trabajos.
Dra. Vargas	—Comprendo por qué está preocupado. Esta tarde hablo con sus profesores y les explico que usted está enfermo.
Juanito	—Muchas gracias, doctora.
Dra. Vargas	—De nada. Adiós.

Ampliación

—**Buenas tardes,**[3] señora Madero.   *Good afternoon,* Mrs. Madero.
   (buenas noches)   (*good evening* or *good night*)
—¿Cómo está su **familia?**   *How's your* **family?**
   (esposa, señora, mujer, marido,   (*wife, wife, wife, husband, husband*)
   esposo)[4]

---

[1] **Acabar de** + *infinitive* means *to have just done something.*

[2] **Cada** is invariable: **cada año, cada semana.**

[3] See the **Notas Culturales** for use of these greetings.

[4] **Marido** and **mujer** for *husband, wife* are more common in Spain. **Esposo** and **esposa** are used everywhere. Some speakers use the more respectful **su señora** when referring to someone else's wife.

—¿Cómo está su **hijo** menor / mayor?
    (hija, hermano, hermana)

How's your youngest / oldest
    (younger / older) son?
    (daughter, brother, sister)

—Está **enfermo.**
    (bien, mal, mejor, peor, grave,
    perfectamente)

*He's **sick.***
    (well, sick, better, worse, seriously ill,
    in perfect health)

—¿Qué tiene?
—Tiene un poco de gripe.

What's the matter with her?
She has a touch of the flu.

—¿Dónde está mi **madre?**[5]
    (mamá, padre, papá, abuelo,
    abuela, tío, tía)

*Where's my **mother?***
    (mother, father, father, grandfather,
    grandmother, uncle, aunt)

—¿Está mi **primo?**
    (prima, amigo, amiga)

*Is my (**male**) cousin in?*
    (female cousin, male friend, female
    friend)

—Ese hombre está **en casa.**
    (aquí, ahí, allí)[6]

*That man is **at home.***
    (here, there, there)

—Mis **padres**[7] están ocupados.
    (papás, hermanos, abuelos, tíos,
    primos)

*My **parents** are busy.*
    (parents, brothers and sisters,
    grandparents, aunt and uncle,
    cousins)

—Los estudiantes están **contentos.**
    (alegres, listos, aburridos, tristes)

*The students are **happy.***
    (cheerful, ready, bored, sad)

—Siempre tengo que tomar **pastillas.**
    (aspirinas, medicina)

*I always have to take **pills.***
    (aspirin, medicine)

—La tienda está **cerrada** hoy.
    (abierta)

*The store is **closed** today.*
    (open)

Preguntas sobre la Presentación

1. ¿Dónde está Juanito?
2. ¿Con quién habla?
3. ¿Necesita Juanito guardar cama?
4. ¿Por cuánto tiempo?
5. ¿Por qué está preocupado Juanito?
6. ¿Qué tiene que entregar?

---

[5] In Spain **madre** and **padre** mean *mother, father* while **mamá, papá** mean *Mom, Dad.* Spanish Americans prefer **mamá, papá** for both meanings.

[6] **Ahí** means *there* (near the person spoken to). **Allí** means *over there* (not near the person spoken to).

[7] The masculine plural in Spanish can refer either to groups composed entirely of males or to groups composed of both males and females.

NOTAS CULTURALES

1. Spanish speakers break up the 24-hour period into three parts. The first, **la mañana,** begins at sunrise and lasts until approximately 1 or 2 P.M. It is followed by **la tarde,** which starts at 1 or 2 P.M. and ends at 8 P.M. **La noche** begins when **la tarde** ends and continues until sunrise.

2. Spanish greetings are related to the divisions of the day: **buenos días** (for **la mañana**), **buenas tardes** (for **la tarde**), and **buenas noches** (for **la noche**). These greetings are used both on arriving and departing.

3. The divisions of the day revolve around Hispanic meal schedules. Lunch, the main meal of the day, is eaten between 2 and 3 P.M. in Spain and either then or earlier in Spanish America. Spain's dinner hour is 10 to 11 P.M.; in Spanish America dinner is eaten somewhat earlier, about 8 P.M.

Vocabulario activo

abierto   open
el **abuelo**   grandfather (cf. **la abuela, los abuelos**)
aburrido   bored
adiós   goodbye
ahí   there
alegre   happy, cheerful
alguno,(-a, -os, -as)   some, a few
allí   there
la **amiga**   friend (*fem.*) (cf. **el amigo**)
aquí   here
la **aspirina**   aspirin
bueno   good
cada   each, every
la **cama**   bed
cansado   tired
la **casa**   house
cerrado   closed
comprender   to understand
contento   happy, content
descansar   to rest
el (la) **doctor,(-a)**   doctor
enfermo   sick
entregar   to hand in
la **esposa**   wife (cf. **el esposo**)
el (la) **estudiante**   student
explicar   to explain
la **familia**   family
frito   washed up, done for, finished; lit. fried

gracias   thank you
grave   serious, seriously ill
la **gripe**   flu
el **hermano**   brother (cf. **la hermana**)
la **hija**   daughter (cf. **el hijo**)
los **hijos**   children
el **hombre**   man
la **hora**   hour
el **hospital**   hospital
la **infección**   infection
listo   ready
la **madre, mamá**   mother
el **marido**   husband
mayor   older, oldest
mejor   better
menor   younger, youngest
la **mujer**   woman, wife
nada   nothing
la **noche**   night
ocupado   busy
el **padre**   father
los **padres, papás**   parents
el **papá**   father
la **pastilla**   pill
peor   worse
perfectamente   well, fine
preocupado   worried
el **primo**   cousin (cf. **la prima**)
pues (*interj.*)   well
siempre   always

la **tarde** afternoon, evening
  tener to have
el **tío** uncle (cf. **la tía**)
  todavía still, yet
el **trabajo** work, job; term paper
  triste sad

EXPRESIONES
acabar de (+ *inf.*) to have just done
  something
buenas noches good evening, good night

buenas tardes good afternoon, good
  evening
buenos días good morning
¡caray! gosh!
de nada you're welcome
en casa at home
guardar cama to stay in bed
muchas gracias thanks a lot
no importa never mind
un poco a little

Estructura 1

Estar (*to be*)

Análisis

▶ **Estar** is an irregular verb of the **-a-** class.

	Stem	Class-vowel	Person-ending	Full form
INFINITIVE				**estar**
Singular				
1st person	est-	—	**oy**	**estoy**
2nd person	est-	**á**	**s**	**estás**
3rd person	est-	**á**	—	**está**
Plural				
1st person	est-	**a**	**mos**	**estamos**
2nd person	est-	**á**	**is**	**estáis**
3rd person	est-	**á**	**n**	**están**

▶ The forms of **estar** are stressed on the class-vowel rather than on the stem.

▶ The **yo**-form ends in **-oy**, not **-o**.

▶ **Estar** is the equivalent of *to be* with phrases of location and with adjectives designating conditions the speaker considers resulting from a change, such as those referring to health, fatigue, or frame of mind.

▶ By itself, **estar** means *to be in, to be at home.*

    Lo siento, pero mi padre no **está**.   *I'm sorry but my father **is not in**.*

Práctica

Form sentences with **estar** as answers to questions, according to the model.

> MODELO: —¿Contento? ¿Tú?   *Happy? You?*
>   —Sí, yo estoy contento.   *Yes, I'm happy.*

1. ¿Graves? ¿Esas señoras?
2. ¿Mejor? ¿Aquel profesor?
3. ¿Aburridos? ¿Uds.?
4. ¿Ocupado? ¿Este ingeniero?

5. ¿Preocupada? ¿La dentista?
6. ¿Contento? ¿Yo?
7. ¿Enfermas? ¿Las señoritas?
8. ¿Cerrada? ¿Aquella universidad?

Estructura 2

Form and agreement of adjectives

Análisis

▶ Spanish adjectives agree with their nouns in gender and number. They are divided into two main categories: four-form adjectives and two-form adjectives.

▶ *Four-form adjectives* have a masculine singular in **-o.** They change their form to agree with the noun they modify in gender and number.

> **El hospital** está **abierto.**   **La tienda** está **abierta.**
> **Los hospitales** están **abiertos.**   **Las tiendas** están **abiertas.**

▶ *Two-form adjectives* end in **-e** or in a consonant in the singular. These adjectives do not change form for gender, only for number.

> Mi **hermano** está **triste.**   Mis **hermanos** están **tristes.**
> Mi **hermana** está **triste.**   Mis **hermanas** están **tristes.**

▶ Gender and number agreement applies even if the noun or the pronoun determining it does not appear in the sentence.

> —¿Está Ud. **contento?** (*to a male*)   —¿Está Ud. **contenta?** (*to a female*)
> —Sí, estoy **contento.** (*male answers*)   —Sí, estoy **contenta.** (*female answers*)
>
> Estamos **listos.** (*two or more males   Estamos **listas.** (*two or more
> or one or more males and one or   females speaking*)
> more females speaking*)

Práctica

Change the subject according to each new cue in the following sentences. Make all necessary changes in the verb and in the form of the adjective.

MODELO: Mi primo está enfermo.   (**mi tía**) → *Mi tía está enferma.*

1. Este muchacho está preocupado.   (aquellas chicas, mi primo, tu mamá)
2. Nuestra prima no está contenta.   (ese médico, los estudiantes, las profesoras)
3. Aquel museo está cerrado.   (esta tienda, las oficinas, esos hoteles)

Estructura 3

Possessive adjectives

Análisis

▸ The possessive adjectives in Spanish are:

mi	*my*	**nuestro**	*our*
tu	*your*	**vuestro**	*your*
su	*his, her, your, its*	**su**	*their, your*

IF NOUN IS PLURAL THEN ADJ IS PLURAL

▸ Possessive adjectives in Spanish agree with the nouns they are associated with, just like any other modifiers.

NOT THE PERSON

nuestro hotel	*our hotel*	**nuestra** tienda	*our store*
nuestros hoteles	*our hotels*	**nuestras** tiendas	*our stores*

▸ **Mi, tu,** and **su** have only two forms, a singular and a plural. **Nuestro** and **vuestro** are four-form adjectives, however (see above examples).

▸ **Su** refers to **él, ella, ellos, ellas, Ud., Uds.** It therefore has five possible English translations: *his, her, its, your, their.* Although to an English speaker **su** seems ambiguous, context usually clarifies the person it refers to.

su casa	*his, her, your, their, its house*
sus casas	*his, her, your, their, its houses*

Práctica

In the following sentences, substitute the cues for the italicized word and make all necessary changes.

MODELO: Mi papá no está.   (primos) → Mis primos no están.

1. Su *tío* trabaja aquí.   (padre, primas, amiga, abuelo)
2. Nuestra *escuela* está abierta.   (tiendas, libros, colegio, oficinas)
3. Necesito hablar con mi *abogado*.   (médico, profesores, madre, papás, hermanos)
4. Tu *mamá* está ocupada.   (abuelos, padre, hermana, profesor, tíos)

Estructura 4

Use and omission of the definite article with titles

Análisis

▶ Spanish titles such as **señor, doctor** must be preceded by the definite article when referring to (but not addressing) the particular person.

—Necesito hablar con **la** señora Salas.	*I have to speak with Mrs. Salas.*
—Lo siento, pero no está. ¿Desea hablar con **los** señores[8] Gómez?	*I'm sorry, but she's not in. Do you want to speak with Mr. and Mrs. Gómez?*

▶ When you address a person by his title you omit the article.

—Doctor Vargas, ¿cómo está Ud.?	*Dr. Vargas, how are you?*
—Muy bien, señorita (Camacho),[9] ¿y Ud.?	*Very well, Miss Camacho, and you?*

Notice that Spanish titles are not capitalized unless they occur at the beginning of a sentence.

Práctica

Your secretary announces that someone is here to see you. Get up, shake hands with your guest, and greet him / her as in the model.

MODELO: Aquí está la señora Camacho.   → Buenos días, señora Camacho.

1. Aquí está el doctor Méndez.
2. Aquí está la señorita Villa.
3. Aquí está la profesora Salas.
4. Aquí está el señor Madero.

---

[8] **Señores** means *Mr. and Mrs.* as well as *gentlemen.*
[9] The use of the family name with a title is very formal in Spanish, like English *sir, madam.* The social equivalent for the English **Mr. Díaz** is merely **señor** without the last name.

Estructura 5

Tener; tener que + *infinitive*

Análisis

▸ The forms of **tener**, *to have*, are irregular. **Tener** is a **-g-** verb; that is, in the **yo**-form it has a **-g-** between the stem (**ten-**) and the person-ending (**-o**).

tener	
Singular	*Plural*
tengo	tenemos
tienes	tenéis
tiene	tienen

Tener + **que** + *infinitive* means *to have to do something.*

▸ There is often no equivalent for English *some* or *any* after forms of **tener**.

Tengo aspirinas.	*I have some aspirins.*
¿Tienes pastillas?	*Do you have any pills?*

Práctica

A. Change the verb to agree with each new subject in the following sentences.

1. Tienes doce primos.
   (yo, usted, nosotros, él, ellos, ella)

2. Tenemos que estudiar más.
   (esos estudiantes, mi primo, tú, yo, Ud., ellos, nosotros)

B. Change **deber** or **necesitar** to the corresponding form of **tener que** in these sentences.

MODELO:	Debemos llegar a tiempo.	*We should arrive on time.*
	→ Tenemos que llegar a tiempo.	*We have to arrive on time.*

1. Debe comprender más.
2. Necesito tomar nueve pastillas.
3. ¿Quién debe estar en el hospital?
4. Necesitas guardar cama.
5. Debo descansar.
6. Necesitamos estudiar mucho.

Comunicando

Preguntas personales

1. ¿Cómo estás hoy?
2. ¿Tiene Ud. que tomar medicina?   (pastillas, aspirinas)

3. ¿Cómo está su familia?
4. ¿Dónde están tus abuelos?   (tíos, primos)
5. ¿Están Uds. alegres o tristes hoy? ¿Por qué?
6. ¿Tienen Uds. mucho trabajo esta semana?

Charlas

1. **—Este año tomo muchas materias.**
   ¿Cuántas tiene?   ¿Para qué clase tiene que leer más?   ¿Está contento con todas las materias?   ¿Enseñan bien sus profesores?

2. **—No estoy bien hoy.**
   ¿Estás cansado?   ¿Estás enfermo?   ¿No crees que debes guardar cama? ¿Deseas hablar con el médico?

Situación

(*Two students*)   You are a doctor in a hospital. Your patient is studying to be an engineer, and she is afraid of missing a lot of work because she has the flu. Tell her what she must do to get well and respond to her worries about missing classes and exams.

Para escribir

A. Answer the following questions using the correct form of **estar.**

   MODELO: ¿Contenta? ¿Ana?   → Sí, Ana está contenta.

1. ¿Sus padres? ¿Listos?   5. ¿El hospital? ¿Cerrado?
2. ¿Tu marido? ¿Alegre?   6. ¿Yo? ¿En casa?
3. ¿Mi primo y yo? ¿Bien?   7. ¿Ustedes? ¿Mal?
4. ¿Tú? ¿Preocupado?

B. Complete each sentence with the correct form of the possessive adjective in parentheses.

1. _____ (*our*) tía está grave. 2. ¿Dónde están _____ (*my*) aspirinas? 3. _____ (*his*) oficina está cerrada los sábados.   4. Acabas de leer _____ (*your*) libros.   5. Alicia y Pablo deben tomar _____ (*their*) exámenes.   6. Aquí está _____ (*your, formal*) prima. 7. _____ (*her*) profesora visita el museo. 8. _____ (*our*) médicos ganan demasiado.

C. Change the noun to the plural and make all necessary changes.

1. Mi hija menor descansa.
2. Elena toma su pastilla ahora.

3. ¿Lees tu composición?
4. Luis lee nuestro libro.
5. Su hotel está abierto.

D. Rewrite each sentence as in the model.

MODELO: Creo que Ud. aprende español, *I think you're learning Spanish,*
señora Tirso. *Mrs. Tirso.*
—La señora Tirso aprende *Mrs. Tirso is learning Spanish.*
español.

1. Creo que Ud. trabaja aquí, señor García.
2. Creo que Ud. enseña bien, profesora Salas.
3. Creo que Uds. no pagan bastante, señores García.
4. Creo que Ud. tiene que descansar, señorita Sánchez.
5. Creo que Ud. visita el museo, doctor Pacheco.

E. Translate the following sentences into Spanish.

1. Good morning, Mrs. Madero, how are your children?
2. If you (*formal, singular*) are sick, you have to stay in bed.
3. I'm not ready yet.
4. We've just taken our medicine.[10]
5. Have you (*pl.*) just written a lot of compositions?[10]
6. I've just read her book.[10]
7. Their younger brother is at home because the school is closed today.

---

[10] Use **acabar de** + *inf.* to translate *have just.*

repaso 1

A. *Present tense.* Supply the correct form of the verb in parentheses in each sentence.

> MODELO: El chico *estudia* (estudiar) español.

1. Tu _____ (entregar) dos trabajos esta semana.
2. Yo _____ (deber) tomar unas pastillas.
3. ¿Por qué _____ (estar) Uds. tan tristes hoy?
4. Profesor, ¿cuántos libros _____ (escribir) Ud.?
5. Nosotros _____ (aprender) mucho en historia.
6. Los abogados _____ (escribir) en esta casa.
7. Ellos _____ (trabajar) lejos de aquí.

B. *Verb + infinitive constructions.* Expand each sentence with the verb in parentheses as shown in the model.

> MODELO: Hablo con el señor Salas.   (desear)
> → *Deseo hablar con el señor Salas.*

1. Llegamos a la universidad a tiempo.   (deber)
2. Los estudiantes leen seis libros.   (desear)
3. Tomo el examen.   (acabar de)
4. Estoy en casa los sábados.   (necesitar)
5. ¿Sacas buenas notas en economía?   (tener que)

C. *Adjective agreement.* Add the correct form of the adjective in parentheses.

> MODELO: La señora está *contenta*. (contento)

1. Este hotel está _____.   (abierto)
2. ¿Están _____ (triste) tus papás?
3. Todas aquellas tiendas están _____.   (cerrado)

4. Su esposa está _____ (enfermo) todavía.
5. ¿Por qué están _____ (aburrido) esos enfermeros?

D. *Possessive adjectives*. Complete each sentence with the correct form of the possessive adjective in parentheses.

MODELO: *Mi* (*my*) casa está aquí.

1. Manolo visita el museo con _____ (*his*) abuelos.
2. No ganamos mucho en _____ (*their*) restaurante.
3. _____ (*our*) tía habla cuatro idiomas.
4. ¿Están alegres _____ (*your, informal*) primas?
5. Tomo _____ (*my*) exámenes la semana que viene.
6. _____ (*your, pl.*) hijo mayor está muy ocupado.

E. Translate the following sentences into English.

1. ¡Acabo de leer tantos libros de historia!
2. Sus estudiantes siempre están aburridos en esta clase.
3. Tienen que trabajar todos los días esta semana.
4. Tomo muchas materias porque estudio para ingeniero.
5. ¿Con quién llegan Uds. al colegio los martes?

F. *Reading passage*. Read the following paragraph carefully and answer the questions in *English*.

Estudio historia y ciencias políticas ahora porque deseo estudiar derecho el año que viene. Estudio como una loca porque necesito sacar muy buenas notas en todas mis materias. Cuando mis amigos visitan los museos y los cafés, yo les explico que tengo que escribir un trabajo o leer unos libros para mis clases. ¡Qué lata! Deseo ir (*to go*) con ellos pero no tengo tiempo. Cuando no tengo que estudiar, trabajo en la biblioteca de la universidad. Trabajo allí los lunes, jueves, viernes y sábados. Necesito trabajar tanto para pagar mis estudios (*studies*). Estoy contenta porque no tengo que pagar la residencia (*dormitory*) también. Vivo (*I live*) en casa de mis padres. Ellos no viven muy lejos (*far*) de la universidad y voy (*I go*) todos los días en autobús (*bus*) a mis clases.

COMPREHENSION CHECK
1. ¿Qué materias estudia esta estudiante?
2. ¿Por qué tiene que sacar muy buenas notas?
3. ¿Pasa mucho tiempo con sus amigos en los museos y en los cafés?
4. ¿Dónde trabaja y por qué?
5. ¿Por qué no necesita pagar la residencia?

lección 4

Objectives

Structure   You will learn the forms of **ser,** the other Spanish verb meaning *to be,* and what Spanish speakers signal when they choose between **ser** and **estar.** You will also see how Spanish and English differ on the position of adjectives and on the expression of possession.

Vocabulary   You will learn the names of countries and nationalities and some words for physical characteristics.

Conversation   After finishing the lesson you will be able to describe yourself and your friends and to tell about your ethnic origins.

Culture   You will learn something about the ethnic variety of Spanish America and about the Hispanic community in the United States. You will also read about Hispanic attitudes towards family life.

Outline

Estructura 1   **Ser** (*to be*)
Estructura 2   Possession
Estructura 3   **Ser** contrasted with **estar**
Estructura 4   Adjectives of nationality
Estructura 5   Position of adjectives

Where Are They From?

1. Why is it hard to believe that this man is Chilean? Because he's so tall and blond? The fact is he's of German background, like many Chileans.
2. This dark-haired woman is my neighbor. She's Argentine, but she's married to an American. She has three very handsome children.
3. Do you think these children are speaking Spanish because they're from South America? You're wrong. They're from Brazil and, of course, Brazilians don't speak Spanish. They speak Portuguese.
4. Those women are Cubans, but they live in the United States. The Spanish-speaking community of this country is very large. Most Spanish speakers are Mexicans, Puerto Ricans, or Cubans, but there are also many from other countries.

Presentación

¿De dónde son?

1. ¿Por qué es difícil creer que este hombre es chileno? ¿Porque es tan alto y rubio? Es que es de origen alemán, como muchos chilenos.

2. Esta mujer morena es mi vecina. Ella es argentina, pero está casada con un norteamericano. Tiene tres hijos muy guapos.

3. ¿Ud. cree que estos niños hablan español porque son de Sudamérica? Está equivocado. Son de Brasil y, claro, los brasileños no hablan español. Hablan portugués.

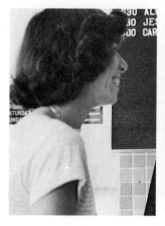

4. Aquellas señoras son cubanas, pero viven en los Estados Unidos. La comunidad hispana de este país es muy grande. La mayor parte de los hispanos son mexicanos, puertorriqueños o cubanos, pero también hay muchos de otros países.

THERE IS
THERE AR

45

Ampliación

Es **difícil** vivir en este país. (fácil)	It's **hard** to live in this country. (*easy*)
—¿De dónde es la novia de Luis? —Es **del Canadá.** (de Cuba, de México, de Hispanoamérica)	*Where is Luis's girlfriend from?* *She's from* **Canada.** (*from Cuba, from Mexico, from Spanish America*)
—¿De qué nacionalidad[1] es Ud.? —Soy **venezolano.** (colombiano, francés, español, italiano)	*What nationality are you?* *I'm* **Venezuelan.** (*Colombian, French, Spanish, Italian*)
—¿De qué origen son Uds.? —Somos de origen **inglés.** (irlandés, ruso, europeo)	*What background, extraction are you?* *We're of* **English** *background.* (*Irish, Russian, European*)
—¿De dónde eres? —Soy de **Francia.** (Inglaterra, España, Italia, Irlanda, Rusia, Alemania, Europa)	*Where are you from?* *I'm from* **France.** (*England, Spain, Italy, Ireland, Russia, Germany, Europe*)
—¿Dónde viven Uds.? —Vivimos en **Colombia.** (Venezuela, Puerto Rico, Chile, Argentina, Latinoamérica)	*Where do you* (pl.) *live?* *We live in* **Colombia.** (*Venezuela, Puerto Rico, Chile, Argentina, Latin America*)
—¿Cómo es tu amigo? —Es **gordo.** (delgado, pequeño, feo)	*What does your friend look like?* *He's* **fat.** (*thin, small, ugly*)
—¿Cómo son tus amigas? —Son **bonitas.** (viejas, jóvenes)	*What are your friends* (fem.) *like?* *They're* **pretty.** (*old, young*)

Preguntas sobre la Presentación

1. ¿Cómo es el chileno?
2. ¿De qué origen es?
3. ¿De dónde es la vecina?
4. ¿Hablan español en el Brasil?
5. ¿Hay muchos hispanos en los Estados Unidos?
6. ¿De dónde son la mayor parte de esos hispanos?

---

[1] **Nacionalidad** in Spanish refers to the country a person is a citizen of. For ethnic background, use **el origen.**

NOTAS CULTURALES

1. **Hispanoamérica** refers to the Spanish-speaking countries of the Western Hemisphere and therefore does not include Brazil and Haiti, for example, where the official languages are Portuguese and French, respectively. **Latinoamérica** includes the Spanish-speaking countries of the New World plus Brazil and Haiti.

   The adjective **hispanoamericano** refers to people from **Hispanoamérica.** **Hispano** means *Spanish-speaking*, whether from a Spanish-speaking country or not (e.g., **chicanos** are **hispanos** as much as Mexicans are).

2. Although the pressures of urbanization are increasing the number of nuclear families in Spain and Spanish America, the presence of other relatives in a household is by no means rare. Grandparents, aunts, and uncles often live with relatives and are treated as integral parts of the family.

3. It is typical of Hispanic countries for people to live near, if not with, their families. Married couples often live a few blocks from their parents. Sisters, brothers, uncles, and aunts are usually nearby as well. Family gatherings occupy a prominent place in the social life of most Spanish-speaking people.

Vocabulario activo

Alemania   Germany
alto   tall; high
la **Argentina**   Argentina[2]
argentino   Argentine
bonito   pretty
el **Brasil**   Brazil[2]
brasileño   Brazilian
el **Canadá**   Canada[2]
casado   married
claro   of course
Colombia   Colombia
colombiano   Colombian
la **comunidad**   community
Cuba   Cuba
cubano   Cuban
Chile   Chile
chileno   Chilean
delgado   thin
difícil   difficult, hard
equivocado   wrong
los **Estados Unidos**   United States[2]
Europa   Europe

europeo   European
fácil   easy
feo   ugly
Francia   France
gordo   fat
grande   big, large
guapo   good-looking
hispano   Spanish-speaking
Hispanoamérica   Spanish America
Inglaterra   England
Irlanda   Ireland
irlandés   Irish
Italia   Italy
joven   young (*pl.* **jóvenes**)
Latinoamérica   Latin America
mexicano   Mexican
México   Mexico
moreno   dark-haired, dark-skinned
la **nacionalidad**   nationality
el (la) **niño,(-a)**   child
norteamericano   American
la **novia**   girlfriend (cf. **el novio**)

---

[2] The definite article is optional with the names of these countries.

el **origen**   origin, background
otro   other
el **país**   country, nation
pequeño   small, little
Puerto Rico   Puerto Rico
puertorriqueño   Puerto Rican
rubio   blond, fair-skinned
Rusia   Russia
ruso   Russian
Sudamérica   South America
tan   so (*before adj. or adv.*)
el (la) **vecino,(-a)**   neighbor
venezolano   Venezuelan

Venezuela   Venezuela
viejo   old
vivir   to live

EXPRESIONES
es que   the fact is that, it's because
estar casado con   to be married to
estar equivocado   to be wrong
hay (+ *noun*)   there is, there are
la mayor parte de   most of
ser de origen francés   to be of French
   extraction

Estructura 1

Ser (*to be*)

Análisis

▶ The forms of the verb **ser,** *to be,* are irregular.

ser	
Singular	*Plural*
soy	somos
eres	sois
es	son

Práctica

A. Change the verb to agree with each new subject.

Somos de Europa.
(tú, él, yo, Ud., Uds., nosotros, ellos)

B. Mr. Paso thinks that you, your family, and your friends are foreign, but you're all from the United States. Tell him so.

MODELO: —Creo que María es de España.
              —Usted está equivocado. María es de los Estados Unidos.

1. Creo que Ud. es de Francia.

2. Creo que sus padres son de Colombia.

3. Creo que su tía es de
   Inglaterra.
4. Creo que su amigo es de
   México.

5. Creo que su médico es
   de Italia.
6. Creo que Uds. son de
   Europa.

Estructura 2

Possession

Análisis

▸ Spanish expresses possession with the preposition **de**. Spanish has no equivalent for the English markers of possession *'s, s'*.

El hermano de Luisa trabaja en la
tienda **del**³ señor Camacho.

*Luisa's brother works in Mr.
Camacho's store.*

Práctica

A. By making the substitutions indicated inquire about where Mrs. Pacheco's relatives come from.

¿De dónde es **el tío** de la señora Pacheco?
(la tía, los abuelos, el papá, la mamá, las primas)

B. Translate the following phrases into Spanish.

1. Mr. and Mrs. Camacho's children
2. the lawyer's office
3. the man's country
4. Dr. Vargas' hospital
5. my cousins' school
6. those teachers' classes

Estructura 3

Ser contrasted with estar

Análisis

Spanish has two verbs that are equivalent to English *be*: **ser** and **estar**.

---

³ **de** + **el** contract to **del** (cf. **a** + **el** → **al**).

SER

▸ **Ser** is used before phrases beginning with **de** that express origin and possession.

> Somos de Puerto Rico.
> *We're from Puerto Rico.*

> El libro es de Carlos.
> *The book is Carlos'.*

▸ **Ser** is used to link two nouns or pronouns. Both nouns or pronouns may appear in the sentence, or one of them (the subject) may be deleted.

> —¿Tu papá es profesor?[4]
> *Is your father a teacher?*
> —No, es dentista.[4]
> *No, he's a dentist.*

▸ **Ser** is used before adjectives to indicate that, for the speaker, the condition expressed by the adjectives does not result from a change.

> Mi amiga es española.
> *My friend is Spanish.*

> Pedro es rubio.
> *Pedro is blond.*

Thus **ser** is usually used with adjectives expressing color, nationality, beauty, and age, which are characteristic of the subject.[5]

▸ The choice of **ser** or **estar** affects the meaning of the sentence.[6]

Mi primo es gordo.

Mi primo está gordo.

ESTAR

▸ **Estar** is used to express location.

> Madrid está en España.
> *Madrid is in Spain.*

> El médico está en el hospital.
> *The doctor is in the hospital.*

SER + DE
ESTAR + EN

JUAN = PROFESOR

▸ **Estar** is used before adjectives to indicate that the speaker perceives the condition expressed by the adjective as resulting from a change.

> Los estudiantes están
> enfermos.
> *The students are sick.*

Thus **estar** is more common with adjectives describing mental or physical states.

My cousin is fat. (No change is perceived; he's a fat person.)
My cousin is fat. (This condition results from a change; he has gotten fat, looks fat to me.)

---

[4] Spanish omits **un, una** between **ser** and a noun of profession or nationality.

[5] **Contento** is used only with **estar.**

[6] Note also **ser listo** (*to be smart*), **estar listo** (*to be ready*).

▸ Notice that the question **¿Cómo está María?** inquires about conditions resulting from a change such as health, while **¿Cómo es María?** inquires about conditions the speaker does not see as resulting from a change and means *What is María like?* or *What does María look like?*

Práctica

A. Practice using **ser** and **estar** in typical sentences by making the substitutions indicated.

1. María es *de los Estados Unidos*.
   (la hija del doctor Camacho, estudiante, alta, morena, bonita, mi prima)

2. Mis primos están *en México*.
   (bien, con su familia, en casa de sus tíos, muy contentos)

B. Answer the following choice questions about an imaginary female friend. Select one of the alternatives in your answer.

1. ¿De dónde es tu amiga, de Francia o de Alemania?
2. ¿Qué es, estudiante o profesora?
3. ¿Cómo está, bien o enferma?
4. ¿Dónde está ahora, en la universidad o en su casa?
5. ¿Cómo es, alta o pequeña?
6. ¿Es rubia o morena?

C. *Oral composition.* Make up five sentences about a friend or relative using **ser** or **estar.** Tell where he (or she) is from, where he is now, what profession he has, what he looks like, and how he feels.

D. Make up an oral composition similar to the one outlined in Exercise C, but instead, talk about two or more people, e.g., your sisters, your cousins, a couple you know, etc.

calle de ud. por favor.

cállate

cállate (tonta)
stupid

Estructura 4

Adjectives of nationality

Análisis

▸ Adjectives of nationality are not capitalized in Spanish.

▸ Adjectives of nationality that end in **-o** have the expected four forms.

   chileno   chilena   chilenos   chilenas

▸ Adjectives of nationality, whose masculine singular form ends in a consonant such as **español,** also have four forms. Note, however, that the masculine plural of these adjectives ends in **-es,** not **-os.**

español	francés	alemán
española	francesa	alemana
españoles	franceses	alemanes
españolas	francesas	alemanas

▸ When accompanied only by an article or other determiner, adjectives of nationality are used as nouns referring to people. The masculine singular form of adjectives of nationality when appearing with the definite article **el** may also refer to the language.

la inglesa	*the Englishwoman*	el italiano	*Italian language, the Italian*
los alemanes	*the Germans*	el ruso	*Russian, the Russian*

Práctica

A. Change the subject in each of the following sentences and then make all other necessary changes.

1. ¿Aquel hombre es francés o alemán?
(esos señores, la muchacha, mis amigas, mi novio)

2. Señor Gómez, ¿es Ud. mexicano?
(Muchachas, Profesora Díaz, Señores Vargas, Alberto y Carlos, Doctor Sánchez)

B. Answer each question affirmatively using the appropriate adjective of nationality as in the model.

MODELO: ¿Es de España tu profesora? *Is your teacher from Spain?*
Sí, es española. *Yes, she's Spanish.*

1. ¿Es de Italia el abogado?
2. ¿Son de la Argentina tus tíos?
3. ¿Son de los Estados Unidos las aspirinas?
4. ¿Es de Irlanda esa niña?
5. ¿Es de Rusia su novia?
6. ¿Son de Europa aquellos libros?

Estructura 5

Position of adjectives

Análisis

▸ In English, adjectives always precede the nouns they are associated with: *a big house.* In Spanish the normal position of adjectives is *after* the nouns they modify.

mi novio mexicano   *my Mexican boyfriend*
una casa grande   *a big house*

However, the following modifiers *precede* their nouns:

1. The articles **el, la, los, las; un, una**

2. Quantifying adjectives: the numbers; **unos, unas; muchos, muchas; poco, poca, pocos, pocas; algunos, algunas**

Tengo $\left\{\begin{array}{l}\textbf{muchos}\\ \textbf{pocos}\\ \textbf{algunos}\\ \textbf{unos}\end{array}\right\}$ amigos.

3. The possessives **mi(-s), tu(-s), su(-s), nuestro(-a, -os, -as), vuestro(-a, -os, -as)**

   Su hermana está casada con **mi** tío.

4. **Este, ese,** and **aquel**

   Esta señora y **esa** señora son españolas.

Práctica

Transform each of the following sentences according to the model.

MODELO: La muchacha es rusa. →   Es una muchacha rusa.

Las muchachas son rusas. →   Son unas muchachas rusas.

1. La materia es difícil.
2. Los médicos son venezolanos.
3. La casa es pequeña.
4. Las composiciones son fáciles.
5. El niño es guapo.
6. El país es grande.

Comunicando

Preguntas personales

1. ¿De qué nacionalidad es Ud.? ¿De qué origen?
2. ¿De qué origen es su familia?
3. ¿Es Ud. alto y moreno (alta y morena)?
4. ¿En qué país viven Uds.?
5. ¿Hay muchos hispanos donde Ud. vive?
6. ¿Tiene Ud. novio (novia)? ¿Cómo es?

Charlas

1. **—Estoy casada con un venezolano.**

   ¿Cómo es él? ¿Viven Uds. en Venezuela? ¿Hay muchos europeos en Venezuela? ¿Qué hablan los venezolanos?

2. **—Un primo de los señores García llega hoy de México.**

   ¿Es mexicano? ¿Cuántos días desea pasar aquí? ¿Vive en casa de los García o en un hotel? ¿Es joven o viejo?

Situación

Your boyfriend (girlfriend) is of a different cultural background from yours. Discuss your friend's background, language, and family. Tell where that person lives and what he or she looks like.

Para escribir

A. In each of these sentences, supply the correct form of the adjective of nationality and the name of the corresponding country as in the model.

   MODELO: Elvira es *española* (español). Es de *España*.

1. Juan y José son _____ (mexicano). Son de _____.
2. Soy _____ (inglés). Soy de _____.
3. Somos _____ (alemán). Somos de _____.
4. Eres _____ (colombiano). Eres de _____.
5. María es _____ (norteamericano). Es de _____.

B. Add the proper form of **ser** or **estar,** as required, to the following sentences.

1. Los señores _____ contentos.
2. Mi tía _____ en Francia.
3. Toda mi familia _____ de Venezuela.
4. Nuestro país _____ grande.
5. Estos libros italianos _____ de nuestro profesor.
6. Yo _____ enfermo.
7. Nosotros necesitamos _____ allí hoy.
8. El no _____ abogado.
9. México y Argentina _____ en Latinoamérica.
10. Todas las tiendas _____ abiertas hoy.

C. Answer each of the following questions in a complete sentence. Your answers will tell something about Gloria Díaz.

1. ¿Cómo es Gloria Díaz, alta y morena o baja y rubia?
2. ¿Es francesa o española?

3. ¿Dónde estudia, en un colegio o en la universidad?
4. ¿Cómo son sus clases, fáciles o difíciles?
5. ¿Para qué estudia, para profesora o para abogado?

D. Translate into Spanish.

1. my grandmother's house
2. that professor's wife
3. Dr. Vargas' brother
4. this hotel's restaurant
5. your uncle's supermarket
6. the student's composition

E. Translate the following sentences into Spanish. Choose carefully between **ser** and **estar** in those sentences having forms of *to be*.

1. What does your friend look like? Is she tall and blond?
2. My neighbor is married to a Cuban (woman).
3. There is a large American community in Italy.
4. That (*far removed*) book is very easy.
5. You're wrong, Pablo. It's very difficult.
6. All the students are bored in that class.
7. England and France are European countries.
8. Most Puerto Ricans study English.
9. There are three good-looking children in that family.
10. Luisa's boyfriend is of French extraction.

lección 5

Objectives

Structure   You will learn some verbs that have changes in the stem vowel. You will also learn how to select the correct direct object pronoun in Spanish. You will be introduced to the two Spanish verbs meaning *to know*, **saber** and **conocer**, and you will practice forming questions.

Vocabulary   The words for several articles of clothing and colors will now become part of your active vocabulary. You will also learn the numbers 21–99.

Conversation   When you finish the lesson, you will be able to buy clothing in a store and discuss your wardrobe.

Culture   You will be able to compare shopping in a Venezuelan department store with your own shopping experience in the United States. You will learn about Hispanic attitudes towards personalized service.

Outline

Estructura 1   Stem-changing verbs (**e → ie, o → ue**)
Estructura 2   Noun objects and personal **a**
Estructura 3   **Ver** (*to see*); **saber** and **conocer** (*to know*)
Estructura 4   Direct object pronouns
Estructura 5   Interrogative words (Summary)
Estructura 6   Question formation; **¿verdad?** and **¿no?**
Estructura 7   Cardinal numbers 21–99

In a Venezuelan Store

Rafael Pereda wants to buy a gift for his girlfriend, Amelia. His friend Enrique Villa goes with him (= accompanies him) to El Bazar Bolívar, where they intend to look for the gift in the blouse department.

R.:   Enrique, I don't know if they sell good clothing here. I don't know this department store well.

E.:   Of course you can find something good and cheap, too.

R.:   Terrific! (= How good!) If I see that the blouses aren't expensive, I can buy two.
   Rafael and Enrique arrive at the blouse department, and they call the saleswoman:

S.:   As you can see, there are several styles and colors. What color do you prefer?

R.:   Maybe that yellow one. Amelia always wears light-colored clothing.

S.:   Here it is. It's made of cotton. And the young woman can wear it with a skirt or pants.

R.:   It's beautiful. And it only costs 60 *bolívares*. It's a bargain!

Presentación

En un almacén venezolano

Rafael Pereda quiere comprar un regalo para su novia, Amelia. Su amigo Enrique Villa lo acompaña al Bazar Bolívar[1] donde piensan buscar el regalo en la sección de blusas.

Rafael	—Enrique, no sé si venden ropa buena aquí. No conozco bien este almacén.
Enrique	—Chico, claro que puedes encontrar algo bueno y barato también.
Rafael	—¡Qué bueno! Si veo que las blusas no son caras, puedo comprar dos.
	Rafael y Enrique llegan a la sección de blusas y llaman a la dependienta:
La dependienta	—Como Ud. puede ver, hay varios modelos y colores. ¿Qué color prefiere?
Rafael	—Quizás esa amarilla. Amelia siempre lleva ropa de color claro.
La dependienta	—Aquí la tiene. Es de algodón. Y la señorita puede llevarla con falda o con pantalón.
Rafael	—Es hermosa. Y sólo cuesta sesenta bolívares. ¡Es una ganga!

Ampliación

—¿De qué color es tu abrigo?
—Es **blanco.**

   (rojo, azul, verde, gris, negro, marrón, café, anaranjado, de un color oscuro)

What color is your overcoat?
*It's **white.***

   (*red, blue, green, gray, black, brown, brown, orange, a dark color*)

---

[1] A large Venezuelan department store with many branches in Caracas.

59

—¿Qué piensa Ud. comprar?	*What do you intend to buy?*
—Pienso comprar **el suéter.**	*I intend to buy **the sweater.***
(el traje, el vestido, el saco,[2] la camisa, los zapatos, las corbatas, los calcetines, los guantes)	*(the suit, the dress, the jacket, the shirt, the shoes, the ties, the socks, the gloves)*
—¿Es cara esta ropa?	*Is this clothing expensive?*
—No, es barata.	*No, it's cheap.*
—Los precios son altos, ¿verdad?	*The prices are high, aren't they?*
—No, son bajos.	*No, they're low.*
—¿A quién conoces?	*Whom do you know?*
—Conozco al cliente.	*I know the customer.*

Alto

Preguntas sobre la Presentación

1. ¿Qué quiere comprar Rafael Pereda?
2. ¿Dónde piensa comprarlo?
3. ¿Quién lo acompaña?
4. ¿Cómo es la ropa en el almacén?
5. ¿La novia de Rafael prefiere colores oscuros?
6. ¿De qué es la blusa amarilla?
7. ¿Cuánto cuesta el regalo para Amelia?

NOTAS CULTURALES

1. Caracas, the capital of Venezuela, is near the northern coast of the country, not far from the Caribbean Sea. Venezuela's oil-rich economy makes it unique in Latin America. Per capita income is higher than in most Latin-American countries, and people have more money to spend on consumer goods. Signs of industrialization and modernization are noticeable in the capital, as new urban areas and modern architecture replace old colonial structures.

2. In spite of the impact of mass-merchandising in Latin America and Spain, many consumer goods, such as custom-made clothing and shoes, have not yet become the nearly unattainable luxuries that they are in the United States.

    In many aspects of everyday life Hispanic culture prefers an alternative that provides an opportunity for personal contact rather than one which, to people in the United States, might seem more efficient but which is depersonalized.

3. The **bolívar** is the monetary unit of Venezuela. It was named for Simón Bolívar (1783–1830), the Venezuelan leader known as "the liberator" because of his efforts in Venezuela's ten-year struggle to free itself from Spanish rule.

---

[2] Some speakers use **la chaqueta** or **la americana** for jacket.

ALTOS

MEDIANOS

NORMALES

Comunes

Vocabulario activo

el **abrigo**   coat, overcoat
acompañar   to go with, to accompany
algo   something
el **algodón**   cotton
el **almacén**   department store
amarillo   yellow
anaranjado   orange
azul   blue
bajo   low; short
barato   cheap
blanco   white
la **blusa**   blouse
el **bolívar**   monetary unit of Venezuela
buscar   to look for
café   brown
el **calcetín**   sock
la **camisa**   shirt
caro   expensive
claro   light (*in color*)
el (la) **cliente**   customer, client
el **color**   color
comprar   to buy
conocer (yo conozco)   to know
la **corbata**   necktie
costar (o → ue)   to cost
el **dependiente**, la **dependienta**
salesperson, clerk
encontrar (o → ue)   to find
la **falda**   skirt
la **ganga**   bargain
gris   gray
el **guante**   glove
hermoso   beautiful
llamar   to call

llevar   to wear; to carry, take
marrón   brown
el **modelo**   style
negro   black
oscuro   dark
el **pantalón (or los pantalones)**   pants
pensar (e → ie)   to think
poder (o → ue)   can, to be able to
el **precio**   price
preferir (e → ie)   to prefer
querer (e → ie)   to want
quizás   maybe, perhaps
el **regalo**   gift
rojo   red
la **ropa**   clothes, clothing
saber (yo sé)   to know
el **saco**   jacket
la **sección**   department (*in a store*)
si   if
sólo   only
el **suéter**   sweater
también   also
el **traje**   suit
varios   several
vender   to sell
ver (yo veo)   to see
verde   green
el **vestido**   dress
el **zapato**   shoe

EXPRESIONES
pensar (+ *inf.*)   to intend to
¡qué bueno!   terrific!

Estructura 1

Stem-changing verbs (e → ie, o →ue)

Análisis

▶ Many Spanish verbs have changes in the vowels of the stem in those forms of the present tense where the stress falls on the stem. The changes are **e → ie** and **o → ue**. Note that these verbs are regular in their class vowels and person endings.

querer (e → ie)		poder (o → ue)	
Singular	*Plural*	*Singular*	*Plural*
quiero	queremos	puedo	podemos
quieres	queréis	puedes	podéis
quiere	quieren	puede	pueden

▸ The **nosotros** and **vosotros** forms and the infinitive are not stressed on the stem and therefore do not have these changes.

▸ Since it is impossible to predict from the infinitive alone which verbs have these changes, it is necessary to memorize any stem changes a verb may have along with its meaning.

Práctica

A. Change the verb according to the cues.

1. Piensan comparlo.
   (yo, ella, nosotros, Uds., Rafael, tú)
2. No puedo llegar a tiempo.
   (ellos, Ud., tú y yo, Amelia, él, tú)
3. Encontramos algo bueno.
   (Uds., yo, tú, el cliente, ellos, Ud.)
4. Quiere estudiar español.
   (yo, nosotros, Ud., mi hija, ellas, Uds.)

B. Answer the following questions using the cue in parentheses according to the model.

MODELO: —¿Qué piensa Ud. vender?   *What do you intend to sell?*
          (mi casa)   *(my house)*
      —Pienso vender mi casa.   *I intend to sell my house.*

1. ¿Qué piensas buscar?   (un abrigo)
2. ¿Qué pueden Uds. escribir?   (una composición)
3. ¿Qué quiere él llevar?   (el traje)
4. ¿Qué encuentran los chicos?   (los zapatos)
5. ¿Qué prefieres ver?   (esa biblioteca)

Estructura 2

*Noun objects and personal **a***

Análisis

▸ The basic element of a sentence is the verb. In English a verb always has a subject and may have one or more objects. The subject is the element of the sentence that helps to determine the form of the verb: *I **work**; John **works.***

▶ The idea or thought expressed by the subject and verb may be completed by a noun object or pronoun. These completion elements are called *complements.* In English a direct object is a complement that cannot be separated from the verb by a preposition.

> He sees the *saleswoman.*   (*direct object noun*)
> He sees *her.*   (*direct object pronoun*)

▶ In Spanish a direct object noun that refers to a specific, *animate* being must be preceded by the preposition **a.**

> Veo **el almacén.**   *I see **the department store.*** (direct object not animate: **a** not required)
>
> Veo **a la dependienta.**   *I see **the saleswoman.*** (direct object specific and animate: **a** required)

This use of the preposition **a** is called *personal* **a.** It has no equivalent in English structure.

NOTE: The personal **a** is not used after **tener.**

Práctica

Construct sentences according to the models. Use personal **a** where necessary.

> MODELO: Comprendo / la materia   → Comprendo la materia.
>   Comprendo / mis abuelos   → Comprendo a mis abuelos.

1. Buscamos / un regalo / los dependientes / Juanito / la ropa
2. Debes conocer / el dentista / este restaurante / mi hermana / esos cubanos
3. ¿Quién lleva? / unos calcetines / los muchachos / el regalo / tu novia
4. Ve / esos estudiantes / nuestra vecina / las tiendas / la doctora

Estructura 3

Ver *(to see);* **saber** *and* **conocer** *(to know)*

Análisis

The verbs **ver, conocer,** and **saber** are irregular in the **yo**-form of the present tense but regular in all other forms.

ver		conocer		saber	
Singular	*Plural*	*Singular*	*Plural*	*Singular*	*Plural*
veo	vemos	conozco	conocemos	sé	sabemos
ves	veis	conoces	conocéis	sabes	sabéis
ve	ven	conoce	conocen	sabe	saben

▸ The meanings of the English verb *to know* are divided between two Spanish verbs, **saber** and **conocer.**

▸ **Saber** means to know something that can be stated or repeated: a fact, a name, a date, an amount. It is used before **que** and before interrogatives such as **¿dónde?, ¿cómo?, ¿quién?,** etc.

    —¿**Saben** Uds. dónde está Enrique?   *Do you know where Enrique is?*
    —No, pero **sabemos que** llega hoy.   *No, but we know he's arriving today.*

▸ **Conocer** refers to knowledge that cannot be stated—familiarity or acquaintance with someone or something. It is used when the direct object is a noun or pronoun referring to a person or a place.[3]

    —¿**Conoce** Ud. a Pablo?   *Do you know Pablo?*
    —No, pero **conozco** a su hermana.   *No, but I know his sister.*
    —Uds. **conocen** Caracas, ¿verdad?   *You're familiar with Caracas, aren't you?*

    —No, no **conocemos** Venezuela.   *No, we don't know Venezuela.*

Práctica

A. Answer each of the following questions selecting one of the choices offered.

    MODELO: —¿Qué ves, el colegio o la *What do you see, the high school or the*
                universidad?   *university?*
             —Veo el colegio.   *I see the high school.*

1. ¿Qué ven Uds., un hotel o un restaurante?
2. ¿Qué ve ella, las aspirinas o las pastillas?
3. ¿Qué veo, la blusa o la camisa?
4. ¿Qué vemos, la tienda o el almacén?
5. ¿Qué ves, tus libros o tus composiciones?

B. Add the correct form of **saber** or **conocer** as required in each of the following items. You will have to add personal **a** in some cases.

---

[3] In addition to *know,* the infinitive **saber** may mean *find out* and **conocer,** *meet.*

MODELOS: Tú / que llego mañana.
→ Tú sabes que llego mañana.   *You know I'm arriving*
tomorrow.

Tú / mis papás.
→ Tú conoces a mis papás.   *You know my parents.*

1. yo / las notas
2. Mario / la dependienta
3. nosotros / dónde viven

4. Uds. / España
5. ella / que están perfectamente
6. Ud. / esos ingenieros

Estructura 4

Direct object pronouns

Análisis

▶ A direct object pronoun replaces a noun that functions as a direct object. The
Spanish direct object pronouns are:

Singular		Plural	
Subject pronoun	*Direct Object pronoun*	*Subject pronoun*	*Direct Object pronoun*
yo	**me**	nosotros	**nos**
tú	**te**	vosotros	**os**
él	**lo**	ellos	**los**
ella	**la**	ellas	**las**
Ud.	**lo, la**	Uds.	**los, las**

▶ Third person direct object pronouns (**lo, la, los, las**) agree in gender and number
with the nouns they replace.

—¿Compras **el saco?**   *Are you buying **the jacket?***
—Sí, **lo** compro.   *Yes, I'm buying **it.***

Lo in the reply replaces a second occurrence of **el saco.** Compare these
sentences.

—¿Compras **la blusa?**   —Sí, **la** compro.
—¿Compras **los pantalones?**   —Sí, **los** compro.
—¿Compras **las corbatas?**   —Sí, **las** compro.

▶ **Lo, la, los, las** refer to people as well as things.

—¿Conocen a María?   *Do you know María?*
—No, no **la** conocemos.   *No, we don't know **her.***

—¿Vendes tu casa?   *Are you selling your house?*
—No, no **la** vendo.   *No, I'm not selling it.*

▶ **Lo, la, los, las** also mean *you* (they replace **usted** and **ustedes**).

—¿Me conoce Ud.?   *Do you know me?*
—No, señor, no **lo** conozco.   *No (sir), I don't know you.*

—¿Nos conoce Ud.?   *Do you know us?*
—No, señoras, no **las** conozco. *No (ladies), I don't know you.*

Note that, in Spanish, object pronouns precede the verb. In English they follow it.

▶ In *verb* + *infinitive* constructions, the object pronouns may either precede the first verb or follow the infinitive. In the latter case, the infinitive and the pronoun are written as one word. There is no difference in meaning.

Lo quiero acompañar. ⎫
                          ⎬ *I want to go* **with him.**
Quiero acompañar**lo.** ⎭

Práctica

A. Repeat each of the following sentences replacing the direct object noun with the corresponding direct object pronoun.

MODELO: Vendo **las blusas.**   *I'm selling the blouses.*
          → **Las** vendo.   *I'm selling them.*

1. Llevas **el abrigo.**   (los calcetines, la corbata, los guantes)
2. Conocen **a la señorita Pereda.**   (a la dependienta, a esos rusos, a su profesor)
3. Buscamos **los regalos.**   (el almacén, la sección, las camisas)
4. No puede encontrar **a Luisa.**   (a los clientes, a su novia, a ese niño)

B. Answer each of the following questions changing the direct object noun to a pronoun as in the model.

MODELO: —¿Visitas a ese hombre?   *Do you visit that man?*
          —Sí, lo visito.   *Yes, I visit him.*

1. ¿Encuentra Ud. los bolívares?   4. ¿Conoces a estas mujeres?
2. ¿Quieres ver a mi esposa?   5. ¿Piensan Uds. vender su restaurante?
3. ¿Ven el libro?   6. ¿Quieres acompañar a Carlos?

C. Answer each of the following questions in the negative as in the model.

MODELO: —¿Me conoce Ud.?   *Do you know me?*
          —No, no **lo (la)** conozco.   *No, I don't know you.*

1. ¿Me acompaña Ud.?
2. ¿Me comprendes?
3. ¿Necesita Ud. verme?

4. ¿Nos llama Ud.?
5. ¿Nos buscas?
6. ¿Nos piensas visitar?

Estructura 5

Interrogative words (Summary)

Análisis

▸ Questions beginning with interrogative words in Spanish usually have the following word order:

interrogative word + verb (+ subject) + remaining elements

The subject position may or may not be occupied since verb endings themselves indicate the subject. The Spanish interrogative words are summarized below.

¿A quién?,		**¿Cuántos?, ¿Cuántas?**	*How many?*
¿A quiénes?	*Whom?*	**¿De quién?, ¿De**	
¿Adónde?	*(To) where?*	**quiénes?**	*Whose?*
¿Cómo?	*How?*	**¿Dónde?**	*Where?*
¿Cuál?,		**¿Por qué?**	*Why?*
¿Cuáles?	*Which?*	**¿Qué?**	*What?*
¿Cuándo?	*When?*	**¿Quién?,**	
¿Cuánto?,		**¿Quiénes?**	*Who?*
¿Cuánta?	*How much?*		

▸ **¿Qué?, ¿Cuál?,** and **¿Cuáles?** may also be used both before nouns (as adjectives) and before verbs (as pronouns).

¿Qué ves?	*What do you see?*
¿Qué día es?	*What day is it?*
¿Cuál debo vender?	*Which one should I sell?*
¿Cuál falda compras?	*Which (what) skirt are you buying?*
¿Cuáles faldas compras?	*Which skirts are you buying?*

▸ **¿Quiénes?** and **¿A quiénes?** are used when the speaker has more than one person in mind. **¿A quién?** and **¿a quiénes?** are used when **who** is the direct object of the verb; compare formal English *whom*.

¿A quién conoces?	*Who (whom) do you know?*
¿A quiénes conoces?	*Who (whom) do you know?*

▸ Prepositions associated with an interrogative word must precede it in Spanish. In English they usually are separated from the question word and may appear at the end of the sentence.

¿Con quién habla Ud.?	*Who are you speaking with?*
¿De dónde es Ud.?	*Where are you from?*
¿De quién es esta casa?	*Whose house is this?*

▸ **¿Dónde?** is replaced by **¿adónde?** with verbs expressing motion.

¿Adónde me llevan?	*Where are they taking me (to)?*

Práctica

A. Your friend tells you something that really surprises you. Respond accordingly to each statement using the appropriate interrogative word. There may be more than one response possible for each statement.

MODELO: —Tomo seis materias.   *I'm taking six subjects.*
—¿Cuántas?   *How many?*

1. Luis está en el almacén.
2. Puedo comprar cuatro blusas.
3. Visitamos el museo mañana.
4. Quiere acompañar a su novio.
5. El examen es muy difícil.
6. La falda cuesta sesenta bolívares.

B. Translate the following sentences into Spanish.

1. Who are you calling?
2. When are you calling?
3. Why are you calling?
4. Which one are you calling?
5. Where do they work?
6. When do they work?
7. Who do they work with?   *(Con quines)*
8. How do they work?

Estructura 6

Question formation; ¿verdad? and ¿no?

Análisis

▸ Spanish statements consisting of *a noun + a form of **to be** + an adjective* are made into questions by placing the subject at the end of the sentence.

noun verb adjective   verb adjective   noun

La **escuela es grande.** → ¿*Es grande* la *escuela*?

▸ The addition of **¿verdad?** to an affirmative or negative sentence or **¿no?** to an affirmative sentence forms a question by asking for confirmation of the content of the original sentence.

No hay muchos abrigos, **¿verdad?**   *There aren't many coats, **are there?***
Es de algodón, **¿no?**   *It's made of cotton, **isn't it?***

Práctica

A. Change each of the following statements into questions.

1. Esa ropa es cara.
2. Los sacos son verdes.
3. Esos chicos son colombianos.
4. Manolo está preocupado.
5. El ingeniero está enfermo.
6. Su hijo está equivocado.

B. Change each of the following statements into questions by adding **¿verdad?** Then do the same by adding **¿no?** to each statement.

1. Quieren comprar un regalo.
2. Es una ganga.
3. La comunidad hispana es grande.
4. El médico trabaja los lunes.
5. Tenemos que entregar un trabajo.
6. Pablo aprende mucha química.

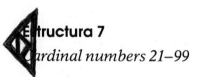

Estructura 7
Cardinal numbers 21–99

Análisis

▸ The numbers 21–99 are formed as follows:

21	**veintiuno**	27	**veintisiete**	40	**cuarenta**
22	**veintidós**	28	**veintiocho**	50	**cincuenta**
23	**veintitrés**	29	**veintinueve**	60	**sesenta**
24	**veinticuatro**	30	**treinta**	70	**setenta**
25	**veinticinco**	31	**treinta y uno**	80	**ochenta**
26	**veintiséis**	32	**treinta y dos**	90	**noventa**

▸ The numbers 21–29 may also be written as three words: **veinte y uno, veinte y dos,** etc.

▸ Forms in **-uno** change to **-un** before a masculine noun and to **-una** before a feminine noun.

veinti**ún** almacenes   veinti**una** clases
cuarenta y **un** estudiantes   cincuenta y **una** familias

Práctica

A. Repeat each number after your instructor. Then say that number *minus* ten.

26   58   43   21   66   84   72   89   31   55   15

B. Repeat Exercise A *adding* ten to each number.

C. Count by fives from 5 to 95.

D. Count by sixes from 6 to 96.

PRFERIR

Comunicando

Preguntas personales

1. ¿Qué ropa llevas todos los días?
2. ¿De qué color es tu **camisa?**   (suéter, blusa, abrigo)
3. ¿De qué color son tus **zapatos?**   (guantes, calcetines, pantalones)
4. ¿Compra Ud. ropa en un almacén? ¿Cómo se llama el almacén?
5. ¿Es buena la ropa allí?
6. ¿Son altos los precios?

Charlas

1. —**Quiero buscar un regalo para mi novio (novia).**
   ¿Piensas comprarlo en un almacén? ¿Buscas ropa? ¿Qué colores prefiere él (ella)? ¿Cuánto puedes pagar?

2. —**Por favor, señor, deseo ver una camisa.**
   ¿Prefiere Ud. un color oscuro o claro? ¿La quiere de algodón? ¿Cuánto desea Ud. pagar? ¿Quiere una de Europa o de Estados Unidos?

Situación

You enter a department store, call a salesperson over, and ask where a certain item of clothing that you want to buy is displayed. Ask him or her to show you the color you want and check the price. Be sure not to miss any bargains.

Para escribir

A. Rewrite each sentence changing the subjects as indicated by the cues.

MODELO: Encuentro al dependiente. **(ellos)** → **Ecuentran** al dependiente.

1. Prefiere algo barato.   (nosotros, tú, yo)
2. ¿Puedes comprar otros guantes?   (ellos, tú y yo, la doctora Vargas)
3. Pensamos tomar el examen.   (Antonio, ellas, Ud.)

B. Answer each of the following questions with the appropriate object pronoun as in the model.

> MODELO: —¿Necesita un suéter?   —Sí, lo necesito.

1. ¿Sabe Ud. el precio?
2. ¿Llaman Uds. a las dependientas?
3. ¿Conoces a Rafael?
4. ¿Vende pastillas?
5. ¿Quiere estudiar idiomas?
6. ¿Ves el colegio?
7. ¿Comprenden a su madre?
8. ¿Piensan Uds. llevar a la señorita?

C. Unscramble each string of elements to form a complete sentence. Make all necessary changes.

> MODELO: él / museo / visitar / desear / el → **Él desea visitar el museo.**

1. yo / ruso / estudiar / querer
2. vender / dependiente / zapatos / aquel
3. una / Amelia / pensar / de / blusa / comprar / algodón
4. la / Francisca / a / sección / acompañar / amiga / de / vestidos / su / a
5. negro / zapatos / buscar / blanco / nosotros / unos / y
6. ella / faldas / color / de / preferir / llevar / oscuro

D. Complete the following sentences by adding personal **a** where necessary. Remember that **a** + **el** contract to **al.**

1. Tengo que llevar _____ mis hermanos.
2. Esta tarde llaman _____ su vecino.
3. Los estudiantes no comprenden _____ la materia.
4. No podemos encontrar _____ la tienda.
5. ¿Buscas _____ los señores García?
6. No conocemos _____ el ingeniero inglés todavía.
7. Antonio prefiere acompañar _____ el hombre al banco.
8. Veo _____ el almacén Bolívar todos los días.

E. Translate the following sentences into Spanish.

1. This jacket is beautiful. I want to buy it.
2. What color is your blouse?
3. We know that they sell expensive clothing.
4. She sees her grandmother on Saturdays.
5. The tie costs only 15 bolívares. It's a bargain!
6. Do you know Juanita?
7. No, I don't know her.

lección 6

Objectives

Structure   You will learn an important construction that expresses future time in Spanish. You will also learn how to use the indirect object of the verb. You will be introduced to a group of very common verbs in Spanish that have entirely different patterns from their English equivalents. You will learn stem-changing verbs of the type **e → i.**

Vocabulary   You will learn how to say you like, love, or care about something. You will also learn the names of the months of the year.

Conversation   After completing the lesson you will be able to express your likes and dislikes and discuss job-hunting.

Culture   You will be introduced to some of the concerns of Puerto Ricans living in New York City.

Outline

Estructura 1   **Ir, dar, decir, venir**
Estructura 2   Stem-changing verbs (**e → i**)
Estructura 3   Prepositional pronouns
Estructura 4   Indirect object pronouns
Estructura 5   Reverse construction verbs

I'm Looking for a Job

Iris Portillo and Consuelo Pérez are two young Puerto Rican women who live in the Barrio in New York City. They're both looking for a job. Iris reads *El Diario* and then shows the newspaper to Consuelo. They begin to talk about the (employment) ads in it.

I.: There are so many ads for waitresses and sewing machine operators. However, I'm not interested in those jobs.

C.: Here's one for a cashier in a restaurant. What do you think of it?

I.: I like it, but I lack experience. And if I don't finish my classes in high school in June, what job will they give me?

C.: You already know that I've been unemployed since October. I want to work as a secretary or typist, but I can't get a job.

I.: Look, if you don't mind traveling to the Bronx, this office needs a receptionist.

C.: I don't have any choice (= no other solution remains for me). I'm going to apply for this job. If I don't, I'm going to end up in a dress factory like my mother.

Presentación

Busco empleo

Iris Portillo y Consuelo Pérez son dos jóvenes puertorriqueñas que viven en el Barrio de Nueva York. Las dos buscan trabajo. Iris lee *El Diario* y luego le enseña el periódico a Consuelo. Empiezan a hablar de los anuncios que hay en él.

Iris	—Hay tantos anuncios para mozas y operarias.[1] Sin embargo, no me interesan esos trabajos.
Consuelo	—Aquí hay uno para cajera en un restaurante. ¿Qué te parece?
Iris	—Me gusta pero me falta experiencia. Y si no termino mis clases en el colegio en junio, ¿qué empleo me van a dar?
Consuelo	—Ya sabes que yo estoy sin trabajo desde octubre. Quiero trabajar de secretaria o mecanógrafa, pero no consigo empleo.
Iris	—Mira, si no te importa viajar al Bronx, esta oficina necesita una recepcionista.
Consuelo	—No me queda más remedio. Voy a solicitar este trabajo. Si no, voy a acabar en una fábrica de vestidos como mi mamá.

Ampliación

—¿Cuándo empieza tu trabajo?
When does your job begin?

—Empieza en **enero.**
    (febrero, marzo, abril, mayo, junio)
*It begins in **January.***
    (*February, March, April, May, June*)

Estoy sin trabajo desde **julio.**
    (agosto, septiembre, octubre, noviembre, diciembre)
*I've been unemployed since **July.***
    (*August, September, October, November, December*)

—¿Adónde vas?
Where are you going?

—Voy a la oficina de empleos.
I'm going to the employment office.

---

[1] New York Spanish for *sewing machine operators*.

—¿Vienen los empleados?	*Are the employees coming?*
—No, sólo viene el jefe.	*No, only the boss is coming.*
—¿Qué te dicen?	*What are they telling you?*
—Me dicen el precio.	*They're telling me the price.*
—¿Qué te parece el sueldo?	*What do you think of the salary?*
—Me parece **bien.** (mal)	*I think it's **all right.** (awful)*
—¿A ella le gusta **este lápiz?**[2]	*Does she like **this pencil?***
(esta pluma)	* (this pen)*
—Sí, le encanta.	*Yes, she loves it.*
—¿Cuánto tiempo le queda para	*How long (how much time) do you*
terminar?	* have left to finish?*
—Me quedan cinco meses.	*I have five months left.*
—¿Cuánto dinero les falta?	*How much money are you (pl.) short?*
—Nos faltan setenta dólares.	*We're short seventy dollars.*
—¿Qué le pides? (pedir)	*What are you asking him for? (to ask*
	* for)*
—Le pido café.	*I'm asking him for coffee.*
—¿Qué me sirven Uds.? (servir)	*What are you serving me? (to serve)*
—Te servimos café.	*We're serving you coffee.*
—¿Sigue con sus clases? (seguir)	*Are you going on with your classes?*
—Sí, sigo con ellas.	*Yes, I'm going on with them.*

NOTA CULTURAL

Also known as Spanish Harlem, New York City's **Barrio** is home to Hispanics from many countries. It extends from 96th Street to 125th Street on the East Side of Manhattan. It is estimated that 50 to 75 percent of the inhabitants are Puerto Rican. The Barrio has its own typical stores, restaurants, and publications. *El Diario*, founded in 1949 and published in New York City, is a daily newspaper in Spanish that caters to New York's Spanish-speaking community.

Preguntas sobre la Presentación

    1. ¿Dónde viven Iris Portillo y Consuelo Pérez?
    2. ¿Qué le enseña Iris a su amiga?
    3. ¿Qué anuncios hay?
    4. ¿A Iris le interesa ser moza?

---

[2] The plural of *lápiz* is *lápices*.

5. ¿Desde cuándo está Consuelo sin trabajo?
6. ¿Qué empleo va a solicitar Consuelo?

Vocabulario activo

abril April
acabar to end up, wind up; to finish
agosto August
el **anuncio** ad
el **café** coffee
el (la) **cajero,(-a)** cashier
conseguir (e → i) to get, obtain
dar to give
decir (*irreg.*) to say, tell
desde since
diciembre December
el **dinero** money
el **dólar** dollar
el **empleado** employee
el **empleo** job
encantar to love (*something*)
enero January
enseñar to show
la **experiencia** experience
la **fábrica** factory
faltar to be missing, be short
febrero February
gustar to like
importar to matter; to mind; to care about (*something*)
interesar to be interested in
ir (*irreg.*) to go
el **jefe** boss
julio July
junio June
el **lápiz** pencil
luego then, afterwards
marzo March
mayo May

la **mecanógrafa** typist
el **mes** month
la **moza** waitress
el **mozo** waiter
noviembre November
octubre October
la **operaria** (*New York Span.*) operator, garment worker
parecer to seem; to think of, have an opinion of
pedir (e → i) to ask for, to order
el **periódico** newspaper
la **pluma** pen
quedar to have left, to remain
el (la) **recepcionista** receptionist
el **remedio** remedy, alternative
el (la) **secretario, (-a)** secretary
seguir (e → i) to follow, continue
septiembre September
servir (e → i) to serve
sin without
solicitar to apply for
el **sueldo** salary
terminar to finish
venir (*irreg.*) to come
viajar to travel

EXPRESIONES

empezar a (+ *inf.*) (**e → ie**) to begin to
¡mira! look!, hey!
no me queda más remedio I have no choice
sin embargo however, nevertheless
trabajar de + *occupation* to work as a _____

Estructura 1

Ir, dar, decir, venir

Análisis

▶ Study the conjugations of the following four irregular verbs:

ir (*to go*)	**dar** (*to give*)	**decir** (*to say, tell*)	**venir** (*to come*)
voy	**doy**	digo	vengo
vas	das	dices	vienes
va	da	dice	viene
vamos	damos	decimos	venimos
vais	dais	decís	venís
van	dan	dicen	vienen

▶ **Ir** and **dar** are conjugated like **-a-** verbs in the present. Their stems are **v-** and **d-**, respectively. Their **yo**-forms are irregular: **voy, doy** (compare **estoy, soy**).

▶ **Decir** and **venir** are **-g-** verbs like **tener:** their **yo**-forms are **digo** and **vengo**, respectively. **Decir** changes the **e** of the stem to **i** in the **yo, tú, él / ella / Ud.** and **ellos / ellas / Uds.** forms. **Venir** changes the **e** of the stem to **ie** in the **tú, él / ella / Ud.** and **ellos / ellas / Uds.** forms.

▶ **Ir a** + *infinitive* corresponds to the English *to be going to do something.* In both languages this construction refers to future time. **Vamos a** + *infinitive* may mean either *we're going to do something* or *let's do something.*

Vamos a solicitar empleo. { *We're going to apply for a job.*

Let's apply for a job.

Práctica

A. Change the verb according to each new cue.

1. Consuelo va a la fábrica.
   (yo, Uds., él, tú, nosotros, ellas, Ud.)

2. Voy a buscar trabajo.
   (nosotros, Amelia, tú, ellos, Ud., el mozo)

3. Le da el empleo.
   (yo, Ud., ellos, Amelia, nosotros, Uds., tú)

4. Les dicen el mes.
   (tú, él, nosotros, yo, Uds., los clientes)

5. Juan viene al hospital.
   (Ud., nosotros, Uds., tú, yo, la médico)

B. Answer each of the following questions using the cue in parentheses.

MODELO: —¿Adónde va Ud.?   (Venezuela)   *Where are you going?*
          —Voy a Venezuela.   *I'm going to Venezuela.*

1. ¿Adónde va ella?   (el almacén)
2. ¿Adónde vamos?   (la universidad)
3. ¿Adónde voy?   (Puerto Rico)
4. ¿Adónde van Uds.?   (el hotel)
5. ¿Adónde vas?   (el Barrio)
6. ¿Adónde van los jefes?
   (la oficina)

C. Expand each of the following sentences by adding the corresponding form of **ir a** + *infinitive*. The sentences will form a connected narrative about a job search.

MODELOS: Trabaja en esta oficina. → Va a trabajar en esta oficina.
   Lo busco. → Voy a buscarlo. OR Lo voy a buscar.

1. Voy al Barrio esta tarde.
2. Solicito empleo en una oficina.
3. Necesitan secretarias en septiembre.
4. Mi amiga Iris me acompaña.
5. Iris trabaja en un banco.
6. Iris empieza en octubre.
7. El sueldo es bueno.

D. Answer the following questions using the cues in parentheses.

MODELOS: —¿Qué le das?   (una pluma)   *What are you giving him?*
   —Le doy una pluma.   *I'm giving him a pen.*

   —¿Qué le dices?   (por qué)   *What are you telling him?*
   —Le digo por qué.   *I'm telling him why.*

1. ¿Qué le das?   (un lápiz)
2. ¿Qué le dan Uds.?   (el periódico)
3. ¿Qué le da ella?   (estos regalos)
4. ¿Qué le damos?   (cincuenta dólares)
5. ¿Qué les dice Ud.?   (el día)
6. ¿Qué les dicen Uds.?   (de dónde es)
7. ¿Qué les digo?   (la hora)
8. ¿Qué les dice él?   (por qué)

Estructura 2

Stem-changing verbs (e → i)

Análisis

▸ Certain verbs of the -i- class, such as **pedir, seguir, conseguir,** and **servir,** change the **e** of their stems to **i** in the **yo, tú, él,** and **ellos** forms.

pedir (*to ask for, order*)	**seguir** (*to follow*)	**servir** (*to serve*)
pido	sigo	sirvo
pides	sigues	sirves
pide	sigue	sirve
pedimos	seguimos	servimos
pedís	seguís	servís
piden	siguen	sirven

▸ The vowel **e** is kept in the stem of the **nosotros** and **vosotros** forms and in the infinitive because in these forms the stress falls on the class vowel and not on the stem.

▸ The sound / g / in **seguir** is written **g** in **sigo** but **gu** in the other forms.

Práctica

A. In the following sentences, change the verb to agree with each new cue.

  1. Consigo empleo en la fábrica.
     (ella, nosotros, tú, ellos, Ud., Uds.)

  2. Le sirven café.
     (yo, ellas, tú y yo, Ud., él, Uds.)

  3. Pedimos unos lápices.
     (Uds., yo, él, él y ella, tú, Ud.)

Estructura 3

Prepositional pronouns

Análisis

▸ Spanish has a special set of pronouns that are used after prepositions. Except for **mí** and **ti,** these prepositional pronouns are identical to the subject pronouns.

PREPOSITIONAL PRONOUNS

Singular	*Plural*
de **mí**	de **nosotros,** de **nosotras**
de **ti**	de **vosotros,** de **vosotras**
de **él,** de **ella**	de **ellos,** de **ellas**
de **Ud.**	de **Uds.**

▶ **Mí** and **ti** combine with the preposition **con** to form **conmigo,** *with me,* and **contigo,** *with you.* The other persons have the expected forms: **con él, con Ud.,** etc.

▶ Note that **él, ella, ellos, ellas** refer to things as well as to people.

No me gusta esa fábrica,　　　　*I don't like that factory,*
　y no quiero trabajar **en ella.**　　*and I don't want to work **in it.***

Práctica

A. Correct your friend's misconceptions by using the cues in parentheses.

MODELO:　—Trabajas para ellas, ¿verdad?　*You work for them, don't you?*
　　　　　　(él)　　　　　　　　　　　　(*him*)
　　　　　　—No, trabajo para él.　　　　*No, I work for him.*

1. Vienes con él, ¿verdad? (tú)
2. El regalo es para ellas, ¿verdad? (Ud.)
3. Estos abrigos son de ellos, ¿verdad? (Uds.)
4. Uds. van con ella, ¿verdad? (Ud.)
5. Ella vive con María, ¿verdad? (yo)
6. Tú compras los libros para ellos, ¿verdad? (nosotros)

B. Restate each sentence replacing the noun following the preposition with the corresponding prepositional pronoun.

MODELO:　Hablan del banco.　*They're talking about the bank.*
　　　　　→ Hablan de él.　　*They're talking about it.*

1. Escribes con el lápiz.
2. Acaban en la fábrica.
3. Hablamos de las faldas.
4. Trabajo para los abogados.
5. Son cajeros en esos restaurantes.
6. No son de este país.

Estructura 4

Indirect object pronouns

Análisis

▶ An indirect object is a complement that is joined to its verb by a preposition (usually *to* or *for* in English).

He told the story *to the children.*
He painted the house *for the old couple.*

NOTE: The indirect object in English appears without the preposition *to* when moved to a position before the direct object. Both nouns and pronouns may function as indirect objects.

He told *the children* the story.   (*indirect object noun*)
He told *them* the story.   (*indirect object pronoun*)

▶ The following table summarizes the Spanish indirect object pronouns. Note that **me, te, nos,** and **os** are identical in form to the direct object pronouns.

INDIRECT OBJECT PRONOUNS

Singular		Plural	
Subject	*Indirect object*	*Subject*	*Indirect object*
yo	**me**	nosotros / nosotras	**nos**
tú	**te**	vosotros / vosotras	**os**
él / ella / Ud.	**le**	ellos / ellas / Uds.	**les**

▶ Indirect object pronouns appear in the same positions as direct object pronouns.

1. They precede the verb they complement.

Le doy el libro.   *I'm giving **him** the book.*

2. In *verb + infinitive* constructions, they stand either before the first verb or after the infinitive. In the latter case, the infinitive and the pronoun are written as one word.

¿**Me** vas a **hablar?**
¿Vas a **hablarme?**   *Are you going to **talk to me?***

▶ In Spanish, an indirect object noun must appear with its corresponding indirect object pronoun. In English this is impossible.

Le vendemos la casa **a este señor.**   *We're selling the house **to this man.***
¿Qué **les** enseñas **a tus amigos?**   *What are you showing **your friends?***
Siempre **le** pide dinero **a su padre.**   *He always asks **his father** for money.*

▶ In order to focus on the indirect object English speakers move the main stress of the sentence to the indirect object pronoun.

He's giving **me** the money, not **you.**

In Spanish, however, the indirect object pronouns are unstressed words. Speakers focus attention on the indirect object pronoun by adding the appropriate corresponding prepositional pronoun:

a mí   a nosotros
a ti   a vosotros
a él   a ellos
a ella   a ellas
a Ud.   a Uds.

—**Le** voy a dar una pluma **a ella.**   *I'm going to give **her** a pen.*
—Y **a mí,** ¿qué **me** vas a dar?   *And what are you going to give **me?***

Práctica

A. Repeat each sentence changing the indirect object pronoun according to the cues.

1. Le enseña el museo.   (me, te, nos, les)
2. Me van a pedir un suéter.   (les, te, le, nos)
3. Quiere venderte la casa.   (le, nos, me, les)

B. Answer each question with a complete sentence containing an indirect object pronoun.

1. ¿A quién le vas a dar un regalo?
2. ¿Qué le vas a dar?
3. ¿Quién te pide dinero?
4. ¿A quién le pides tú dinero?
5. ¿Quiénes les venden sus libros viejos a Ud. y a sus amigos?
6. ¿A quién le dices siempre la verdad?
7. ¿A quiénes les entregan Uds. sus composiciones?
8. ¿A quién le vas a pedir trabajo?

Estructura 5

Reverse construction verbs

Análisis

▸ These Spanish verbs have the following meanings when they appear with an indirect object.

CpmER

encantar	to love (something)
faltar	to be missing, to be short (*money*)
gustar	to like
importar	to matter, to care about (something)
interesar	to be interested in
parecer	to seem, to think of, have an opinion of
quedar	to have left

hacer nada

morir

▸ If you compare Spanish:

indirect object	verb	subject
Me	**gusta**	**el libro.**

with English:

subject	verb	direct object
I	like	*the book.*

you will see that the *English subject* corresponds to a *Spanish indirect object* and that the *English direct object* corresponds to the *Spanish subject.* We refer to verbs like **gustar** as *reverse construction verbs.* These verbs form a special category only when contrasted with their English counterparts. There is nothing unusual about them for Spanish speakers.

▸ When an indirect object noun appears with a reverse construction verb, the corresponding indirect object pronoun must also be used.

¿Qué **les** gusta **a tus hijos?**   *What do your children like?*

▸ Speakers focus on the indirect object by adding a phrase consisting of **a** + *corresponding prepositional pronoun.*

A él le faltan diez dólares, pero **a**   *He's missing ten dollars, but **we're***
nosotros nos faltan treinta.   *missing thirty.*

▸ It is most common for the subject to follow a reverse construction verb. The verb is usually in the third person singular or third person plural. Note, in the following example, that it is the subject **(el libro, los libros)** and not the indirect object pronoun **(me)** that determines the form of the verb.

Me gusta **el libro.**   *I like the book.*
Me gustan **los libros.**   *I like the books.*

▸ If the subject of a reverse construction verb is an infinitive, then the third person singular form of the verb is used.

No me gusta **trabajar.**   *I don't like to work.*

Práctica

A. Repeat each sentence changing the subject to the plural.

MODELO: Me gusta la blusa.   *I like the blouse.*
         → Me gustan las blusas.   *I like the blouses.*

1. Me falta un dólar.
2. Le importa la comunidad.
3. Te encanta su hermana.
4. Nos interesa ese saco.
5. Me queda una semana para terminar.
6. Le parece bien el anuncio.

B. Answer the following questions affirmatively.

MODELO: —¿Te gusta estudiar?   *Do you like to study?*
—Sí, me gusta estudiar.   *Yes, I like to study.*

1. ¿A Ud. le falta un dólar?
2. ¿Te quedan unos exámenes?
3. ¿A Uds. les gusta viajar?
4. ¿A él le interesan los periódicos?
5. ¿A ellas les importa el idioma?
6. ¿Te interesa solicitar empleo?
7. ¿Te va a gustar el regalo?
8. ¿Te van a gustar sus amigas?

C. Answer each of the following questions using a reverse construction verb.

1. ¿Qué color te gusta más?
2. ¿Qué le parece el almacén?
3. ¿Cuánto dinero te falta?
4. ¿Te interesa trabajar de secretario?
5. ¿Te parece bien el sueldo que te pagan?
6. ¿Te gusta escribir con pluma o con lápiz?

Comunicando

Preguntas personales

1. ¿Trabajas de moza?   (dependienta, recepcionista, secretaria)
2. ¿Qué te parece el jefe?
3. ¿Cuántos empleados hay donde trabajas?
4. ¿Le escriben sus amigos?
5. ¿Qué le dicen?
6. ¿Cuándo les escribe a ellos?

Charlas

1. —**Solicito empleo en un almacén.**
¿Desde cuándo estás sin trabajo?   ¿Te interesa trabajar de dependiente o de cajero?   ¿Te dan un sueldo bueno allí?   ¿En qué sección te gusta trabajar?   ¿Qué vas a venderles a los clientes?

2. —**Voy a terminar mis clases en el colegio este año.**
¿En qué mes vas a terminarlas?   ¿Tus papás te van a dar dinero o vas a buscar trabajo?   ¿Es difícil encontrar empleo ahora?   ¿Qué trabajos te gustan?

Situación

You have been out of work since October. You are worried because you cannot find another job. As you look through the employment ads in the newspaper, you find many positions available. Discuss these job possibilities, telling which ones interest you (or don't interest you) and why. Decide on one job you really like and tell how you are going to apply for it.

Para escribir

A. Expand each sentence by adding the corresponding form of **ir a** + *infinitive*. Your sentences will form a connected narrative.

> MODELO: Termino mis clases en diciembre.
> → Voy a terminar mis clases en diciembre.

1. Hoy busco empleo.
2. Vienes conmigo, ¿verdad?
3. Conseguimos empleo en aquella fábrica.
4. ¿Te interesa trabajar allí?
5. Podemos empezar a trabajar en enero.
6. Nos pagan un sueldo muy alto.

B. Answer the following questions about history class either affirmatively or negatively.

> MODELO: —¿A Ud. le gusta esta materia?
> —Sí, me gusta. OR No, no me gusta.

1. ¿Te gusta la clase de historia?
2. ¿A tu amigo le gusta también?
3. ¿A los otros estudiantes les parece bien el profesor?
4. ¿Les interesan los libros que leen?
5. ¿A Uds. les importa estudiar en la biblioteca?
6. ¿Cuántas semanas de clase les quedan?

C. Answer the following questions selecting one of the two choices given.

> MODELO: —¿A Pedro le gusta más la física o la química?
> —Le gusta más la física. OR Le gusta más la química.

1. ¿A tu hermana le gusta más Chile o México?
2. ¿A ese hombre le importa más el tiempo o el dinero?
3. ¿Nos quedan más dólares o bolívares?
4. ¿Cuántos exámenes le faltan a María, uno o dos?

D. Translate the following sentences into Spanish.

1. I've been unemployed since October. *estoy sin trabajo desde octubre*
2. We're going to the employment office.
3. I like those pencils. *me gustan esos lapices*
4. She's giving me the newspaper. *me da periodico*
5. How much money are you short? *cuanto dinero les hace falta*
6. He doesn't mind working as a waiter. *no le importa trabajar como mozo*

7. These employees lack experience.. Estos empleados les falta experiencia
8. What do you think of this factory? que te parece esta fabrica
9. We love the salary! nos encanta suleldo
10. Is he going to serve you coffee? va serventicofe
11. Yes, I always ask him for coffee. si te pido

si siempre le pido cafe

repaso 2

(Lecciones 4–6)

A. Complete the following dialogue and paragraph with the correct forms of **ser** or **estar**.

1. —¿De dónde _____ Luis?
2. —Luis _____ chileno. _____ casado con una profesora argentina.
3. —Creo que sus padres _____ de origen europeo.
4. —No, (tú) _____ equivocado. Toda su familia _____ de Hispanoamérica.

   Esa tienda _____ del señor Vargas. Hoy _____ domingo y la tienda _____ cerrada. Puedes verla mañana. La tienda del señor Vargas _____ muy bonita.

B. Answer each of the following questions in the affirmative, changing the direct object noun to a pronoun.

   MODELO: —¿Compras el abrigo?   —Sí, lo compro.

1. ¿Conoces al señor Pereda?
2. ¿Visita Ud. a sus primos?
3. ¿Encuentran Uds. las camisas?
4. ¿Puedo llamar a la dependienta?
5. ¿Piensan buscar los regalos?
6. ¿Quieren Uds. vender su casa?
7. ¿Tiene los bolívares?
8. ¿Comprendes a las profesoras?

C. Add a personal **a** where necessary in each of the following sentences.

1. Buscamos _____ el suéter gris.
2. No conocen _____ esos abogados.
3. Deben llevar _____ su abuela al hospital.
4. ¿No encuentras _____ la sección de blusas?
5. Pienso ver _____ Amelia esta tarde.
6. No puedo visitar _____ el museo hoy.

D. Complete the following dialogue about Mercedes' boyfriend with the correct forms of **saber** or **conocer**.

1. —¿_____ (tú) al novio de Mercedes?
2. —Sí, pero no _____ si llega hoy o mañana.
3. —Creo que mañana. Él no _____ nuestro país.
4. —¿_____ (tú) si piensa buscar un empleo aquí?
5. —No creo. Él y Mercedes no _____ todavía si van a vivir aquí o en Venezuela.
6. —Si él quiere trabajar, yo _____ una tienda donde necesitan dependientes.
7. —Pero nosotros no _____ si le interesa trabajar de dependiente.

E. Write answers to the following questions using the cues in parentheses as in the model.

   MODELO: —¿Qué te dan? (un periódico) —Me dan un periódico.

1. ¿Qué te decimos? (los precios)
2. ¿Qué nos das? (veinte dólares)
3. ¿Qué les enseña Ud.? (el Barrio)
4. ¿Qué le pido? (las composiciones)
5. ¿Qué me sirven Uds.? (un café)
6. ¿Qué le vendemos a Ud.? (unas blusas)

F. Pretend you are studying to be an engineer. Answer each of the following questions using reverse construction verbs.

1. ¿Le interesa la ingeniería?
2. ¿Qué materia le gusta más?
3. ¿Le importa si saca malas notas?
4. ¿Cuántos años le faltan todavía?
5. ¿Le quedan muchos exámenes?
6. ¿Qué le parecen sus profesores?

G. Translate the following sentences into Spanish.

1. He's been unemployed since January.
2. They love to buy clothing in that department store.
3. What does your brother look like?
4. I'm going to give her some pencils.
5. We're from Spain, but we're in Venezuela now.

H. Translate the following sentences into English. They will form a connected paragraph.

1. ¿Conoce Ud. al señor Durán?
2. Quiero trabajar de secretaria en su oficina, pero me falta experiencia.
3. En su oficina todos los empleados tienen que saber español.
4. Yo, por desgracia, no lo hablo.

5. No me queda otro remedio.
6. Voy a estudiar español para poder conseguir un empleo allí.

I. *Reading passage.* The following reading passage deals with an important difference in United States and Hispanic cultures—the attitudes towards work and personal relationships. In this selection many cognate words that have not been presented in the preceding chapters have been used. Since their form and meaning are similar to English words, you should be able to guess their meaning. These cognates are marked with a raised degree sign (°).

The passage also contains some new words. Study the following vocabulary items until you can give the English equivalent for each Spanish word or phrase. After reading the paragraph try to answer the multiple choice comprehension questions that follow it.

afirmar to strengthen	**hacer** to make, do
casi almost	**hispanoamericano** de
la **ciudad** city	Hispanoamérica
el **comerciante** un señor que tiene una	**ir de compras** to go shopping
tienda	el **poblado** ciudad pequeña
las **compras** shopping (*cf.* **comprar**)	**recibir** conseguir
eficaz (*pl.* **eficaces**) efficient	**todo lo que** all that
la **gente** people (*singular in Span.*)	

Las tiendas en los países hispanos

¿Sabe Ud. cómo y dónde compra la gente en los países hispanoamericanos? Las compras pueden ser muy diferentes.° En los Estados Unidos los supermercados y los almacenes grandes son muy populares.° En muchas partes° del país hay muy pocas tiendas pequeñas y la gente hace casi todas sus compras en los supermercados y almacenes grandes. En Hispanoamérica existen° también estas tiendas modernas,° pero es fácil encontrar otro sistema° comercial,° el sistema° tradicional.° En las partes viejas de las ciudades y en los poblados las tiendas están especializadas.° Cada tienda vende sólo algunas cosas y el cliente tiene que ir a muchas tiendas para comprar todo lo que necesita. Los comerciantes° conocen a sus clientes y cada cliente recibe mucha atención° personal.° Parece que los hispanos prefieren la atención personal cuando compran, y no les importa tanto si sus compras toman más tiempo. Al norteamericano no le interesan tanto las relaciones° personales cuando va de compras. A él le gustan las compras rápidas° y eficaces. Sin embargo, la cultura° hispanoamericana es una cultura muy personalizada.° La gente busca en todos los aspectos° de su vida cómo afirmar sus relaciones personales. Ve en la familia, en los amigos y en el trabajo una oportunidad° de contactos° con la gente. Podemos decir que en Latinoamérica la mayor parte de la gente cree que las relaciones personales son la cosa más importante° de la vida. En Estados Unidos es el trabajo que más le importa a la gente. Las dos culturas son muy diferentes.

Los clientes pueden encontrarlo todo en esta tienda.

COMPREHENSION CHECK

1. En Hispanoamérica hay
   a. sólo supermercados y almacenes grandes.
   b. dos sistemas comerciales—el sistema moderno y el tradicional.
   c. sólo tiendas especializadas.

2. ¿Qué quiere el norteamericano cuando va de compras?
   a. Tener relaciones personales.
   b. Un comerciante tradicional.
   c. Comprar en poco tiempo.

3. ¿Por qué sigue tan popular el sistema tradicional de las compras en Hispano-américa?
   a. Los países de Hispanoamérica son primitivos° y la gente no sabe que los supermercados son mejores.
   b. A los hispanoamericanos no les gusta pasar mucho tiempo en las tiendas.
   c. A los hispanoamericanos les gusta la atención personal de los comerciantes de las tiendas pequeñas.

4. ¿Qué podemos decir de las relaciones personales en los Estados Unidos?
   a. Para los norteamericanos no son la cosa más importante de la vida.
   b. A la gente le interesan más los contactos personales.
   c. La cultura norteamericana es una cultura muy personalizada.

5. ¿Por qué podemos decir que a los hispanoamericanos les importa mucho el contacto personal?
   a. Lo buscan en todos los aspectos de su vida.
   b. Creen que el trabajo es más importante.
   c. No les gustan las tiendas pequeñas.

lección 7

Objectives

Structure   You will learn how to form the preterit, one of the past tenses in Spanish. You will learn new **-g-** verbs including **hacer** (*to do, to make*).

Vocabulary   You will learn some idioms with the verb **hacer,** weather expressions, and how to tell time in Spanish.

Conversation   You will be able to talk about the weather and your vacation and travel plans. Now you will even be able to discuss a trip you took *last* year!

Culture   You will learn about two cities in Mexico—Mexico City and Veracruz—with regard to their weather and points of interest.

Outline

Estructura 1   **Hacer, salir, traer**
Estructura 2   Weather expressions
Estructura 3   The preterit of regular verbs
Estructura 4   **Hacer . . . que** + *present* (*has been* . . .); **hace . . . que** + *preterit* (*ago*)
Estructura 5   Telling time
Estructura 6   Diminutives (For recognition)
Estructura 7   **Al** + *infinitive* (For recognition)
Estructura 8   Spelling changes in the preterit (For recognition)

On Vacation

Elena Reyes takes a trip to Veracruz where she spends her vacation. Her cousin, Jorge Fernández, is on vacation in Mexico City. Here are their letters.

Dear Jorgito,

I've been in Veracruz for four days. As you know, I took the plane in Mexico City and arrived here on Thursday at 2:30 P.M. It's very sunny and very hot every day. My hotel is near the beach and it has a pool, too. I spend the whole day in my bathing suit and I'm going to come home very sunburned. At night I go out to eat. Last night I ate in a restaurant in the Plaza de la Constitución. I liked the food a lot and I paid only 20 pesos. Today I'm going back to the Plaza to buy gifts. I intend to bring a lot of things for everyone. See you soon.

Love,
Elena

Dear Elenita,

I received your letter today and I see that you like Veracruz a lot. I love the capital (city). I have so many things left to see. Two days ago I visited the Museum of Anthropology, which is very interesting. This afternoon I'm going to go to the Merced Market. The weather's nice here during the morning, but between four and five in the afternoon it rains every day. However, it stops quickly. You tell me that in Veracruz you wear a bathing suit; well, here I need a raincoat and umbrella. At night it's cool.

I love Mexican food, although it's spicy. There are restaurants all over the city and I read the guidebook to find them. Yesterday I went into one, but I didn't like it and I left. I walk through the downtown streets every day and in this way I get to know the city better. I see that it's already a quarter to twelve. I have to leave now. I'll write to you soon.

Love,
Jorge

Presentación

De vacaciones

Elena Reyes hace un viaje a Veracruz donde pasa sus vacaciones. Su primo, Jorge Fernández, está de vacaciones en la Ciudad de México. Aquí están sus cartas.

Querido Jorgito,
    Hace cuatro días que estoy en Veracruz. Como sabes, tomé el avión en la Ciudad de México y llegué aquí el jueves a las dos y media de la tarde. Hace mucho sol y hace mucho calor todos los días. Mi hotel queda cerca de la playa y tiene piscina también. Paso todo el día en traje de baño y voy a volver a casa muy bronceada. Por la noche salgo a comer. Anoche comí en un restaurante de la Plaza de la Constitución. Me gustó mucho la comida y sólo pagué 20 pesos. Hoy vuelvo a la Plaza para comprar regalos. Pienso traer muchas cosas para todos. Hasta pronto.

Cariños de
Elena

Querida Elenita,
    Recibí tu carta hoy y veo que te gusta mucho Veracruz. A mí me encanta la capital. Me quedan tantas cosas que ver. Hace dos días visité el Museo de Antropología que es muy interesante. Esta tarde voy a ir al Mercado de la Merced. Aquí hace buen tiempo durante la mañana, pero entre las cuatro y las cinco de la tarde llueve todos los días. Sin embargo, pasa pronto. Me dices que en Veracruz llevas el traje de baño, pues aquí me hacen falta el impermeable y el paraguas. Por la noche hace fresco.
    Me encanta la comida mexicana aunque es picante. Hay restaurantes por toda la ciudad y leo la guía para encontrarlos. Ayer entré en[1] uno pero no me

---

[1] **Entrar a** is also used.

gustó y salí. Voy por las calles del centro todos los días y así llego a conocer la ciudad mejor. Ya veo que son las doce menos cuarto. Ahora tengo que salir. Te escribo pronto.

Cariños de
Jorge

Ampliación

—¿Qué tiempo hace?	*How's the weather?*
—Hace mal tiempo.	*The weather's bad.*
—Hace frío.	*It's cold.*
—Hace fresco.	*It's cool.*
—Hace viento.	*It's windy.*
—Nieva.	*It's snowing.*
—Nevó mucho el año pasado.	*It snowed a lot last year.*
—Está nublado.	*It's cloudy.*
—¿Cuántos grados hace?	*What's the temperature?*
—Hace veintiún grados.[2]	*It's 21 degrees.*
—¿Cómo van al aeropuerto?	*How are you going to the airport?*
—Vamos en **coche.**	*We're going by car.*
(taxi, autobús, tren)	*(taxi, bus, train)*
—¿Queda **cerca** de aquí?	*Is it near here?*
—No, queda lejos.	*No, it's far.*
—¿Qué hora es?	*What time is it?*
—Son las cinco de la tarde.	*It's five P.M.*
—¿Cuánto (tiempo) hace que viajan por México?	*How long have they been traveling in Mexico?*
—Hace un mes que viajan por México. (Viajan por México hace un mes.)	*They've been traveling in Mexico for a month.*
—¿Cuánto (tiempo) hace que viajaron por México?	*How long ago did they travel in Mexico?*
—Hace un mes que viajaron por México. (Viajaron por México hace un mes.)	*They traveled in Mexico a month ago.*

Preguntas sobre la Presentación

1. ¿A quién le escribe Elena?
2. ¿Cuánto tiempo hace que Elena está en Veracruz?

---

[2] The metric system is used throughout the Hispanic world. Twenty-one degrees Celsius (centigrade) equals 70 degrees Fahrenheit.

3. ¿Cómo llegó a Veracruz?
4. ¿Qué tiempo hace en Veracruz?
5. ¿Qué hace Elena todos los días?
6. ¿Cuándo visitó Jorge el Museo de Antropología?
7. ¿Adónde va Jorge esta tarde?
8. ¿Qué tiempo hace en la capital?
9. ¿Qué le hace falta a Jorge?
10. ¿Cómo encuentra Jorge la comida mexicana?

NOTAS CULTURALES

1. Veracruz, a famous vacation resort and one of Mexico's main commercial ports, is on the Gulf Coast. The state of Veracruz is an important source of oil for the nation.

2. Mexico City, the capital of Mexico, is built upon the remains of Tenochtitlán, the Aztec capital that was conquered by the Spaniards in 1521. The National Museum of Anthropology, which opened in 1964, has outstanding exhibits of pre-Hispanic culture dating back over 2,000 years. In the Mercado de la Merced, the largest market in the city, can be found the ruins of the eighteenth-century La Merced Monastery.

Vocabulario activo

el **aeropuerto** airport
  anoche last night
la **antropología** anthropology
  así like this (that), thus
el **autobús** bus
el **avión** airplane
  ayer yesterday
  bronceado sunburned
el **calor** heat
la **calle** street
la **capital** capital (*city*)
el **cariño** affection
la **carta** letter
el **centro** downtown
  cerca (de) near
la **ciudad** city
el **coche** car
  comer to eat
la **comida** food; meal
la **cosa** thing
  durante during
  entre between
  entrar (en / a) to enter, go in

el **frío** cold (*weather*)
el **grado** degree (*temperature*)
la **guía** guidebook
  hacer (yo hago) to do, to make
  hasta until
el **impermeable** raincoat
  interesante interesting
  lejos (de) far (from)
  llover (o → ue) to rain
la **mañana** morning
el **mercado** market
  nevar (e → ie) to snow
  nublado cloudy
el **paraguas** umbrella
  pasado past
el **peso** monetary unit of Mexico
  picante spicy
la **piscina** swimming pool
la **playa** beach
la **plaza** square, plaza
  pronto soon
  quedar to be (*located*)
  querido dear

recibir   to receive
salir (yo salgo)   to leave, go out
el **sol**   sun
el **taxi**   taxi
el **tiempo**   weather
traer (yo traigo)   to bring
el **traje de baño**   bathing suit
el **tren**   train
las **vacaciones**   vacation
el **viaje**   trip
el **viento**   wind

volver (o → ue)   to return, go
(come) back

EXPRESIONES
estar de vacaciones   to be on vacation
hacer falta (*rev. const.*)   to need
hacer un viaje   to take a trip
llegar a (+ *inf.*)   to get to do something
¿qué hora es?   what time is it?
¿qué tiempo hace?   how's the weather?

Estructura 1

Hacer, salir, traer

Análisis

▶ **Hacer** (*to do, to make*), **salir** (*to go out, to leave*), and **traer** (*to bring*) are all **-g-**
verbs: the **yo**-forms are **hago, salgo, traigo,** respectively. All other forms are
regular in present tense.

hacer (*to do, make*)	**salir** (*to leave, go out*)	**traer** (*to bring*)
hago	salgo	traigo
haces	sales	traes
hace	sale	trae
hacemos	salimos	traemos
hacéis	salís	traéis
hacen	salen	traen

Práctica

A. Change the verb in each sentence according to the cues.

1. Hago un viaje en avión.
    (Ud., nosotros, ella, tú, Uds., ellos)

2. Salen de la fábrica.
    (nosotros, él, ellas, yo, tú, Ud.)

3. Le traemos el paraguas.
    (yo, Uds., Ud. y yo, tú, ellos, ella)

B. Answer each of the following questions using the cue in parentheses in your
answer.

HACER FALTA → TO MAKE A LACK OF "TO NEED"

MODELO: —¿Qué te hace falta?   (**una piscina**)   *What do you need?*
          —Me hace falta una piscina.   *I need a swimming pool.*

1. ¿Qué te hace falta?   (quince pesos)
2. ¿Qué les hace falta a Uds.? (conseguir empleo)
3. ¿Qué le hace falta a ella?   (unos lápices)
4. ¿Qué nos hace falta?   (unas vacaciones)
5. ¿Qué me hace falta?   (comer algo)
6. ¿Qué le hace falta a Ud.?   (una guía)

Estructura 2

Weather expressions

Análisis

nouns

▸ The third person singular of **hacer—hace—**is used in many expressions of weather conditions. The words **calor, frío, fresco, sol, viento** are nouns and **mucho** and **poco** (not **muy**) are used to modify them. **Muy** is used, however, before **buen** and **mal** and with **estar nublado.**

Hace mucho sol.   *It's very sunny.*
Hace muy buen tiempo.   *The weather's very good.*

Práctica

A. Your friend asks you about today's weather on the telephone, before he takes a trip to your city. Tell him it's either better or worse than he thinks!

MODELO: —¿Hace frío hoy?   *Is it cold today?*
          —Hace mucho frío hoy.   *It's very cold today.*
     OR: —Hace poco frío hoy.   *It's not very cold today.*

1. ¿Hace viento hoy?
2. ¿Está nublado hoy?
3. ¿Hace fresco hoy?
4. ¿Hace buen tiempo hoy?
5. ¿Nieva hoy?
6. ¿Llueve hoy?

B. Answer these questions about the weather.

1. ¿Qué tiempo hace hoy?
2. ¿Qué tiempo va a hacer mañana?
Temp— 3. ¿Cuántos grados hace hoy?
4. ¿Qué tiempo hace por aquí en **julio?** (enero)
5. ¿En qué mes **llueve** mucho? (nieva)
6. ¿Te gusta **el calor?** (el frío) ¿Por qué?

Estructura 3

The preterit of regular verbs

Análisis

▸ The preterit tense is used to designate an event that the speaker sees as completed in the past.

▸ Verbs of the **-a-** class (**-ar** verbs) have the following endings in the preterit.

a-CLASS VERBS

trabajar		
Preterit endings	*Preterit*	
-**é**	trabaj**é**	*I worked*
-**aste**	trabaj**aste**	*you worked*
-**ó**	trabaj**ó**	*he, she, you worked*
-**amos**	trabaj**amos**	*we worked*
-**asteis**	trabaj**asteis**	*you worked*
-**aron**	trabaj**aron**	*they, you worked*

▸ The forms of the preterit of **-a-** class verbs are all stressed on the endings. **Trabajo** (*I work*) and **trabajó** (*he, she, you worked*) are distinguished solely by the difference in stress placement. **Trabajamos** means both *we are working* and *we worked*. Context clarifies which tense is meant. (In English, *we put* is both present and past.)

▸ Verbs of the **-e-** class (**-er** verbs) and **-i-** class (**-ir** verbs) have the following endings in the preterit.

-e- *and* **-i- CLASS VERBS**

	vender	**vivir**
Preterit endings		
-**í**	vend**í**	viv**í**
-**iste**	vend**iste**	viv**iste**
-**ió**	vend**ió**	viv**ió**
-**imos**	vend**imos**	viv**imos**
-**isteis**	vend**isteis**	viv**isteis**
-**ieron**	vend**ieron**	viv**ieron**

▸ For **-i-** class verbs, the **nosotros** form (**vivimos**) is the same in both the present and preterit. For **-e-** class verbs the forms are different: **vendemos** (present) / **vendimos** (preterit).

▸ Verbs of the **-a-** class and **-e-** class that have changes in the vowel of the stem (**e →
ie, o → ue**) in the present do not have these changes in any of the forms of the
preterit.

pensar	volver
pensé	volví
pensaste	volviste
pensó	volvió
pensamos	volvimos
pensasteis	volvisteis
pensaron	volvieron

▸ **Ver** (*to see*) is regular in the preterit. The written accent is not used in the first
and third singular forms. **Dar** (*to give*) is conjugated like an **-e-** or **-i-** verb in the
preterit rather than like an **-a-** verb. Like **ver,** it has no accent mark in the first
and third person singular forms.

ver	dar
vi	di
viste	diste
vio	dio
vimos	dimos
visteis	disteis
vieron	dieron

Práctica

A. Change the verb in each sentence according to the cues.

1. Viajaron en tren.
   (yo, tú, ellas, nosotros, él)

2. ¿Dónde comiste anoche?
   (Uds., ella, nosotros, yo, Ud.)

3. Recibí las cartas.
   (nosotros, ella, tú, Uds., él y ella)

4. No vimos esa playa.
   (él, ellas, tú, yo, Ud.)

B. Repeat each sentence changing the verb from the present to the preterit
tense. The sentences in past time will form a connected paragraph.

   Lead sentence: Viajé a Venezuela el año pasado.

1. Paso las vacaciones allí.
2. Salgo de Nueva York.
3. Tomo el avión a Caracas.
4. Encuentro un hotel en la ciudad.
5. Conozco a muchos venezolanos.
6. Un amigo venezolano me lleva a
   su casa.

7. Un día él y yo seguimos por las calles del centro.
8. Entro en el Bazar Bolívar para comprar regalos.
9. Veo muchas cosas y lo paso bien en Venezuela.
10. También aprendo un poco de español.

C. Your friend asks you if you and other people are going to do certain things on Monday. Tell her you did them yesterday.

> MODELO: —¿Vas a visitar el museo el lunes?   *Are you going to visit the museum on Monday?*
>
>   —Visité el museo ayer.   *I visited the museum yesterday.*

1. ¿Vas a solicitar empleo el lunes?
2. ¿Tus tíos van a volver el lunes?
3. ¿Juan va a darte el dinero el lunes?
4. ¿Vamos a salir a comer el lunes?
5. ¿Vas a tomar el tren el lunes?
6. ¿Tu prima va a escribirte el lunes?

Estructura 4

Hace . . . que + present (has been); hace . . . que + preterit (ago)

Análisis

▸ Sentences whose structure consists of **hace** + *expression of time* + **que** + *verb in present tense* are equivalent to *have / has been doing (something).*

> —¿Cuánto (tiempo) hace que vive Ud. en Veracruz?
> —**Hace cuatro años que vivo** en Veracruz.
> —**Vivo** en Veracruz **hace cuatro años.**
>
> *How long have you been living in Veracruz?*
>
> *I've been living in Veracruz for four years.*

In these constructions, **hace** + *expression of time* may appear at the end of the sentence, in which case **que** is omitted.

▸ Sentences whose structure consists of **hace** + *expression of time* + *verb in the preterit tense* mean *ago.* As above, **hace** + *expression of time* may appear at the end of the sentence, in which case **que** is omitted.

> —¿Cuánto (tiempo) hace que vivió Ud. en Veracruz?
> —**Hace cuatro años que viví** en Veracruz.
> —**Viví** en Veracruz **hace cuatro años.**
>
> *How long ago did you live in Veracruz?*
>
> *I lived in Veracruz four years ago.*

—¿Cuánto (tiempo) hace que lo
   vieron?

How long ago did you
   see him?

—**Hace un mes que** lo vimos
—**Lo vimos hace un mes.**

We saw him a month ago.

Práctica

A. You arrived in Mexico City five weeks ago to study Spanish. The Mexican family you're living with wants to know more about you. Answer their questions using a time expression.

MODELOS: —¿Cuánto tiempo hace que
           comió aquí?

How long ago did you eat
   here?

—Hace dos semanas que comí
   aquí.

I ate here two weeks ago.

—¿Cuánto tiempo hace que
   come aquí?

How long have you been eating
   here?

—Hace tres días que como
   aquí.

I've been eating here for three
   days.

1. ¿Cuánto tiempo hace que vive en Nueva York?
2. ¿Cuánto tiempo hace que estudia español?
3. ¿Cuánto tiempo hace que vio el Museo de Antropología?
4. ¿Cuánto tiempo hace que les escribió a sus padres?
5. ¿Cuánto tiempo hace que no recibe cartas de sus amigos?
6. ¿Cuánto tiempo hace que busca regalos para su familia?

Estructura 5

Telling time

Análisis

▸ *Spanish uses a form of* **ser** + **la(s)** + *number* to tell time. Time past the hour—up to half-past the hour—is expressed by **y** + *the number of minutes*. A quarter after and half-past the hour are usually expressed by special terms: **y cuarto** and **y media,** respectively. Time after half-past the hour is deducted from the following hour by the word **menos** (*less, minus*).

—¿Qué hora es?[3]
—Es la una.
—Son las seis y cuarto.

What time is it?
It's one o'clock.
It's 6:15.

---

[3] Some Spanish speakers say **¿Qué horas son?**

—Son las dos y media.   *It's 2:30.*
—Son las diez menos veinte.   *It's twenty to ten. (a quarter)*
    (cuarto)[4]

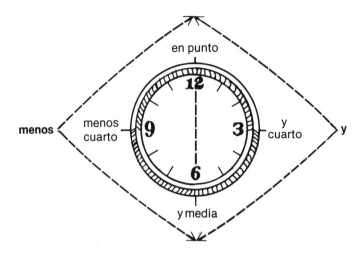

▶ *At a certain time* is expressed by the preposition **a.** The phrases **de la mañana, de la tarde, de la noche** specify a part of the day; when the hour is not expressed, the prepositions **por** or **en** are used in place of **de.**

—¿A qué hora sale el tren?   *What time does the train leave?*[5]
—Sale a las ocho y diez **de la**   *It leaves at 8:10 A.M.*
    mañana.
—¿Van Uds. **por la mañana?**   *Are you going in the morning?*
—¡Qué va! Vamos a las tres **de la**   *Are you kidding? We're going at 3*
    tarde.   *P.M.*

Práctica

A. Express the following times in Spanish.

It's:
1. 8:00   7. 12:30 P.M.
2. 1:00   8. 11:50 P.M.
3. 10:30   9. 2:10
4. 3:15   10. 6:55
5. 7:45   11. 9:27
6. 5 A.M.

---

[4] Many Spanish Americans use the verb **faltar: Faltan veinte para las diez.**
[5] In official time (timetables, movie, television and theater schedules), a 24-hour clock is often used: **El tren sale a las 18 y 25,** *The train leaves at 6:25.*

B. Your new roommate asks you questions about your daily schedule. As you answer her, you form a connected paragraph.

1. ¿A qué hora comes por la mañana?
2. ¿A qué hora sales de casa?
3. ¿A qué hora tomas el autobús?
4. ¿A qué hora llegas a tus clases?
5. ¿A qué hora te gusta ir a la biblioteca?
6. ¿A qué hora vas al supermercado?
7. ¿A qué hora prefieres llamar a tus papás?
8. ¿A qué hora vuelves a casa?

Estructura 6

Diminutives (For recognition)

Análisis

▸ The diminutive suffixes add to the noun the idea of smallness or endearment. The most widely used diminutive suffix in Spanish is **-ito (-ita)**; **-ico, -illo** are also used. The final vowel of nouns ending in **-o** or **-a** is replaced by **-ito (-ita)** to form the corresponding diminutive. The gender of the noun remains the same.

   el niño→el niñ**ito**   la carta→la cart**ita**

▸ If the noun ending in **-o** or **-a** has two syllables and its stem has **ie** or **ue**, the final **-o** or **-a** is replaced by **-ecito (-ecita)**.

   la tienda → la tiend**ecita**   el viento → el vient**ecito**

▸ Nouns ending in a consonant (other than **-n** or **-r**) add **-ito (-ita)**. Nouns ending in **-n, -r,** a stressed vowel, or **-e** add **-cito (-cita)**.

   el lápiz → el lap**icito**[6]   el tren → el tren**cito**   el café → el café**cito**

▸ Diminutive endings are very commonly added to proper names, adjectives, and even adverbs.

   Robertito (Roberto)   **pequeñito** (pequeño)
   Elenita   (Elena)   **cerquita**   (cerca)[7]

_____

[6] **Z** changes to **c** before **e, i.**
[7] **C** changes to **qu** before **e, i.**

APAGAR — TO TURN OFF
ENSEN DAR —
SOPLAR —
VELA — CANDLE
SERILLA —

Práctica

Give the diminutive forms of the following nouns, adjectives, and adverbs.

el traje	el guante	morena	el regalo	delgado
el avión	el sueldo	rubio	la plaza	tarde
azul	joven	baja	temprano	el autobús
la mujer	la playa	el suéter	claro	verde

Estructura 7

Al + *infinitive* (For recognition)

Análisis

▸ The Spanish **al** + *infinitive* construction literally means *upon (on) doing something.* Its colloquial English equivalent is a clause beginning with *when.*

—¿Cuándo encontró Ud. al recepcionista?   *When did you find the receptionist?*

—**Al volver** a la oficina, lo encontré.   ***When I got back*** *to the office, I found him.*

Práctica

Make sure you can translate these sentences into English.

1. Al llegar a la fábrica, empezó a trabajar.
2. Al verme en el Barrio, me llamaron.
3. Al hacer un viaje a Veracruz, conocí a los señores Díaz.
4. Al salir el médico, vio a los enfermeros.
5. Al traernos Iris el periódico, le pagamos dos pesos.

Estructura 8

Spelling changes in the preterit (For recognition)

Análisis

▸ Verbs of the **-a-** class whose stems end in the letters **c, g, z** have spelling changes in the **yo**-form of the preterit. While these verbs are regular in speech, spelling changes are required by the rules of the writing system. The sounds / k /, / g / and / s / (written **z**) are spelled differently before **e** and **i:** / k / —**que, qui;** / g / —**gue, gui;** / s / —**ce, ci.**

> buscar → **busqué**
> empezar → **empecé**
> pagar → **pagué**

Práctica

Rewrite these sentences in the preterit.

1. Saco buenas notas.
2. Pago noventa pesos.
3. Busco la sección de trajes.
4. Explico historia.
5. Empiezo el empleo en mayo.
6. Llego el domingo.

Comunicando

Preguntas personales

1. ¿Adónde vas a hacer un viaje este año?
2. ¿Cómo vas a llegar allí?
3. ¿Vas a salir o a descansar?
4. ¿Qué tiempo hace hoy?
5. ¿Qué hora es?
6. ¿Cuánto hace que Ud. salió de casa?

Charlas

1. —**Pasé las vacaciones en México.**
   ¿Cuánto hace que viajaste allí? ¿Cómo llegaste al país? ¿Conociste la capital y Veracruz? ¿Cuál ciudad te gustó más? ¿Por qué?

2. —**Salí a comer anoche.**
   ¿A qué hora saliste? ¿Dónde comiste? ¿Te gustó la comida? ¿Cuánto costó? ¿Quién te acompañó? ¿A qué hora volviste a casa?

Situación

You have just returned from a vacation in Mexico. Tell about your trip: how you traveled, what you saw, where you lived, what you liked best.

Para escribir

A. Rewrite the following sentences changing the verbs from present to preterit.

1. Comemos en el centro.
2. Roberto ve la piscina.
3. Vuelvo a la capital en tren.
4. ¿Te dan un traje de baño?
5. Tomas el avión, ¿verdad?
6. Salimos a las nueve menos cuarto.
7. Pasa las vacaciones en Veracruz.
8. Piensa venir temprano.

B. Answer the following questions in the preterit using the cues in parentheses. Change direct object nouns to pronouns and make necessary spelling changes.

MODELO: —¿No tienes que llegar a las dos?   (a la una)
—No, llegué a la una.

1. ¿No tienes que explicar matemáticas?   (ayer)
2. ¿No quieres empezar este libro?   (hace tres días)
3. ¿No debes buscar al jefe?   (esta mañana)
4. ¿No te hace falta pagar en abril?   (en enero)

C. Answer the following questions negatively using the cues in parentheses.

MODELO: —¿Son las dos y media?   (las tres y cuarto)
—No, son las tres y cuarto.

1. ¿Hace buen tiempo?   (mal)
2. ¿Viajaron en autobús?   (taxi)
3. ¿Son las doce y veinte?   (la una menos diez)
4. ¿El museo queda cerca del centro?   (lejos)
5. ¿Hace frío durante el día?   (calor)
6. ¿Hace 14 grados?   (19 grados)
7. ¿Traes comida a casa?   (café)
8. ¿Hace un mes que estás de vacaciones?   (tres semanas)

D. Translate the following sentences into Spanish.

1. How's the weather today?
   It's cold and windy. I think its going to rain.
2. We have to take the train at 7:30 P.M.
3. Elena takes a trip to Mexico every year.
4. How long ago did you eat?
   I ate three hours ago.
5. What time is it?
   It's 10:45.
6. I spent my vacation at the beach last year.
7. They returned to the pool in the afternoon.
8. How long have you (**Uds.**) been in Veracruz?
   We've been here for five years.
9. I went into the café because it began to rain.
10. You (**Ud.**) need (*use* **hacer falta**) 75 pesos for food.

lección 8

Objectives

Structure   You will learn the preterit of stem-changing and irregular verbs. You will practice the use of double object pronouns and learn how to form relative clauses.

Vocabulary   You will learn the names of several foods and eating utensils.

Conversation   By the end of the lesson you will be able to talk about some foods you eat and to relate your restaurant experiences.

Culture   You will learn about some foods eaten by Spanish speakers.

Outline

Estructura 1   The preterit of stem-changing verbs of the **-i-** class (**-ir** verbs)
Estructura 2   Irregular preterits
Estructura 3   Double object pronouns
Estructura 4   The suffix **-ísimo** (the absolute superlative)
Estructura 5   The compound sentence: relative pronouns **que, quien**

The Cooking Enthusiast

Eduardo Valdés studies engineering at the University of Chile in Santiago. On Saturdays he helps his parents in their restaurant because cooking is his hobby.

On Saturday I worked a lot because so many people came to have lunch and dinner. After serving lunch, I set the tables for dinner. A waiter helped me with the plates, glasses, and napkins. I went to the kitchen where I prepared a meat and vegetable stew. My mother tasted it and found it delicious. The other cook made some chicken and rice dishes that were (tasted) delicious. I spent the whole afternoon in the kitchen and afterwards I served dinner in the dining room. I brought the menus and the food. The customers ordered soup, fish, salad, eggs, and the stew I made. Many people preferred fruit, cheese, and ice cream for dessert. They drank water, wine, and beer. When the customers finished dinner, they asked me for the check and I brought it to them. Everyone left me a tip. I was very happy!

Presentación

El aficionado a la cocina

Eduardo Valdés estudia ingeniería en la Universidad de Chile en Santiago. Los sábados ayuda a sus papás en el restaurante de ellos porque es aficionado a la cocina.

El sábado trabajé mucho porque tanta gente vino a almorzar y cenar. Después de servir el almuerzo puse las mesas para la cena. Un mozo me ayudó con los platos, los vasos y las servilletas. Fui a la cocina donde preparé una cazuela de carne y legumbres. Mi mamá la probó y la encontró riquísima. El otro cocinero hizo unos platos de pollo y arroz que estuvieron ricos. Pasé toda la tarde en la cocina y después serví la cena en el comedor. Traje las cartas y la comida. Los clientes pidieron sopa, pescado, ensalada, huevos y la cazuela que hice yo. Mucha gente prefirió fruta, queso y helado de postre. Bebieron agua, vino y cerveza. Cuando terminaron la cena, los clientes me pidieron la cuenta y se la traje. Todos me dejaron una propina. ¡Estuve contentísimo!

Ampliación

—¿Tomaste el desayuno?
—Sí, desayuné antes de salir.

Did you eat breakfast?
Yes, I ate breakfast before I went out.

—¿Qué tomaron con la comida?
—Tomamos **leche.**
    (jugo, té, soda)

What did you drink with the meal?
*We drank **milk.***
    (juice, tea, soda)

—¿Prueban el sandwich?
—No, sólo probamos **la torta.**
    (el pan, la manzana, el plátano)

Are you tasting the sandwich?
*No, we're only tasting **the cake.***
    (the bread, the apple, the banana)

—Moza, **otro cuchillo,** por favor.
    (otro tenedor, otra cuchara, otra cucharita, otra taza)

*Waitress, **another knife,** please.*
    (another fork, another spoon, another teaspoon, another cup)

—¿Durmió Ud. bien anoche?   *Did you sleep well last night?*
—No, dormí mal.   *No, I slept badly.*

—¿Cuándo murió el señor Salas?   *When did Mr. Salas die?*
—Murió el año pasado.   *He died last year.*

Preguntas sobre la presentación

1. ¿Dónde estudia Eduardo?
2. ¿Cómo ayuda Eduardo a sus papás?
3. ¿Qué plato hizo Eduardo?
4. ¿Qué comieron los clientes?
5. ¿Qué tomaron con la comida?
6. ¿Por qué estuvo Eduardo contento?

Vocabulario activo

el **aficionado**   fan, devotee
el **agua** (*fem.*)   water
  almorzar (o → ue)   to have lunch
el **almuerzo**   lunch
  antes (de)   before
el **arroz**   rice
  ayudar   to help
  beber   to drink
la **carne**   meat
la **carta**   menu
la **cazuela**   stew; stew pot
la **cena**   dinner
  cenar   to have dinner
la **cerveza**   beer
la **cocina**   kitchen; cooking
el **cocinero**   cook
el **comedor**   dining room
la **cuchara**   spoon
la **cucharita**   teaspoon
el **cuchillo**   knife
la **cuenta**   check, bill
  dejar   to leave
  desayunar   to have breakfast
el **desayuno**   breakfast
  después (de)   after
  dormir (o → ue; o → u)   to sleep
la **ensalada**   salad
la **fruta**   fruit

la **gente**   people
el **helado**   ice cream
el **huevo**   egg
el **jugo**   juice
la **leche**   milk
la **legumbre**   vegetable
la **manzana**   apple
la **mesa**   table
  morir (o → ue; o → u)   to die
el **pan**   bread
el **pescado**   fish
el **plátano**   banana
el **plato**   plate, dish
el **pollo**   chicken
  poner (yo pongo)   to put
el **postre**   dessert
  preparar   to prepare
  probar (o → ue)   to taste, to try
la **propina**   tip
el **queso**   cheese
  rico   delicious
el **sandwich**   sandwich
la **servilleta**   napkin
la **soda**   soda
la **sopa**   soup
la **taza**   cup
el **té**   tea
el **tenedor**   fork

la **torta**   cake
el **vaso**   glass
el **vino**   wine

EXPRESIONES
poner la mesa   to set the table
por favor   please

Estructura 1

*The preterit of stem-changing verbs of the **-i-** class (**-ir** verbs)*

Análisis

▸ Verbs of the **-i-** class that have a change in the vowel of the stem in the present tense (**e → i, e → ie**) have to change to **i** in the stems of the third person singular and third person plural of the preterit.

seguir	preferir
seguí	preferí
seguiste	preferiste
siguió	prefirió
seguimos	preferimos
seguisteis	preferisteis
siguieron	prefirieron

▸ **Dormir** (*to sleep*) and **morir** (*to die*) have a change of **o → ue** in the present tense. They change **o → u** in the third person singular and third person plural of the preterit.

dormir		morir	
Present	*Preterit*	*Present*	*Preterit*
d**ue**rmo	dormí	m**ue**ro	morí
d**ue**rmes	dormiste	m**ue**res	moriste
d**ue**rme	d**u**rmió	m**ue**re	m**u**rió
dormimos	dormimos	morimos	morimos
dormís	dormisteis	morís	moristeis
d**ue**rmen	d**u**rmieron	m**ue**ren	m**u**rieron

Práctica

A. Change the verb in each sentence according to the cues.

   1. Dormí bien en el hotel.
      (ella, nosotros, Ud., ellos, tú, Uds.)

2. Preferimos ir en coche.
   (ellas, yo, él, tú, Ud., Uds.)

B. Your friend asks you who will be doing certain things. Tell her that Eduardo did them already.

> MODELO: —¿Quién va a conseguir el empleo?   *Who's going to get the job?*
>   —Ya lo consiguió Eduardo.   *Eduardo already got it.*

1. ¿Quién va a servir el pollo?
2. ¿Quién va a dormir en esta cama?
3. ¿Quién va a seguir con esa clase?
4. ¿Quién va a pedir otro jugo?

C. Repeat Exercise B using **Eduardo y Carlos** as your answer.

> MODELO: —¿Quiénes van a conseguir el empleo?
>   —**Ya lo consiguieron Eduardo y Carlos.**

Estructura 2

Irregular preterits

Análisis

▸ Many Spanish verbs have preterits that contain both an irregular stem plus a special set of endings. Study the conjugation of the following irregular preterits.

	estar	tener	poder	saber	traer
Preterit endings					
-e	estuve	tuve	pude	supe	traje
-iste	estuviste	tuviste	pudiste	supiste	trajiste
-o	estuvo	tuvo	pudo	supo	trajo
-imos	estuvimos	tuvimos	pudimos	supimos	trajimos
-isteis	estuvisteis	tuvisteis	pudisteis	supisteis	trajisteis
-ieron	estuvieron	tuvieron	pudieron	supieron	trajeron

	decir	venir	hacer	querer	poner
Preterit endings					
-e	dije	vine	hice	quise	puse
-iste	dijiste	viniste	hiciste	quisiste	pusiste
-o	dijo	vino	hizo	quiso	puso
-imos	dijimos	vinimos	hicimos	quisimos	pusimos
-isteis	dijisteis	vinisteis	hicisteis	quisisteis	pusisteis
-ieron	dijeron	vinieron	hicieron	quisieron	pusieron

▶ The stem **hic-** (from **hacer**) is spelled **hiz-** in the third person singular. The irregular preterits whose stem (**dij-, traj-**) ends in **-j** have **-eron** and not **-ieron** in the third person plural: **dijeron, trajeron.**

▶ Verbs of the **-e-** and **-i-** class such as **leer, creer,** whose stems (**le-, cre-**) end in a vowel, change the **-i-** of the third person singular and third person plural endings to **-y-: leyó, leyeron; creyó, creyeron.** A written accent is used on the **-i-** of the endings of the **tú, nosotros,** and **vosotros** forms of **-e-** verbs whose stems end in a vowel: **leíste, leímos, leísteis; creíste, creímos, creísteis.**

▶ **Ser** and **ir** have the same conjugation in the preterit.

ser / ir	
fui	fuimos
fuiste	fuisteis
fue	fueron

▶ The preterit of **hay** is **hubo.**

Práctica

A. Change the verb in each sentence according to the cues.

1. Vine a las dos.
   (nosotros, ella, tú, Uds., ellos)

2. Le dijeron el precio.
   (yo, él, nosotros, Ud., Uds.)

3. Trajo otro plato.
   (ellas, yo, tú, él y yo, Uds.)

4. Hicimos la sopa.
   (tú, él y ella, yo, Uds., Ud.)

5. Fuiste cocinero.
   (él, yo, nosotros, ellos, Ud.)

6. Tuvo tres exámenes.
   (Uds., tú, ella, nosotros, yo)

7. Ya puso la mesa.
   (ellos, yo, Uds., tú, nosotros)

8. No pudieron venir a comer.
   (yo, Ud., ellas, ella, tú, Uds.)

9. No supe dónde viven.
   (ella, nosotros, tú, Ud., yo, Uds.)

10. No quisimos cenar con ellos.
    (tú, yo, nosotros, él, Uds., ella)

B. Answer the following questions affirmatively. Change any direct object nouns to pronouns.

MODELO: —¿Hizo Ud. el desayuno?
            —Sí, lo hice.

1. ¿Supiste la nota?
2. ¿Quisieron Uds. almorzar?
3. ¿Estuvo Ud. en el comedor?
4. ¿Pusiste la mesa?
5. ¿Tuvimos unos tenedores?
6. ¿Pudo dejar una propina?
7. ¿Fueron a la cocina?
8. ¿Trajeron Uds. el paraguas?

Estructura 3

Double object pronouns

Análisis

▶ When two object pronouns are used with the same verb, the indirect object *precedes* the direct object. The following combinations are possible:

me lo	me la	me los	me las
te lo	te la	te los	te las
nos lo	nos la	nos los	nos las
os lo	os la	os los	os las

NOTE: Both **le** and **les** change to **se** before **lo, la, los, las: se lo, se la, se los, se las.**

▶ Out of context, **se lo sirvo** may mean *I serve it to him, to her, to you* (**Ud.** or **Uds.**), or *to them* (**ellos** or **ellas**). This **se** may seem ambiguous, but context usually indicates who is referred to. Should the speaker wish to focus on the person **se** refers to, he adds a phrase consisting of **a** plus a prepositional pronoun.

Se lo sirvo
- a él.
- a ella.
- a Ud.
- a ellos.
- a ellas.
- a Uds.

▶ In *verb + infinitive* constructions, double object pronouns (like single ones) either precede the first verb or follow the infinitive. In the latter case, the infinitive and the pronouns are written as one word. A written accent is added over the class-vowel of the infinitive (the vowel before the **-r**).

¿El pescado? **Me lo** puedes servir.
¿El pescado? Puedes servír**melo**.   *The fish? You can serve **it to me.***

Práctica

A. Repeat each sentence changing the indirect object pronoun according to the cues.

1. ¿El vino? **Se** lo pido.   (a ella, a ti, a ellos, a Ud.)
2. ¿Las servilletas? No **me** las quiso dar.   (a él, a nosotros, a Uds., a ti)
3. ¿La piscina? **Nos** la enseñaron.   (a ti, a ellos, a mí, a Ud.)
4. ¿Los guantes? No pudo vendér**telos**.   (a Uds., a ella, a mí, a Ud.)

B. Your friend wants to know who you're getting a series of things from. Tell her in each case that it's Teresa who's giving them to you.

MODELO:　(*Tu amiga*)—¿Quién te da su suéter?　*Who's giving you her sweater?*

—Me lo da Teresa.　*Teresa's giving it to me.*

1. ¿Quién te da sus tazas?
2. ¿Quién te da sus lápices?
3. ¿Quién te da un regalo?
4. ¿Quién te da su pluma?
5. ¿Quién te da el arroz?
6. ¿Quién te da unas cartas?

Estructura 4

The suffix -ísimo (the absolute superlative)

Análisis

▸ The suffix **-ísimo** added to the stem of an adjective is equivalent to **muy** + adjective.

delicious — very commonly used

—¿Estuvo rico el arroz?　　　　　*Was the rice delicious?*
—Sí, estuvo **riquísimo.**　　　　*Yes, it was most delicious.*

Adjectives ending in **-ísimo** are four-form adjectives: **riquísimo, riquísima, riquísimos, riquísimas.** Note the spelling change **c → qu** before **-ísimo.**

▸ **Muchísimo** and **poquísimo** also function as adverbs: **Me gustó muchísimo el plato** (*I liked the dish very much*).

Práctica

Your friend asks you what you think about certain things. Give her your opinion using the suffix **-ísimo** in your answers.

MODELO:　—¿Es bueno ese libro?　*Is that book good?*
　　　　　—Sí, es buenísimo.　　*Yes, it's very good.*

1. ¿Es grande tu oficina?
2. ¿Es hermosa tu novia?
3. ¿Estuvieron ricas las tortas?
4. ¿Fue interesante el viaje?
5. ¿Son fáciles los exámenes?
6. ¿Está preocupado tu papá?

Estructura 5

*The complex sentence: relative pronouns **que, quien***

Análisis

▸ Two sentences that share an identical element can be combined into one by means of a *relative pronoun*.

Veo al mozo. El mozo trabaja aquí.	*I see the waiter. The waiter works here.*
main clause relative clause	main clause relative clause
Veo al mozo *que* **trabaja aquí.**	*I see the waiter **who** works here.*

There are two clauses in the new sentence: the main clause and the relative clause, which begins with a relative pronoun. A sentence consisting of these two types of clauses is called a complex sentence.

▸ In Spanish, the relative pronoun **que** replaces both animate and inanimate nouns, that is, nouns referring to both people and things.

Conozco a la dependienta. **La dependienta** vende blusas.	*I know the saleswoman. **The saleswoman** sells blouses.*
Conozco a la dependienta *que* **vende blusas.**	*I know the saleswoman **who** sells blouses.*
Conozco la ciudad. Vas a visitar **la ciudad.**	*I know the city. You're going to visit **the city.***
Conozco la ciudad *que* **vas a visitar.**	*I know the city **that** you're going to visit.*

▸ In Spanish, a preposition may not be separated from its noun and therefore precedes the relative pronoun.

Aquí están los platos. Hablamos **de los platos.**	*Here are the plates. We talked **about the plates.***
Aquí están los platos *de que* **hablamos.**	*Here are the plates we talked about.*

▸ After prepositions **quien** (**quienes** for plurals) is used instead of **que** at the beginning of the relative clause to replace a noun referring to a person.

Aquí está la cocinera **para quien** trabajo.	*Here's the cook I work for.*
Aquí están las cocineras **para quienes** trabajo.	*Here are the cooks I work for.*

Nouns referring to persons that are preceded by a personal **a** in the original sentence may appear either as **a quien** (**a quienes**) or as **que** at the beginning of a relative clause.

El hombre $\left\{\begin{array}{l}\textbf{que} \\ \textbf{a quien}\end{array}\right\}$ Ud. conoció es mi tío.   *The man you met is my uncle.*

In Spanish, the relative pronouns **que** and **quien (quienes)** are never omitted as *who, whom, which, that* often are in English.

el autobús **que** tomé   *the bus I took*
las niñas **con quienes** vino   *the girls she came with*

Práctica

Combine each pair of sentences into a single sentence replacing the identical element of the second by the appropriate relative pronoun.

MODELO: Acompañas a los estudiantes.   *You're going with the students.*
Los estudiantes estudian   *The students study*
sicología.   *psychology.*
→ Acompañas a los   *You're going with the students*
estudiantes que estudian   *who study psychology.*
sicología.

1. Llamé a mi amiga. Mi amiga vive en el Barrio.
2. Prueba la cazuela. La cazuela está en la cocina.
3. Aquí está la profesora. Estudio derecho con la profesora.
4. Murió el hombre. Hablaste del hombre.
5. Los muchachos están perfectamente. Vimos a los muchachos.
6. La pluma es gris. Escriben con la pluma.

Comunicando

Preguntas personales

1. ¿A qué hora desayunas? (almuerzas, cenas) ¿Qué comes?
2. ¿Eres aficionado(-a) a la cocina? ¿Qué te gusta preparar?
3. Para comer, ¿qué pones en la mesa?
4. Cuando fue al restaurante, ¿qué pidió?
5. ¿Qué trajo el mozo (la moza)?
6. ¿Dejó Ud. una propina?

Charlas

1. **—Preparé una comida el sábado.**
¿Qué serviste? ¿Qué pusiste en la mesa? ¿Quiénes vinieron a comer?
¿Dónde comieron Uds., en la cocina o en el comedor?

2. —**Almorzamos en un restaurante ayer.**

¿Qué pidieron? ¿Qué bebieron con la comida? ¿Sirvió bien el mozo? ¿Les gustó la comida?

Situación

Talk about the foods and beverages you usually have for breakfast, lunch, and dinner. Tell where you ate these meals yesterday and what you had.

Para escribir

A. Rewrite the following sentences changing the verb from the present to the preterit.

1. El hombre muere.
2. Prefieren cenar en casa.
3. Eduardo pone la mesa.
4. Piden un sandwich de queso.
5. ¿Qué sirvo de postre?
6. Todos leen la carta.
7. Vamos al comedor.
8. No tienes tenedores.
9. No podemos dormir cn csc hotcl.
10. La cazuela está riquísima.

B. Answer the following questions changing all direct object nouns to pronouns in your answers. Make all necessary changes.

MODELO: —¿Vas a servirle el té?
—Ya se lo serví.

1. ¿Vas a traerles la cuenta?
2. ¿Uds. van a hacerme la ensalada?
3. ¿Ud. va a darnos los huevos?
4. ¿Voy a enseñarte las tazas?
5. ¿Vamos a pedirle más jugo?
6. ¿Van a venir a las once y cuarto?

C. Supply the correct form of the adjective ending in **-ísimo** in each of the following sentences.

1. Aquellos libros son _____ (difícil).
2. Las niñas son _____ (pequeño).
3. Fuimos a ese almacén _____ (grande).
4. La falda amarilla es _____ (barato).
5. Los señores Valdés son _____ (guapo).
6. Esa calle es _____ (feo).

D. Fill in the blanks with the appropriate relative words.

1. Allí está el tren en _____ viajamos.
2. No vimos la carta _____ trajo la moza.
3. ¿Probaste el plato de _____ te hablé?

4. Los abogados ＿＿＿ llamé vinieron.
5. ¿Dónde está el amigo con ＿＿＿ haces el viaje?
6. Conozco al cocinero ＿＿＿ hizo el pan.

E. Translate the following sentences into Spanish.

1. I ate lunch before I went out.
2. The cook made a chicken dish.
3. We put knives, forks, spoons, and napkins on the table.
4. The waitress served the meal after she brought the menu.
5. Are you trying the vegetable soup and the meat?
6. I ordered a glass of milk, but the waiter didn't bring it to me.
7. I love to cook.
8. The chicken was most delicious.
9. Did you (**Ud.**) order an apple or a banana?
10. They didn't sleep well because they ate too much.

lección 9

Objectives

Structure   You will learn the forms and functions of reflexive verbs in Spanish. You will also practice the **vosotros**-form of the verb and learn the group of words called "neuters."

Vocabulary   You will learn how to express in Spanish that you are hungry, thirsty, cold, lucky, etc. You will learn many verbs that describe everyday activities such as washing, dressing, combing one's hair, or waking up.

Conversation   By the end of the lesson you will be able to describe your daily activities in detail, from getting up to going to bed. You will also be able to discuss your physical states—hungry, tired, comfortable—as well as your emotional states—angry, insulted, fearful, etc.

Culture   In your first introduction to Spain you will learn something about the country's geography and about some of its cultural features.

Outline

A Trip to Cordoba

Mr. and Mrs. Suárez live in Madrid. When their daughter Paloma got married in May, 1980, she moved to Cordoba with her husband. Her parents are visiting her now for the first time.

P.:   You made such a long trip, 300 kilometers. You're hungry and thirsty, aren't you?

D.J.:   Yes (daughter), I feel tired. I'm anxious to take a shower and lie down for a while.

D.F.:   I'm fine, but I'm very hot. What I want is to wash up and change my clothing.

P.:   Of course. Here's the bathroom if you want to wash up. Next to it is your room, where you can take a nap.

D.F.:   Fine. But we're not going to waste time this way. I intend to see as much as possible before I leave Cordoba. So we should wake up early tomorrow.

D.J.:   My goodness, Felipe, why are you in such a hurry? Are you forgetting that we're going to stay with Paloma all month long? You can wait a little, can't you?

P.:   Mom's right. Manolo and I intend to take you everywhere. Tonight we're taking you out to get to know the city.

D.F.:   Terrific! And I'm dying to see the Mezquita. You'll show it to me tomorrow, won't you?

P.:   O.K., Dad . . . Oh, I hear Manolo. He's coming from the office. Let's say hello to him.

Presentación

Un viaje a Córdoba

Los señores Suárez viven en Madrid. Cuando su hija Paloma se casó en mayo de 1980, se mudó a Córdoba con su marido. Sus papás la visitan ahora por primera vez.

Paloma	—Hicisteis un viaje tan largo, de trescientos kilómetros.[1] Tenéis hambre y sed, ¿verdad?
Doña Josefa[2]	—Sí, hija, me siento cansada. Tengo ganas de ducharme y echarme un rato.
Don Felipe[2]	—Yo me encuentro bien pero tengo mucho calor. Lo que deseo es lavarme y cambiarme la ropa.
Paloma	—Cómo no. Aquí está el baño si queréis lavaros. Al lado está vuestro cuarto para dormir la siesta.[3]
Don Felipe	—Bien. Pero no vamos a perder tiempo así. Pienso ver lo más posible antes de irme de Córdoba. Por eso debemos despertarnos temprano mañana.
Doña Josefa	—Por Dios, Felipe, ¿por qué tienes tanta prisa? ¿Te olvidas que vamos a quedarnos con Paloma todo el mes? Puedes esperar un poco, ¿no?
Paloma	—Mamá tiene razón. Manolo y yo pensamos llevaros a todas partes. Esta noche os sacamos a conocer la ciudad.
Don Felipe	—¡Estupendo! Y tengo muchísimas ganas de ver la Mezquita. Mañana me la enseñas, ¿no?
Paloma	—De acuerdo, papá . . . Ah, oigo a Manolo. Llega de la oficina. Vamos a saludarlo.

---

[1] A kilometer (1,000 meters) equals approximately 5/8 of a mile.

[2] **Don,** used before masculine given names, and **doña,** used before feminine given names, are titles of respect.

[3] While not as universal as it once was, the after-lunch nap is still customary in many Spanish-speaking countries.

Ampliación

—¿Cuántos cuartos tiene la casa?	*How many rooms does the house have?*
—Tiene tres. Una sala y dos dormitorios.[4]	*It has three. A living room and two bedrooms.*
—¿Dónde queda Córdoba?	*Where's Cordoba?*
—Queda a cien millas de aquí.	*It's 100 miles from here.*
—¿Es largo el viaje?	*Is the trip **long**?*
—No, es corto.	*No, it's short.*
—¿De qué te quejas?	*What are you complaining about?*
—Me quejo de **esto.**	*I'm complaining about **this.***
(eso, aquello)	*(that—near you, that—over there)*
—¿Se acuerdan Uds. de Felipe?	*Do you remember Felipe?*
—Sí, nos acordamos de él.	*Yes, we remember him.*
—**¿Se ofenden** ellos? (se enfadan)	*Do they **get insulted**? (get angry)*
—No, **ofenden** a Josefa.	*No, **they insult** Josefa.*
(enfadan)	*(they make Josefa angry)*
—¿Se puso Ud. el abrigo?	*Did you put on your overcoat?*
—No, me lo quité.	*No, I took it off.*
—¿A qué hora **se levantaron?**	*What time **did you get up?***
(se acostaron, se bañaron, se peinaron, se vistieron)	*(did you go to bed, did you take a bath, did you comb your hair, did you get dressed)*
—**Nos levantamos** a las ocho.	***We got up** at eight o'clock.*
(nos acostamos, nos bañamos, nos peinamos, nos vestimos)	*(we went to bed, we took a bath, we combed our hair, we got dressed)*
—¿Tienes miedo de viajar en avión?	*Are you afraid of travelling by plane?*
—Sí, los aviones me dan miedo.	*Yes, planes scare me.*
—Paloma tiene **suerte,** ¿verdad?	*Paloma's **lucky,** isn't she?*
(éxito, frío, sueño)	*(successful, cold, sleepy)*
—Sí, tiene **mucha.**	*Yes, **very.***

Preguntas sobre la Presentación

1. ¿Por qué hacen los señores Suárez un viaje a Córdoba?
2. ¿Cómo se encuentran los señores Suárez cuando llegan a casa de Paloma?
3. ¿Por cuánto tiempo van a quedarse en Córdoba?

---

[4] Other words for bedroom in Spanish-speaking countries are **el cuarto, la alcoba, la recámara** (Mexico).

4. ¿Adónde lleva Paloma a sus papás esta noche?
5. ¿Qué le interesa ver a don Felipe?
6. ¿Qué oye Paloma?

NOTA CULTURAL

Spain is a country of great regional diversity. Madrid, the capital of Spain, is located in the center of the country in the region called **Castilla. Córdoba,** an important city in south central Spain, is in the vast agricultural region **Andalucía.** La **Mezquita de Córdoba** is a magnificent mosque that dates from the arrival of the Arabs in Spain; it was started in 786. A chapel was added within the structure in the sixteenth century for Christian worship.

Vocabulario activo

acordarse (o → ue) to remember
acostarse (o → ue) to go to bed
bañarse to take a bath
el **baño** bathroom
cambiar to change
casarse (con) to get married (to)
corto short
el **cuarto** room; bedroom
despertarse (e → ie) to wake up
don masculine title of respect
doña feminine title of respect
el **dormitorio** bedroom
ducharse to take a shower
echarse to lie down
encontrarse (o→ue) to be (= **estar**)
enfadarse to get angry
esperar to wait
irse to go away
el **kilómetro** kilometer
largo long
lavarse to wash
levantarse to get up
la **milla** mile
mudarse to move
ofenderse to get insulted
oír (yo oigo) to hear
olvidarse to forget
peinarse to comb one's hair
perder (e → ie) to lose
ponerse to put on (*article of clothing*)
posible possible
quedarse to stay, to remain

quejarse to complain
quitarse to take off (*article of clothing*)
el **rato** while (*n.*)
sacar to take out
la **sala** living room
saludar to greet, to say hello to
sentirse (e → ie) to feel
la **siesta** nap
vestirse (e → i) to get dressed

EXPRESIONES

a todas partes everywhere
al lado (de) next door, next to
cómo no of course
de acuerdo OK, agreed
¡estupendo! terrific!
por eso therefore, that's why
por primera vez for the first time
tener calor to be warm (*referring to people*)
tener éxito to be successful
tener frío to be cold (*referring to people*)
tener ganas de (+ *inf.*) to feel like doing something
tener hambre to be hungry
tener miedo to be afraid
tener prisa to be in a hurry
tener razón to be right
tener sed to be thirsty
tener sueño to be sleepy
tener suerte to be lucky

Estructura 1

Vosotros

Análisis

▸ In contrast to Spanish America, where **Uds.** is used as the plural of both **tú** and **Ud.,** Spain uses **vosotros** with its corresponding verb endings as the plural of **tú.** In Spain, **Uds.** is the plural of **Ud.** only.

▸ The person ending for **vosotros** is **-is.** The **vosotros** form always has the same form of the stem as the **nosotros** form. The present tense forms for **-ar, -er,** and **-ir** verbs are:

> habl**áis**   com**éis**   viv**ís**

1. The written accent is used on all present-tense **vosotros** forms except those of one syllable: **dais (dar), vais (ir), sois (ser), veis (ver).**

2. The class-vowel **-i-** or **-ir** verbs merges with the **-i-** of the **-is** person ending: **vivís, escribís, pedís.** For the preterit tense, add **-is** to the **tú** form of the preterit:

> hablaste**is**   comiste**is**   viviste**is**

▸ The subject pronoun is **vosotros** (or **vosotras** for groups consisting solely of females). The direct and indirect object pronoun is **os.** The possessive adjectives for **vosotros** are: **vuestro, vuestra, vuestros, vuestras.**

—¿Cuándo nos das el paraguas?	*When are you giving us the umbrella?*
—**Os** lo doy mañana.	*I'll give it to you tomorrow.*
—¿Dónde están **vuestras** tazas?	*Where are your cups?*
—Están en la cocina.	*They're in the kitchen.*

Práctica

A. Make the following sentences plural by replacing the **tú**-form of the verbs with the corresponding **vosotros**-form in the same tense, as shown in the models.

MODELOS: Viajas a Córdoba. → Viajáis a Córdoba.
              Viajaste a Córdoba. → Viajasteis a Córdoba.

1. Tienes hambre.
2. Saludas a mis papás.
3. Sales de la ciudad.
4. Duermes la siesta.
5. Dejaste una propina.
6. Pusiste la mesa.
7. Recibiste unas cartas.
8. Fuiste a Madrid.

B. Answer the following questions using the correct form of the possessive adjective **vuestro** in your answer.

MODELO: —¿Es nuestra comida?   *Is it our meal?*
              —Sí, es vuestra comida.   *Yes, it's your meal.*

1. ¿Es nuestro autobús?
2. ¿Son nuestras aspirinas?
3. ¿Son nuestros ingenieros?
4. ¿Es nuestra pluma?
5. ¿Son nuestros supermercados?
6. ¿Es nuestro dormitorio?

C. Answer the following questions using the object pronoun **os** in your answer.

> MODELO: —¿Nos vas a llamar?   *Are you going to call us?*
> —Sí, os voy a llamar.   *Yes, I'm going to call you.*

1. ¿Nos sacas esta noche?
2. ¿Nos hace falta una guía?
3. ¿Nos saludó don Carlos?
4. ¿Nos quedan cien kilómetros de viaje?
5. ¿Nos trajiste té?
6. ¿Quisiste escribirnos?

Estructura 2

Reflexive verbs

Análisis

▶ When the subject of a verb and its direct object pronoun refer to the same person, the direct object appears as a *reflexive pronoun*. The reflexive pronouns for the first two persons are the same as the direct and indirect object pronouns. The reflexive pronoun for the third person singular and plural is **se.**

levantarse (*to get up*)	
me levanté *I got up*	**nos** levantamos
te levantaste	**os** levantasteis
se levantó	**se** levantaron

Reflexive verbs appear in vocabulary lists with **-se** attached to the infinitive. This **se** must change to agree with the subject of a *verb + infinitive* construction. Like other object pronouns, the **se** may stand either after the infinitive or before the first verb.

No quiero **levantarme** ahora.
No quieres **levantarte** ahora.
No quiere **levantarse** ahora.
No queremos **levantarnos** ahora.
No queréis **levantaros** ahora.
No quieren **levantarse** ahora.

No **me** quiero **levantar** ahora.
No **te** quieres **levantar** ahora.
No **se** quiere **levantar** ahora.
No **nos** queremos **levantar** ahora.
No **os** queréis **levantar** ahora.
No **se** quieren **levantar** ahora.

▶ Reflexive verb forms in English are followed by a pronoun ending in *-self* or *-selves*: *I wash myself. They hurt themselves.* Most Spanish reflexives, however, correspond either to English intransitive verbs (verbs without a direct object) or to English verb constructions with *get* or *be*, which deemphasize the performer of the action.

Se lavó esta mañana.	*She washed up this morning.* (intransitive)
Me enfadé mucho.	*I got very angry.* (performer of action deemphasized; person who made me angry not mentioned)

▶ Some reflexive constructions in Spanish have a reflexive pronoun that is an indirect object rather than a direct object. English equivalents of these sentences have a possessive adjective (*my*) where Spanish has a reflexive pronoun. In the following examples **los zapatos** and **la camisa** are the direct objects.

Me pongo los zapatos.	*I put on **my** shoes.*
Se quitaron la camisa.	*They took off **their** shirts.*

The reflexive pronoun may be replaced by an indirect object pronoun. This will require a change in the possessive adjective of the English equivalent.

reflex. pron. **Se** puso el abrigo.	*He put on his overcoat.*
i.o. **Le** puso el abrigo.	*He put on her overcoat.* (He helped her on with it.)

The direct object noun may be replaced by the appropriate object pronoun.

Me pongo **los zapatos.**	→ Me **los** pongo.	*I put them on.*
Se quitaron **la camisa.**	→ Se **la** quitaron.	*They took it off.*
Se puso **el abrigo.**	→ Se **lo** puso.	*He put it on.*
Le puso **el abrigo.**	→ Se **lo** puso.	*He helped her on with it.*

In the sentence **Se lo puso** (from **Le puso el abrigo**), **a ella** may be added to focus on who **se** refers to.

Se lo puso a ella.	*He helped **her** on with it.*

▶ Spanish uses a singular object for articles of clothing even when more than one subject is involved. If each subject has one item, for example, one suit each, Spanish uses the singular; if each subject has more than one item, Spanish uses the plural.

Se pusieron **el traje.**	*They put on **their suits.***
Se pusieron **los guantes.**	*They put on **their gloves.***

▶ The verbs **acordarse, olvidarse, quejarse** require **de** before a noun object:

Me acuerdo *de* la playa.	*I remember the beach.*
Se olvidó *de* eso.	*You forgot that.*

The **de** may be omitted before **que**: **¿Te olvidas (de) que viene hoy?** (*Are you forgetting he's coming today?*)

▸ The use of the reflexive pronouns with some verbs changes the English equivalents considerably.

acordar to agree, to resolve	**acordarse** to remember
dormir to sleep	**dormirse** to fall asleep
encontrar to find	**encontrarse** to be (**estar**)
ir to go	**irse** to go away
quedar to remain, to be left	**quedarse** to stay, to remain (*location*)
sentir to regret	**sentirse** to feel

Práctica

A. Change the verb in each sentence according to the cues.

1. Se casó en febrero.
   (ellos, tú, yo, nosotros, vosotros)

2. Me acuesto a las diez.
   (Ud., ellas, nosotros, él, Uds.)

3. Se visten en el cuarto.
   (yo, vosotros, ella, tú y yo, tú)

4. No debéis ofenderos.
   (nosotros, Ud., yo, ellos, él)

B. Answer the following questions in Spanish.

1. ¿Cómo te encuentras hoy?
2. ¿A qué hora te despertaste hoy?
3. ¿A qué hora te acostaste anoche?
4. ¿Prefiere Ud. ducharse o bañarse?
5. ¿Qué se pone Ud. para salir?
6. ¿En qué cuarto **te lavas?** (te peinas, te vistes)
7. ¿Piensas casarte?
8. ¿Adónde queréis mudaros?
9. ¿De qué te quejas?
10. ¿De qué **te acuerdas**? (te olvidas)

Estructura 3

Neuters

Análisis

▸ Spanish has a series of forms of the demonstrative pronouns ending in **-o** that are called *neuters*. **Esto** (*this*), **eso** (*that*), and **aquello** (*that*) correspond to the three demonstratives **este, ese,** and **aquel.** They mean *this* or *that* in the sense of *this or that business, matter, stuff.*

Se queja de **eso.**	*He's complaining about **that** (matter).*
¿Qué es **esto?**	*What's **this** (stuff)?*

English sentences that have equivalents for **esto, eso,** and **aquello** cannot have the word *one* inserted after the demonstratives:

No me gusta *esto.*	*I don't like **this.***
No me gusta *este.*	*I don't like **this one.***

▸ **Lo,** often called the neuter article, is used in a variety of situations:
1. In the phrase **lo más (menos) posible** (*as much [little] as possible*).

2. Before the masculine singular form of adjectives it means *that which is*: **lo bueno** (*the good part, what's good*).

3. Before a **de** phrase it means *the matter concerning*: **lo del almacén** (*the department store matter, affair, situation, thing*).

4. In the phrase **lo que** it means *what* (but not as an interrogative).

Lo que deseo es dormir la siesta.	*What I want is to take a nap.*
Nos acordamos de lo que dijo.	*We remember what he said.*

Práctica

A. *Patterned translation drill.* Translate each sentence following the pattern of the Spanish model.

MODELO: *They eat as much as possible.*   Comen lo más posible.

1. They complain as much as possible.
2. They wait as much (long) as possible.
3. They bathe as much as possible.
4. They visit us as much as possible.
5. They help me as much as possible.

Now perform the same drill with **lo menos posible.**

B. Form complete sentences connecting each pair of elements by means of **lo** and **de** or **lo que.**

MODELOS: comprendo / el colegio. →   Comprendo lo del colegio.
I understand the high school matter.

comprendo / dices →   Comprendo lo que dices.
I understand what you're saying.

1. sabéis / el cocinero
2. tomamos / pedimos
3. nos gustó / nos enseñó
4. le interesa / la comunidad
5. no recibo / espero
6. vimos / hicisteis
7. no vas a creer / mis hermanos
8. no quisieron beber / les servimos

Estructura 4

*Idioms with **tener** and **dar***

Análisis

▸ The construction **tener** + *noun* appears as the equivalent of English phrases with both *to be* and *to have*. Many English equivalents consist of *to be* + *adjective*.

Tengo hambre. (sueño)	*I'm hungry. (sleepy)*
Tiene éxito.	*She's successful.*

There is considerable variety in the English phrases that correspond to some **tener** + *noun* phrases.

Tienen prisa.	*You're in a hurry.*
¿Tenéis ganas de salir?	*Do you feel like going out?*

Since the words following **tener** are all nouns, forms of **mucho** and **poco** rather than **muy** must be used to modify them.

Eduardo tiene **mucha** suerte.	*Eduardo's **very** lucky.*
Tengo **poca** sed.	*I'm **not very** thirsty.*
Tenemos **muchas** ganas de cenar.	*We **really** feel like having dinner.*

▸ Most of the nouns used with **tener** can also be used with **dar** + *an indirect object pronoun* to mean *to cause someone to have hunger, thirst, desire*, etc. As with the **tener** idioms, the nouns must be modified by forms of **mucho** and **poco**.

Me da miedo.	*It scares me.*
Os da **mucha** hambre.	*It makes you **very** hungry.*

Práctica

Answer the following questions in Spanish.

1. ¿Tienes **hambre** ahora?   (sed)
2. ¿Qué tomas cuando tienes sed?
3. Ud. se acostó tarde. ¿Tiene sueño?
4. ¿Cree que tiene **suerte?**   (éxito)
5. Te levantaste tarde hoy. ¿Tienes prisa?
6. ¿Qué te da **miedo?**   (hambre, sueño)
7. ¿Qué **te pones** (te quitas) cuando tienes **frío?**   (calor)
8. ¿Tenéis ganas de quedaros en esta ciudad?

Estructura 5

Cardinal numbers 100–10,000

Análisis

100	**ciento**	400	**cuatrocientos**	700	**setecientos**
200	**doscientos**	500	**quinientos**	800	**ochocientos**
300	**trescientos**	600	**seiscientos**	900	**novecientos**

1,000 **mil**	5,000 **cinco mil**	10,000 **diez mil**

▶ **Ciento** (100) shortens to **cien** before a noun—**cien lápices** (*100 pencils*)—but not before another number—**ciento un lápices** (*101 pencils*). In isolation, either **ciento** or **cien** may be used.

NOTE: **Un** never appears before **ciento (cien)** or **mil,** as in English *one hundred* or *one thousand*.

—¿Cuántos lápices tienes?   *How many pencils do you have?*
—Ciento. OR Cien.   *One hundred.*

▶ The numerals 200–900 agree in number with the noun that follows.

trescien**tos** tenedores   *300 forks*
trescien**tas** cucharas   *300 spoons*
seiscien**tos** cuarenta tenedores   *640 forks*
seiscien**tas** cuarenta cucharas   *640 spoons*

Numerals ending in *one* (**un, una**) also agree in gender with the noun that follows.

quinientos setenta y ***un* kilómet*ros***   571 kilometers
quinientas setenta y ***una* mill*as***   571 miles

▶ Spanish uses a period where English uses a comma in writing numbers over a thousand: 1,000 = 1.000. Spanish speakers do not count by hundreds above 1,000 as do English speakers. Thus, 1,800 is rendered only as **mil ochocientos.**

Práctica

Read the following phrases aloud.

1. 100 dormitorios	5. 415 hoteles	9. 946 mecanógrafos
2. 101 vasos	6. 579 materias	10. 1.000 kilómetros
3. 101 servilletas	7. 731 calles	11. 4.600 calcetines
4. 221 manzanas	8. 893 ingenieros	12. 9.871 recepcionistas

Estructura 6

Oír *(to hear)*

Análisis

▶ **Oír** (*to hear*) is a **-g-** verb; the **yo**-form in the present tense is **oigo.** The verb is irregular in both the present and the preterit.

oír	
Present	*Preterit*
oigo	oí
oyes	oíste
oye	oyó
oímos	oímos
oís	oísteis
oyen	oyeron

Práctica

Change the verb in each sentence according to the cues.

1. Oigo el viento.
   (ella, tú, nosotros, ellos, vosotros)

2. No oyeron a los niños.
   (Ud., yo, Uds., tú y yo, vosotros)

Comunicando

Preguntas personales

1. ¿Qué te pones cuando hace **calor?**   (frío)
2. ¿Qué hacéis antes de tomar el desayuno todos los días?
3. ¿Te gusta **ducharte** por la mañana o por la noche?   (bañarte, peinarte)
4. ¿Se echa un rato cuando tiene sueño?
5. ¿Cree que **sus papás** tienen razón siempre?   (sus amigos, sus profesores)
6. ¿Qué os **enfada?**   (ofende)
7. ¿A cuántas millas de aquí queda tu casa?

Charlas

1. —**Tengo ganas de mudarme a otra casa.**
   ¿Por qué te quejas de tu casa?   ¿Cuántos cuartos tiene?   ¿Cuáles son?
   ¿Cuánto dinero puedes pagar por otra casa?   ¿Cuándo quieres mudarte?

2. —**Hicimos un viaje largo hace dos meses.**
   ¿Cuántos kilómetros viajasteis?   ¿Fuisteis allí por primera vez?   ¿Dormisteis la siesta cuando llegasteis?   ¿Os duchasteis y os cambiasteis la ropa?
   ¿Os acordáis bien del viaje?

Situación

Tell what your typical schedule is on a school day. Mention what you do and when you do it from the time you get up until the time you go to sleep. Tell how your schedule is different on Saturdays and Sundays by stating some things you never do as well as those you usually do.

Para escribir

A. Make the following sentences plural by replacing the **tú**-form of the verbs with the **vosotros**-form. Make all necessary changes in the possessive adjectives (**tu → vuestro**) and direct and indirect object pronouns (**te → os**).

> MODELOS: Estudias con tus amigos. → Estudiáis con vuestros amigos.
> ¿Te gustan tus primos? → ¿Os gustan vuestros primos?

1. Dormiste la siesta en tu cuarto.
2. Pierdes mucho tiempo así.
3. Te quejas de tus hermanas.
4. ¿Te interesó la Mezquita?
5. Te llevamos a ver a tus tíos.
6. Te encuentras perfectamente hoy.
7. ¿Le vas a poner el abrigo?
8. ¿Te dan miedo los hospitales?
9. Te despiertas a las siete.
10. Puedes esperarme en tu dormitorio.

B. Answer the following questions in complete Spanish sentences.

1. ¿Se sienten Uds. alegres hoy?
2. ¿Te enfadas si un amigo te ofende?
3. ¿A qué hora se acuestan Uds.?
4. ¿Qué ropa le pusiste al niño?
5. ¿Cuándo pensáis casaros?
6. ¿Os acordasteis del viaje que hicisteis?
7. ¿Te peinas antes o después de vestirte?
8. ¿A qué hora se levantó hoy?
9. ¿Queréis bañaros o ducharos?
10. ¿Se vistió en el baño o en el dormitorio?

C. Construct complete sentences by connecting each pair of elements with **lo** and **de** or **lo que.**

> MODELOS: Sabe / los empleos → Sabe lo de los empleos.
> Sabe / compramos → Sabe lo que compramos.

1. perdió / le dimos
2. no comprendemos / las materias
3. les encantó / el supermercado
4. coméis / os hago
5. me importa / los empleados
6. quisiste saber / el regalo
7. oigo / dicen
8. no encuentran / buscan

D. Supply the correct form of **mucho** or **poco** in these sentences.

1. Tenemos _____ (mucho) sed.
2. Tenéis _____ (poco) suerte.
3. Nos da _____ (mucho) hambre.
4. ¿Tienes _____ (mucho) ganas de irte?
5. Le da _____ (poco) éxito.
6. Tengo _____ (mucho) prisa.

E. Write the following numbers in Spanish.

1. _____ (100) tazas
2. _____ (584) kilómetros
3. _____ (3.916) plumas
4. _____ (101) mozas
5. _____ (778) millas
6. _____ (9.999) estudiantes
7. _____ (351) días
8. _____ (1.000) aviones
9. _____ (10.000) ciudades

F. Translate the following sentences into Spanish.

1. Madrid is **(quedar)** 701 kilometers from here.
2. I'm very sleepy. That's why I feel like taking a nap.
3. You **(vosotros)** always complain about that.
4. He said "hello" to me (*greeted me*) and went away.
5. We took off our jackets and we stayed a while.
6. Your (de **vosotros**) bedroom is next to the bathroom.
7. You're **(vosotros)** very cold but we're very warm.
8. You **(Ud.)** should shower in the morning and take a bath at night.
9. You **(tú)** got up, washed, combed your hair, and got dressed before having breakfast.
10. They're wasting **(perder)** a lot of time this way.

repaso 3

(Lecciones 7–9)

A. Answer each of the following questions using the cue in parentheses.

1. ¿Qué les hace falta a Uds.?   (unas vacaciones)
2. ¿Adónde piensan hacer un viaje?   (a Veracruz)
3. ¿Qué nos van a traer de México?   (unos libros)
4. ¿Qué día salen?   (el jueves)
5. ¿Cuándo vuelven de allí?   (en dos semanas)

B. Answer each of the following questions using the preterit in your response. Change direct object nouns to pronouns and make all necessary changes.

> MODELO: —¿Va él a seguir con esas clases?
> —Ya siguió con ellas.

1. ¿Van ellos a servirle el postre?
2. ¿Vas a decirme el día?
3. ¿Vamos a hacerles la cazuela?
4. ¿Va ella a traernos unas blusas?
5. ¿Vais a venir con Eduardo?
6. ¿Van (ellos) a pedirle una cuchara al mozo?
7. ¿Vas a darle una pluma a Elena?
8. ¿Van Uds. a ver al cocinero hoy?

C. Supply the correct present tense form of the verb in parentheses. The sentences form a connected narrative about a day at the beach.

1. Yo _____ (despertarse) a las siete.
2. Mis amigos _____ (levantarse) temprano también.
3. (Yo) _____ (vestirse) en el dormitorio y _____ (peinarse) en el baño.
4. (Yo) _____ (ponerse) el traje de baño.
5. Todos _____ (quejarse) del tiempo.
6. Marta y yo _____ (irse) a la playa.
7. Alberto y Elena _____ (quedarse) en casa.
8. (Ellos) _____ (sentirse) cansadísimos.

9. Cuando Marta y yo llegamos a la playa _____ (echarse) para descansar.
10. Después _____ (salir) el sol y nosotros _____ (bañarse = here, *go for a swim*) en el agua.

D. Rewrite Exercise C using the preterit of each of the verbs.

E. Answer each of the following questions with a complete Spanish sentence.

1. ¿A qué hora se acostó Ud. anoche?
2. ¿Qué te pones cuando hace mucho frío?
3. ¿De qué te quejas más en tu colegio (universidad)?
4. ¿Te duchaste o te bañaste esta mañana?
5. ¿Qué te enfada?
6. ¿Durmió Ud. la siesta ayer?

F. Complete each of the following sentences with **que** or **quien(es)**.

1. Vi a mis tíos _____ viven en Madrid.
2. La recepcionista con _____ trabajo recibe un sueldo muy bueno.
3. ¿Puedes enseñarme el avión _____ tomaron?
4. Murieron los señores de _____ te hablé.
5. Aquí está el jefe para _____ trabajamos.
6. La señora _____ conocisteis es mi abuela.
7. Probaron la carne _____ está en la mesa.
8. ¿No te gustó el tren en _____ hiciste el viaje?

G. Translate the following sentences into Spanish. They form a connected narrative.

1. It's 1:45 P.M. now.
2. I had lunch with my friends an hour ago.
3. We ordered fish; it was delicious.
4. Today it's cold and cloudy and it's going to snow.
5. When we left the restaurant we went (back) home.
6. We stay home as much as possible in the winter.

H. Translate the following sentences into English.

1. No me acuerdo de lo de tus vecinos.
2. ¿Pusisteis la mesa antes o después de vestiros?
3. Siempre tienen mucha prisa cuando se despiertan tarde.
4. Jorge nos dijo que Felipe lo ofendió.
5. Hace mucho tiempo que están en la piscina.
6. ¿No tenéis ganas de probar un plato picante?

I. Reading passage. The following passage deals with the traditional Spanish meal schedule as experienced by an American student living with a Spanish family.

Cognates will again be marked with a raised degree sign°. New words are listed below. Study them until you can give the English equivalent for each Spanish word or phrase. After reading the passage, do the comprehension exercise that follows it.

el **aperitivo** apéritif, predinner drink	la **mermelada** jam
la **costumbre** custom	**mismo** same
la **criada** servant	el **pan tostado** toast
charlar to chat	**por fin** finally
dije para mí I said to myself	**precisamente** precisely
dormirse to fall asleep	**primer(o)** first
el **embotellamicnto** traffic jam	**raro** strange
era it was	**segundo** second
estaban they were	**sentarse** to sit down
la **estancia** stay, period of residence	la **sobremesa** afterdinner conversation
juntos together	la **tortilla** omelet
el **membrillo** quince jelly	**último** last

Las comidas en España

Me llamo Cynthia Smith y el año pasado hice un viaje a España. Mi idea fue estudiar español en la Universidad de Madrid. Como parte del programa,° viví con una familia española. Aprendí muchas cosas interesantes sobre la vida española durante mi estancia. Encontré que las costumbres españolas eran muy diferentes° de las costumbres norteamericanas, especialmente la hora de las comidas. Me acuerdo de mi primer día en España. Llegué a la casa de mi familia española un domingo por la tarde. El lunes me desperté a las siete, me lavé y me vestí. Fui al comedor para tomar el desayuno. Me lo sirvió una criada. No fue un desayuno norteamericano con huevos y cereales.° La criada me dio pan tostado con mantequilla y mermelada, y un café con leche. Me pareció poco, pero no quise pedir nada más.

Después de desayunar, salí para la universidad. Fui a tres clases y a la una salí de la universidad para volver a casa. Vi que todas las tiendas estaban cerradas, y no comprendí por qué. Tomé un autobús, y fue muy difícil llegar a casa por el tráfico. Todo Madrid quiere volver a casa para tomar el almuerzo y puedes imaginarte° los embotellamientos que hay en las calles de la capital. Dicen que ahora hay muchos españoles que ya no vuelven a sus casas para comer precisamente porque no tienen tiempo con ese tráfico tan horrible. Por fin llegué a casa y a las dos la criada puso la mesa. Empezamos a comer a las dos y media. El almuerzo fue enorme.° El primer plato fue una sopa de legumbres, y el segundo, un arroz con pescado. La criada nos sirvió pan y vino con la comida. De postre comimos queso, membrillo y fruta. Después de comer nos quedamos en la mesa para charlar. Me dijeron que esto era la sobremesa. A las cuatro menos cuarto los señores fueron a echarse a dormir la siesta. ¡Qué raro! dije para mí. Echarse después del almuerzo. En Estados Unidos el almuerzo es una

Una comida tan rica: sopa, pescado, ensalada y fruta.

comida tan corta y aquí la gente pasa tres o cuatro horas con su comida, su sobremesa y su siesta. Yo pasé a mi cuarto y me eché también. Descansé media hora antes de volver a la universidad para oír mi última clase del día.

Volví a la casa de mi familia española a las ocho y a las nueve la señora me llamó para tomar un aperitivo con todos ellos. —Vamos a cenar a las diez —me dijo. —A las diez —pensé— ¡qué tarde! No sé si puedo esperar. A las diez nos sentamos a la mesa y comimos una ensalada y una tortilla de patatas. De postre hubo una torta riquísima. Después, un café y la sobremesa. Me acosté a las doce. Las costumbres de comida son muy diferentes aquí, pensé, pero me gustan. Los miembros° de la familia pasan mucho tiempo juntos con esas comidas tan largas y hablan mucho durante la sobremesa. No va a ser difícil vivir como los españoles, pensé, y me dormí contenta.

COMPREHENSION CHECK

¿Qué aprendió Ud. sobre (*about*) la vida española?

Tell whether each of the following statements is true or false based on the information contained in the passage.

1. Los norteamericanos y los españoles comen a la misma hora.
2. El desayuno español es enorme.
3. La señora de la casa sirve las comidas.
4. Los españoles prefieren volver a casa para almorzar.

5. Muchos españoles ya no pueden volver a sus casas porque hay demasiado tráfico.
6. Cierran todas las tiendas y oficinas a la una de la tarde.
7. En el almuerzo la gente come poco.
8. El membrillo es un plato principal.°
9. La gente vuelve a su trabajo o a sus clases entre (*between*) las cuatro y las cinco de la tarde.
10. Los españoles se quedan en la mesa para conversar después de comer.
11. Es costumbre descansar después del almuerzo.
12. Los españoles cenan muy tarde.

lección 10

Objectives

Structure   You will learn another past tense—the imperfect—and will practice using the imperfect and preterit to signal different ways of looking at past events.

Vocabulary   You will learn words relating to your dreams, ambitions, and family traditions. You will also learn how to express dates and say the numbers above 10,000.

Conversation   By the end of the lesson, you will be able to talk about important dates (your birthday, for example), the seasons, how you hope to fulfill your dreams and expectations, and your values.

Culture   You will be introduced to a Cuban family living in the United States and will see, through their eyes, some of the conflicts they face as younger members of the family adopt American values.

Outline

Estructura 1   The imperfect tense
Estructura 2   **Hacía . . . que** + *imperfect* (*had been*)
Estructura 3   Use of the definite article
Estructura 4   Dates
Estructura 5   Numbers above 10,000
Estructura 6   **Y → e** before **i, hi; o → u** before **o, ho** (For recognition)

Two Cuban Women: Mother and Daughter

The mother:
When José and I decided to leave Cuba in 1965, we didn't know what awaited us in the U.S. We found another world in this country that clashed with our customs, and although we wanted to continue our Cuban traditions, it wasn't easy. For my husband and me, it was very difficult to adjust. For our daughters, on the other hand, American life was wonderful. Although Marisa and Patricia were born in Cuba, they were little when we left. They adjusted almost immediately to life here, and they no longer wanted to follow our customs. They even preferred not to speak Spanish. We used to talk to them about how important it was to continue their grandparents' traditions, but they had their ideas. Marisa got married, and as they do here, she got divorced. That makes me ashamed. Now Patricia is going to get married this summer, on July 28. Her fiancé is American. Heaven knows what kind of life she can expect in this country!

The daughter:
My mother is worried because my sister is going to marry an American. I married a Cuban and that turned out badly. But she thinks the country is to blame for the things that work out badly. I was 13 when I arrived in the United States and soon I began to think like an American. My parents, however, followed Cuban traditions and they weren't happy here. I had been going out with Cuban boys for several years . . . until I married one. In spite of our both being Cuban, we didn't get along well and, finally, we got divorced. I feel happier now and I look to the future optimistically. I devote myself to my son at the same time that I am studying to be an engineer. I know in this country of so many opportunities, my ambitions and dreams can be realized. It's a new life we're living here, a life of different and modern ideas in which women can be successful in all professions. And in my personal life, I don't intend to get married again for now. I'm going to be very careful before getting married again. Perhaps some day my parents are going to realize how good the values of American culture are.

Presentación

Dos mujeres cubanas: madre e hija

La madre:

Cuando José y yo decidimos irnos de Cuba en 1965, no sabíamos lo que nos esperaba en los Estados Unidos. Encontramos otro mundo en este país que chocaba con nuestras costumbres y aunque queríamos seguir nuestras tradiciones cubanas, no era cosa fácil. Para mi esposo y para mí era dificilísimo adaptarnos. Para nuestras hijas, al contrario, la vida norteamericana era maravillosa. Aunque Marisa y Patricia nacieron en Cuba, eran pequeñas cuando nos fuimos. Se adaptaron casi en seguida a la vida aquí y ya no querían seguir nuestras costumbres. Incluso preferían no hablar español. Hablábamos con ellas sobre lo importante que era seguir las tradiciones de sus abuelos, pero ellas tenían sus ideas. Marisa se casó, y como hacen aquí, se divorció. Eso me da vergüenza. Ahora Patricia va a casarse este verano, el 28 de julio. Su novio es norteamericano. ¡Dios sabe la vida que le espera en este país!

La hija:

Mi mamá está preocupada porque mi hermana se va a casar con un norteamericano. Yo me casé con un cubano y salió mal. Ella, sin embargo, cree que el país tiene la culpa de las cosas que salen mal. Yo tenía 13 años cuando llegué a Estados Unidos y pronto comencé a pensar como una norteamericana. Mis papás, sin embargo, seguían las tradiciones cubanas y no estaban contentos aquí. Hacía varios años que salía con chicos cubanos . . . hasta que me casé con uno. A pesar de que los dos éramos cubanos, no nos llevábamos bien y por fin nos divorciamos. Me siento más contenta ahora y miro hacia el futuro con optimismo. Me dedico a mi hijo al mismo tiempo que estudio para ingeniera. Sé que en este país de tantas oportunidades, puedo realizar mis sueños y ambiciones. Es una vida nueva que vivimos aquí, una vida con ideas diferentes y modernas, en que la mujer puede tener éxito en todas las profesiones. Y en la vida personal, no pienso volver a casarme por ahora. Voy a tener mucho cuidado antes de casarme otra vez. Quizás algún día mis papás van a darse cuenta de lo bueno de los valores de la cultura norteamericana.

Ampliación

—¿En qué estación estamos?	*What season is it?*
—Estamos en **verano.**	*It's **summer.***
(otoño, invierno, primavera)	*(fall, winter, spring)*
—¿Qué fecha es hoy?[1]	*What's today's date?*
—Hoy es **el primero** de agosto.	*Today is August **first.***
(el dos, el quince, el veinticinco)	*(2nd, 15th, 25th)*
—¿Cuándo nació Ud.?	*When were you born?*
—Nací el 6 de junio de 1964.	*I was born on June 6, 1964.*
—¿En qué pensaban Uds.?	*What were you thinking about?*
—Pensábamos en **el futuro.**	*We were thinking about **the future.***
(el pasado, el presente)	*(the past, the present)*
—¿Dónde estaba el jefe?	*Where was the boss?*
—Estaba fuera de la oficina.	*He was out of the office.*
—¿Cómo eran sus ideas?	*What were her ideas like?*
—Eran **nuevas.** (viejas)	*They were **new.** (old)*

Preguntas sobre la Presentación

1. ¿En qué pensaba la madre cuando salió de Cuba?
2. ¿Cómo era la vida para ella en Estados Unidos?
3. ¿Cómo se adaptaron Marisa y Patricia a la vida norteamericana?
4. ¿Cuántos años tenía Marisa cuando llegó a Estados Unidos?
5. ¿Cuáles valores de la cultura norteamericana le gustan a Marisa?
6. ¿Qué hace Marisa ahora y qué va a hacer en el futuro?

NOTA CULTURAL

When Fidel Castro came to power and imposed a Communist system of government on Cuba in 1959, many Cubans went into exile in other countries. Over the years, hundreds of thousands of Cubans have come to the United States, bringing with them the values of pre-Castro Cuba, a traditional Hispanic society with cultural patterns similar to those of other Spanish-speaking countries. While the Cubans who have taken up residence in the United States have usually chosen to maintain their traditions and customs, their children have straddled the two cultures (Hispanic patterns with family, American patterns outside the home) and have generally ended up embracing United States cultural norms. Cuban parents in the United States have seen their authority challenged by American society when their children choose to live like their American-born peers, even giving up their mother tongue for English.

---

[1] Also said for *What's today's date?*: **¿Cuál es la fecha de hoy?** and **¿A cuántos estamos?** The latter is answered **Estamos a treinta.** (*It's the 30th.*)

Vocabulario activo

adaptarse (a) to adjust to
la **ambición** ambition
aunque although
casi almost
comenzar (e → ie; z → c/e) to begin
la **costumbre** custom
la **cultura** culture
chocar to clash
decidir to decide
dedicarse (a) to devote oneself (to)
diferente different
divorciarse to get divorced
la **estación** season
la **fecha** date (*calendar*)
fuera (de) outside (of), away from
el **futuro** future
hacia toward
la **idea** idea
importante important
incluso even
el **invierno** winter
maravilloso wonderful
el **millón** million
mirar to look at
mismo same
moderno modern
el **mundo** world
nacer (yo nazco) to be born
nuevo new
la **oportunidad** opportunity
el **optimismo** optimism

el **otoño** fall, autumn
el **pasado** past
personal personal
el **presente** present (*time*)
la **primavera** spring
la **profesión** profession
realizar to realize (to achieve);
    to fulfill
sobre about
el **sueño** dream
la **tradición** tradition
el **valor** value
el **verano** summer
la **vergüenza** shame

EXPRESIONES

a pesar de in spite of
al contrario on the contrary
algún día some day
darse cuenta de to realize
en seguida immediately
llevarse bien (mal) con to get along well
    (not get along well) with
otra vez again
por fin finally
salir mal to turn out badly
tener cuidado to be careful
tener _____ años to be _____ years old
tener la culpa to be to blame
volver a (+ *inf.*) to do something again
ya no no longer

Estructura 1

The imperfect tense

Análisis

1. While both the preterit and the imperfect refer to past time, the two tenses express different ways of looking at past actions. The preterit designates the action as completed in the past while the imperfect designates an action as going on in the past without any reference to when it began or if it was completed. Common English equivalents for the Spanish imperfect are *used to do, was doing.*

Since the imperfect is not concerned with the beginning or the end of an action, it is the ideal tense for expressing repeated actions in past time. Adverbs and adverbial phrases such as **todos los días, siempre, muchas veces** are often clues for the selection of the imperfect rather than the preterit.

✳ For telling time in the past, only the imperfect is used, never the preterit. Some examples:

Trabajaba en el almacén **todos los días.**	She **used to work** in the department store **every day.**
Trabajó en el almacén **ayer.**	She **worked** in the department store **yesterday.**
—¿Qué hora **era?**	What time **was it?**
—**Era** la una.	It **was** one o'clock.

▸ The endings of the imperfect tense for -a- class verbs are formed by inserting **-aba-** between the stem and the person ending.

▸ The endings for both **-e-** and **-i-** class verbs are formed by inserting **-ía-** between the stem and the person ending.

hablar			
Stem	*Insert*	*Person-ending*	*Full form*
habl-	**aba**	—	**hablaba**
habl-	**aba**	s	**hablabas**
habl-	**aba**	—	**hablaba**
habl-	**ába**	mos	**hablábamos**
habl-	**aba**	is	**hablabais**
habl-	**aba**	n	**hablaban**

comer				escribir			
Stem	*Insert*	*Person-ending*	*Full form*	*Stem*	*Insert*	*Person-ending*	*Full form*
com-	**ía**	—	**comía**	escrib-	**ía**	—	**escribía**
com-	**ía**	s	**comías**	escrib-	**ía**	s	**escribías**
com-	**ía**	—	**comía**	escrib-	**ía**	—	**escribía**
com-	**ía**	mos	**comíamos**	escrib-	**ía**	mos	**escribíamos**
com-	**ía**	is	**comíais**	escrib-	**ía**	is	**escribíais**
com-	**ía**	n	**comían**	escrib-	**ía**	n	**escribían**

The first and third person singular forms are identical in -a-, -e-, and -i- verbs.

▸ All verbs are regular in the imperfect except **ir, ser,** and **ver.** The imperfect of **hay** is **había.**

ir	ser	ver
iba	era	veía
ibas	eras	veías
iba	era	veía
íbamos	éramos	veíamos
ibais	erais	veíais
iban	eran	veían

2. **The preterit and imperfect used in the same sentence.** When the imperfect and the preterit appear in a single sentence, the imperfect expresses the background (a continuing action or state) against which a completed event (expressed by the preterit) takes place. In the following model, *our leaving* is an event completed in past time that occurs against a background of *their being little*. No indication is given by the imperfect form **eran** as to when the *being little* began or ended.

> Eran pequeñas cuando nos fuimos.   *They were little when we left.*

3. **Changes in meaning in the preterit and imperfect.** Entirely different English verbs are used to express the difference between the imperfect and preterit of *some* Spanish verbs. The change in English equivalents merely expresses the difference (described above) between the imperfect and preterit. In the following pairs of sentences, the sentence in the imperfect expresses the action as being not yet concluded. In contrast, the sentence in the preterit expresses the action as being over and done with.

Sabía la fecha.	*I **knew** the date.*
Supe la fecha.	*I **found out** the date.*
Tenía una idea.	*She **had** an idea.*
Tuvo una idea.	*She **got** an idea.*
Conocía a Patricia.	*I **knew** Patricia.*
Conocí a Patricia.	*I **met** Patricia.*
No **podíamos** adaptarnos.	*We **couldn't** (weren't able to) adjust.*
No **pudimos** adaptarnos.	*We **(tried but) couldn't** adjust.*
No **querían** ir en verano.	*They **didn't want** to go in summer.*
No **quisieron** ir en verano.	*They **refused** to go in summer.*

Práctica

A. Change the verbs in each sentence according to the cues.

1. No veía a Patricia.
   (ellos, tú, nosotros, yo, ella)

2. Leíamos todos los días.
   (yo, Ud., Uds., tú, él y ella)

3. ¿Ibas a sacarlo?
   (Ud., ellos, Uds., yo, tú y yo)

4. Quería vivir en Cuba.
   (nosotros, él, vosotros, Uds., tú)

5. Siempre desayunaban en casa.
   (él, ellas, nosotros, tú, yo)

6. Eran pequeños.
   (Ud., ella, vosotros, yo, ellos)

B. Repeat each of the following sentences changing the first verb into the imperfect and the second into the preterit.

MODELO: Me habla cuando su hermano llega.
           → Me hablaba cuando su hermano llegó.
           He was talking to me when his brother arrived.

1. Marisa está fuera cuando vengo.

2. Estudian cuando los vemos.

3. Hago la torta cuando se acuestan.

4. Miramos la playa cuando comienza a llover.

5. Son las seis cuando decido ducharme.

6. ¿Tienes hambre cuando te trae la carta?

7. Esperáis cuando viene el avión.

8. Estoy en casa cuando se levantan.

C. Translate the following sentences into Spanish.

1. We didn't know your aunt and uncle. / We met them yesterday.
2. He didn't have any idea. / This morning he got an idea!
3. I didn't want to think about the past. / I refused to think about the past.
4. —Did you (tú) know the price of the suit?
   —No, I found it out this afternoon.
5. They couldn't (weren't able to) adjust to life in this country. / They (tried to but) couldn't adjust to life in this country.

D. Change the verbs in the following sentences to the imperfect or preterit as required. You will form a connected paragraph.

1. Salgo de Cuba con mi familia en 1963.
2. Tengo 15 años y mi hermano tiene 13.
3. Llegamos a Estados Unidos en otoño.
4. Buscamos una casa en Nueva York.
5. Por fin mi papá encuentra una.
6. A mis papás no les gusta la vida aquí.
7. Pero mi hermano y yo estamos contentísimos.
8. Aprendemos a hablar inglés.
9. Conocemos a muchos jóvenes.
10. Nos encanta la vida norteamericana.

1. (Anoche) Enrique me saca a cenar.
2. Me lleva a un restaurante muy bonito.
3. Ya tenemos hambre cuando viene el mozo.
4. Él nos trae la carta.
5. Hay tantos platos ricos en la carta.
6. Yo no sé qué quiero.
7. Enrique decide pedir el arroz con pollo.
8. Miro los platos que comen los clientes.

9. Por fin decido pedir el pescado.

10. Después de comer, vamos a casa de un amigo.

Estructura 2

Hacía . . . que + *imperfect (had been)*

Análisis

▸ **Hacía** + *expression of time* + **que** + *verb in the imperfect* is equivalent to the English phrase *had been (doing something)*.

—¿Cuánto (tiempo) hacía que Ud. esperaba?	*How long had you been waiting?*
—**Hacía dos meses que** yo esperaba.	*I had been waiting **for two months**.*

Práctica

When your friend asks whether you wanted to do certain things, you reply that you did and that you hadn't done them for a certain length of time.

MODELO: —Querías ver a Raúl, ¿verdad? **(tres semanas)**
—Claro, **hacía tres semanas** que no lo veía.

You wanted to see Raul, didn't you?
*Of course. I hadn't seen him **for three weeks**.*

1. Querías viajar a Córdoba, ¿verdad?   (dos años)
2. Querías comer comida francesa, ¿verdad?   (seis meses)
3. Querías saludar a tus vecinos, ¿verdad?   (mucho tiempo)
4. Querías preparar una ensalada, ¿verdad?   (varios días)
5. Querías comprarle un regalo a tu mamá, ¿verdad?   (un año)
6. Querías descansar, ¿verdad?   (12 horas)

Estructura 3

Use of the definite article

Análisis

▸ In Spanish the definite article is used before a noun that refers to something in general terms or that refers to all of something.

Las costumbres son diferentes.	*Customs are different.*
Me interesan los idiomas.	*I'm interested in languages.* (languages in general or the languages they spoke)

▸ The definite article **el** is used before the names of languages. It is not used directly after **hablar** and after **de, en.** Many speakers also omit the article with the names of languages that occur directly after verbs such as **leer, estudiar, aprender, enseñar.**

> **El** español es el idioma de Puerto Rico.
> Hablamos español. BUT Hablamos bien **el** español.
> Escribió el libro **en** inglés.
> Estudio (el) inglés pero enseño (el) español.

Práctica

A. Translate the following sentences into Spanish. They will form a connected paragraph.

MI MADRE HABLA INGLES Y MI PADRE HABLA ESPANOL
1. My mother speaks English and my father speaks Spanish.
2. I like languages very much. *ME GUSTAN LOS ILLOMAS MUY MUCHO*
3. I'm studying French and I'm learning Russian in the university.
4. I read Spanish books and I understand Portuguese. *LEO LIBRO ELESPAÑOL Y COMPRENDO PORTUGES*

ESTUDIO FRANCHESA Y APRENDO RUSO EN LA UNIVERSIDAD

B. Translate the following sentences into Spanish.

LOS VALORES SON IMPORTANDE
1. Values are important.
2. I care about traditions. *ME IMPORTAN LAS TRADICION*
3. Spanish-speaking cultures are interesting.
4. We love spring. *NOS EN QUENTA LA PRIMAUERA*
5. Apples are cheap. *LAS MANZANAS SAN BAR*
6. People have ambitions.
LA GENDE TIENE AMBITINES

Estructura 4

Dates

Análisis

▸ Years in Spanish are expressed by the masculine forms of cardinal numbers. The year 1789 is rendered **mil setecientos ochenta y nueve.** Days of the month are also expressed by cardinal numbers **(dos, quince, veinticuatro),** except for *the first,* **el primero. El** precedes the date and **de** precedes both the month and the year: *March 29, 1974,* is read **el veintinueve de marzo de mil novecientos setenta y cuatro.**

▸ In writing abbreviations for the dates in Spanish-speaking countries, Roman numerals are often used for the months. The day is written first. **El veinticinco de agosto de mil novecientos cuarenta y cuatro** is written *25 VIII 1944* (= 8/25/44).

Práctica

A. Read the following dates in Spanish.

1. June 6, 1943
2. October 19, 1809
3. July 4, 1776
4. 13 II 1963
5. October 12, 1492

6. 1 VIII 1957
7. January 1, 1918
8. 11 XI 1084
9. May 30, 1650
10. 31 XII 1521

B. Answer these questions in Spanish.

1. ¿En qué año naciste?
2. ¿En qué año nacieron tus hermanos?

3. ¿Cuándo se casaron tus papás?
4. ¿Qué fecha es hoy?

Estructura 5

Numbers above 10,000

Análisis

▶ The numbers between 10,000 and 100,000 are formed as follows: **diez mil** (10.000), **veinte mil** (20.000), **setenta mil** (70.000), **cien mil** (100.000). After 100,000 multiples of **ciento** agree in gender with the noun that follows: **quinientos mil kilómetros** (*500,000 kilometers*), **quinientas mil millas** (*500,000 miles*). Between **un millón** (and its multiples) and a following noun the preposition **de** is used: **un millón (dos millones) de empleados,** *one million* (*2 million*) *employees*. If another number intervenes, however, **de** is not used: **dos millones setecientos mil empleados** (*2,700,000 employees*).

Práctica

A. Answer the following questions using approximate figures.

1. ¿Cuántos estudiantes hay en la universidad?
2. ¿Cuánto dinero pagas durante los cuatro años en tu universidad?
3. ¿Cuántos libros hay en la biblioteca de la universidad?
4. ¿Cuántos hispanos viven en Estados Unidos?

B. Read the following phrases aloud.

1. 700.000 bolívares
2. 372.000 mujeres

3. 5.000.000 coches
4. 8.500.000 millas

5. 49.568 kilómetros
6. 15.947 enfermeras

7. 1.000.000 pesos
8. 35.000 libros

Estructura 6

Y → e before i, hi; o → u before o, ho (For recognition)

Análisis

▶ The Spanish word **y** (*and*) changes from **y** to **e** when it precedes a word that begins with the sound / i /, represented in writing by **i** or **hi.** Similarly, **o** (*or*) changes from **o** to **u** when it precedes a word that begins with the sound / o /, represented in writing by **o** or **ho.**

Práctica

Transform the following sentences by changing the order of the elements and by then changing **y** to **e** or **o** to **u** as necessary.

MODELO: Estudiaba idiomas y biología. → Estudiaba biología e idiomas.

1. La materia era interesante y difícil.
2. Traían impermeables y abrigos.
3. Tenías que oír o ver.
4. Iban a Veracruz en invierno y verano.
5. Va a nevar en octubre o noviembre.
6. Tenían ideas y oportunidades.

Comunicando

Preguntas personales

1. ¿Es importante seguir las tradiciones y costumbres de nuestros abuelos? ¿Por qué?
2. ¿Qué valores son más importantes para ti? ¿Para tu familia?
3. ¿Cuáles son tus ambiciones en la vida personal? ¿En tu profesión?
4. ¿Cómo piensas realizar tus sueños y ambiciones?
5. ¿Miras hacia el futuro con optimismo? ¿Por qué?
6. ¿Qué fecha es hoy?
7. ¿Cuándo naciste? ¿Cuándo nacieron tus papás?

Charlas

1. **—Mi esposo y yo no nos llevamos bien.**
   ¿Quién tiene la culpa?　¿A qué te dedicas?　¿A qué se dedica él?　¿Cuándo se casaron?　¿Van a divorciarse?　¿No les queda más remedio?

2. **—Era difícil adaptarme a la vida norteamericana.**
   ¿Cuándo llegó Ud. a Estados Unidos?　¿De dónde?　¿Cómo eran diferentes sus costumbres?　¿Qué oportunidades tenía Ud. en su país?　¿Y en Estados Unidos?　¿Pudo realizar sus ambiciones?

Situación

Tell about your dreams and ambitions for the future and how you plan to fulfill them. Discuss your values and how they influence your personal and professional lives. Mention if your ambitions and values differ from those of your family.

Para escribir

A. Rewrite the following sentences changing the verbs to the imperfect or preterit. You will form a connected paragraph in past time.

1. **(Ayer)** Voy a casa de mi amiga Susana.
2. Susana hace el almuerzo cuando entro.
3. Yo tengo sed y le pido un jugo.
4. Está ocupadísima pero puede servírmelo.
5. Me dice que sus papás van a venir a comer.
6. Ya es la una.
7. Susana tiene mucha prisa.
8. Empiezo a ayudarla con la ensalada.
9. Ella y yo hablamos cuando llegan sus papás.
10. Los saludamos y todos comenzamos a almorzar.

B. Fill in the blanks supplying the imperfect or the preterit of the verbs in parentheses.

Yo _____ (venir) a Nueva York el año pasado. Antes _____ (vivir) con mis padres en Miami. Cuando _____ (llegar) aquí, yo _____ (tener) dieciocho años. La nueva ciudad me _____ (chocar), pero por fin me _____ (gustar). En Miami yo _____ (ir) todos los fines de semana a la playa. Mis amigos y yo _____ (pasar) toda la mañana allí y después _____ (tomar) el almuerzo en un restaurante. Cuando yo _____ (irse) de Miami, _____ (darse) cuenta de que la vida _____ (ir) a ser muy diferente en Nueva York. Yo _____ (tener) razón. No estoy muy contenta aquí. No miro hacia el futuro con el mismo optimismo que _____ (tener) en Miami.

C. Combine each string of elements into a complete sentence adding **hacía, que,** and **cuando** in the appropriate order. Put the first verb into the imperfect and the second into the preterit.

> MODELO: dos horas / yo / estudiar / dormirme
> → Hacía dos horas que yo estudiaba cuando me dormí.
> *I'd been studying for two hours when I fell alseep.*

1. 15 años / ella / tener / esa ambición / realizarla
2. muchos años / ellos / dedicarse / al abuelo / él / morir
3. 4 horas / tú / estar / en la playa / comenzar / a hacer frío
4. diez días / vosotros / buscarme / encontrarme
5. una semana / yo / preparar / la comida / el cocinero / llegar
6. 25 años / Andrés / ser / abogado / cambiar / su profesión

D. Supply the correct form of the definite article, as required, in the following sentences.

_____ costumbres son diferentes en todos _____ países del mundo. También _____ tradiciones y _____ valores que tiene _____ gente son diferentes. A mí me gusta mucho _____ cultura hispana y me interesa _____ español. Estudio _____ español en la universidad y comienzo a leer libros de _____ español. Ya puedo escribir un poco en _____ español. Me encanta hablar _____ español con mis amigos puertorriqueños y algún día quiero hacer un viaje a Puerto Rico. Claro que antes de ir voy a estudiar _____ costumbres del país.

E. Translate the following sentences into Spanish.

1. I was 28 years old when I got married.
2. When were you (**Ud.**) born?
   I was born September 25, 1964.
3. We were out of the country when he got the idea.
4. Traditions and customs are important.
5. Patricia had been cold for a long time when she put on her sweater.
6. Did you (**tú**) meet Mr. and Mrs. Suárez when you were living in Cuba?
7. Fall is the season I like best.
8. Some day he's going to realize our values are different.
9. We found out (**saber**) that they had several million dollars.
10. You (**Uds.**) were adjusting to life in the United States when you went back to Chile.

lección 11

Objectives

Structure You will learn the forms of the present subjunctive and its use in noun clauses. You will also practice the formation of adverbs.

Vocabulary You will learn many words relating to bank transactions. You will also learn important words and expressions that will enable you to talk about your wants, needs, doubts, expectations, and emotional states.

Conversation By the end of the lesson you will be able to cash a check in a bank, deposit and withdraw money, fill out a bank form, and count your bills and change.

Culture You will be introduced to bank transactions in Caracas, Venezuela, and will be able to compare the experience with your own in the United States.

Outline

Estructura 1 The present subjunctive forms of regular verbs
Estructura 2 The present subjunctive forms of stem-changing verbs
Estructura 3 The present subjunctive forms of irregular verbs
Estructura 4 Use of the present subjunctive in noun clauses
Estructura 5 Formation of adverbs
Estructura 6 Spelling changes in the present subjunctive (For recognition)

At the Caracas Bank

Isabel Alameda meets her friend Victoria del Arce in the Caracas Bank (Caracas, Venezuela). Isabel is waiting in line when she sees Victoria.

V.: I've just deposited my salary (check) and I cashed a check, too. I hope the money will be enough for the month!

I.: I have the same problem. I spend so much money that I then have to withdraw more from the account.

V.: It's good that we have credit cards, then. That way we can buy things without really having funds in the bank.

I.: I should say so! . . . Ah, it's my turn. I can go to that window now. See you later. (*She speaks with the teller.*) Good morning. I want to close my savings account, please.

Teller: Of course. I need you to give me your withdrawal slip and your passbook, please.

I.: Here they are. Since it's a joint account, is it necessary for my husband to sign also?

Teller.: Exactly. We require that the two of you fill out and sign this white card.

I.: Well, I'll take it to my husband and I'll be back tomorrow. For now, I'll ask you to compute my interest.

Teller: I'll be happy to. One minute please. I'll be back right away.

Presentación

En el Banco Caracas

Isabel Alameda se encuentra con su amiga Victoria del Arce en el Banco Caracas (Caracas, Venezuela). Isabel espera en la cola cuando ve a Victoria.

Victoria	—Acabo de depositar mi sueldo y cobré un cheque también. ¡Ojalá que el dinero sea suficiente para el mes!
Isabel	—Chica, tengo el mismo problema. Gasto tanta plata que después tengo que retirar más de la cuenta.
Victoria	—Es bueno que tengamos tarjetas de crédito, entonces. Así podemos comprar cosas sin tener realmente los fondos en el banco.
Isabel	—Ya lo creo . . . Ah, me toca a mí. Ya puedo ir a esa ventanilla. Hasta luego, pues. (*Habla con el cajero.*) Buenos días. Quiero cerrar mi cuenta de ahorros, por favor.
El cajero	—Cómo no. Necesito que me dé su planilla de retiro y su libreta de ahorros, por favor.
Isabel	—Aquí las tiene. Ya que es una cuenta conjunta, ¿es necesario que firme mi esposo también?
El cajero	—Efectivamente. Exigimos que los dos llenen y firmen esta tarjeta blanca.
Isabel	—Bueno, se la llevo a mi esposo y vuelvo mañana. Por ahora, le pido que me calcule los intereses.
El cajero	—Con mucho gusto. Un minuto, por favor. Vuelvo inmediatamente.

Ampliación

Prefiero que Uds. abran una cuenta corriente. (espero que, insisto en que, dudo que, permito que, siento que)	*I prefer that* you open a checking account. (*I hope that, I insist that, I doubt that, I permit that, I'm sorry that*)

Nos alegramos (de) que él solicite un préstamo.
(nos gusta que, nos sorprende que, tenemos miedo [de] que)

We're happy he's applying for a loan.

(*we're pleased that, we're surprised that, we're afraid that*)

Es posible que tenga la planilla de depósito.
(es imposible, es probable, es improbable)

It's possible that she has the deposit slip.
(*it's impossible, it's probable, it's improbable*)

Te **aconsejo** que cambies el billete de diez dólares.
(mando, prohibo, digo, impido)

I advise you to change the ten-dollar bill.
(*I order, I forbid, I tell, I prevent*)

No es verdad que traigamos monedas.
(no es evidente, no es cierto, no creo, no pienso)

It's not true we're bringing coins.

(*it's not evident, it's not certain, I don't believe, I don't think*)

Tal vez ellos sean **ricos.**
(quizás)   (pobres)

Perhaps they're **rich.**
(*perhaps*)   (*poor*)

—¡Qué lástima que Ud. no ahorre plata!
—Es que no gano suficiente.

What a pity you don't save money!

It's that I don't earn enough.

Preguntas sobre la Presentación

1. ¿Qué hizo Victoria del Arce en el banco?
2. ¿Por qué dice Victoria que es bueno que tengan tarjetas de crédito?
3. ¿Qué le pide el cajero a Isabel Alameda?
4. Para cerrar la cuenta de ahorros, ¿qué tiene que hacer Isabel?
5. ¿Qué le pide Isabel al cajero antes de salir del banco?
6. ¿Por qué tiene que volver Isabel al banco mañana?

NOTA CULTURAL

Bank transactions and procedures in Venezuela are very similar to those in the United States. The banks, however, are owned and operated by the Venezuelan government. Because of their prosperous, oil-rich economy Venezuelans have more money to spend on consumer goods. If cash is not immediately available, people can buy on credit by presenting one of their credit cards at the time of purchase as in the United States.

Vocabulario activo

abrir   to open
aconsejar   to advise
ahorrar   to save
los **ahorros**   savings
alegrarse   to be happy
el **billete**   bill (*money*)
el **cajero**   teller
calcular   to compute
cerrar (e→ie)   to close
cierto   certain, true
cobrar   to cash
la **cola**   line (*of people*)
conjunto   joint
el **crédito**   credit
la **cuenta**   (*bank*) account
el **cheque**   check
dejar   to let (*somebody do something*)
depositar   to deposit
el **depósito**   (*bank*) deposit
dudar   to doubt
efectivamente   exactly, indeed
entonces   then
esperar   to hope
evidente   evident
exigir (g→j/a,o)   to demand, require
firmar   to sign
los **fondos**   funds
gastar   to spend
impedir   to prevent
imposible   impossible
improbable   improbable
inmediatamente   immediately
insistir   to insist
el **interés**   interest
la **libreta**   passbook

llenar   to fill (out)
mandar   to order
el **minuto**   minute
la **moneda**   coin
necesario   necessary
ojalá   I hope
permitir   to permit
la **planilla**   form, slip
la **plata**   money
pobre   poor
el **préstamo**   loan
probable   probable
el **problema**   problem
prohibir   to forbid
realmente   really
retirar   to withdraw
el **retiro**   (*bank*) withdrawal
rico   rich
sentir (e→ie; e→i)   to be sorry
sorprender   to surprise
suficiente   enough, sufficient
la **tarjeta**   card
la **ventanilla**   window (*of bank*)

EXPRESIONES
con mucho gusto   gladly
la **cuenta corriente**   checking account
encontrarse con   to meet, run into
   somebody
hasta luego   see you later
me toca a mí   it's my turn
¡qué lástima!   what a pity!
tal vez   perhaps
¡ya lo creo!   I should say so!

Estructura 1

The present subjunctive forms of regular verbs

Análisis

▸ The forms of the present subjunctive of regular verbs are as follows:

Model verb		Stem	Class-vowel	Person-ending	English equivalent
trabajar		trabaj-	e	—	*He wants me to work.*
		trabaj-	e	s	*He wants you to work.*
	Quiere que	trabaj-	e	—	*He wants him to work.*
		trabaj-	e	mos	*He wants us to work.*
		trabaj-	é	is	*He wants you to work.*
		trabaj-	e	n	*He wants them to work.*
comer		com-	a	—	*He wants me to eat.*
		com-	a	s	*He wants you to eat.*
	Quiere que	com-	a	—	*He wants him to eat.*
		com-	a	mos	*He wants us to eat.*
		com-	á	is	*He wants you to eat.*
		com-	a	n	*He wants them to eat.*
escribir		escrib-	a	—	*He wants me to write.*
		escrib-	a	s	*He wants you to write.*
	Quiere que	escrib-	a	—	*He wants him to write.*
		escrib-	a	mos	*He wants us to write.*
		escrib-	á	is	*He wants you to write.*
		escrib-	a	n	*He wants them to write.*

The present subjunctive is signaled by changing the class-vowel **-a-** of the present indicative to **-e** in **-a** verbs and the class-vowels **-e-** and **-i-** of the present indicative to **-a** in **-e** and **-i** verbs.

▸ In the present subjunctive the **yo**-form and the **él**-form are identical; neither has a person-ending.

▸ Verbs of the **-e-** and **-i-** classes have the same endings in the present subjunctive.

Estructura 2

The present subjunctive forms of stem-changing verbs

Análisis

▸ Verbs of the **-a-** and **-e-** classes that have changes in the vowel of the stem in the present indicative have these same changes in the present subjunctive.

    Quiere que se ac**ue**sten.   *She wants you to go to bed.*
    Prefiero que p**ie**nse más.   *I prefer him to think more.*

▸ Verbs of the **-i-** class that change either **e** → **ie** or **e** → **i** in the present indicative have, in addition to these changes, **i** as the stem vowel of the **nosotros-** and

vosotros-forms of the present subjunctive.

sentir	seguir	dormir
sienta	siga	duerma
sientas	sigas	duermas
sienta	siga	duerma
sintamos	sigamos	durmamos
sintáis	sigáis	durmáis
sientan	sigan	duerman

NOTE: **Dormir** and **morir** have **u** as the stem vowel of the **nosotros-** and **vosotros-** forms of the present subjunctive in addition to the **o → ue** change in the other forms.

Estructura 3

The present subjunctive forms of irregular verbs

Análisis

The forms of the present subjunctive of irregular verbs are shown in the following table. Any irregularity such as **-g-** or **-zc-** that appears in the **yo**-form of the present indicative appears in all persons of the present subjunctive. Since these irregularities exist only in **-e-** and **-i-** verbs, the present subjunctive endings of these verbs all have the class-vowel **-a-**.

Infinitive	*Pres. ind.* (**yo**-form)	*Present subjunctive*
decir	**digo**	diga digas diga digamos digáis digan
hacer	**hago**	haga hagas haga hagamos hagáis hagan
oír	**oigo**	oiga oigas oiga oigamos oigáis oigan
poner	**pongo**	ponga pongas ponga pongamos pongáis pongan
salir	**salgo**	salga salgas salga salgamos salgáis salgan
tener	**tengo**	tenga tengas tenga tengamos tengáis tengan
traer	**traigo**	traiga traigas traiga traigamos traigáis traigan
venir	**vengo**	venga vengas venga vengamos vengáis vengan
conocer	**conozco**	conozca conozcas conozca conozcamos conozcáis conozcan
nacer	**nazco**	nazca nazcas nazca nazcamos nazcáis nazcan
parecer	**parezco**	parezca parezcas parezca parezcamos parezcáis parezcan
ver	**veo**	vea veas vea veamos veáis vean

NOTE: **Dar** and **estar** have the expected class-vowel **-e-** in the present subjunctive, but the forms are all stressed as in the present indicative:

dé des dé demos deis den
esté estés esté estemos estéis estén

The present subjunctive stems of **haber, ir, saber, ser** are completely irregular. The endings are regular, however.

Infinitive	*Stem*	*Present subjunctive*
haber	**hay-**	haya hayas haya hayamos hayáis hayan
ir	**vay-**	vaya vayas vaya vayamos vayáis vayan
saber	**sep-**	sepa sepas sepa sepamos sepáis sepan
ser	**se-**	sea seas sea seamos seáis sean

Estructura 4

Use of the present subjunctive in noun clauses

Análisis

▶ Until now you have been using Spanish verbs in the indicative to express events that are perceived as experienced realities—events that the speaker sees as factual, definite or part of his experience. Note the use of the present and preterit indicative in the following dependent noun clauses.[1]

Veo que hace sol. *I see that it's sunny.*
Nos parece que se fueron. *We think they went away.*

▶ The present subjunctive in Spanish is used almost exclusively in those dependent noun clauses that designate events or states that the speaker sees as not being part of reality or of his or her own experience. These clauses are dependent on main verbs that express the following:

1. expectations, skepticism, uncertainty, doubt:

esperar *to hope*
dudar *to doubt*

Espero **que vengan mañana.** *I hope **they'll come tomorrow.***
Dudo **que lo sepan.** *I doubt **that they know it.***

---

[1] A noun clause is a clause that functions as a noun; that is, it can be either the subject or the direct object of a verb.

2. demands, wants, needs, insistence, advice, and other impositions of will:

> **querer, desear, necesitar** *to need*, **preferir, insistir (en que)** *to insist (that)*, **permitir** *to allow, permit*, **exigir** *to demand*, **pedir** *to ask someone to do something*, **aconsejar** *to advise*, **mandar** *to order someone to do something*, **prohibir** *to forbid*, **decir** *to tell someone to do something*, **impedir (e → i)** *to prevent someone from doing something*, **dejar** *to let someone do something*

> Quiere **que yo escriba una carta.**   *She wants **me to write a letter.***

NOTE: The verbs **permitir, exigir, pedir, aconsejar, mandar, prohibir, decir,** and **impedir** may be accompanied by an indirect object pronoun. **Dejar** may be accompanied by a direct object pronoun.

> (Me) piden **que cobre un cheque.**   *They ask **me to cash a check.***
> **I.O.**

> No (la) dejamos **que gaste plata.**   *We don't let **her spend money.***
> **D.O.**

If the dependent clause has the same subject as the main clause it appears as an infinitive.

> **Yo quiero + Tú vas → Yo quiero** *que tú vayas.*
> *I want you to go.*
> **Yo quiero + Yo voy. → Yo quiero** *ir.*
> *I want to go.*

All of these verbs (except **decir**) may also be followed by the infinitive instead of the subjunctive. When followed by the infinitive the indirect object pronoun (or, in the case of **dejar,** the direct object pronoun) must appear.

> (Les) permito **que salgan.** } *I allow **them** to go out.*
> **Les** permito **salir.**

> (Los) deja **que descansen.** } *He lets **you rest.***
> **Los** deja **descansar.**

3. an emotional state, an attitude, a bias: **alegrarse (de) que** *to be happy*, **sorprender** *to surprise*, **tener miedo (de) que, gustar, sentir** *to be sorry*

> Te alegras **que haya una piscina.**   *You're happy **there's a pool.***

4. negated facts: **no es verdad, no es cierto, no es evidente** *it's not evident*, **no es que** *it's not that*. Note, however, that when these are affirmative (e.g. **es verdad, es cierto**) the present indicative is used in the dependent clause.

> No es que él **tenga** vergüenza.   *It's not that **he's ashamed.***

▸ There are some Spanish expressions with no overt subject (impersonal expressions) that require the subjunctive in dependent noun clauses. These impersonal expressions also imply that the event mentioned in the dependent noun clause is

1. not yet a part of reality: **es necesario que**   *it's necessary that,* **es importante que, es posible**   *it's possible that,* **es probable que**   *it's probable that,* **es improbable que**   *it's improbable that,* **ojalá que**   *I hope that.*

    Es necesario que nos **ayudes.**   *It's necessary for **you to help us.***

2. they express a bias or emotional attitude on the speaker's part toward the event mentioned in the dependent noun clause: **es bueno (malo, mejor, peor) que, es triste que.**

    Es bueno que **lleves** un suéter.   *It's good **you're wearing** a sweater.*

Both the indicative and the subjunctive may appear after interrogative or negative forms of **pensar** and **creer,** after **quizás, tal vez**   *perhaps,* and after **¡qué lástima que . . . !**   *what a pity that . . . !* If a speaker chooses the subjunctive in these cases she signals her lack of knowledge or her uncertainty (non-experience) about the event in the dependent clause. If the speaker chooses the indicative in the dependent clause, she signals that she considers the event closer to the realm of fact.

No creo que **viaje.**	*I don't think **she's traveling.** (I'm uncertain.)*
No creo que **viaja.**	*I **really** don't think **she's traveling.** (I'm quite sure.)*
Tal vez **traigan** monedas.	*Perhaps they **might be bringing** coins.*
Tal vez **traen** monedas.	*Perhaps **they're bringing** coins.*

Práctica

A. Change the verb of the dependent clause in each sentence according to the cues.

1. Quiere que cambies el billete.
   (yo, ellos, ella, Uds., nosotros, Ud.)
2. Es posible que ellos cierren el banco.
   (nosotros, yo, Uds., ella, tú, vosotros)
3. Insisten en que llenemos la planilla.
   (Ud., ellas, yo, vosotros, tú, Uds.)
4. Tal vez yo vaya al museo.
   (tú y yo, él, ellos, tú, Ud., Uds.)

B. Change each of the following sentences into a noun clause dependent on **prefiere que.** Change the verb to present subjunctive.

MODELO: Estudio para médico.   *I'm studying to be a*
                                                   doctor.

   → Prefiere que estudie para médico.   *He prefers that I study to*
                                          be a doctor.

1. Vivimos en la playa.   5. Uds. ponen la mesa.
2. Se casan este invierno.   6. No gasto mucha plata.
3. Tiene una profesión.   7. Estamos de vacaciones.
4. Comes en la cocina.   8. Ella las conoce.

C. Now do the same exercise using **se alegra que, espera que,** and **le sorprende que.**

D. Combine each pair of sentences into a single sentence following the model. When **eso** or **lo** occurs in the main clause, it is replaced by the dependent clause.

MODELO: Compras guantes. / Yo quiero eso.   *You're buying gloves. / I*
                                              want that.

   → Yo quiero que compres guantes.   *I want you to buy gloves.*

1. Solicitan un préstamo. / Nece-   4. Se despierta temprano. / Ojalá.
   sita eso.
2. El cajero viene. / Eso no es   5. Ayudo a Isabel. / Me aconse-
   cierto.   jan eso.
3. Doña Josefa es argentina. / Lo   6. Abrimos una cuenta. / No lo
   dudamos.   cree.

E. You and your friend are in business together. He wants to know if you will be handling certain monetary affairs. Tell him you will not; then tell him who will be doing so by using the cue in the parentheses in your answer.

MODELO: —¿Quieres ir al banco?   (tú)   *Do you want to go to the*
                                            bank?

   —No, quiero que tú vayas al banco.   *No, I want you to go to*
                                        the bank.

1. ¿Deseas hablar con el cajero?   (tú)
2. ¿Esperas depositar la plata?   (la recepcionista)
3. ¿Necesitas cobrar un cheque?   (los empleados)
4. ¿Tienes miedo de perder la libreta de cheques?   (el secretario)
5. ¿Prefieres llenar la planilla?   (el mecanógrafo)
6. ¿Te gusta firmar las tarjetas?   (Rafael y tú)

F. Substitute the corresponding form of each of the verbs in parentheses for the original verb in the dependent clause.

MODELO: No piensa que ahorremos dinero.   *She doesn't think we save*
       (depositar)   *money.*
       → No piensa que depositemos   *She doesn't think we deposit*
       dinero.   *money.*

1. No es evidente que lo tenga.   (encontrar, decir, ver, saber)
2. Me prohiben que venda el coche.   (comprar, buscar, lavar, mirar)
3. Le digo que vuelva al hotel.   (llegar, viajar, entrar, ir)
4. Nos dejan que estudiemos el libro.   (firmar, leer, traer, abrir)

Estructura 5

Formation of adverbs

Análisis

▸ Adverbs are formed from adjectives in English by the addition of *-ly: happy* →
happily. The Spanish equivalent of this process is the addition of the suffix
-mente to the *feminine* form of the adjective:

abierto → abierta → **abiertamente**

Two-form adjectives, such as **fácil, alegre, personal,** have no special feminine
form:

fácil → **fácilmente**

▸ When two or more adverbs are used together, **-mente** is deleted from all but the
last one:

Gastaron la plata *fácil* y   *They spent the money easily and*
alegremente.   *happily.*

▸ Some common adverbs not formed in this way are: **bien** (from **bueno**), **mal**
(from **malo**), **mejor, peor, mucho, poco, más, menos.**

Práctica

Finish each sentence by adding the correct adverb derived from the adjective
in parentheses.

MODELO: Los estudiantes aprendieron español . . .
       (fácil).
       → Los estudiantes aprendieron español   *The students learned*
       fácilmente.   *Spanish easily.*

1. Les dice el precio . . . (triste).

2. Preparó la comida . . . (maravilloso).

3. Voy al banco . . . (inmediato).

4. Dudamos que sea rico . . . (real).

5. Siempre se vestía . . . (hermoso).

6. ¿Habló con el jefe . . . (personal)?

Estructura 6

Spelling changes in the present subjunctive (For recognition)

Análisis

▶ Verbs with stems ending in the letters **c, g, z, j,** although regular in speech, have spelling changes in the present subjunctive. These changes are similar to those occurring in the **yo**-form of the preterit. According to Spanish spelling conventions, the sounds / k /, / g /, / s / (written **z,** not **s**) and / x / are written differently before **e** and **i** than before **a, o, u** in the conjugations of certain verbs.

/ k /	ca	**que**	**qui**	co	cu	busca – busque
/ g /	ga	**gue**	**gui**	go	gu	paga – pague
/ s /	za	**ce**	**ci**	zo	zu	comienza – comience
/ x /	ja	**ge**	**gi**	jo	ju	escoge – escoja (**escoger** *to choose*)

Verbs of the **-a-** class whose stem ends in **j** do not change **j** to **g** before **e:**

Es imposible que traba**je** más.

Práctica

Rewrite each pair of sentences as a single sentence. Change the verbs of the dependent clauses to the present subjunctive. Make all required spelling changes.

MODELO:　Comienzas a ducharte. /　*You're beginning to take a shower. /*
　　　　　Eso es mejor.　　　　　*That's better.*
　→ Es mejor que　　　　　*It's better for you to begin to take a*
　　　comiences a ducharte.　*shower.*

1. Sacan nueve en los exámenes. / Ojalá.
2. Les pago el sueldo los viernes. / Lo dudan.
3. Realizamos nuestras ambiciones. / Eso es necesario.
4. Buscas unos pantalones nuevos. / Me alegro de eso.
5. Felipe almuerza a las ocho. / Quizás.
6. Seguimos por esta calle a la Mezquita. / Nos aconsejan eso.

Comunicando

Preguntas personales

1. ¿Para qué va Ud. al banco?
2. ¿Es necesario que cobres un cheque hoy?
3. ¿Es bueno que haya tarjetas de crédito? ¿Por qué?
4. ¿Qué tienes que hacer para abrir (o cerrar) una cuenta de ahorros (o una cuenta corriente)?
5. ¿Quieres que te calculen los intereses todos los meses?
6. ¿Te aconsejan tus papás que ahorres plata? ¿Por qué?

Charlas

1. **—¡Ojalá que me den el préstamo!**
   ¿A quién se lo pediste?   ¿Para qué lo solicitaste?   ¿Cuánta plata esperas que te den?   ¿Qué vas a hacer si no te dan la plata?
2. **—Señora, Ud. ya puede venir a la ventanilla.**
   ¿Es necesario que yo llene esta tarjeta para depositar mi sueldo?   ¿Exige Ud. que le dé mi libreta de ahorros?   ¿Puede Ud. calcularme los intereses?   ¿Qué tengo que hacer para abrir una cuenta corriente?

Situación

Tell about a banking experience you have had. Discuss the nature of the transaction—making a withdrawal or deposit, cashing a check, etc.—including what the teller did and said, how much money was involved, etc.

Para escribir

A. Combine each pair of sentences into a single sentence. When **eso** or **lo** occurs in the main clause, it is replaced by the dependent clause. Change the verb to either the subjunctive or indicative.

MODELO: Enseño francés. / Se   *I teach French. / They're happy about*
            alegran de eso.   *that.*
       → Se alegran (de) que   *They're happy that I teach French.*
            enseñe francés.

1. Vamos a la piscina esta tarde. / Nos impide eso.
2. Son las diez menos veinte. / Sé eso.
3. Vienes al colegio en autobús. / ¿Eso es necesario?

4. Estamos en primavera. / Eso es verdad.
5. Buscáis unos regalos en el Bazar Bolívar. / Os pido eso.
6. Ud. consigue un empleo pronto. / Lo esperamos.
7. Iris llega en diciembre. / Les parece eso.
8. Eduardo y Victoria se casan en Veracruz. / Me gusta eso.

B. Supply the correct form of the adverb derived from the adjective in parentheses.

MODELO: Leyeron esos libros . . . (difícil). → Leyeron esos libros difícilmente.

1. En el Barrio viven . . . (pobre).
2. Recibió el regalo . . . (alegre).
3. Quiero que me lo expliquéis . . . (diferente).
4. Comimos el postre . . . (inmediato).
5. Cuando él se enfadaba, nos miraba . . . (triste).
6. ¡Qué lástima que no nos hablen . . . (personal)!

C. Translate the following sentences into Spanish.

1. It's necessary for Isabel to wait in line.
2. I doubt that the teller is opening the window.
3. I want to close my savings account.
4. We prefer you (**Ud.**) to fill out and sign this form.
5. They're sorry I can't change the $20 bill.
6. I hope you'll (**tú**) cash this check.
7. She's happy her family is rich.
8. It's sad you're (**vosotros**) applying for a loan.
9. Enrique finished his composition easily and happily.
10. It's improbable we'll run into our friends.

lección 12

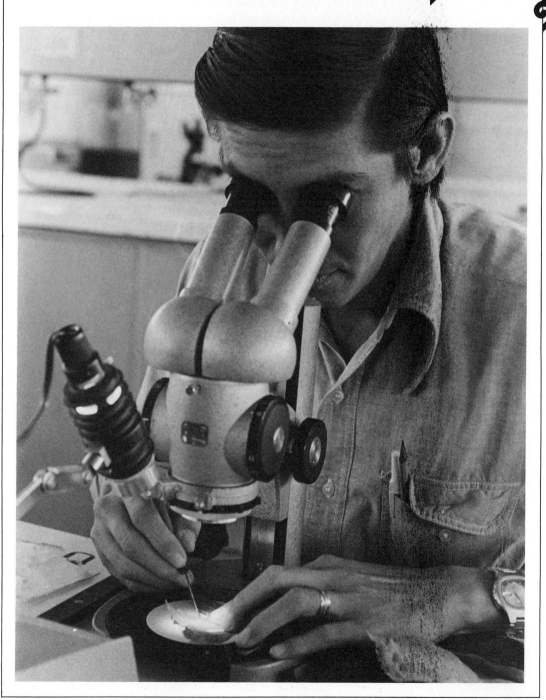

Objectives

Structure   You will increase your knowledge of the subjunctive by practicing it in adjective clauses. You will learn a new tense, the present perfect (*I've gone*).

Vocabulary   You will learn the Spanish words for the parts of the body and many terms related to health care.

Conversation   By the end of the lesson, you will be able to go to a Spanish-speaking doctor and describe your symptoms.

Culture   You will be introduced to the practice of modern medicine in a clinic in Bogota, Colombia. You will also be made aware of a feature of traditional healing methods practiced throughout Colombia and all of Spanish America.

Outline

Estructura 1   Negatives and indefinites
Estructura 2   The present subjunctive in adjective clauses
Estructura 3   The present perfect
Estructura 4   The **-do** form (past participle) used as an adjective
Estructura 5   The past perfect (For recognition)

Diary of a Colombian Doctor

For three months Antonio María Pérez has been working in a clinic in Bogota, the capital of Colombia. He's young and he lacks experience, but nobody is more enthusiastic about his profession than he.

April 22, 1982
I've never seen so many sick people. Several have complained of a headache and of being nauseous. Some people had stomachaches and sore throats. I took their temperature and I examined their hearts and lungs. Some children had fever. I realized they had the flu. I've given them some prescriptions and I've ordered them to rest as much as possible and drink a lot of water.

May 14, 1982
The boy with the broken arm has come back. He broke it four weeks ago, but he's recovering slowly. I've also seen someone who has an ear infection. First he went to the **curandero,** who treated him with herbs. When he began to get worse, he came to the clinic. I've given him antibiotics and I know he's going to get better quickly. Today I've examined many patients with so many different illnesses. I'm very tired.

June 5, 1982
Some patients with colds and others with injuries of the eye, legs, feet, and hands have come today. One man's whole body ached after a car accident. I did some tests on him and I gave him some pills for the pain. There's nothing more I can do for him now. Several children had sore throats and I've had to take throat cultures. It's probable they have a virus.

July 17, 1982
I've said a thousand times that you have to take good care of yourself. Health is the most important thing. Sometimes I get very sad when I see how people suffer. Today one of my patients died. Also today another patient's child was born. As a doctor I see everything. Fortunately I can almost always help my patients.

Presentación

El diario de un médico colombiano

Hace tres meses que Antonio María Pérez trabaja en una clínica de Bogotá, capital de Colombia. Es joven y le falta experiencia, pero no hay nadie que tenga más entusiasmo por su profesión.

22 de abril de 1982

Nunca he visto a tantas personas enfermas. Varias se han quejado de dolor de cabeza y de tener náuseas. A algunas les dolían el estómago y la garganta. Les tomé la temperatura y les examiné el corazón y los pulmones. Unos niños tenían fiebre. Me di cuenta que sufrían de la gripe. Les he dado unas recetas y les he mandado que descansen lo más posible y que tomen mucha agua.

14 de mayo de 1982

Ha vuelto el niño que tiene el brazo roto. Se lo rompió hace cuatro semanas pero mejora lentamente. He visto también a alguien que tiene una infección del oído.[1] Primero fue al curandero[2] que lo trataba con hierbas. Cuando empezó a empeorar, vino a la clínica. Le he dado antibióticos y sé que va a mejorar rápidamente. Hoy he examinado a muchos pacientes con tantas enfermedades diferentes. Estoy cansadísimo.

5 de junio de 1982

Hoy han venido algunos pacientes con catarro y otros con los ojos enfermos y con heridas en las piernas, los pies y las manos. A un señor le dolía todo el cuerpo después de un accidente de coche. Le hice unos análisis y le di unas

---

[1] **Oído** refers to the inner ear (hearing mechanism); **oreja** is the visible outer ear.

[2] The **curandero** or local healer has a large following among the poor of Latin America, who often trust him more than they do doctors and modern medicine. Relying on folk remedies such as herbs, amulets and psychological insights, the **curandero** is often effective in treating illnesses.

pastillas para el dolor. No hay nada más que yo pueda hacer por él ahora. A varios niños les dolía la garganta y he tenido que hacerles un cultivo. Es probable que tengan un virus.

17 de julio de 1982

He dicho mil veces que hay que cuidarse bien. La salud es lo más importante. A veces me pongo muy triste cuando veo cómo sufre la gente. Hoy ha muerto uno de mis pacientes. Hoy también ha nacido el hijo de otra paciente. Como médico lo veo todo. Menos mal que casi siempre puedo ayudar a mis pacientes.

Ampliación

—Señora, ¿le duele la nariz o el oído? *Does your nose or ear hurt?*
—No me duelen ni la nariz ni el oído, *Neither my nose nor my ear hurts,*
    doctor. *doctor.*

—Necesito **perder peso.** *I have to **lose weight.***
    (aumentar de peso) *(gain weight)*
—¡Pero no hay ninguna dieta que *But you don't want to follow any*
    quieras seguir! *diet!*

—¿Tienes sangre en **la herida?** *Is your **wound** bleeding?*
    (la boca) *(mouth)*
—No. Y no me duele tampoco. *No. And it doesn't hurt me either.*

Preguntas sobre la Presentación

1. (en abril) ¿Qué les ha mandado el doctor Pérez a las personas que tienen gripe?
2. (en mayo) ¿Adónde fue primero el paciente que tenía la infección del oído?
3. ¿Qué le ha dado el doctor Pérez?
4. (en junio) ¿De qué sufren los pacientes?
5. ¿Cómo trata el médico al señor que tuvo el accidente de coche?
6. ¿Por qué les hace el médico un cultivo a los niños?
7. ¿Por qué se pone triste a veces Antonio María Pérez?

Vocabulario activo

el **accidente**   accident
   alguien   someone
el **análisis**   (*medical*) test
el **antibiótico**   antibiotic
la **boca**   mouth
el **brazo**   arm
la **cabeza**   head
el **catarro**   cold (*illness*)

la **clínica**   clinic
el **corazón**   heart
el **cuerpo**   body
   cuidarse   to take care of oneself
el **cultivo**   culture (*of germs*)
el **curandero**   native healer
el **diario**   diary
la **dieta**   diet

doler (o→ue)   to hurt, ache
el dolor   ache, pain
  empeorar   to get worse
la enfermedad   sickness, disease
el entusiasmo   enthusiasm
el estómago   stomach
  examinar   to examine
la fiebre   fever
la garganta   throat
la herida   injury, wound
la hierba   herb
  lentamente   slowly
la mano   hand
  mejorar   to get better
  nadie   nobody
la nariz   nose
  ni   neither, nor
  ningún (-o, -a)   no, none, not any
    not any
  nunca   never
el oído   (*inner*) ear
el ojo   eye
el (la) paciente   patient
  la persona   person

el peso   weight
el pie   foot
la pierna   leg
el pulmón   lung
  rápidamente   quickly, fast
la receta   prescription
  romper   to break, rip, tear
la salud   health
la sangre   blood
  sufrir (de)   to suffer (from), have a
    disease
  tampoco   neither, not either
la temperatura   temperature
  tratar   to treat (*illness*)
la vez   time (*occasion*)
el virus   virus

EXPRESIONES
aumentar de peso   to gain weight
hay que (+ *inf.*)   one must, has to _____
menos mal   fortunately
ponerse (+ *adj.*)   to get, become _____
tener náuseas   to be nauseous
tener sangre   to bleed

Estructura 1

Negatives and indefinites

Análisis

▸ Here are some Spanish negative words and their affirmative counterparts:

Negative	Affirmative
nunca *never, not ever*	**alguna vez** **algunas veces** } *sometimes* **a veces** **muchas veces** *often* **siempre** *always*
nada *nothing* **tampoco** *neither, not either* **ni** *neither, nor, not even* **ni . . . ni**[3] *neither . . . nor* **nadie** *no one, nobody, not anyone* **ninguno** *none*	**algo** *something* **también** *also* **o** *either, or* **o . . . o**[3] *either . . . or* **alguien** *someone, somebody* **alguno** *some*

---

[3] A plural verb is used after a subject joined by **ni . . . ni**. The first **o** in **o . . . o** can be omitted.

▸ **Ninguno** and **alguno** are four-form adjectives before a noun. They become **ningún** and **algún** before a masculine singular noun. **Ninguno** is hardly ever used in the plural; **ningún cheque** means *no check* or *no checks.*

Me dio **algún** billete.	He gave me *some* (*a particular*) *bill.*
(**algunos** billetes)	(*some bills*)
Me dio **alguna** moneda.	He gave me *some* (*a particular*) *coin.*
(**algunas** monedas)	(*some coins*)
No tengo **ningún** saco.	I have *no* jacket.
No tengo **ninguna** receta.	I have *no* prescription.

▸ A personal **a** is required before **alguien** and **nadie** (as well as **alguno** and **ninguno** when they refer to people) when these words are used as direct objects.

—¿Conoces **a algunas** de estas personas?	*Do you know **some** of these people?*
—No, no conozco **a ninguna**.	*No, I don't know **any**.*
—¿Vieron **a alguien**?	*Did you see **anyone**?*
—No, no vimos **a nadie**.	*No, we didn't see **anyone**.*

▸ When a negative word precedes the verb, the negative particle **no** does not appear. If the negative word appears after the verb, **no** must precede the verb.

—¿Cuándo tomas antibióticos?	*When do you take antibiotics?*
—**Nunca** tomo antibióticos. OR	*I never take antibiotics.*
No tomo **nunca** antibióticos.	

Práctica

A. Word order changes. Change each of the following sentences by moving the negative word to a position after the verb. Add **no** before the verb.

MODELO: Nadie va a la clínica. *Nobody goes to the clinic.*
→ No va nadie a la clínica.

1. Nunca aumentas de peso.
2. Ningún cajero abrió la ventanilla.
3. Tampoco tiene fiebre.
4. Nada sabían de sus ideas.
5. Nadie se acuerda del pasado.
6. Ni el curandero ni el médico lo trataron.

B. Answer each of the following questions using the negative counterpart of the affirmative word in the sentence.

MODELO: ¿Vas a Bogotá alguna vez? *Do you ever go to Bogota?*
—No, no voy nunca a Bogotá. *No, I never go to Bogota.*

1. ¿Es posible que Ud. vea a alguien?
2. ¿Le dijisteis algo?
3. ¿Hicieron Uds. algún análisis?
4. ¿Siempre te despiertas a las seis?

5. ¿Prefieres llamar el viernes o el
   sábado?

6. ¿Patricia nació en Colombia
   también?

Estructura 2

The present subjunctive in adjective clauses

Análisis

▶ A clause may modify a noun in the same way an adjective does; such a clause is called an adjective clause. All relative clauses—that is, those introduced by relative pronouns such as **que, quien,** etc.—are adjective clauses. For example, in **un niño que tiene el brazo roto** (*a child who has a broken arm*), **que tiene el brazo roto** modifies **un niño** in the same way that **enfermo** does in **un niño enfermo**. The noun modified by an adjective clause is called the **antecedent.** In the preceding example **niño** is the antecedent of the **que**-clause.

▶ Spanish distinguishes between two types of antecedents—those that are part of reality and those that are not. In the sentence **Tengo un médico que sabe mucho** (*I have a doctor who knows a lot*), the antecedent, **médico,** is part of reality; that is, the speaker could tell you the doctor's name. Therefore, the indicative is used.

   For antecedents that are not part of reality—that is, for negative and indefinite (undetermined) antecedents—the subjunctive must be used in modifying adjective clauses.

No conocemos a nadie **que estudie** para médico.	*We don't know anyone **who's studying to be** a doctor.*
No hay hospital **que me guste.**	*There's no hospital **I like.***

| Buscamos
Queremos
Necesitamos } | un médico **que sepa** mucho. | *We're looking for
We want
We need* } | *a doctor **who knows** a lot.* |

Verbs such as **buscar, querer,** and **necesitar** may also have direct objects that are definite and therefore part of reality. Adjective clauses modifying these objects are in the indicative.

Buscamos al médico que sabe mucho.	*We're looking for the doctor who knows a lot.* (*Dr. Pérez knows a lot and we're looking for him.*)

▶ Other relative words such as **quien** and **donde** also introduce adjective clauses.

Necesita un banco **donde den** préstamos.	*He needs a bank **where they give** loans.*

Quieren unas personas **con quienes**   *They want some people **they can***
puedan viajar.   *travel with.*

Práctica

A. Change the form of **tener** to the corresponding form of **buscar.** The verb in the dependent adjective clause will then change from indicative to subjunctive.

MODELO: Tengo algo que te interesa.   *I have something you're interested in.*

→ Busco algo que te interese.   *I'm looking for something you're interested in.*

1. Tengo una medicina que te ayuda.
2. Tiene un vecino que no se queja.
3. Tenemos un plato que nos gusta.
4. Tienes un médico que trata varias enfermedades.
5. Tienen un almacén donde venden ropa.
6. Tenéis una vida en que hay muchas oportunidades.

B. Make each of the following sentences negative. The adjective clause will require the subjunctive.

MODELO: Hay alguien que tiene entusiasmo.   *There's someone who's enthusiastic.*

→ No hay nadie que tenga entusiasmo.   *There's nobody who's enthusiastic.*

1. Hay algo que me duele.
2. Conozco a alguien que realiza sus sueños.
3. Hay algún vino que beben.
4. Vemos algo que nos gusta.
5. Hay algún mozo que trabaja bien.
6. Viene alguien que escribe un diario.

C. You are setting up a clothing store and are looking for several employees. You call up the employment office, and the clerk there tells you what people are looking for work. Tell her in each case that you need someone like that.

MODELO: (*la señora*) —Aquí hay unos señores   *There are some men here*
que pueden trabajar los sábados.   *who can work on Saturdays.*

(*usted*) —Me alegro. Necesito   *I'm glad. I need some*
unos señores que puedan trabajar   *men who can work*
los sábados.   *on Saturdays.*

1. Aquí hay unos cajeros que calculan muy bien.
2. Aquí hay una mecanógrafa que quiere trabajar todos los días.

3. Aquí hay una secretaria que habla inglés.
4. Aquí hay unos dependientes que saben vender ropa.
5. Aquí hay una recepcionista que tiene mucha experiencia.
6. Aquí hay unas operarias que hacen modelos hermosos.

Estructura 3

The present perfect

Análisis

▸ The present perfect is used in both Spanish and English to mark past events that the speaker sees as having some effect or influence upon the present.[4]

▸ The present perfect consists of a conjugated form of the auxiliary verb **haber** + *past participle*, which is the form of the verb ending in **-do.** The **-do** form is invariable; that is, it shows no gender and number agreement when it follows a form of **haber.**

▸ The **-do** form consists of the *stem + class vowel + **do.*** Both **-e-** and **-i-** verbs have **-i-** as class vowel: **hablado, comido, vivido.**[5]

▸ The **-do** forms of **ser** and **ir** are **sido** and **ido,** respectively.

		Present perfect	
Auxiliary	*Past participle*	*Model sentences*	
he		**He mejorado.**	*I've gotten better.*
has		**Has mejorado.**	*You've gotten better.*
ha		**Ha mejorado.**	*She's gotten better.*
hemos	mejor**ado**	**Hemos mejorado.**	*We've gotten better.*
habéis		**Habéis mejorado.**	*You've gotten better.*
han		**Han mejorado.**	*They've gotten better.*

▸ Object pronouns precede the forms of **haber** in the present perfect. They are not attached to the **-do** form. No elements may be placed between auxiliary and past participle.

—¿El enfermero te ha tomado la   *Has the nurse taken your tempera-*
    temperatura?   *ture?*
—Sí, **me la ha tomado.**   *Yes, he's taken it.*

---

[4] The use of this tense is similar in both languages except in sentences such as **Hace una semana que tengo un catarro** (*I've had a cold for a week*), where Spanish may also use the present tense.
[5] Verbs of the **-e-** class that have stems ending in a vowel have an accent over the **-i-** in the **-do** form: **leído (leer), creído (creer).** The same is true for **oír: oído.**

▶ The following verbs have irregular past participles that must be learned through memorization.

abrir	**abierto**	hacer	**hecho**	romper	**roto**
decir	**dicho**	morir	**muerto**	ver	**visto**
escribir	**escrito**	poner	**puesto**	volver	**vuelto**

Práctica

A. Change the verb in these sentences according to each new cue.

1. Han perdido peso.
   (yo, Uds., vosotros, ella, tú, Ud.)
2. Me he lavado las manos.
   (Uds., él, tú y yo, Ud., ellas, tú)
3. Ha roto todos los vasos.
   (ellos, yo, tú, nosotros, ellas, vosotros)
4. Hemos abierto una cuenta corriente.
   (tú, él y ella, Ud., yo, Uds., vosotros)

B. Your friend is very concerned about you because you have missed classes due to colds and flu. She asks you what you are going to do to check out your health. Tell her you have already done everything she asks about.

MODELO: —¿Cuándo vas a hablar con la   *When are you going to talk with*
         enfermera?   *the nurse?*
         —Ya he hablado con ella.   *I've already talked with her.*

1. ¿Cuándo vas a ir al médico?
2. ¿Cuándo va a examinarte los pulmones?
3. ¿Cuándo van a hacerte unos análisis?
4. ¿Cuándo van a hacerte un cultivo de la garganta?
5. ¿Cuándo van a darte medicina?
6. ¿Cuándo vas a volver al médico?

C. Change the following sentences to the present perfect. You will have a connected paragraph about someone's illness.

1. Aunque me cuido mucho, me siento mal.
2. Por eso voy al médico.
3. El médico me examina.
4. Me hace unos análisis.
5. Me dice que sufro de una infección.
6. Me da una receta para unos antibióticos.
7. Descanso mucho y tomo mucho jugo.
8. Ya comienzo a mejorar.

Estructura 4

*The **-do** form (past participle) used as an adjective*

Análisis

▸ The past participle (**-do** form) can be used as an adjective after forms of **estar** (or other verbs such as **parecer** and **sentirse**) or in association with a noun. When used in this way it has four forms like any other adjective.

El plato está **roto.**   Los platos están **rotos.**
La taza está **rota.**   Las tazas están **rotas.**

▸ You have already encountered past participles used as adjectives: **pasado** (*past, last*), **cerrado** (*closed*), **abierto** (*open*), **preocupado** (*worried*), **ocupado** (*busy*).

Práctica

A. Change the present perfect construction to one containing the same past participle used as an adjective in each of the following sentences.

MODELO: El profesor ha cerrado la   *The professor has closed the*
                 biblioteca.   *library.*
           → La biblioteca está cerrada.   *The library is closed.*

1. Mi esposo ha cobrado un cheque.
2. Los muchachos han ofendido a sus tíos.
3. Antonio ha escrito unas composiciones.
4. Iris y yo hemos lavado la blusa.
5. Paloma ha leído esos libros.
6. Yo he vestido a la niñita.

B. Your friend has been studying Spanish in Mexico for the last six months, and now that he is home, he wants to catch up on the news. Answer his questions using the cues in parentheses in your answers.

MODELO: —¿Qué tal está Juanita? (preocupado) *How's Juanita?*
           —Juanita está preocupada.   *Juanita's worried.*

1. ¿Qué tal están Amelia y Luis? (casado)
2. ¿Qué tal está Eduardo? (ocupado)
3. ¿Qué tal están los Pereda? (divorciado)
4. ¿Qué tal está doña Ana? (muerto)
5. ¿Qué tal está tu prima? (enfadado)
6. ¿Qué tal están mis profesoras? (sorprendido)

Estructura 5

The past perfect (*For recognition*)

Análisis

▸ The past perfect tense designates an event as having happened prior to another past event, that is, further back in the past. The past perfect consists of the imperfect of the auxiliary verb **haber** + past participle.

		Past Participle	
Auxiliary	*Past participle*	*Model sentences*	
había		Ya **había comido.**	*I'd already eaten.*
habías		Ya **habías comido.**	*You'd already eaten.*
había	comido	Ya **había comido.**	*She'd already eaten.*
habíamos		Ya **habíamos comido.**	*We'd already eaten.*
habíais		Ya **habíais comido.**	*You'd already eaten.*
habían		Ya **habían comido.**	*They'd already eaten.*

Práctica

In each of the following sentences change the first verb from present to preterit and the second from present perfect to past perfect. Make sure you can translate each sentence.

MODELO: Creo que han salido. *I think they've gone out.*
→ Creí que habían salido. *I thought they'd gone out.*

1. Veo que han puesto la mesa.
2. Dicen que has escrito un diario.
3. Piensa que nos hemos acostado.
4. Nos parece que habéis hecho cola.
5. ¿Oyes que ha ido a Bogotá?
6. Les escribo que he visto a Marisa.
7. Se acuerda que han sido pobres.
8. Comprendemos que han gastado mucha plata.

Comunicando

Preguntas personales

1. ¿Qué te duele hoy?
2. ¿Qué te aconseja hacer el médico cuando tienes **un catarro?** (una infección, un virus, náuseas)

3. ¿Qué hace Ud. para cuidarse bien?
4. ¿Qué dieta sigues para **perder peso?**   (aumentar de peso)
5. ¿Ha tenido Ud. una herida en el cuerpo? ¿Dónde?
6. ¿De qué enfermedades sufren sus papás y sus abuelos?   (del corazón, del pulmón, del estómago, de la sangre, etc.)

Charlas

1. —**Hace una semana que me duele la garganta.**
   ¿Has empeorado?   ¿Te ha examinado el médico?   ¿Te ha hecho un cultivo y unos análisis?   ¿Te ha dado una receta?

2. —**Ud. tiene que perder peso, señor.**
   Doctor, ¿por qué es necesario que sea delgado?   ¿Sufro de una enfermedad del corazón?   ¿Qué dieta debo seguir?   ¿Quiere Ud. que tome pastillas?

Situación

(*Two students*)   One takes the role of the doctor; the other, the role of the patient. The patient describes his symptoms and the doctor asks him questions while she examines him. The doctor tells the patient step by step what she is doing; recommends tests, cultures, etc., if necessary; makes a diagnosis; and tells the patient at least three things to do to get well.

Para escribir

A. Complete each sentence with either the present indicative or the subjunctive of the verb in parentheses.

1. No hay nadie que _____ (mejorar) rápidamente.
2. Conozco a un curandero que _____ (dar) hierbas.
3. Buscamos algo que les _____ (gustar).
4. Tiene unos pacientes que _____ (estar) muy graves.
5. Necesitan unas personas con quienes _____ (poder) almorzar.
6. Quieres un médico que te _____ (hacer) unos análisis.
7. No hay ninguno que _____ (cuidarse).
8. Es una clínica adonde _____ (ir) muchos pacientes.
9. No hay nada que me _____ (doler).
10. Ese es el hombre que _____ (seguir) la dieta.

B. Your friend wants to know whether you have already done certain things. Tell her you have not, using the present perfect in your reply. Replace direct object nouns with the corresponding pronouns.

MODELO: —¿Ya tomaste los antibióticos?
—No. Todavía no los he tomado.

1. ¿Ya hiciste cola en el banco?
2. ¿Ya te pusiste el traje de baño?
3. ¿Ya perdiste peso?

4. ¿Ya te peinaste?
5. ¿Ya preparaste la ensalada?
6. ¿Ya viste las tarjetas de crédito?

C. Fill in the blank with the proper present form of **haber** or **estar** as required.

1. El restaurante _____ abierto.
2. Su hija se _____ casado.
3. Las cartas _____ escritas.

4. Su novio _____ vuelto.
5. Esa falda _____ rota.
6. Todos los vasos _____ lavados.

D. Answer the following questions negatively, using the cues in parentheses in your answers.

MODELO: —¿Vas a estudiar ruso algún día? (nunca)
—No, no voy a estudiar ruso nunca.

1. ¿Necesitas que alguien venga? (nadie)
2. ¿Uds. han ahorrado algo? (nada)
3. ¿Te hemos dicho el precio también? (tampoco)
4. ¿Siempre os echábais a las cuatro? (nunca)
5. ¿Te interesa ver algún periódico? (ninguno)
6. ¿Llovió o nevó el miércoles? (ni)

E. Translate the following sentences into Spanish.

1. There's no doctor who has more patients.
2. He's gotten better, but his throat still hurts.
3. I don't know anyone who's going to the clinic.
4. You have to (**hay que**) take good care of yourself.
5. She broke her nose in the car accident.
6. They never get sad when they gain weight.
7. The doctor hasn't done tests or a culture on you (**Ud.**).
8. Have you (**vosotros**) written your diary?
   Yes, it's written.
9. We've examined their lungs and heart. Fortunately they have no infection.
10. You've (**tú**) been nauseous and your stomach hurts; you have (**sufrir de**) a virus.

repaso 4

A. Rewrite each of the following sentences changing the verbs from the present to the imperfect.

1. Piensa en el futuro.
2. No ven las planillas.
3. Voy a dedicarme a mi profesión.
4. Es el médico que trabaja allí.
5. Le duele la garganta.
6. Te encuentras con Antonio María.

B. Rewrite the following paragraph in past time. Change each of the verbs to the imperfect or the preterit, as required.

El martes Raúl *se despierta* a las siete para ir a la oficina. *Tiene* dolor de cabeza y le *duele* la garganta. Se *da* cuenta que *sufre* de alguna enfermedad. Por fin *se levanta* y *va* al baño donde *se lava* y *se viste*. Se *toma* la temperatura y cuando *ve* que *tiene* fiebre *vuelve* a acostarse. *Decide* guardar cama porque *cree* que *tiene* gripe. En seguida *llama* a su jefe para decirle que no *puede* ir a la oficina.

C. Rewrite each of the following sentences adding the verb or impersonal expression in parentheses and changing the first verb to the present subjunctive. The sentences form a narrative of a doctor concerned about a patient.

MODELO: Podemos ayudar a este paciente. (espero que)
→ Espero que podamos ayudar a este paciente.

1. A este paciente le duele la cabeza. (dudo que)
2. Sin embargo, tiene un poco de fiebre. (es posible que)
3. Toma un antibiótico. (es necesario que)
4. Pierde peso. (le voy a aconsejar que)
5. Le doy una dieta. (me va a pedir que)
6. La sigue. (ojalá que)

7. Se pone peor si no sigue la dieta.   (tengo miedo de que)
8. Mis pacientes mejoran.   (yo siempre quiero que)

D. Rewrite the following paragraph choosing either the present indicative or the present subjunctive of the verbs in parentheses.

Hoy yo _____ (tener) que ir al banco. Yo _____ (necesitar) cobrar un cheque y depositar plata en mi cuenta de ahorros. (Yo) _____ (esperar) que no _____ (haber) cola. (Yo) _____ (preferir) que mi esposo _____ (ir), pero es posible que él _____ (estar) ocupado todo el día. Mi esposo me pide que _____ (depositar) su sueldo, pero yo no _____ (creer) que la plata _____ (ser) suficiente para el mes. ¡Qué lastima que nosotros no _____ (poder) ahorrar plata para el futuro, pero todos los meses (nosotros) _____ (tener) que gastar todo lo que _____ (ganar)!

E. Complete the following sentences choosing either the present indicative or the present subjunctive of the verbs in parentheses. The sentences form a connected story about two overweight people seeking medical help.

1. Nos hace falta un médico que _____ (dar) una buena dieta.
2. Buscamos médicos que _____ (saber) mucho.
3. No hemos encontrado a nadie que _____ (tener) experiencia.
4. Pero mi tía conoce a un médico que _____ (tratar) a la gente gorda.
5. Trabaja en una clínica adonde _____ (ir) muchos pacientes.
6. Él tiene dietas y pastillas que _____ (ayudar) a la gente gorda.
7. Ese médico, dice mi tía, quiere pacientes que _____ (cuidarse) mucho.
8. Vamos a ver si tiene pastillas que no nos _____ (dar) dolores de estómago.

F. Supply the proper form of **haber** or **estar** in each sentence.

1. La ventanilla no _____ abierta todavía.
2. Yo _____ retirado cien dólares de mi cuenta de ahorros.
3. Ellos _____ solicitado un préstamo.
4. Las planillas de depósito _____ firmadas.
5. Todo el dinero _____ depositado.
6. ¿Vosotros _____ escrito vuestro cheque?
7. Los intereses _____ calculados.
8. Nosotros _____ esperado en la cola.

G. Translate the following story into Spanish.

1. Patricia and Pedro were going to get married this summer.
2. Pedro met Patricia in a bank. She was a teller.
3. But in June Patricia felt (*preterit*) sick.
4. The doctors did medical tests on her and said she had to rest for three months.
5. I hope she gets better quickly!

H. Translate the following story into English.

1. Hacía cuatro años que mi primo y su esposa no se llevaban bien cuando decidieron divorciarse.
2. Mi tía se puso enferma cuando lo supo.
3. Tuvieron que llevarla al médico porque le dolían el estómago y la cabeza.
4. Le dio algunas pastillas y mejoró bastante.
5. ¡Ojalá que no vuelva a ponerse enferma por los problemas de sus hijos!

I. Reading passage. The following passage deals with an extended family situation. Extended family living patterns are far more common in Spanish-speaking countries than in English-speaking ones.

Cognates are marked with a raised degree sign (°). New words are listed below. Study them until you can give the English equivalent for each Spanish word or phrase. After reading the passage, do the comprehension exercise that follows it.

el **amor** love	el **lugar** place
apretado crowded	la **muerte** death
consentir to spoil (children)	el (la) **nieto, (a)** grandchild
la **cuadra** (*city*) block	el **principio** beginning
cuidar to take care of	la **reunión** gathering
débil weak	**reunirse** to get together
extrañar to miss (*someone*)	**sentarse (e→ie)** to sit down
el **gasto** expense	**sería** it would be
hacerle caso pay attention to, heed	el **sobrino** nephew
jugar (u→ue) to play (*a game*)	**soltero** unmarried

Claudia González habla de su familia

En mi casa somos ocho personas—mi abuela, mi tía Rosalia, mis papás, mi hermano Carlos Antonio, mis hermanas Aurora y Beatriz y yo. Todos nuestros parientes, cuando hablan de mi casa, dicen «la casa de la abuela Eugenia». ¿Cómo llegaron la abuela y la tía a vivir con nosotros? Voy a explicarles un poco la cosa.

Mis abuelos tenían un apartamento a dos cuadras de nuestra casa. Cuando éramos pequeños, mis hermanos y yo pasábamos muchísimo tiempo en su casa. Comíamos y jugábamos allí con nuestros primos. ¡Cómo nos consentían los abuelos! La abuela siempre nos hacía los postres que más nos gustaban, y el abuelo, que siempre decía que la abuela nos consentía demasiado, nunca se olvidaba de traernos algún regalito todas las semanas. No sería una exageración° decir que nuestros abuelos nos cuidaban tanto como nuestros papás, y que eran muy importantes en nuestra vida.

Sin embargo, este mundo maravilloso no pudo seguir para siempre. Sabíamos que el abuelo sufría del corazón y que su enfermedad era incurable.° Él se ponía peor, más débil, hasta que un día se sentó en el patio° para leer el periódico y no se levantó más. Nos fue muy difícil aceptar° su muerte y ver el dolor de la abuela y de la tía Rosalia. La tía Rosalia es soltera. Ella es la hija mayor de mis abuelos y nunca se casó porque se dedicaba a mis abuelos y a sus sobrinos.

Mi papá ayudó a mi abuela a vender su apartamento y ella y la tía Rosalia pasaron a vivir a nuestra casa. —No quiero que tú y mi hermana tengan que vivir solas, mamá —le dijo mi padre. —Es necesario que vengas a vivir con nosotros. —Pero, Jaime —le dijo mi abuela— la casa de ustedes no es tan grande. No puedo permitir que mis nietos vivan apretados por mí. Pero papá insistió y por fin la abuela y la tía se mudaron a nuestra casa. La tía Rosalia quería ir a vivir con su hermana, mi tía Felisa, porque creía que no iba a haber lugar para ella, pero mi padre le dijo —tú has vivido toda la vida con nuestros padres y te has dedicado a cuidarlos. ¿Cómo puedes pensar que no hay lugar para ti en mi casa? A mí me parece que no hay nadie en este mundo que sea más bueno ni más generoso° que mi padre.

Mi tía, que ha trabajado toda su vida como cajera en un banco, decidió seguir con su empleo para poder ayudar a mi padre con los gastos. Mi papá no quería eso. —Has trabajado bastante —le dijo— ahora ha llegado el momento° de descansar. Pero a mi tía le gusta trabajar y se dio cuenta de que económicamente° la presencia° de dos personas más en la casa iba a ser difícil.

Somos una familia grande: mamá, papá, los abuelos, los tíos y yo.

Ahora, cuando toda la familia se reúne, la reunión es en nuestra casa. Pero, como dije al principio, todo el mundo dice que va a casa de la abuela. Ella es la cabeza de la familia y todo el mundo le tiene mucho amor y respeto.° Sus quince nietos la quieren mucho y todos saben que hay que hacerle caso a ella tanto como a sus papás. Y la abuela hace muchas cosas importantes para la familia. Aquí nadie sabe lo que es un «baby-sitter». Si uno de mis tíos tiene que salir, va mi abuela a cuidar a los niños. Cuando mi tío Ernesto y su esposa fueron a pasar quince días en Europa, sus dos hijos vinieron a vivir en nuestra casa y mi abuela los cuidaba. A pesar de que ella extraña mucho al abuelo, el amor de sus hijos y de sus nietos es para ella una consolación.°

COMPREHENSION CHECK.

1. ¿Quiénes son las personas que viven con Claudia?
2. ¿Dónde vivía antes la abuela Eugenia?
3. ¿Qué hacían los niños en casa de sus abuelos?
4. ¿Cómo los trataban los abuelos?
5. ¿De qué murió el abuelo?
6. ¿Dónde murió?
7. ¿Qué hacía cuando murió?
8. ¿Cómo se sintieron los niños cuando murió su abuelo?
9. ¿Quién es Rosalia?
10. ¿Por qué no se casó nunca?
11. ¿Adónde fueron a vivir la abuela y la tía Rosalia después de la muerte del abuelo?
12. ¿Dónde trabaja Rosalia?
13. ¿Por qué no quería dejar el trabajo?
14. ¿Qué piensa Claudia de su padre?
15. Explique la importancia de la abuela en la familia González.

lección 13

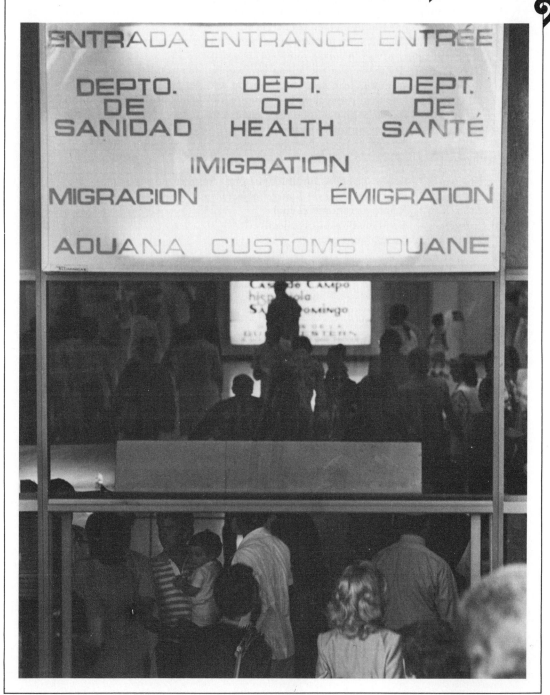

Objectives

Structure   You will learn to use **se** with the third person of the verb to deemphasize the importance of the person performing the action. You will also learn to use this structure in combination with an indirect object to produce the commonly used constructions for unplanned occurrences.

Vocabulary   You will learn terms that have to do with official procedures such as birth certificates, drivers' licenses, marriage licenses, etc.

Conversation   By the end of the lesson you will be able to talk about some aspects of United States immigration and citizenship and describe your own official papers.

Culture   You will be introduced to the situation of the illegal alien in the United States and learn one way in which he may legalize his status. You will also study a map of Latin America and talk about it in Spanish.

Outline

Estructura 1   **Se**-*constructions* for indefinite or deemphasized subjects
Estructura 2   **Se**-*construction* + *indirect object pronoun* for unplanned occurrences
Estructura 3   Relative pronoun: **el cual**
Estructura 4   Shortened forms of adjectives
Estructura 5   Ordinal numbers

An Illegal Alien

Francisco Colón left the Dominican Republic in 1978 and entered the United States illegally. He went to New York in order to live better and be able to send money to his family in Santo Domingo. He found only bad jobs because he didn't have the necessary papers. He worked in hotels and restaurants downtown and picked fruit on the farms of northern New Jersey. Today Francisco is speaking with an official in the Immigration Office in New York.

O.:   You know that without the necessary papers you're not permitted to work or live in this country.

F.:   I know. It became unbearable for me to go on as an illegal alien. Now that I've married an American citizen everything can be straightened out.

O.:   I see in these papers that your wife is Puerto Rican. That's fine. We also need your marriage license and your wife's birth certificate.

F.:   Here's the license, but it never dawned on me to bring her birth certificate.

O.:   Well, you can bring it another day. I'm going to give you an appointment to talk to the government agents.

F.:   Meanwhile, should these forms be filled out and signed?

O.:   Yes, please. Afterwards we'll give you the green card.

F.:   Great! At last I'm going to get a good job.

Presentación

Un inmigrante indocumentado

Francisco Colón salió de la República Dominicana[1] en 1978 y entró en Estados Unidos ilegalmente. Fue a Nueva York para vivir mejor y para poder mandarle plata a su familia en Santo Domingo.[2] Solamente encontraba empleos malos porque no tenía los documentos necesarios. Trabajaba en los hoteles y restaurantes del centro y recogía fruta en las fincas del norte de New Jersey. Hoy Francisco habla con un funcionario de la Oficina de Inmigración de Nueva York.

El funcionario —Ud. sabe que sin los documentos necesarios no se permite ni trabajar ni vivir en el país.

Francisco —Así es. Se me hizo insoportable seguir como inmigrante indocumentado. Ahora que me he casado con una ciudadana norteamericana, todo se arregla.

El funcionario —Veo en estos papeles que su esposa es puertorriqueña. Muy bien. Se necesitan también el certificado de matrimonio y la partida de nacimiento de la señora.

Francisco —Aquí tiene Ud. el certificado, pero nunca se me ocurrió traer la partida.

El funcionario —Bueno, Ud. puede traerla otro día. Le voy a dar una cita para hablar con los agentes del gobierno.

Francisco —Mientras tanto, ¿se deben llenar y firmar estos formularios?

El funcionario —Sí, por favor. Después le damos la tarjeta verde.

Francisco —¡Chévere! Por fin voy a conseguir un buen empleo.

---

[1] The Dominican Republic, to the west of Puerto Rico, comprises, along with Haiti, the island of Hispaniola (La Española).

[2] Santo Domingo is the capital of the Dominican Republic.

Ampliación

—¿Se les olvidó **el pasaporte?** (la tarjeta de indentidad, la licencia de manejar)	*Did you forget your **passport?** (ID card, driver's license)*
—Sí, y se nos olvidaron los otros documentos también.	*Yes, and we forgot our other papers, too.*
—¡Caray! ¡Se le cayeron **los anteojos!** (los lentes de contacto)	*Gosh! She dropped her **eyeglasses!** (contact lenses)*
—¿Se le rompieron?	*Did they break?*
—¿Has estado en el extranjero?	*Have you been abroad?*
—No, pero voy al extranjero en la primavera.	*No, but I'm going abroad in the spring.*
—¿Ese obrero extranjero entró al país legalmente?	*Did that foreign worker enter the country legally?*
—Sí. Tiene una visa.	*Yes. He has a visa.*
—¿La tarjeta verde le da los derechos de ciudadano?	*Does the green card give him a citizen's rights?*
—Sí, todos menos el derecho de votar.	*Yes, all of them except the right to vote.*
—¿Se abrió una oficina de turismo en el norte?	*Did a tourist office open in the north?*
—Sí, y se abrió otra en **el sur.** (el este, el oeste)	*Yes, and another opened in **the south.** (the east, the west)*
—¿Es el primer **policía** que ha llegado? (bombero)	*Is it the first **policeman** who's arrived? (firefighter)*
—No. Es **el segundo.** (el tercero, el cuarto, el quinto, el sexto, el séptimo, el octavo, el noveno, el décimo)	*No. It's **the second.** (the third, the fourth, the fifth, the sixth, the seventh, the eighth, the ninth, the tenth)*
Allí está **la oficina** hacia **la cual** caminan. (el banco, el cual)	*There's **the office** they're walking towards. (the bank)*
Son **los documentos** por **los cuales** he ido a la oficina de inmigración. (las cartas, las cuales)	*They're **the papers for which** I've gone to the immigration office. (the letters, for which)*

Preguntas sobre la Presentación

1. ¿Para qué fue Francisco Colón a Estados Unidos?
2. ¿Por qué tenía Francisco solamente empleos malos?
3. ¿Por qué va Francisco a la Oficina de Inmigración?
4. ¿Qué documentos le pide el funcionario a Francisco? ¿Francisco los tiene?
5. ¿Qué tiene que hacer Francisco antes de recibir la tarjeta verde?

6. ¿Por qué quiere Francisco conseguir una tarjeta verde?

NOTA CULTURAL

Of the five major Hispanic groups living in New York City—Puerto Ricans, Dominicans, Colombians, Ecuadorians, and Cubans—Dominicans make up the second largest group. While the Puerto Ricans are United States citizens and the Cubans are welcomed as political refugees, the other nationalities have not found emigration to the U.S. an easy procedure and consequently many Dominicans, Colombians, and Ecuadorians have found illegal entry the only avenue open to them. Because illegal aliens have no papers they are forced to accept jobs that pay poorly and offer no benefits or security—jobs in hotels, restaurants and other service businesses, in the apparel trade, or picking fruits and vegetables in farms in northern New Jersey and other farm areas close to New York City.

One way an illegal alien may legalize his status is by marrying a United States citizen. By so doing he can acquire a green card that enables him to compete for better jobs and that grants him all rights of a United States citizen except the right to vote.

Vocabulario activo

el **agente**   agent
los **anteojos**   eyeglasses
arreglar   to arrange, to fix, straighten out
el **bombero**   firefighter
caer   to fall
caminar   to walk
el **certificado**   license, certificate
la **cita**   appointment, date
el (la) **ciudadano, (-a)**   citizen
el **derecho**   right, privilege
el **documento**   document; (*pl.*) papers
el **este**   east
extranjero   foreign
la **finca**   farm
el **formulario**   form (*paper*)
el **funcionario**   official, public employee
el **gobierno**   government
la **identidad**   identification, identity
ilegalmente   illegally
indocumentado   without papers, illegal
la **inmigración**   immigration
el (la) **inmigrante**   immigrant
insoportable   unbearable
legalmente   legally

la **licencia**   license
mandar   to send
manejar   to drive
el **matrimonio**   marriage
el **norte**   north
el **obrero**   worker
el **oeste**   west
el **papel**   paper
el **pasaporte**   passport
el (la) **policía**   policeman, policewoman
recoger   to pick (*crops*)
la **república**   republic
solamente   only
el **sur**   south
el **turismo**   tourism
la **visa**   visa
votar   to vote

EXPRESIONES
¡chévere! (*Caribbean*)   great!, terrific!
estar en el extranjero   to be abroad
ir al extranjero   to go abroad
la partida de nacimiento   birth certificate
los lentes de contacto   contact lenses
mientras tanto   meanwhile
ocurrírsele   to dawn on someone

Estructura 1

Se-*constructions* for indefinite or deemphasized subjects

Análisis

▶ It is necessary to distinguish between the grammatical subject (the element of the sentence that determines the ending of the verb) and the performer of the action. In the sentence **Vendo anteojos** (*I sell eyeglasses*), the grammatical subject and the performer of the action refer to the same person. In the sentence **Se venden anteojos** (*Eyeglasses are sold*), the grammatical subject is not the performer of the action.

▶ The speaker uses the **se**-construction (**se** + *verb*) to signal that he considers the identity of the performer of the action unimportant or that he cannot identify the performer of the action. In English, there are a variety of ways for speakers to deemphasize the subject. **Se venden anteojos** might be rendered as *Eyeglasses are sold, You sell eyeglasses, They sell eyeglasses, People sell eyeglasses, One sells eyeglasses.*

▶ The verb in the **se**-construction is either third-person singular or third-person plural depending on whether the grammatical subject is singular or plural: **se oye un tren, se oyen trenes.**

▶ Intransitive verbs—those that do not take a direct object—may also be used in the **se**-construction. In this case, the verb is always third person singular.

Se camina por aquí.	*You walk around here.*
Se trabajaba los lunes.	*People were working on Mondays.*

Práctica

A. Change each of the following sentences to a **se**-construction. Notice that the original direct object becomes the new grammatical subject.

MODELO: Compro una camisa. *I buy a shirt.*
→ Se compra una camisa. *A shirt is bought.*

1. Mandan plata a su familia.
2. Arreglamos los documentos.
3. Recojo fruta en la finca.
4. Necesitas formularios.
5. Tomó antibióticos.
6. Buscaron la partida de nacimiento.

B. Answer the following questions by deleting the first verb in the *verb + infinitive* construction and changing the second verb (infinitive) to the preterit. Add **ya** as in the model.

MODELO: —¿Se va a entregar el pasaporte? *Is the passport going to be handed in?*
—Se entregó ya. *It was already handed in.*

1. ¿Se quieren realizar los sueños?
2. ¿Se necesita hacer un análisis?
3. ¿Se deben visitar los almacenes?

4. ¿Se piensa solicitar un préstamo?
5. ¿Se van a probar los platos españoles?
6. ¿Se puede conseguir la licencia?

Estructura 2

Se-construction + *indirect object pronoun* for unplanned occurrences

Análisis

▶ Indirect object pronouns are commonly added to sentences with **se**-construction verbs in Spanish. The indirect object pronoun designates the person the speaker sees as being affected in some way by the action of the verb. A common function of these sentences is to deemphasize the performer of the action, thereby diminishing or softening his participation or responsibility in the action. Compare theses sentences:

Rompí la taza.	*I broke the cup.*
Se me rompió la taza.	*The cup broke (on me).*

▶ It is easier for English-speaking students to learn to use these constructions if they remember that the indirect object pronoun is added to a reflexive construction that already has its own meaning and that the verb must be either third-person singular or third-person plural.

Se olvidó la fecha	*The date was forgotten.*
Se **le** olvidó la fecha.	*She forgot the date.*
Se perdieron los documentos.	*The papers got lost.*
Se **nos** perdieron los documentos	*We lost the papers.*
Se acabó la leche.	*The milk ran out.*
Se **les** acabó la leche.	*They ran out of milk.*

Práctica

A. You and your friends must present some papers at the immigration office. When the official asks for them, tell him you and everyone else left them at home.

MODELO: —¿Trajo Ud. el certificado de matrimonio?
          —No. Se me quedó en casa.

Did you bring your marriage license?
No. I left it at home.

1. ¿Trajo Ud. la partida de nacimiento?

2. ¿Trajeron Uds. los documentos?

3. ¿Trajo él la visa?
4. ¿Trajeron ellas la tarjeta de identidad?
5. ¿Trajeron ellos los papeles?
6. ¿Trajo ella la tarjeta verde?

B. Repeat Exercise A using the following response:

MODELO: —¿Trajo Ud. el certificado *Did you bring the marriage license?*
de matrimonio?
—No. Se me olvidó. *No. I forgot it.*

C. Answer each of the following questions using the cue in parentheses in your response.

MODELO: —¿Qué se le rompió? *What did he tear?* (*his overcoat*)
(**el abrigo**)
—Se le rompió el abrigo. *He tore his overcoat.*

1. ¿Qué se te cayó? (los platos)
2. ¿Qué se me perdió? (el paraguas)
3. ¿Qué se les olvidó a Uds.? (depositar el cheque)
4. ¿Qué se le rompió a Ud.? (los lentes de contacto)
5. ¿Qué se le hizo imposible a él? (vivir en el extranjero)
6. ¿Qué se os acabó? (los ahorros)

D. Your friend is very careless, so when you see him carrying things that he might drop, you try to caution him.

MODELO: —Aquí está el vaso de agua. *Here's the glass of water.*
—¡Cuidado! Se te va a caer. *Careful! It's going to fall.*

1. Aquí están los anteojos.
2. Aquí está la comida.
3. Aquí están las monedas.
4. Aquí están las cucharas.
5. Aquí está la taza.
6. Aquí está la sopa.

E. Just as you thought! Ask your friend what happened to the items in Exercise D. He'll tell you he dropped them!

MODELO: —¿Dónde está el vaso de agua? *Where's the glass of water?*
—Lo siento. Se me cayó. *I'm sorry. I dropped it.*

Estructura 3

*Relative pronoun: **el cual***

Análisis

▸ As you will remember from the discussion of relative pronouns (see Lesson 8,

Estructura 5), two sentences that share an identical element can be combined into one by means of a relative pronoun. The new sentence has two clauses—the main clause and the relative clause, which begins with a relative pronoun. To **que** and **quien** we now add another relative pronoun: **el cual, la cual, los cuales, las cuales.**

▸ After prepositions other than **a, con, de,** and **en** (and sometimes even after these), nouns *not* referring to humans[3] are replaced by **el cual, la cual, los cuales, las cuales,** and not by **que.** After compound prepositions such as **antes de** and **después de, el cual (la cual, los cuales, las cuales)** is generally used.

Estos son los documentos **por los cuales** he venido.	*These are the papers I've come for.*
Una comida **durante la cual** hablaron de sus problemas.	*A meal **during which** they talked about their problems.*
El viaje **después del cual** me llamó.	*The trip **after which** he called me.*

Práctica

A. Combine each pair of sentences into a single sentence replacing the identical element of the second by **el cual, la cual, los cuales,** or **las cuales.**

MODELO: Allí están los restaurantes.   *There are the restaurants.*
          Vamos hacia los restaurantes.   *We're going towards the restaurants.*

→ Allí están los restaurantes   *There are the restaurants we're*
  hacia los cuales vamos.   *going towards.*

1. Miro la playa. Él camina hacia la playa.
2. No conocen los museos. Entramos en los museos.
3. Fue el viaje. Se casó después del viaje.
4. Tomó el examen. Se puso enferma durante el examen.
5. Tengo las planillas. Viene por las planillas.
6. Es la fecha. Retiráis la plata antes de la fecha.

B. Substitute each cue in parentheses and make all necessary changes.

1. Veo **la calle** hacia la cual camina.
   (el colegio / los hoteles / las tiendas / la clínica)
2. Son **los papeles** por los cuales volvió.
   (las cartas / la licencia de manejar / la tarjeta de identidad / los periódicos)

---

[3] Some Spanish speakers use **el cual, la cual, los cuales, las cuales** to refer to people as well.

Estructura 4

Shortened forms of adjectives

Análisis

▸ The following adjectives lose their final **-o** before a masculine singular noun.

Adjective		Shortened form before masculine singular noun
uno	*one, a*	**un** pasaporte
alguno	*some*	**algún** papel
ninguno	*no*	**ningún** gobierno
bueno	*good*	un **buen** obrero
malo	*bad*	un **mal** funcionario
primero	*first*	el **primer** día
tercero	*third*	el **tercer** mes

▸ **Uno, alguno,** and **ninguno** become **un, algún,** and **ningún,** respectively, also before masculine singular adjectives: ***un* buen obrero** *a good worker;* ***algún* otro papel** *some other paper;* ***ningún* mal gobierno,** *no bad government.*

▸ **Grande** shortens to **gran** before both masculine and feminine singular nouns. **Grande** means *great* when it is placed *before* a noun. When it comes *after* a noun, it means *big.*

un **gran** hombre	*a great man*	una **gran** mujer	*a great woman*
grandes hombres	*great men*	una mujer **grande**	*a big woman*

Práctica

Change each of the following sentences according to the cue in parentheses and make all necessary changes.

MODELO:　Conocí a una buena profesora.　*I met a good teacher.*
　　　　　(profesor)
　　　　　→ Conocí a un buen profesor.　*I met a good teacher.*

1. Han estado en una buena clínica.　(hospital)
2. ¡Qué mala república!　(gobierno)
3. Había grandes doctores en la ciudad.　(doctoras)
4. ¿Has tenido algunas enfermedades?　(virus)
5. Aquí está la primera moneda.　(billete)
6. No llené ninguna planilla.　(formulario)
7. Ese policía fue un gran hombre.　(esa policía)
8. Se pide la tercera cosa en la carta.　(plato)

Estructura 5

Ordinal numbers

Análisis

▶ Cardinal numbers are used for counting: *one, two, three,* etc. Ordinal numbers are used for ranking: *first, second, third,* etc. The Spanish ordinals are:

primero	*first*	**sexto**	*sixth*
segundo	*second*	**séptimo**	*seventh*
tercero	*third*	**octavo**	*eighth*
cuarto	*fourth*	**noveno**	*ninth*
quinto	*fifth*	**décimo**	*tenth*

The ordinal numbers are all four-form adjectives: **el** *cuarto* **mes, la** *cuarta* **semana. Primero** and **tercero** lose their final **-o** before masculine singular nouns.

▶ In Spanish ordinal numbers are rarely used beyond *tenth;* cardinal numbers are used instead.

Se lee el **décimo** libro.	*The **tenth** book is read.*
Se lee el libro **quince**.	*The **fifteenth** book is read.*

For dates Spanish uses only cardinal numbers except for the *first.*

Hoy es el **primero** de febrero.	*Today is February **1st**.*
Mañana es el **dos** de febrero.	*Tomorrow is February **2nd**.*

Práctica

There's really one more of everything your friend mentions. Tell him so, using the appropriate ordinal number.

MODELO: —¿Ese es el quinto libro que   *Is that the fifth book that you*
           compraste?   *bought?*
         —No, es el sexto libro.   *No, it's the sixth book.*

1. ¿Ayer tuviste tu tercera cita con el dentista?
2. ¿La química es la octava materia que tomaste?
3. ¿España es el cuarto país que visitaste?
4. ¿Tu prima es la novena persona de aquella cola?
5. ¿Él es el primer bombero que llegó?
6. ¿Éste es tu sexto préstamo?

Preguntas personales

1. ¿Qué documentos se necesitan para entrar a un país extranjero?
2. ¿Qué derechos te da **la tarjeta de identidad?**   (la licencia de manejar, la tarjeta verde)

3. ¿Llevas unos documentos siempre? ¿Qué se dice en cada uno?   (la tarjeta de identidad, la tarjeta de crédito, la licencia de manejar, la partida de nacimiento)
4. ¿Se te **olvidó** algo importante? ¿Qué fue?   (ocurrió)
5. ¿Qué se le cayó a Ud.? ¿Se le rompió?
6. Study the map and then answer these questions.
   a. ¿Queda México al norte de Venezuela?
   b. ¿Queda la República Dominicana al oeste de Cuba?
   c. ¿Queda Colombia al sur de Chile?
   d. ¿Queda Chile al este de la Argentina?

Charlas

1. —**Señor, quiero conseguir una tarjeta verde.**

   ¿Cuándo entró Ud. en Estados Unidos?   ¿De dónde viene Ud.?   ¿Por qué solicita Ud. la tarjeta?   ¿Ya tiene Ud. una visa?

2. —**¡Caray! ¡Se me ha caído un lente de contacto!**

   ¿Se te ha perdido?   ¿Se te ha roto?   ¿Se te quedaron los anteojos en casa?   ¿El médico va a volver a examinarte los ojos?

Situación

(*Two students*)   One student is an illegal alien who has recently married a United States citizen. She goes to the Immigration Office to declare her status and apply for a green card. The other student, the government agent, asks her where she is from, when she entered the United States, and why she wants to remain in this country. He then asks to see her birth certificate, her marriage license and her husband's birth certificate, and tells her what the procedure involves.

Para escribir

A. Form complete sentences using the **se**-construction as in the model.

MODELO: comer / arroz   →   Se come arroz.
          comer / legumbres   →   Se comen legumbres.

1. buscar / esa sección del almacén
2. perder / los lápices
3. poner / la mesa
4. seguir / una tradiciones
5. leer / los anuncios del periódico
6. pedir / un plato picante

B. Answer the questions on p. 206 using the cues in parentheses in your answers.

MODELO: —¿Se abre el hotel hoy?   (la semana que viene)
   —No, se va a abrir la semana que viene.

1. ¿Se arreglaron los papeles ayer?   (pasado mañana)
2. ¿Se cierra la ventanilla a las tres?   (a la una y media)
3. ¿Se recogen manzanas en agosto?   (en septiembre)
4. ¿Se caminó por la finca en la mañana?   (en la tarde)
5. ¿Se sirvió la cena a las siete?   (a las nueve)
6. ¿Se durmió bien anoche?   (esta noche)

C. Construct sentences expressing unplanned occurrences out of the following strings of elements as in the model. Use the preterit tense.

MODELO: a él / caerse / los anteojos → Se le cayeron los anteojos.

1. a ella / olvidarse / entregar la libreta de ahorros
2. a nosotros / perderse / los billetes
3. a mí / hacerse difícil / seguir sus tradiciones
4. a Ud. / acabarse / el jugo
5. a ellas / ocurrirse / una idea
6. a él / romperse / la pierna
7. a vosotros / quedarse en la oficina / la tarjeta de crédito
8. a ti / caerse / los tenedores

D. Supply the correct form of the adjective in parentheses in the following sentences.

1. El señor Suárez era un _____ (grande) profesor.
2. Es el _____ (tercero) pasaporte que ha recibido.
3. Te aconsejo que llenes _____ (alguno) formulario.
4. Ese agente es realmente _____ (bueno).
5. Se viaja durante la _____ (séptimo) semana.
6. No hay _____ (ninguno) _____ (malo) estudiante en esa clase.
7. Doña Teresa es una mujer _____ (grande).
8. Hemos mandado la _____ (primero) partida de nacimiento.

E. Translate the following sentences into Spanish.

1. Some illegal aliens pick fruit.
2. Did you (**Ud.**) forget your ID card at home?
3. They need your birth certificate and your marriage license. (*use **se**-con-struction*)
4. I dropped a glass of milk yesterday and it broke.
5. Did they ask for your passport when you went abroad? (**tú**)
6. The green card doesn't give them the right to vote.
7. A tourist office opened up to the east of the city.
8. The first firefighters have arrived; the policemen haven't arrived yet.
9. It became unbearable for us to work illegally.
10. Her papers got straightened out in the immigration office.

lección 14

Objectives

Structure You will learn and practice the command forms of verbs so that you can tell someone else to do or not to do something.

Vocabulary You will learn the words for many pieces of furniture, electrical appliances, and other important household items.

Conversation By the end of the lesson, you will be able to tell your friends where to place the furniture they are helping you to move. You will be able to understand them when they tell you to shut off the TV and straighten up your room!

Culture You will learn something about the layout and furnishings of an apartment in Madrid and will observe a Spanish family on moving day. You will be able to compare this experience to your own.

Outline

Estructura 1 Command forms for **Ud., Uds., tú, nosotros**
Estructura 2 Comparative and superlative constructions
Estructura 3 **¡Qué!** in exclamations
Estructura 4 Command forms for **vosotros** (For recognition)

Moving Day

The Gómezes, a Spanish family from Madrid, are moving to a new apartment today. Julia and Alejandro and their two children, Ricardo and Carmen, are trying to get settled, but it is not at all easy.

In the living room:

Mover: Where do you want us to put the chair, ma'am? Next to the couch or in front of the window?

Mrs. G.: Please, first move the rug to the right and then put the chair near the door. Over there, behind the table.

Mover: There it is. Now, where should we take the washing machine and dryer?

Mrs. G.: Go this way, please. The kitchen's in the back. Leave them against the wall where the refrigerator and the dishwasher are. If you don't find the spot, ask my husband.

In Ricardo's room:

Mr. G.: Ricardo, shut off the stereo, please, and help me with these boxes. We have to put these small appliances in a closet.

R.: OK, Dad. But Carmen is still watching television. I'm working more than she is. Why doesn't she have to do as much as I do?

Mr. G.: Don't worry, son. Soon your sister is going to be as busy as you. She has to paint the furniture in her room.

Upstairs in the bedroom, late at night:

Mrs. G.: What a difficult day! I can't stand it anymore. Tomorrow I'll put the clothing away in the chest of drawers. Now let's go to bed.

Mr. G.: Shut off the light and go to bed. I'm not as tired as you. I'm going to hang up the mirror and some paintings downstairs.

Mrs. G.: Nothing doing! We'll do all that tomorrow, darling.

Mr. G.: But Julia, I'm very restless tonight. I can't relax . . . I have an idea. Make me a cup of tea, please. Let's see if I fall asleep.

Mrs. G.: OK. And you, sit down and put the radio on. I'll make you the tea right now.

Presentación

Día de mudanza

Los Gómez, familia española de Madrid, se mudan a un apartamento nuevo hoy. Julia y Alejandro y sus dos hijos, Ricardo y Carmen, tratan de instalarse, pero no es nada fácil.

En la sala:

Cargador	—¿Dónde quiere Ud. que pongamos la silla, señora? ¿Al lado del sofá o delante de la ventana?
Sra. Gómez	—Por favor, primero corran la alfombra a la derecha y luego pongan la silla cerca de la puerta. Allí, detrás de la mesa.
Cargador	—Ya está. Ahora, ¿adónde llevamos la máquina de lavar y la secadora?
Sra. Gómez	—Sigan Uds. por aquí. La cocina está al fondo. Déjenlas contra la pared donde están la nevera y el lavaplatos. Si no encuentran el lugar, pregúntenle a mi marido.

En el cuarto de Ricardo:

Sr. Gómez	—Ricardo, apaga el estéreo, por favor, y ayúdame con estos cajones. Hay que guardar los aparatos eléctricos pequeños en un armario.
Ricardo	—De acuerdo, papá. Pero Carmen mira la televisión todavía. Yo trabajo más que ella. ¿Por qué no tiene que hacer ella tanto como yo?
Sr. Gómez	—No te preocupes, hijo. Pronto va a estar tu hermanita tan ocupada como tú. Ella tiene que pintar los muebles de su cuarto.

Arriba en el dormitorio, tarde en la noche:

Sra. Gómez	—¡Qué día más difícil! No puedo más. Mañana guardo la ropa en la cómoda. Ahora acostémonos.

Sr. Gómez	—Apaga la luz y acuéstate tú. Yo no estoy tan cansado como tú. Voy a colgar el espejo y unos cuadros abajo.
Sra. Gómez	—¡Ni hablar! Hagamos todo eso mañana, mi amor.
Sr. Gómez	—Pero Julia, es que estoy muy inquieto esta noche. No puedo relajarme . . . Tengo una idea. Hazme un té, por favor. A ver si me duermo.
Sra. Gómez	—Bueno. Y tú, siéntate y pon la radio. Te hago el té ahora mismo.

Ampliación

—La cocina está a la derecha, ¿verdad?	*The kitchen is to the right, isn't it?*
—No, está a la izquierda.	*No, it's to the left.*
—¿Te doy la lámpara verde?	*Shall I give you the green lamp?*
—Sí, dámela.	*Yes, give it to me.*
—¿Les decimos el precio de las cortinas?	*Shall we tell you the price of the curtains?*
—No, no nos lo digan.	*No, don't tell us (it).*
—¿Quiere Ud. que le compre el reloj?	*Do you want me to buy you the watch?*
—Sí, cómpremelo, por favor.	*Yes, please buy it for me.*
—¿Debo arreglarle el apartamento?	*Should I fix up his apartment?*
—Sí, arrég</selo.	*Yes, fix it up for him.*
—¿Guardamos los papeles en la gaveta?	*Shall we put the papers away in the drawer?*
—No, guardémoslos en el cajón.	*No, let's put them in the box.*
—Estoy cansada. No trabajemos más.	*I'm tired. Let's not work anymore.*
—De acuerdo. Vamos a sentarnos un rato.	*OK. Let's sit down a while.*

Preguntas sobre la Presentación

1. ¿Dónde quiere la señora que los cargadores pongan la silla?
2. ¿Qué aparatos eléctricos se encuentran en la cocina?
3. ¿Qué le pide el señor a su hijo?
4. ¿De qué se queja Ricardo?
5. ¿Por qué no puede Alejandro dormirse?
6. ¿Qué le aconseja Julia a su marido?

Vocabulario activo

abajo downstairs
la **alfombra** rug, carpet

apagar to shut off
el **aparato** appliance

el **apartamento** apartment
el **armario** closet
  arriba upstairs
el **cajón** box
el **cargador** mover, carrier
  colgar (o→ue) to hang
la **cómoda** chest of drawers
  contra against
  correr to move; to run
la **cortina** curtain
el **cuadro** painting, picture
  dormirse to fall asleep
  eléctrico electrical
el **espejo** mirror
el **estéreo** stereo
la **gaveta** drawer
  guardar to put away
  inquieto upset, restless
  instalarse to get settled in
la **lámpara** lamp
el **lavaplatos** dishwasher
el **lugar** place
la **luz** light
la **máquina** machine
la **mudanza** moving
los **muebles** furniture
la **nevera** refrigerator

la **pared** wall
  pintar to paint
  poner to turn on (*an appliance*)
  preguntar to ask a question
  preocuparse to worry
la **puerta** door
la (el) **radio** radio
  relajarse to relax
el **reloj** watch, clock
la **secadora** dryer
  sentarse (e→ie) to sit down
la **silla** chair
el **sofá** couch
la **televisión** television
la **ventana** window

EXPRESIONES
a la derecha to the right
a la izquierda to the left
ahora mismo right now
al fondo in the back
delante de in front of
detrás de behind
mi amor dear, darling
¡ni hablar! nothing doing!
no puedo más I can't stand it anymore
tratar de (+ *infinitive*) to try to . . .

Estructura 1

Command forms for *Ud., Uds., tú, nosotros*

Análisis

▶ Command forms for **Ud.** and **Uds.** are derived from the present subjunctive. Negative commands (i.e., telling someone not to do something) are formed by placing **no** in front of the affirmative command. The addition of **Ud.** or **Uds.** after a command form adds a polite tone to the command, much as the addition of *please* does to English command forms.

—¿Con quién debo hablar?   *Who should I talk with?*
—**Hable** con Alejandro.   *Talk with Alejandro.*

—¿Debo trabajar arriba?   *Should I work upstairs?*
—No, **trabaje** abajo.   *No, work downstairs.*

—¿Dónde esperamos?   *Where shall we wait?*
—**Esperen** en la puerta.   ***Please wait** at the door.*

OR

—**Esperen Uds.** en la puerta.   ***Please wait** at the door.*

▶ Negative informal commands for **tú** are derived from the present subjunctive.

—¿Estudio con Julia?   *Shall I study with Julia?*
—No, **no estudies** con ella.   *No, **don't study** with her.*

—¿Debo caminar al centro?   *Should I walk downtown?*
—No, **no camines** allí.   *No, **don't walk** there.*

▶ Affirmative informal commands are *not* taken from the present subjunctive but are formed from the present indicative **tú**-form by dropping the person ending **-s.**

STATEMENT

Arreglas los armarios.
You're straightening up the closets.

Comes a las dos.
You eat at two o'clock.

COMMAND

Arregla los armarios.
***Straighten up** the closets.*

Come a las dos.
***Eat** at two o'clock.*

▶ The following verbs have irregular affirmative **tú** commands. Note, however, that the negative **tú** commands of these verbs are *regular;* that is, they are drawn from the present subjunctive.

Verb	*Affirmative tú*-command
decir	**di**
hacer	**haz**
ir	**ve**
poner	**pon**
salir	**sal**
ser	**sé**
tener	**ten**
venir	**ven**

Note that the affirmative **tú** commands for **ir** and **ver** are the same: **ve.**

▶ The present subjunctive **nosotros**-forms are used as commands (English: *let's, let's not*).

—¿Qué hacemos ahora?   *What should we do now?*
—**Miremos** la televisión.   *Let's watch TV.*

The affirmative **nosotros** command (*let's do something*) but *not* the negative one is often replaced by **vamos a** + *infinitive.*

Vamos a mirar la televisión.   *Let's watch TV.* OR ***We're going to watch** TV.*

NOTE: **Vamos** is used instead of **vayamos** for *let's go.*

Vamos a la derecha.   ***Let's go** to the right.*

▶ Object pronouns (direct, indirect, reflexive) appear in their usual position before the verb in negative commands.

—No tenemos dinero.	*We have no money.*
—No **se** preocupen.	*Don't worry.*

—¿Me lavo las manos?	*Shall I wash my hands?*
—No, no **te las** laves.	*No, don't wash them.*

Object pronouns *follow* affirmative commands and are attached to the command form in writing.[1]

—¿Te enseñamos las cortinas?	*Shall we show you the curtains?*
—Sí, enséñen**melas.**	*Yes, **show them to me.***

—¿Te pongo el saco?	*Shall I help you on with your jacket?*
—Sí, pón**melo.**	*Yes, **help me on with it.***

Note that affirmative **nosotros** command forms lose their final **-s** when the object pronouns **nos** and **se** are added.

Sentémonos. (sentemos + nos)   *Let's sit down.*
Pidámoselo. (pidamos + se + lo)   *Let's ask her for it.*

Práctica

A. The moving company is bringing your furniture and other household items into your new apartment. The mover asks you what he should do with certain belongings of yours. Answer him using an affirmative **Ud.** command in each case.

MODELO: —¿Debo poner el sofá contra   *Should I put the couch against*
                 la pared?   *the wall?*
              —Sí, póngalo contra la pared.   *Yes, put it against the wall.*

1. ¿Debo poner la lámpara en la mesa?
2. ¿Debo dejar el estéreo en la sala?
3. ¿Debo llevar estos cajones arriba?
4. ¿Debo darle la cuenta a su marido?
5. ¿Debo traer esta alfombra al cuarto?
6. ¿Debo instalar el lavaplatos ahora?

---

[1] When object pronouns are attached to command forms, an accent is added to the stressed syllable, except when a single object pronoun is added to a one-syllable command form: **dime** (*tell me*) vs. **dímelo** (*tell it to me*). **Dé** loses the accent mark when one pronoun is added but retains it when two are added: **deme** (*give me*) vs. **démelo** (*give it to me*).

B. Now tell the mover not to do the things he asks about. Repeat Exercise A using negative **Ud.** commands.

> MODELO: —¿Debo poner el sofá contra la pared?
> —No, no lo ponga contra la pared.

C. Your friends are helping you fix up your new house and want you to approve their decorating ideas. Answer their questions using affirmative **Uds.** commands.

> MODELO: —¿Dónde dejamos la silla? ¿Cerca de la puerta?
> —Sí, déjenla cerca de la puerta.

1. ¿Dónde ponemos la televisión? ¿Al lado del sofá?
2. ¿Dónde colgamos las cortinas? ¿En aquella ventana?
3. ¿Dónde guardamos los tenedores? ¿En esta gaveta?
4. ¿Adónde llevamos el espejo? ¿Al dormitorio?
5. ¿Adónde corremos el lavaplatos? ¿A otro lugar?

D. Now tell your friends not to do what they suggest. Repeat Exercise C using negative **Uds.** commands.

> MODELO: —¿Dónde dejamos la silla? ¿Cerca de la puerta?
> —No, no la dejen cerca de la puerta.

E. Your friend tells you all the things she must do today. Since you are anxious for her to stay with you, you tell her not to do them today but rather to do them tomorrow.

> MODELO: (*your friend*)—Voy a comprar una   *I'm going to buy a refriger-*
> nevera hoy.   *ator today.*
> (*you*)—No la compres hoy.   *Don't buy it today.*
> Cómprala mañana.   *Buy it tomorrow.*

1. Voy a pintar el cuarto hoy.
2. Voy a colgar el espejo hoy.
3. Voy a ir a la oficina de turismo hoy.
4. Voy a cerrar la cuenta de ahorros hoy.
5. Voy a visitar la clínica hoy.
6. Voy a mandarle un regalo a mi hermano hoy.

F. Your roommate tells you some things he wants to do right now. You like his suggestions and say *let's do it* in each case.

> MODELO: (*roommate*)—Debemos arreglar los armarios ahora mismo.
> (*you*)   —De acuerdo. Arreglémoslos.

1. Debemos hacerle la comida a Carmen ahora mismo.
2. Debemos mirar la televisión ahora mismo.
3. Debemos buscar unos periódicos ahora mismo.
4. Debemos abrir las ventanas ahora mismo.

5. Debemos apagar el estéreo ahora mismo.
6. Debemos salir a comer algo ahora mismo.

G. Repeat Exercise F telling your roommate that you don't like his suggestions. Ask him why all the rush and say, *Let's not do it now.*

> MODELO: (*roommate*)—Debemos arreglar los armarios ahora mismo.
> (*you*)   —¿Por qué tanta prisa? No los arreglemos ahora.

H. Patterned translation drill. Translate each sentence following the pattern of the Spanish model.

> MODELO: Let's wash up. *Lavémonos.*

1. Let's sit down.
2. Let's fall asleep.
3. Let's get married.
4. Let's relax.

5. Let's get dressed.
6. Let's take a shower.
7. Let's get up.

I. Do the sentences of Exercise H in the negative.

> MODELO: Let's not wash up. *No nos lavemos.*

Estructura 2

Comparative and superlative constructions

Análisis

▶ Adjectives in English form the comparative either by the addition of the suffix **-er** (*younger*) or by the use of the word *more* (*more interesting*) or its opposite, *less*. In Spanish the comparative is formed by placing **más** (*more*) or **menos** (*less*) before the adjective. *Than* is translated by **que.**

> Esta idea es **más** / **menos** intere-   *This idea is **more** / **less** interesting*
>   sante **que** esa idea.   ***than** that idea.*

▶ The **más . . . que** and **menos . . . que** constructions may also modify nouns, verbs, and adverbs.

> Hay **más** / **menos** ventanas en   *There are **more** / **fewer windows***
>   este cuarto **que** en ese cuarto.   *in this room **than** in that room.*

> Nosotros descansamos **más** /   *We rest **more** / **less than** they do.*
>   **menos que** ellos.

> Él se duerme **más** / **menos rápida-**   *He falls asleep **more** / **less quickly***
>   **mente que** yo.   ***than** I do.*

‣ **Que** is followed by negative words where English uses indefinites.

> Fue más difícil **que nunca.**   *It was harder **than ever.***

Que is replaced by **de** before a numeral.

> He depositado **más de** mil dólares.   *I've deposited **more than $1,000.***

‣ Some comparative forms are irregular.

> mejor *better*   mayor *older, greater*
> peor   *worse*   menor *younger, lesser*

The corresponding regular constructions also exist but have specialized meanings. **Más bueno** and **más malo** refer to moral qualities while **más grande** and **más pequeño** refer to physical size.

‣ Comparisons of equality (*as . . . as, as much / many . . . as*) are rendered in Spanish by forms of **tanto** and **como.** With verbs, **tanto** is invariable.

> Vosotros hacéis **tanto como** él.   *You do **as much as** he does.*

Tanto agrees with a following noun in gender and number.

> Llenamos **tantos formularios como** tú.   *We filled out **as many forms as** you did.*

Tanto shortens to **tan** before adjectives and adverbs.

> Estas blusas no son **tan bonitas como** las otras.   *These blouses are not **as pretty as** the other ones.*

‣ In English the superlative is formed by adding **-est** to the adjective (*youngest*) or by placing the word *most* in front of it (***most interesting***). The superlative in Spanish is identical to the comparative, except for the addition of the definite article or a possessive adjective.[2]

> Es **la** alfombra **más hermosa.**   *It's the **most beautiful** carpet.*
> Fue su **mejor / peor** trabajo.   *It was his **best / worst** job.*

No article is used with the superlative of adverbs, making the comparative and superlative identical.

> Ud. comió **más lentamente.**   *You ate **the slowest.***

Práctica

A. Combine each pair of sentences into a single one containing a comparative construction. Give two answers for each—one using **más,** one using **menos.**

---

[2] English *in* after a superlative = **de,** not **en** in Spanish: **Es la alfombra más hermosa *de* la tienda** (*It's the most beautiful carpet **in** the store*).

MODELO: La silla es grande. / El sofá es más grande.

→ El sofá es más grande que la silla. OR La silla es menos grande que el sofá.

1. La secadora es cara. / El lavaplatos es más caro.
2. La infección se trató fácilmente. / El virus se trató menos fácilmente.
3. El apartamento es grande. / La casa es más grande.
4. Ellos estudiaban. / Nosotros estudiábamos más.
5. Antonio era delgado. / Iris era más delgada.
6. Elena perdió peso. / Felipe perdió más peso.

B. Your friend wants to know who in your family did the most in fixing up your new house. Answer his questions with complete sentences that contain comparative constructions.

MODELO: —¿Quién llevó más   *Who carried more boxes, your*
cajones, tu hermana o tú?   *sister or you?*
—Yo llevé más cajones que   *I carried more boxes than my*
mi hermana.   *sister.*

1. ¿Quién guardó más cosas, Alejandro o tú?
2. ¿Quiénes colgaron más cuadros, tus papás o tus tíos?
3. ¿Quién pintó más cuartos, Victoria o Isabel?
4. ¿Quién lavó más ventanas, Eduardo o tú?
5. ¿Quién descansaba más, tu papá o tu mamá?
6. ¿Quién trabajó más, tu abuelo o tu tío?

C. Now when your friend asks you who did what in fixing up the new house, tell him that everyone did about the same amount of work. Answer the questions of Exercise B with comparisons of equality.

MODELO: —¿Quién llevó más   *Who carried more boxes, your*
cajones, tu hermana o tú?   *sister or you?*
—Yo llevé tantos cajones   *I carried as many boxes as my*
como mi hermana.   *sister.*

D. Your friend asks you your opinion about certain people and things. You respond with great enthusiasm using a superlative construction and incorporating each cue as in the model.

MODELO: —Este chico es alto, ¿verdad?   *This boy is tall, isn't he?*
(el colegio)
—¡Claro! Es el chico más   *Of course. He's the tallest boy in*
alto del colegio.   *the school.*

1. Estas manzanas son buenas, ¿verdad?   (la finca)
2. Aquellos mozos son pobres, ¿verdad?   (el restaurante)
3. Este libro es importante, ¿verdad?   (la biblioteca)

4. Este cuadro es hermoso, ¿verdad?   (el mundo)
5. Esta falda es barata, ¿verdad?   (el almacén)

Estructura 3

¡Qué! in exclamations

Análisis

▶ **¡Qué!** is used in exclamations before adjectives and nouns.

¡Qué chévere!	*How terrific!*
¡Qué idea!	*What an idea!*
¡Qué relojes!	*What watches!*

When there is both an adjective and a noun the usual pattern is **¡qué!** + noun + **tan / más** + *adjective.* The pattern **¡qué!** + *adjective* + *noun* is also used.

¡Qué idea más interesante!	*What an interesting idea!*
¡Qué relojes tan bonitos!	*What pretty watches!*
¡Qué maravillosa oportunidad!	*What a wonderful opportunity!*

Práctica

A. Restate each sentence as an exclamation consisting of **¡qué!** + *noun* + **más** + *adjective.*

MODELO: Es una enfermera muy buena.   *She's a very good nurse.*
      → ¡Qué enfermera más buena!   *What a good nurse!*

1. Son heridas muy graves.
2. Es una persona muy inquieta.
3. Es un examen muy fácil.
4. Son unas paredes muy oscuras.
5. Son platos muy picantes.
6. Es un apartamento muy moderno.

B. Now restate each sentence in Exercise A as an exclamation consisting of **¡qué!** + *noun* + **tan** + *adjective.*

MODELO: Es una enfermera muy buena.   →   ¡Qué enfermera tan buena!

C. Your friend gives you several pieces of news, some good, others bad. React to each one with an appropriate exclamation using the cues provided.

MODELO: —¿Sabes? Recibo un sueldo más alto ahora.   (bueno)
      —¡Qué bueno!

1. ¿Sabes? Voy a hacer un viaje a Veracruz.   (maravilloso)
2. ¿Sabes? He comprado un estéreo.   (chévere)
3. ¿Sabes? Saqué una mala nota en el examen.   (triste)
4. ¿Sabes? Paso la vida en la biblioteca.   (lata)
5. ¿Sabes? Mi hermano se ha divorciado.   (lástima)
6. ¿Sabes? Mi abuela ha mejorado.   (estupendo)

Estructura 4

Command forms for **vosotros** *(For recognition)*

Análisis

▶ Negative informal commands for **vosotros** (like negative **tú**-commands) are derived from the present subjunctive. Affirmative commands for **vosotros** are formed by replacing the **-r** of the infinitive by **-d.** This **-d** drops in reflexive commands before the addition of **-os** (except in **idos,** *go away*).

No pintéis las paredes. **Pintad** las paredes.	***Don't paint*** *the walls.* ***Paint*** *the walls.*
No corráis la silla. **Corred** la silla.	***Don't move*** *the chair.* ***Move*** *the chair.*
No salgáis del lugar. **Salid** del lugar.	***Don't leave*** *the place.* ***Leave*** *the place.*
No os sentéis en el sofá. **Sentaos.**	***Don't sit*** *on the couch.* ***Sit down.***

Práctica

Translate the following **vosotros** commands into English.

1. Mandadle las planillas.
2. Guardadlos en la gaveta.
3. No os pongáis los zapatos marrones.
4. Idos ahora mismo.
5. No se los hagáis.
6. Acostaos a las diez.

Comunicando

Preguntas personales

1. ¿Vives en un apartamento? ¿Cuántos cuartos hay en él?
2. ¿Qué muebles hay en **la sala?** (el comedor, el dormitorio)

3. ¿Qué aparatos eléctricos hay en la cocina?
4. ¿Qué hace Ud. cuando no puede dormirse?
5. ¿Qué hace Ud. para relajarse?
6. Hable de su cuarto (dónde se encuentran las ventanas, la puerta, los muebles).

Charlas

1. —**Nos instalamos hoy en nuestro apartamento nuevo.**

   ¿Dónde está **la sala?** (el dormitorio, el comedor, la cocina, el baño)   ¿Qué cosas tienen que guardar?   ¿Qué tienen que colgar?   ¿De qué color van a pintar las paredes?

2. —**Busco algunos muebles para la sala.**

   ¿Qué muebles necesita Ud.?   ¿Qué colores prefiere Ud.?   ¿Le interesa comprar unas lámparas también?   ¿Quiere ver unas cortinas y una alfombra también?

Situación

It's moving day for you and your roommate! Tell the movers where to put your furniture and other household items. Tell your roommate where she should put things too. Have her tell you what you should do to help get settled into the new apartment.

Para escribir

A. Tell someone you do not know very well to do something for you. Use **Ud.** command forms.

   MODELO: abrir / la puerta → Abra la puerta.

1. poner / la televisión
2. llevar / estos cajones
3. colgar / el espejo
4. sentarse / en esa silla
5. apagar / las luces
6. escribir / unas cartas

B. Now tell two people you do not know very well to perform the actions in Exercise A. Use **Uds.** command forms.

C. Tell your brother what he should do to help you. Use **tú** command forms. Change each direct object noun to a pronoun.

   MODELO: instalar / la secadora → Instálala.

1. correr / las mesas
2. pintar / la pared
3. irse / de aquí

4. hacerme / la cena
5. poner / el estéreo
6. darme / el reloj

D. Now tell your brother what he should not do based on the items in Exercise C. Use negative **tú** commands.

E. Translate the following sentences into Spanish.

1. Turn the radio on. Shut it off. (**tú**-*commands*)
2. Let's hang the paintings on the white wall.
3. No, let's not hang them there.
4. Go to the right. (**Ud.** *command*)
5. And you stay to the left. (**Ud.** *command*)
6. Sit down and relax. (**Uds.** *command*)
7. I put away more boxes than he did.
8. Her dreams are as interesting as their dreams.
9. They painted better than we did.
10. The radio is cheaper than the stereo.
11. Try to move the furniture next door. (**tú** *command*)
12. Should I fix up your apartment?
    Yes, fix it up for me.

lección 15

Objectives

Structure   You will learn the Spanish equivalent of English verb forms ending in *-ing* and the progressive tenses formed with it. You will also learn how to make parts of speech other than nouns function as nouns.

Vocabulary   You will learn words that have to do with the entertainment media: theater, film, concerts, and dance.

Conversation   After finishing the lesson you will be able to talk about your experiences with plays and movies, your criteria for judging them and your favorite performers, playwrights, and directors. You will also be able to discuss your own musical talent and what instruments you play.

Culture   You will be introduced to Buenos Aires as an important cosmopolitan cultural center. You will also learn something about the ethnic composition of Argentina.

Outline

Estructura 1   The **-ndo** form (the gerund)
Estructura 2   The progressive (**estar** + **-ndo** form)
Estructura 3   Nominalizations
Estructura 4   Long-form possessives (possessive pronouns)
Estructura 5   The passive voice (For recognition)

Having a Good Time in Buenos Aires

Radio Buenos Aires presents "Today's Entertainment Listings" with your announcer, Blanca Franzetti.

Dear listeners, good afternoon to you. If you and your friends are thinking about seeing each other today to spend the evening downtown, I suggest you attend one of the shows that are being presented in the theaters and movie houses of our city.

At the Opera Theater they're showing a new film by our great director Carlos Alemán Felloni. "Night Dreams" is very original and interesting and the photography is excellent. The shows begin this evening at 6:30, 8:45, and 11:55.

At the América Theater you can see two films of the famous American actor Lance Taylor. One is a police film and the other, a horror film; both are dubbed in Spanish. Call 47–9268 for more information.

The smash hit of the year continues at the Ateneo Theater. Tickets can still be bought for the two shows of "Let's Get Married Tomorrow." It's a very amusing comedy, perhaps the most original of all those (written) by the intelligent playwright Alberto Peralta.

This evening at the Regina Theater a debut is being presented. The drama "The Red Beach" has a simple and sensitive plot. In this play two very talented actresses, Bárbara Arce and Angélica Kraus, are performing together for the first time. The show begins at 9:30 P.M.

For you music lovers there's a concert at 8:30 P.M. at the Colón Theater. The famous musician Isaac Péretz is going to play the piano with the National Orchestra.

At the National Theater a very lovely folkloric show is being presented, in which the Venezuela Group dances and sings. There are still some tickets at the box office for the ten o'clock show.

I hope these announcements give you an idea of the magnificent shows from which you can choose today. And now, my friends, a very good afternoon to you from your announcer, Blanca Franzetti, who hopes that we can get together again tomorrow at the same time for "Today's Entertainment Listings."

Presentación

Divirtiéndose en Buenos Aires

Radio Buenos Aires presenta «La Cartelera de Hoy» con su locutora Blanca Franzetti.[1]

Queridos radioyentes, muy buenas tardes. Si Uds. y sus amigos están pensando en verse[2] hoy para pasar la tarde en el centro, les aconsejo que asistan a uno de los espectáculos que se están presentando en los teatros y cines de nuestra ciudad.

En el Cine Opera están pasando una película[3] nueva del gran director nuestro Carlos Alemán Felloni. «Sueños de noche» es muy original e interesante y la fotografía es excelente. Las funciónes comienzan a las 18.30, 20.45 y 23.55.[4]

En el Cine América se pueden ver dos películas del famoso actor norteamericano Lance Taylor. Una es policíaca y la otra, de terror; las dos están dobladas al español. Llame Ud. al teléfono 47-9268 para más información.[5]

Sigue el exitazo del año en el Teatro Ateneo. Todavía se pueden comprar boletos para las dos funciones de «Casémonos mañana.» Es una comedia muy divertida, quizás la más original de todas las del inteligente dramaturgo Alberto Peralta.

Esta tarde en el Teatro Regina se está presentando un estreno. El drama «La playa roja» tiene un argumento sencillo y sensible. En esta obra trabajan juntas por primera vez dos actrices de mucho talento, Bárbara Arce y Angélica Kraus. Empieza la función a las 21.30.

---

[1] There are large numbers of people of Italian and German descent living in Argentina.

[2] Plural reflexive forms may convey the idea of "each other." **Se ven** may mean either *they see themselves* or *they see each other* depending on context.

[3] **El film** and **el filme** are also used.

[4] The 24-hour clock is often used for theater and movie show times. See Lesson 7, *Estructura* 5, note 5.

[5] Most Spanish speakers give phone numbers by breaking them into a series of two-digit numbers: *47–9268* is read **cuarenta y siete, noventa y dos, sesenta y ocho.**

Para los aficionados a la música hay un concierto a las 20.30 en el Teatro Colón.[6] El famoso pianista Isaac Péretz va a tocar el piano con la Orquesta Nacional.

En el Teatro Nacional se está presentando un espectáculo folklórico lindísimo en el cual el Grupo Venezuela baila y canta. Quedan todavía algunos boletos en la taquilla para la función de las 22 horas.

Espero que estos anuncios les den a Uds. una idea de los magníficos espectáculos entre los cuales pueden escoger hoy. Y ahora, amigos míos, les desea muy buenas tardes su locutora Blanca Franzetti, quien espera que podamos encontrarnos otra vez mañana a la hora de «La Cartelera de Hoy.»

Ampliación

—¿Están tocando la guitarra?	*Are they playing the guitar?*
—Sí, siguen tocándola.	*Yes, they're still playing it.*
—¿Pasaste el día mirando la televisión?	*Did you spend the day watching television?*
—¡Qué va! Pasé todo el día leyendo.	*Are you kidding? I spent the whole day reading.*
—¿La oyó cantando?	*Did he hear her singing?*
—Sí, y la vio bailando también.	*Yes, and he saw her dancing too.*
—¿Los escuchasteis cantar algo?	*Did you listen to them sing something?*
—Sí, los escuchamos cantar una canción linda.	*Yes, we listened to them sing a lovely song.*
—¿Les gustan los discos de este músico?	*Do they like this musician's records?*
—Sí, pero les gustan más los del otro músico.	*Yes, but they like the ones of the other musician better.*
—¿Qué les parece su fotografía?	*What do you think of his photography?*
—Nos interesa, pero nos gusta más la tuya.	*We're interested in it but we like yours better.*

Preguntas sobre la Presentación

1. ¿Qué les aconseja Blanca Franzetti a los radioyentes?
2. ¿Cómo es la película "Sueños de noche"?
3. ¿Qué otras películas están pasando hoy?

---

[6] Buenos Aires has a rich and varied cultural life. The famous **Teatro Colón** is the city's opera house and home of the National Symphony Orchestra.

4. ¿Qué obra se está presentando en el Teatro Ateneo? ¿Cómo es?
5. ¿Qué estreno se puede ver esta tarde? ¿Cómo es la obra?
6. ¿Qué espectáculos hay para los aficionados a la música?

Vocabulario activo

el **actor**   actor
la **actriz**   actress
el **argumento**   plot (*of play*)
   asistir (a)   to attend
   bailar   to dance
el **boleto**   ticket
la **canción**   song
   cantar   to sing
la **cartelera**   entertainment listings
el **cine**   movies, movie theater
la **comedia**   comedy, play
el **concierto**   concert
el **director**   director
el **disco**   record
   divertido   amusing
   divertirse (e→ie)   to have a good time, to enjoy oneself
   doblar   to dub (*film*)
el **drama**   drama
el **dramaturgo**   playwright
   encontrarse (con)   to get together with someone
   escoger (g→j/a,o)   to choose
   escuchar   to listen to
el **espectáculo**   show
el **estreno**   debut
   excelente   excellent
el **exitazo**   smash hit (*success*)
   famoso   famous
   folklórico   folkloric
la **fotografía**   photography; photograph

la **función**   show
el **grupo**   group
la **guitarra**   guitar
la **información**   information
   inteligente   intelligent
   juntos   together
   lindo   pretty, lovely
la **locutora**   announcer
   magnífico   magnificent
la **música**   music
el **músico**   musician
   nacional   national
la **obra**   play (*theater*)
   original   original
la **orquesta**   orchestra
   pasar   to show (*film*)
la **película**   film
el **pianista**   pianist
el **piano**   piano
   policíaco   police (*adj.*)
   presentar   to present
el **radioyente**   radio listener
   sencillo   simple
   sensible   sensitive
el **talento**   talent
la **taquilla**   box office
el **teatro**   theater
el **teléfono**   telephone
el **terror**   terror, horror
   tocar   to play (*an instrument*)

Estructura 1

The **-ndo** *form (the gerund)*

Análisis

▸ The Spanish **-ndo** form corresponds roughly to the English *-ing* form, although its use in Spanish is more restricted. To form the gerund, verbs of the **-a-** class add **-ando** to the stem, while verbs of the **-e-** and **-i-** class add **-iendo: hablar** → **hablando; comer** → **comiendo; vivir** → **viviendo**.

Verbs of the **-e-** and **-i-** class that have stems ending in a vowel add **-yendo** rather than **-iendo:**

creer → **creyendo**	traer → **trayendo**
leer → **leyendo**	oír → **oyendo**

Verbs of the **-i-** class that have a vowel change in the third person of the preterit have the same change in the **-ndo** form:

sentir → **sintiendo**	decir → **diciendo**
pedir → **pidiendo**	venir → **viniendo**

NOTE: The **-ndo** forms of **poder** and **ir** are irregular: **pudiendo, yendo.**

▸ The **-ndo** form in Spanish is usually the equivalent of a clause or *-ing* phrase beginning with *if, when, because, while, by* in English.

—¿Cómo pasaron Uds. la tarde? *How did you spend the afternoon?*
—Yo pasé la tarde **escuchando** *I spent the afternoon **listening** to*
discos. Mi mamá la pasó *records. My mother spent it*
viendo una película y mi papá ***seeing** a film and my father*
pasó el día **escribiendo** cartas. *spent the day **writing** letters.*

Práctica

Answer each of the following questions with a gerund using the cue in parentheses.

MODELO: —¿Ganaste mucha plata?   (trabajar en el teatro)
—Sí, gané mucha plata trabajando en el teatro.

1. ¿Leía Ud. la cartelera?   (viajar en tren)
2. ¿Aprendieron Uds. español?   (vivir en Buenos Aires)
3. ¿Te pusiste enfermo?   (pintar la casa)
4. ¿Juan se rompió la mano?   (recoger manzanas)
5. ¿Se les cayeron los vasos?   (servir la comida)

Estructura 2

*The progressive (**estar** + **-ndo** form)*

Análisis

▸ The **-ndo** form may be preceded by present or past forms of the verb **estar** to form the progressive tenses. The present and imperfect progressive differ from the corresponding simple tenses in that they emphasize that the action is or was in progress. They may also imply that the action is temporary from the point of view of the speaker. The preterit progressive designates an action that was in progress in the past but that is now over.

Escucho la radio.	*I **listen** to the radio.* (habitual action)
Estoy escuchando la radio.	*I'm **listening**[7] to the radio.* (at this moment)
Estaba escuchando la radio.	*I was **listening** to the radio.*
Estuve escuchando la radio hasta que él la apagó.	*I was **listening** to the radio until he turned if off.*

▸ While the English present progressive is commonly used to refer to future time, the Spanish present progressive can never refer to future time. The simple present or the **ir a** + *infinitive* construction is used.

> **Presentan** el concierto mañana. 〈 *They're **presenting** the concert*
> **Van a presentar** el concierto mañana. 〉 *tomorrow.*

▸ **Seguir** + the **-ndo** *form* means *to be still doing something, to keep on doing something:*

> **Ud. seguía leyendo** la cartelera.   *You **kept on reading** the entertainment listings.*

▸ In the progressive tenses the object pronouns may either precede the form of **estar** or be attached to the gerund. If attached, a written accent is added to the **a** or **e** preceding the **-ndo.**

> **Nos estamos divirtiendo** mucho. ⎫
>   OR   ⎬ *We're having a very good time.*
> **Estamos divirtiéndonos** mucho. ⎭

Práctica

A. Change the verb of each sentence from present to present progressive.

MODELO: Viajo por Estados Unidos. → Estoy viajando por Estados Unidos.

1. Doblamos la película rusa.
2. Duerme en el dormitorio.
3. Cuelgan el espejo.
4. Me lavo las manos.
5. Os instaláis en el apartamento.
6. Pides más información.

---

[7] The simple present in Spanish can also be used to express actions that are going on at the present time. The Spanish progressive, however, can *never* be used to express habitual action.

B. Repeat Exercise A changing all direct object nouns to direct object pronouns. State each answer twice, once with the direct object pronoun preceding the form of **estar,** once with it following the **-ndo** form.

C. Change the verb of each sentence from imperfect to imperfect progressive.

MODELO: Estudiaban economía. → Estaban estudiando economía.

1. Realizaba sus ambiciones.
2. Te ponías el vestido.
3. Vendíamos todos los muebles.
4. Sufría de un virus.
5. Peinabais a la niña.
6. Iban al supermercado.

D. Repeat Exercise C changing all direct object nouns to direct object pronouns. State each answer twice, once with the direct object pronoun preceding the form of **estar,** once with it following the **-ndo** form.

E. Your friend hasn't seen you for a long time, and she wants to know if you and people you know are still doing certain things. Tell her that you are still doing everything she asks about, using **seguir** + **-ndo** *form* in your answer. Change all direct object nouns to direct object pronouns.

MODELO: —¿Todavía tomas química?   *Are you still taking chemistry?*
          —¿Sí, sigo tomándola.   *Yes, I'm still taking it.*

1. ¿Todavía tocas la guitarra?
2. ¿Todavía trabaja de secretario tu hermano?
3. ¿Todavía viven tus papás en Buenos Aires?
4. ¿Todavía lees la cartelera todos los días?
5. ¿Todavía canta canciones españolas tu hermana?
6. ¿Todavía se preocupan por tu primo tus tíos?

Estructura 3

Nominalizations

Análisis

▸ Nominalization is the process through which a word that is not a noun is made to *function* as a noun. In English an adjective is nominalized by replacing the noun it modifies by *one* or *ones: the foreign films* → *the foreign ones.* In Spanish an adjective is nominalized by *deleting* the noun it modifies:

la película extranjera → **la extranjera**
las películas extranjeras → **las extranjeras**

▸ Noun deletion is also used to nominalize adjective clauses and prepositional phrases (usually beginning with **de**).

la directora que dobló la película *the director who dubbed the film*
  → la que dobló la película   *→ the one who dubbed the film*

¿Cuál te gustó más? ¿La música *Which did you like better? The Mexican*
  del grupo mexicano o **la del**   *group's music or the Venezuelan*
  venezolano?   *group's?*

▸ In Spanish, demonstrative adjectives are also nominalized by noun-deletion. Nominalized demonstrative adjectives are called *demonstrative pronouns.* In the written language an accent mark may be added to demonstrative pronouns.

Este lucotor ha hablado más que *This announcer has talked more than*
  ese locutor. → Este locutor   ***that announcer.*** *→ This announcer*
  ha hablado más que **ése (ese).** *has talked more than **that one.***

Estas obras son mas divertidas *These plays are more amusing than **those***
  que **aquellas obras.** → Estas   ***plays.*** *→ These plays are more*
  obras son más divertidas que   *amusing than **those.***
  aquéllas (aquellas).

Práctica

A. Answer each of the following questions deleting the second occurrence of the noun in your response.

MODELO: —¿Esta silla es **la silla** de la sala?
      —Sí, esta silla es **la** de la sala.

1. ¿Esta película es la película del nuevo director inglés?
2. ¿Este lavaplatos es el lavaplatos de tu hija?
3. ¿Estos músicos son los músicos de la orquesta?
4. ¿Estas libretas son las libretas del banco?
5. ¿Este piano es el piano del señor Peralta?
6. ¿Estos documentos son los documentos del director?

B. Answer each of the following questions negatively. Delete the noun in your answer.

MODELO: —¿Hablas de la obra que viste *Are you talking about the play*
      ayer?   *you saw yesterday?*
      —No, no hablo de la que vi   *No, I'm not talking about the*
      ayer.   *one I saw yesterday.*

1. ¿Hablas de las planillas que vas a llenar?
2. ¿Hablan Uds. de los discos que estaban escuchando?

3. ¿Habla Alberto de la comedia que ha visto?
4. ¿Habláis del sofá que escogisteis?
5. ¿Hablan los empleados del sueldo que están ganando?
6. ¿Habla Ud. de la pluma que se perdió?

C. You are a drama and film critic being asked to make some judgments about the theater and movies. Respond to the questions using a nominalized construction.

MODELO: —¿La película italiana es mejor   *Is the Italian movie better than*
                   que la película francesa?   *the French movie?*
              —Sí, la película italiana es mejor   *Yes, the Italian movie is better*
                   que la francesa.   *than the French one.*

1. ¿El argumento de esta obra es más sencillo que el argumento de esa obra?
2. ¿La fotografía de Blanca es más original que la fotografía de Julia?
3. ¿Eran más hermosas las actrices argentinas o las actrices alemanas?
4. ¿Asistieron más personas a estos estrenos o a esos estrenos?
5. ¿Dónde están presentando mejores espectáculos? ¿En este teatro o en aquel teatro?
6. ¿Quiénes tienen más talento? ¿Estos actores o esos actores?

Estructura 4

Long-form possessives (possessive pronouns)

Análisis

▸ In addition to the short-form possessives (**mi, tu, su, nuestro, vuestro**), which always precede the noun and are unstressed, Spanish has a set of long-form possessives that follow the noun. They are all four-form adjectives:

mío	**nuestro**
tuyo	**vuestro**
suyo	**suyo**

They are used when the speaker wishes to focus on or emphasize the possessor. In English this is done by a shift of the main stress of the sentence to the possessive. Compare English *This is my **ticket*** → *This is **my** ticket (not **your** ticket)* to Spanish **Este es mi boleto** → **Este es el boleto mío (no el boleto tuyo).** Long-form possessives occur in the pattern: *definite article + noun + long-form possessive.*

los libros **tuyos**	*your* pencils
la nevera **nuestra**	*our* refrigerator

▸ The definite article may be replaced by **un, una;** a numeral; a quantifier (**tanto, mucho, algunos,** etc.); a demonstrative. When the long-form possessive is nominalized, it is called a *possessive pronoun.*

una vecina **nuestra**	*a neighbor **of ours***
quince libros **míos**	***fifteen** books **of mine***
algunos papeles **suyos**	***some** papers **of theirs***
esta tarjeta **tuya**	***this** card **of yours***

▸ The exact referent of **suyo** may be focused upon by replacing **suyo** by **de él, de ella, de Ud., de ellos, de ellas, de Uds.**

algunos papeles **suyos**	→	algunos papeles **de ella**	*some of her papers*
esta guitarra **suya**	→	esta guitarra **de ellos**	*this guitar of theirs*

The masculine singular of the long-form possessives may be used with the neuter article **lo** and with **algo** and **nada.**

Lo suyo es divertirse.	***His lot*** *(role, part) is to have a good time.*
No tienes **nada tuyo.**	*You have **nothing of yours** (your own).*

Práctica

A. Answer each of the following questions using a long-form possessive. Form a comparison as in the model using the words in parentheses as cues.

MODELO: —¿Es grande tu cuarto? (su cuarto)
—Sí, el mío es más grande que el suyo.

Is your room big? (her room)
Yes, mine is bigger than hers.

1. ¿Es interesante su libro?   (tu libro)
2. ¿Son originales tus ideas?   (sus ideas)
3. ¿Son difíciles sus exámenes?   (nuestros exámenes)
4. ¿Es sencilla tu composición?   (vuestra composición)
5. ¿Son bonitas sus cortinas?   (mis cortinas)
6. ¿Es caro tu abrigo?   (su abrigo)

B. Your friend asks you whether you like certain people and things. You tell him you do but that you like someone else's better (the person in the cue in parentheses).

MODELO: —¿Te gusta el cine de él? (ella)
—Sí, pero me gusta más el de ella.

Do you like his movie theater?
Yes, but I like hers better.

1. ¿Te gustan las obras de ellos? (Uds.)
2. ¿Te gusta la fotografía nuestra? (él)

3. ¿Te gustan los dramas de él?
   (ellas)
4. ¿Te gusta el paraguas mío?
   (doña Blanca)

5. ¿Te gustan las tradiciones tuyas?
   (ellos)
6. ¿Te gustan los amigos de ella?
   (Uds.)

Estructura 5

The passive voice (*For recognition*)

Análisis

▸ The passive voice in Spanish enables the speaker to focus on the direct object by making it the subject of the passive sentence. A verb in the passive voice may be considered a rephrasing of a verb in the active voice. The passive voice consists of a form of **ser** + **-do** *form* (past participle) often followed by an "agent phrase" introduced by **por** that tells who the performer of the action is. The **-do** form agrees in number and gender with the grammatical subject.

(active)	El director **dobló** la película.	*The director **dubbed** the film.*
(passive)	La película **fue doblada** por el director.	*The film **was dubbed** by the director.*

Remember that Spanish uses **se** + *verb* without the "agent phrase" for indefinite or deemphasized subjects (see Lesson 13, *Estructura 1*): **Se dobló la película** (*The film was dubbed*).

Práctica

Be sure you can translate the following sentences into English.

1. El piano fue tocado por el señor Alemán.
2. ¿Su máquina de lavar fue instalada por ti?
3. Esa información fue dada por los agentes.
4. Todos los platos picantes fueron hechos por aquel cocinero.
5. Varias cartas han sido escritas por mí.
6. La televisión fue puesta por su papá.

Comunicando

Preguntas personales

1. ¿Qué obras de teatro te gustan más? (los dramas, las comedias, etc.)
2. ¿Te importa *la fotografía* en las películas? (el argumento, la música, etc.)

3. ¿Cuáles *actores* te gustan más? (actrices, directores, músicos)
4. ¿Qué canciones y discos prefieres? ¿Te gusta cantar y bailar?
5. ¿Toca Ud. *el piano?* (la guitarra)
6. ¿Cómo escoge Ud. los espectáculos que ve?

Charlas

1. **—Soy actor.**
   ¿Trabaja Ud. en el teatro o en el cine? ¿En qué obras y películas ha traba-jado? ¿Qué le importa más al escoger una obra o una película? ¿Ud. canta y baila? ¿Tiene Ud. mucho talento?

2. **—Vimos una película muy original ayer.**
   ¿Qué les pareció el argumento? (la fotografía, el director) ¿Fue difícil con-seguir boletos en la taquilla? ¿Fue un estreno? ¿Se divirtieron Uds.? ¿Dónde están pasando la película? ¿A qué hora hay funciones?

Situación

You are an announcer on a radio program that offers information about the entertainment possibilities in the city. Talk about the plays, films, and concerts being presented, describing some of the features your listeners would be interested in knowing about: types of plays and films; actors, musicians and directors; interesting elements in the shows; information about theaters, schedules, etc.

Para escribir

A. Rewrite the following sentences changing the verbs from present to present progressive. Change all direct object nouns to pronouns. Write each sentence in two ways as in the model.

MODELO: Arreglamos los dormitorios.
          → Estamos arreglándolos.
          → Los estamos arreglando.

1. Asisto a un espectáculo magnífico.
2. Escojo la música de guitarra.
3. Pasan unas películas inglesas en este cine.
4. Escuchamos al locutor en la radio.
5. Le pedís más información.
6. ¿Nos traes la cartelera?

B. Rewrite the sentences written in the present progressive in Exercise A in the imperfect progressive.

MODELO: Estamos arreglándolos.   → Estábamos arreglándolos.
          Los estamos arreglando.   → Los estábamos arreglando.

C. Write an answer for each of the following questions using the proper form of the adjective in parentheses in your answer.

> MODELO: —¿Qué película te gustó más? (argentino)
> —Me gustó más la argentina.

1. ¿Qué argumentos le interesaban? (triste)
2. ¿Qué tarjetas se te olvidaron? (amarillo)
3. ¿Con qué abogados estábamos hablando? (guapo)
4. ¿Qué canción habéis escuchado? (portugués)
5. ¿Qué estéreo prefieren Uds.? (barato)
6. ¿Qué materias va a tomar? (difícil)

D. Rewrite each of the following sentences deleting the nouns in italics.

> MODELO: La *oficina* de aquel profesor está abierta.
> → La de aquel profesor está abierta.

1. Esas *películas* suyas de terror eran las mejores.
2. El *concierto* de este grupo fue divertido.
3. Hagamos cola para la *función* de las cuatro y media.
4. Estamos comprando los *muebles* de las amigas suyas.
5. Varios *cines* nuestros se han cerrado.
6. Dos *pacientes* de esa doctora están mejorando.
7. La *hija* de aquellos señores es famosa.

E. Translate the following sentences into Spanish.

1. They're showing an excellent film at that movie theater. (*use present progressive*)
2. Regina and Ricardo saw each other yesterday.
3. The film is dubbed, but the plot is original and the photography is beautiful.
4. We were watching a police film and a horror film. (*use imperfect progressive*)
5. She always had a good time playing the piano in the orchestra.
6. His plays are more amusing than theirs.
7. These playwrights are more intelligent than those.
8. Are you talking about the actors who are dancing in this smash hit?
9. No, I'm talking about the ones who are singing.
10. Come here. You (**tú**) can hear her sing a song.
11. I can't. I'm taking a bath.
12. Are you still listening to that announcer on the radio?

repaso 5

A. Rewrite each of the following sentences changing the italicized verb phrase to the corresponding **se**-construction. Use the same tense as in the original sentence and eliminate the subject, if any. The sentences form a connected paragraph about moving day.

MODELO: Mi papá corrió la alfombra.   → Se corrió la alfombra.

1. *Llevan* los muebles al apartamento.
2. Uno de los cargadores *trajo* la alfombra.
3. Mamá *guardó* la ropa en un armario.
4. —¿Dónde *van a poner* la televisión? —pregunté.
5. —*Deben dejar* la televisión en la sala por ahora, —contestó papá.
6. —*Tenemos que pintar* la cocina, —dijo mamá.
7. —Y *tenemos que colgar* tres cuadros en la sala, —dije yo.
8. —¿Los cargadores ya *han traído* todo? —preguntó papá.
9. —¿*Podemos terminar* la mudanza hoy? —preguntó mi hermana.
10. —¡Ni hablar! —dijo mamá. Ahora *pongo* la televisión para que nos relajemos un poco.

B. Form positive and negative commands in the **tú**-form relating to entertainment and the arts.

MODELO: _____ (ver) esa película.   → Ve esa película.

1. _____ (leer) la cartelera de hoy.
2. No _____ (escoger) una comedia.
3. _____ (decirme) quién es el director.
4. No _____ (asistir) a ese espectáculo.
5. _____ (venir) con nosotros al teatro.
6. _____ (escuchar) esta linda canción.
7. No _____ (ir) al cine esta tarde.
8. _____ (divertirse) mucho en el concierto.

C. Form commands in the **Ud.**-form relating to official procedures.

>   MODELO: _____ (firmar) los papeles.   → Firme los papeles.

1. _____ (arreglar) el pasaporte.
2. _____ (ir) a la cita.
3. _____ (explicárselo) al agente de inmigración.
4. _____ (solicitar) la tarjeta verde.
5. _____ (traer) la partida de nacimiento.
6. _____ (mandarnos) los documentos.
7. _____ (llenar) estos formularios.
8. _____ (darme) la licencia de manejar.

D. Form plural commands (**Uds.**) related to the home environment.

>   MODELO: _____ (lavar) las cortinas.   → **Laven** las cortinas.

1. _____ (colgar) el cuadro en la pared azul.
2. _____ (correr) la cómoda a la izquierda.
3. _____ (poner) la luz en la sala.
4. _____ (sentarse) en el sofá.
5. _____ (venir) a ver esta alfombra.
6. _____ (apagar) el estéreo ahora mismo.
7. _____ (relajarse) antes de seguir el trabajo.
8. _____ (guardar) sus abrigos en el armario.

E. Answer the following questions with sentences that contain comparative constructions.

1. ¿Quién vio más obras de teatro, tú o tu amigo?
2. ¿Quiénes miran menos televisión, Uds. o sus papás?
3. ¿Quién tenía más documentos, Ud. o él?
4. ¿Quién era mejor actriz, Blanca o Julia?
5. ¿Dónde pasan más películas dobladas, en el cine Argentina o en el cine Colón?
6. ¿Dónde hay menos muebles, arriba o abajo?

F. Rewrite each sentence changing the verb from present to present progressive. The sentences form a narrative about moving.

>   MODELO: Abro la puerta de su casa.   → Estoy abriendo la puerta de su casa.

1. Uds. se instalan en su nuevo apartamento.
2. Tus hermanos traen los cajones.
3. Tú cuelgas algunos cuadros en tu cuarto.
4. Todos trabajan mucho.
5. Tu papá, muy cansado, se duerme en el sofá.
6. Yo les preparo un café para que descansen un poco.

G. Supply the correct form of the long form of the possessive adjective in each sentence.

> MODELO: Mi libro es más interesante que _____ (*his*).
> Mi libro es más interesante que el suyo.

1. Mis documentos son más importantes que _____ (*yours*—**tú**)
2. Mi nevera es más grande que _____ (*theirs*).
3. Sus guitarras son mejores que _____ (*ours*).
4. Mi lámpara es más cara que _____ (*yours*—**vosotros**).
5. Tu obra es más original que _____ (*mine*).

H. Answer each of the following questions deleting the second occurrence of the noun in your response.

> MODELO: —¿Este cuadro es el cuadro del comedor?
> —Sí, es el del comedor.

1. ¿Esta obra es la obra del dramaturgo alemán?
2. ¿Estos anteojos son los anteojos de doña Carmen?
3. ¿Estas monedas son las monedas de los niños?
4. ¿Este actor es el actor del espectáculo que vimos?

I. Answer each of the following questions deleting the noun in your response.

> MODELO: —¿Hablas de los exámenes que tomaste ayer?
> —Sí, hablo de los que tomé ayer.

1. ¿Habla Ud. del disco que compró ayer?
2. ¿Hablan ellos de los muebles que se escogen?
3. ¿Habláis de las películas que habéis visto?
4. ¿Habla ella de la blusa que se puso anoche?

J. Rewrite the original sentence, step by step, using each of the cues provided and making all necessary changes.

1. She forgot the appointment.   → Se le olvidó la cita.
2. (they)   → Se les olvidó la cita.
3.   (their eyeglasses)
4. (we)   (our)
5.   (dropped)
6. (you—**tú**)   (your)
7.   (broke)
8.   (the plate)
9. (I)
10. (you—**Ud.**)
11.   (lost)
12.   (your papers)

K. Translate the following story about moving day into Spanish.

1. We're going to spend the day getting settled into our new apartment.
2. Help us (**tú**). Move the chair to the left and leave the couch in front of the window.
3. Pedro and Francisco, go out to (=**a**) buy (some) coffee.
4. We can't. We left (= forgot) our driver's license at home.
5. I can go, then. But I think you prefer me to buy beer.
6. Good idea. Beer is better than coffee when you're moving.   (*progressive*)
7. Moving day is difficult, but everyone is having a good time.   (*progressive*)

L. Translate the following story about getting ready to go to the movies into English.

1. Se está presentando el estreno de una película policíaca hoy.
2. Apaguen esa tele y vengan conmigo a verla.
3. Si no salimos ahora se van a acabar los boletos en la taquilla.
4. Se me ocurre que debemos ir en taxi.
5. Pónganse los abrigos mientras yo busco mi dinero.

M. *Reading passage.* The following passage will give you an idea of the culture shock experienced by Spanish-speaking people living in the United States.

Cognates are marked with a raised degree sign (°). New words in the passage are listed below. Study them until you can give the English equivalent for each Spanish word or phrase. After reading the passage, do the comprehension exercise that follows it.

contar (o→ue) to tell, to relate	**molestar** to bother
de repente suddenly	**ofrecer** to offer
el **desempleo** unemployment	la **pena** sorrow, grief
distinto different	**quitarse** to go away, scram
en cambio on the other hand	**raro** strange
entender (e→ie) to understand	la **razón** reason
el **escaparate** shop window	**reclamar** to complain (*officially*)
extrañar to miss (*someone*)	el **seguro** insurance
faltar to be absent	el **seguro social** social security
indicar to point	la **señal** sign
jugar (u→ue) to play	**soportar** to stand, to bear
el **latino** Latin American	**valer** to be worth
la **manera: no hay manera** it's impossible, there's no way	**ver mal a alguien** not to like, to think ill of

Tres latinoamericanos en los Estados Unidos

Una conversación entre un puertorriqueño (Diego), un cubano (Raúl) y un colombiano (Jairo) en un barrio latino de Nueva York. Jairo, el colombiano, es inmigrante indocumentado.

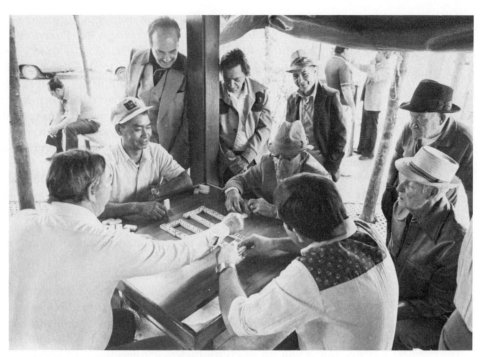

Estos hombres se divierten mucho jugando dominó.

Diego —¿Cómo pueden soportar el frío del invierno aquí? Yo extraño mucho el sol y el calor de mi Isla.

Raúl —Yo ni pienso en el clima.° A mí no me quedó más remedio. Salí de Cuba por razones políticas. Tú por lo menos puedes volver a Puerto Rico cuando te dé la gana si no te gusta la vida aquí.

Diego —Eso es cierto. Sin embargo, yo vivía tan mal en San Juan que salí para mejorar mi situación° económica.° Pero miren Uds. cómo son las cosas. Aunque gano más plata en la fábrica donde estoy trabajando ahora, no vivo bien porque todo está tan caro.

Jairo —Por lo menos a ti te pagan el sueldo mínimo° porque eres ciudadano norteamericano. Yo, en cambio, soy inmigrante indocumentado y tengo que aceptar° el sueldo que me ofrezcan. No recibo nada, ni seguro social, ni seguro por desempleo, nada.

Raúl —Lo que a mí me causa° mucho problema es la lengua. Cuando estoy en el barrio entre amigos, no me hace falta el inglés, pero para hablar con los funcionarios de mi oficina, o con los jefes, no hay manera. Gracias a Dios que varios americanos de mi oficina se expresan° más o menos en español.

Jairo —Tienes más suerte que yo. Donde yo trabajo los americanos no saben decir ni «Buenos días», aunque casi todos los empleados son de países hispanos. Así que si me tratan mal o si no me pagan no hay manera de reclamar. Los jefes no me entienden a mí ni yo a ellos.

Diego —Yo estudié un poco de inglés en el colegio en Puerto Rico. Nos obligan° a estudiarlo. Pero ya se me olvidó casi todo. Entonces, ¿saben lo que hago cada vez que tengo que ir al banco o a hablar con algún funcionario público? Pues, saco a mi hijo mayor del colegio y lo llevo conmigo de intérprete.° Su maestro se pone furioso cada vez que falta a la clase, pero en realidad,° no me queda más remedio. Sin él, no puedo arreglar mis cosas. A mí me parece que lo más importante es que un muchacho ayude a su papá, pero aquí no quieren saber nada de eso.

Raúl —A mí me lo dices. Aquí un padre no vale nada. Escúchenme esto. Mi hija, que tiene dieciocho años, me dijo el otro día que ella tiene el derecho de salir con quien ella quiera, sin que yo conozca al muchacho. Y que no quiere que su tía la acompañe cuando sale. No me digan que una muchacha de dieciocho años puede salir sola con un muchacho.

Jairo —Es que aquí todo es distinto. Déjenme contarles algo que pasó el verano pasado cerca de mi casa. Hacía mucho calor esa tarde y un grupo° de latinos estaban hablando en la esquina. No molestaban a nadie. Llegaron dos policías y les dijeron a los latinos que tenían que quitarse de ahí. Los latinos no comprendieron por qué, y uno de ellos, que sabía un poco de inglés, les preguntó a los dos policías lo que él y sus amigos habían hecho. Uno de los policías indicó una señal que decía «no loitering». Los muchachos se fueron sin saber lo que esa señal significaba.° Todavía no comprendo lo que pasó allí ese día.

Raúl —«No loitering» significa algo como «se prohibe estar en las calles sin hacer nada». Explíquenme a mí, por favor, para qué son las calles si la gente no puede estar en ellas hablando o leyendo el periódico o jugando dominó.° Pero aquí ven las cosas de una manera muy rara.

Diego —Y eso no es lo peor. Aquí ven muy mal al latino. La semana pasada yo fui a una agencia° para ver si podía conseguir un apartamento más grande en un barrio un poco mejor. Se me ocurrió que me podían ayudar allí. Entré y pregunté y me dijeron que no tenían nada. Cuando oyeron mi pobre inglés y se dieron cuenta de que yo era latino, de repente se les olvidó que tenían una lista° de casi cincuenta apartamentos en el escaparate. Muy bonito, ¿verdad?

Jairo —Muchachos, estos problemas no los vamos a solucionar° hoy. ¿Por qué no vamos al bar de la esquina a tomar una cerveza? Allí siempre ponen música latina y podemos olvidarnos de todas nuestras penas. ¿Qué les parece?

COMPREHENSION CHECK

Choose the correct response based on the information contained in the reading passage.

1. ¿Por qué no piensa el cubano en el frío?
   a. No puede volver a Cuba aun (=*even*) si no le gusta.
   b. El frío es lo que más le gusta de los Estados Unidos.
   c. Siempre puede ir a Puerto Rico.

2. ¿Por qué no vive Diego mucho mejor que antes?
   a. Porque gana más plata.
   b. Porque los precios han subido.
   c. Porque trabaja en una fábrica.

3. ¿Por qué no gana Jairo el sueldo mínimo?
   a. Quiere más dinero.
   b. Es un inmigrante ilegal.°
   c. Está sin trabajo.

4. ¿Cómo habla Raúl con los americanos de su oficina?
   a. Trata de no hablarles.
   b. Raúl les habla en inglés.
   c. Ellos saben algo de español.

5. ¿Qué hace Jairo si no le pagan?
   a. Se expresa en español y todos le entienden.
   b. Reclama su dinero y siempre le pagan.
   c. Nada, porque es indocumentado y no habla inglés.

6. ¿Por qué sabe Diego un poco de inglés?
   a. En Puerto Rico todos tienen que estudiarlo.
   b. Se lo enseñó su hijo.
   c. Tomó clases en Nueva York.

7. ¿Por qué no le parece mal a Diego sacar a su hijo de su colegio?
   a. Es un papá muy irresponsable.°
   b. Para él, un hijo tiene que ayudar a su padre.
   c. No le gusta el maestro de su hijo.

8. ¿Qué quiere la hija de Raúl?
   a. Conocer a un muchacho.
   b. Salir con su tía.
   c. Salir sola con un amigo.

9. ¿Por qué tuvo que irse de la esquina donde estaban hablando ese grupo de latinos?
   a. La policía tenía otra idea sobre la función° de las calles.
   b. Los latinos molestaban a todo el mundo que pasaba.
   c. Es que sabían muy poco inglés esos latinos.

10. ¿Para qué son las calles, según los hispanos?
    a. Son para los policías.
    b. Se prohibe estar en ellas si uno no tiene nada que hacer.
    c. Allí se puede hablar o ver a los amigos.

11. ¿Por qué le fue difícil a Diego encontrar un apartamento?
    a. No hay apartamentos en la agencia.
    b. Nadie quiere tener vecinos hispanos.
    c. Es muy pobre y no puede pagar mucho.

12. ¿Por qué cree Diego que no lo ayudaron en la agencia porque era latino?
    a. Le dijeron que no había apartamentos disponibles (= *available*), pero él sabía que sí.
    b. Les gustó mucho el inglés que hablaba.
    c. Había una señal que decía que veían mal a los latinos.

lección 16

Objectives

Structure   You will learn how to use the subjunctive in adverb clauses. You will also learn to distinguish between two closely related prepositions: **por** and **para.**

Vocabulary   You will learn words related to sports and party-giving.

Conversation   By the end of the lesson you will be able to discuss the sports you like to watch and play. You will also be prepared to discuss the celebration of your birthday.

Culture   You will learn about the enthusiasm of Puerto Ricans for baseball, and you will find out about "La Feria del Caribe," the Caribbean baseball championship.

Outline

Uncle Roberto Celebrates His Birthday

This afternoon I'm going to my sister Veronica's to pick up my nephew Alejandro. I'm going today precisely because it's February 20, my birthday and Alejandro's. I'm going so that we can celebrate the day together. How happy I was that day eight years ago when my nephew was born! What a beautiful coincidence! Since Alejandro was three, I have taken him out for his birthday. Two years ago I took him to the zoo and last year we went skating. Today, after we eat in his favorite restaurant, I'll take him to see a baseball game. Alejandro loves sports and he's a terrific baseball player (=he knows how to play baseball wonderfully). We're going to Hiram Bithorn Stadium so my nephew can see the Bayamón Cowboys, the team he likes best, play against the Venezuela Tigers. For the first time he's going to see the *Feria del Caribe.* I hope it's going to be an exciting game and that there are a lot of home runs! Before we return home, I'm going to take him to a store so that he can choose a gift. Later I'm going out with my girlfriend to Old San Juan. Alejandro wants to go with us, but I told him that he's still a little young to go out at night. Besides, his parents want to celebrate the day with him.

I'm glad that Alejandro still wants to spend his birthday with me. I know that someday he'll prefer to go out with his friends or his girlfriend. Well, until that day comes I'll keep on making plans for the two of us for the twentieth of February. Next year I'll invite him to the theater or maybe to the country or maybe . . .

Presentación

El tío Roberto celebra su cumpleaños

Esta tarde voy a casa de mi hermana Verónica para buscar a mi sobrino Alejandro. Voy hoy precisamente porque es el 20 de febrero, día de mi cumpleaños y también el de Alejandro. Voy para que celebremos el día juntos. ¡Qué feliz me puse ese día hace ocho años cuando nació mi sobrino! ¡Qué hermosa casualidad! Desde que Alejandro cumplió tres años, yo lo he sacado para su cumpleaños. Hace dos años lo llevé al jardín zoológico y el año pasado fuimos a patinar. Hoy, después que almorcemos en su restaurante favorito, lo voy a llevar a ver un partido de béisbol. A Alejandro le encantan los deportes y sabe jugar béisbol maravillosamente. Vamos al estadio Hiram Bithorn[1] para que mi sobrinito vea jugar al equipo que más le gusta, los Vaqueros de Bayamón[2] contra los Tigres de Venezuela. Por primera vez va a ver la Feria del Caribe.[3] ¡Ojalá que sea un partido emocionante y que haya muchos jonrones! Antes que volvamos a casa lo voy a llevar a una tienda para que escoja un regalo. Más tarde voy a salir con mi novia al Viejo San Juan.[4] Alejandro quiere acompañarnos, pero le he dicho que es muy niño todavía para salir de noche. Además, sus papás quieren celebrar el día con él.

Me alegro que Alejandro todavía quiera pasar su cumpleaños conmigo. Yo sé que algún día va a preferir salir con sus amigos o con su novia. Bueno, hasta que llegue ese día sigo haciendo planes para nosotros dos para el 20 de febrero. Para el año que viene voy a invitarlo al teatro o quizás al campo o quizás . . .

---

[1] The Hiram Bithorn Stadium in San Juan bears the name of a well-known Puerto Rican baseball player.

[2] One of Puerto Rico's best baseball teams. Bayamón is a city in the northern part of the Island, not far from San Juan.

[3] After the end of the baseball season in Puerto Rico (late January or early February), Caribbean countries participate in the regional baseball championship known as **La Feria del Caribe.**

[4] Old San Juan, now declared an historic zone, is a section of the capital that conserves the quaint charm and picturesque atmosphere of Puerto Rico's Spanish colonial heritage.

Ampliación

—¿Vas a la fiesta de Alejandro?	*Are you going to Alejandro's party?*
—Sí, a menos que no me invite.	*Yes. Unless he doesn't invite me.*
—¿Invitaste a Pedro?	*Did you invite Pedro?*
—Sí, es tan **simpático.**	*Yes, he's so **nice.***
(amable, gracioso, encantador)	(*pleasant, witty, delightful*)
—No, es **antipático.**	*No, he's **not nice.***
(aburrido, tonto, desagradable)	(*boring, stupid, unpleasant*)
—¿Cuándo vas a cortar la torta?	*When are you going to cut the cake?*
—Tan pronto como lleguen todos los invitados.	*As soon as all the guests arrive.*
—¿Dónde debo colgar la piñata?	*Where should I hang the piñata?*
—Donde ellos te digan.	*Wherever they tell you.*
—¿Qué hicieron por la tarde?	*What did you do in the afternoon?*
—Jugamos (al) **fútbol.**	*We played **soccer.***
(tenis, baloncesto, volley-ball, fútbol americano)	(*tennis, basketball, volleyball, football*)
—¿Cómo son los jugadores?	*What are the players like?*
—Según nos dijo Ana, son fantásticos.	*According to what Ana told us, they're great.*
—Vamos a jugar al tenis, ¿verdad?	*We're going to play tennis, aren't we?*
—Con tal que encuentre **la raqueta.**	*Provided that I find my **tennis racket.***
(la pelota, los zapatos de tenis)	(*ball, sneakers*)
—¿Cuál equipo ganó el partido?	*Which team won the match?*
—Ninguno. Es que empataron.	*Neither one. They tied.*
—¿Qué ejercicio le gusta más a Ud.?	*Which exercise do you like best?*
—A mí me gusta **correr.**	*I like to **run.***
(andar en bicicleta)	(*ride a bicycle*)

Preguntas sobre la Presentación

1. ¿Para qué va el tío Roberto a casa de su hermana?
2. ¿Cuál es la «hermosa casualidad» de que habla Roberto?
3. ¿Adónde fueron Roberto y su sobrino el año pasado? ¿Adónde fueron hace dos años?
4. ¿Qué planes tiene Roberto para hoy?
5. ¿Por qué no va a acompañar Alejandro a su tío al Viejo San Juan?
6. ¿De qué se alegra Roberto?

Vocabulario activo

aburrido boring
además besides
amable pleasant
andar to walk; to go (*pret.* **anduv-**)
antipático not nice, unlikable
el **baloncesto** basketball
el **béisbol** baseball
buscar to pick up (*someone*)
el **campo** country, field
la **casualidad** coincidence
celebrar to celebrate
cortar to cut
el **cumpleaños** birthday
el **deporte** sport
desagradable unpleasant
el **ejercicio** exercise
emocionante exciting
empatar to tie (*score*)
encantador delightful
el **equipo** team
el **estadio** stadium
fantástico great
favorito favorite
feliz happy
la **feria** fair
la **fiesta** party
el **fútbol** soccer
ganar to win
gracioso witty
el **invitado** guest

invitar to invite
el **jardín** garden
el **jardín zoológico** zoo
el **jonrón** home run
el **jugador** player
jugar (u→ue) to play
el **partido** match, game
patinar to skate
la **pelota** ball
la **piñata** paper receptacle filled with candies and toys and broken with a stick at children's parties
el **plan** plan
precisamente exactly, for that reason
la **raqueta** tennis racket
según according to
simpático nice, likable
la **sobrina** niece
el **sobrino** nephew
el **tenis** tennis
tonto stupid, silly
el **volley-ball**, el **volibol** volleyball
el **zapato de tenis** sneaker

EXPRESIONES
andar en bicicleta to ride a bicycle
cumplir ___ años to become ___ years old
saber (+ *inf.*) to know how to do something

Estructura 1

The present subjunctive in adverb clauses

Análisis

▸ Adverbial clauses modify verbs in the same way adverbs do. Adverbial clauses are introduced by adverbial conjunctions, such as *when, while, since:*

> **adverb**
> I arrived at the party **late.**

> **adverbial**
> **conjunction**   **adverb clause**
> I arrived **when** *the party was over.*

▸ In Spanish, the following adverbial conjunctions are always followed by the indicative; they introduce clauses which the speaker considers as part of reality.

conjunctions expressing cause

puesto que, ya que, como   *since*
porque   *because*

conjunctions expressing time

ahora que   *now that*
desde que   *since (from the time that)*

Other adverbial conjunctions introduce adverb clauses in which the verb must appear in the subjunctive.

a menos que *unless*	**para que** *in order that, so that*
antes (de) que *before*	**sin que** *without*
con tal (de) que *provided that*	

▸ There also exists in Spanish a group of conjunctions that may be followed by either the indicative or the subjunctive, depending on the meaning the speaker wishes to convey.

Adverbial conjunctions of manner and location are followed by the *indicative* when the speaker regards the action of the subordinate clause as an established, known fact. The speaker selects the *subjunctive* to signal that he regards the action of the subordinate clause as not yet fixed or identifiable, that is, not part of reality.

como *how, as, the way in which*	**donde** *where*
según *according to, the way in which*	**aunque** *although, even though*

Corta la torta **como** ellos **dicen.**	*Cut the cake **the way** they **say.*** (You know how they want it cut.)
Corta la torta **como** ellos **digan.**	*Cut the cake **whichever way** they **say.*** (You don't know how they want it cut.)
Voy a salir **aunque llueve.**	*I'm going to go out **even though it's raining.***
Voy a salir **aunque llueva.**	*I'm going to go out **even though it may rain.***

▸ The following adverbial conjunctions of time are followed by the subjunctive when the main clause refers to future time or is a command.

después (de) que *after*	**tan pronto como** *as soon as*
cuando *when*	**en cuanto** *as soon as*
hasta que *until*	

Note that when the speaker sees the action of the subordinate clause as a habitual occurrence (thus part of reality), the subjunctive is not used.

Van a jugar tenis **hasta que llegue** la hora de la comida.	*They're going to play tennis until dinner time (comes).*
Juegan tenis **hasta que llega** la hora de la comida.	*They play tennis until dinner time (comes). (usually, habitually)*

When the main clause is in the past tense, the subjunctive is not used after adverbial conjunctions of time; past actions are accomplished facts and therefore part of experience.

Jugaron tenis **hasta que llegó** Roberto.	*They played tennis until Robert arrived.*

Práctica

A. Use the cue in parentheses as the subject of the subordinate clause. Change the infinitive to the appropriate form of the present subjunctive.

MODELO:	Vamos al teatro después de cenar. (Uds.)	*Let's go to the theater after eating.*
	→ Vamos al teatro después de que cenen.	*Let's go to the theater after you eat.*

1. Rompo la piñata para sacar los regalos.   (ellos)
2. Lean Uds. hasta tener que irse.   (nosotros)
3. Vas a llamarlos antes de acostarte.   (ella)
4. Va a asistir al concierto sin comprar boletos.   (yo)
5. Pinta el cuarto después de lavarlo.   (ellos)
6. Ganáis el partido sin saberlo.   (nosotros)
7. Van a estar contentos con tal de ganar el partido.   (yo)

B. The following sentences form a connected narrative about how you settle into your new apartment. Add the cues in parentheses to involve other people in your move and change each of the infinitives to the appropriate form of the present subjunctive.

MODELO:	Vas a comprar esa casa para vivir mejor. (ellos)	*You're going to buy that house to live better.*
	→ Vas a comprar esa casa para que ellos vivan mejor.	*You're going to buy that house so they can live better.*

1. Vas a pintar las paredes después de lavarlas.   (yo)
2. Vas a correr los muebles después de traerlos.   (tus amigos)
3. Abres todos los cajones antes de guardarlos.   (nosotros)
4. Te instalas en el apartamento sin trabajar demasiado.   (nosotros)

5. Vas a arreglar las cortinas hasta salir a comer.   (nosotros)
6. Pones el radio para relajarte.   (yo)

C. Your friend asks you if you or some other people will do certain things. Tell him that these things will be done under certain conditions by adding an appropriate clause in the indicative or subjunctive as required.

1. ¿Vas a jugar fútbol?
    Sí, voy a jugar fútbol cuando . . .
                           antes que . . .
                           tan pronto como . . .
2. ¿Tus hermanas piensan ver esa película extranjera?
    Sí, piensan verla después que . . .
                         en cuanto . . .
                         cuando . . .
3. ¿Tu amiga celebra su cumpleaños hoy?
    Sí, lo celebra hoy a menos que . . .
                           con tal que . . .
                           después que . . .
4. ¿Vas a asistir al concierto de piano esta tarde?
    Sí, voy a asistir al concierto tan pronto como . . .
                                  antes que . . .
                                  sin que . . .

D. Your friend asks you if you're doing certain things for yourself. Explain to her that you are actually doing them for your children.

MODELO: —¿Vas al centro para patinar?   *Are you going downtown to skate?*

          —No, voy para que mis hijos   *No, I'm going so that my children*
          patinen.   *can skate.*

1. ¿Trabajas para vivir mejor?
2. ¿Te mudas a otra casa para tener más cuartos?
3. ¿Compras un piano para aprender a tocarlo?
4. ¿Vas al cine para divertirte?
5. ¿Ahorras dinero para ir a la universidad?
6. ¿Apagas el estéreo para poder estudiar?

Estructura 2

Por and *para*

Análisis

▶ **Por** and **para** are both equivalent to English *for* in certain contexts.

1. **Para** designates a real or figurative goal or destination:

Tomaron el autobús **para** el estadio. (destination)	*They took the bus **for** the stadium.*
Vamos a estar allí **para** las tres. (temporal goal)	*We'll be there **by** three o'clock.*
Trabajaba **para** esos jefes. (figurative goal)	*She was working **for** those bosses.*
Estudio **para** profesora.	*I'm studying **to be a** teacher.*
Hay mucho trabajo **para** esa clase.	*There's a lot of work **for** that class.*
¡Qué oportunidad **para** ellos!	*What an opportunity **for** them!*
Trajimos torta **para** la fiesta.	*We brought cake **for** the party.*

NOTE: **A** and **para** contrast in designating the physical destination.

Voy **al** jardín zoológico.	*I'm going **to** the zoo.*
Voy **para** el jardín zoológico.	*I'm going **toward** the zoo.*

2. **Para** often designates an infinitive as the goal or destination of the action.

Fuimos al jardín **para** jugar.	*We went to the garden **to play**.*

3. **Para** labels the standard of comparison and the holder of an opinion:

Para profesor no sabe mucho.	***For** a teacher he doesn't know much.*
Para mí, el partido fue emocionante.	***In my opinion**, the game was exciting.*

▶ **Por** expresses motion or passage through or location within certain boundaries.

1. When referring to space **por** labels motion through something or imprecise location.

Se entra **por** esta puerta.	*You go in **through** this door.*
Perdimos la pelota **por** aquí.	*We lost the ball **around** here.*

2. When referring to time **por** designates either duration or imprecise location in a period of time.

Ha vivido en San Juan **por** muchos años.	*He's lived in San Juan **for** many years.*
Vino **por** la mañana.	*He came **in** (= sometime during) the morning.*

3. When used figuratively **por** designates cause or reason.

No le gustó la película **por** los actores.	*He didn't like the film **because of** the actors.*

4. **Por** may designate the means.

Viajé **por** avión.	*I traveled **by** plane.*

5. **Por** labels motivation and inducement, exchange, and substitution:

Ahorran dinero **por** sus hijos.	*They save money **for** their children's sake.*
Pagasteis mucha plata **por** los boletos.	*You paid a lot of money **for** the tickets.*
Alejandro jugó baloncesto **por** su amigo.	*Alejandro played basketball **for** (= instead of, in place of) his friend.*

▸ **Por** appears in the following expressions you have already learned.

por desgracia *unfortunately*	**¡Por Dios!** *Gosh!*
por eso *therefore, that's why*	**por favor** *please*
por fin *finally*	**por primera vez** *for the first time*
por todas partes *everywhere*	

Práctica

A. You have just returned from a shopping trip and your husband (wife) inquires about the prices of some items. Tell your spouse that he or she is right about the costs.

MODELO: —¿Estos libros te costaron 8 dólares?
—Sí, pagué 8 dólares por ellos.

1. ¿Estos zapatos de tenis te costaron 20 dólares?
2. ¿Este vestido te costó 75 dólares?
3. ¿Esta lámpara te costó 147 dólares?
4. ¿Estas cortinas te costaron 283 dólares?
5. ¿Estos boletos te costaron 66 dólares?
6. ¿Este suéter te costó 100 dólares?

B. Your friend asks why you do certain things. Answer each of her questions appropriately using a sentence containing **para** + *infinitive.*

MODELO: —¿Para qué trabajas tanto? *Why (= for what purpose) do you work so much?*
—Trabajo para ganar dinero. *I work to earn money.*

1. ¿Para qué juegas tenis con Alejandro?
2. ¿Para qué estudias español?
3. ¿Para qué depositas tu sueldo en el banco?
4. ¿Para qué vas al centro esta tarde?
5. ¿Para qué sigues esta dieta?
6. ¿Para qué haces la fiesta?

Estructura 3

The present perfect subjunctive (*For recognition*)

Análisis

▶ The present perfect subjunctive is used in the same types of dependent clauses as the present subjunctive. It consists of the present subjunctive of **haber** + *the past participle:*

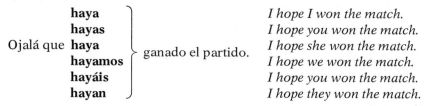

	haya	*I hope I won the match.*
	hayas	*I hope you won the match.*
Ojalá que	**haya** ganado el partido.	*I hope she won the match.*
	hayamos	*I hope we won the match.*
	hayáis	*I hope you won the match.*
	hayan	*I hope they won the match.*

The present perfect subjunctive signals that the action of the dependent clause happened before the action of the main clause.

Espero que ganen.	*I hope they win.*
	(actions are simultaneous)
Espero que hayan ganado.	*I hope they won.*
	(action of dependent clause happened prior to action of main clause)

Práctica

Be sure you can translate the following sentences into English.

1. Dudamos que·hayan vuelto de la fiesta.
2. Es posible que su sobrino haya ido al jardín zoológico.
3. Busco un jugador que haya jugado con ese equipo.
4. No hay nadie que haya roto la piñata.
5. Es bueno que os hayáis mudado de esa casa.
6. Esperan que hayamos hecho la cena.
7. Se alegra que ya hayas visto esa obra de teatro.
8. No creo que haya puesto la radio.

Comunicando

Preguntas personales

1. ¿Qué deporte te gusta más **jugar?**   (ver)
2. ¿Le gusta **andar en bicicleta?**   (correr)
3. ¿Cuál equipo de **béisbol** le gusta más?   (fútbol, baloncesto)

4. ¿Cuál jugador de tenis le gusta más? ¿Por qué?
5. ¿Cómo celebras tu cumpleaños?
6. ¿Invitas a tus amigos a tu casa? ¿Para qué los invitas?

Charlas

1. **—Fui a una fiesta el sábado.**
   ¿Quién te invitó? ¿Para qué fue? ¿Cómo eran los invitados? ¿Había una **piñata**? (música) ¿Qué se sirvió?

2. **—Somos aficionados al tenis.**
   ¿Asisten a los partidos de tenis? ¿Saben jugar tenis también? ¿Qué les hace falta para jugarlo? ¿Quién es su jugador favorito?

Situación

Your birthday. Tell when you were born. Discuss how you celebrated your birthday last year and how you plan to celebrate it next time: with a party, special meal, trip, visit to the theater or sports event, etc.

Para escribir

A. Join each pair of sentences by means of the conjunction in parentheses. Not all verbs of the subordinate clauses will be in the subjunctive.

MODELO: Tenemos una fiesta en casa. Es su cumpleaños. (porque)
→ Tenemos una fiesta en casa porque es su cumpleaños.

1. Vamos a ver la obra. Compras los boletos. (tan pronto como)
2. Pienso jugar volibol con ellos. No saben jugarlo. (a menos que)
3. Se puede tratar de romper la piñata. Están todos los invitados. (con tal que)
4. Tocaron la canción. Ella dijo. (como)
5. Saca buenas notas. Estudia mucho. (ahora que)
6. Los llevamos al partido. Ven su equipo favorito. (para que)
7. Miraba la televisión. Llegó su hermano. (hasta que)
8. Ponte los zapatos de tenis. Salimos al jardín. (cuando)

B. Complete each of the following sentences with **para** or **por** as required.

1. Voy a llegar al cine _____ las ocho.
2. Viajamos _____ (*in the direction of*) San Juan.
3. Felipe trabaja _____ su abuelo. (*the grandfather is his employer*)
4. Hice una piñata _____ la fiesta.
5. Habéis jugado fútbol _____ muchos años.
6. No se realizó el partido _____ el frío.

7. Nos invitaron al campo _____ andar en bicicleta.
8. No quiere que pagues tanta plata _____ el sofá.
9. Se entra _____ aquella puerta.
10. Hacemos todo lo posible _____ los niños.

C. Translate the following sentences into Spanish.

1. We're going to play tennis provided that she finds her racket.
2. He knows how to play basketball very well.
3. She has returned so that they can celebrate their birthday together.
4. Did you invite Julia to the party?
5. Yes, she's nice and charming.
6. Cut the cake as soon as all the guests arrive.
7. What a coincidence for them!
8. The baseball team is looking for a player who has a lot of home runs.
9. In my opinion (**para**), their niece and nephew are boring and unpleasant.
10. Hang the piñata where they tell you to.
11. We spent fifty dollars for the tickets.

lección 17

Objectives

Structure   You will learn two new tenses in this lesson—the future and the conditional—and will practice some of their special uses.

Vocabulary   You will learn words for several different types of stores and for the items you can purchase in them.

Conversation   After finishing this lesson you will be able to buy stamps in the post office, bread in the bakery, and take your car to a gas station for repairs in a Spanish-speaking country.

Culture   You will learn about traditional shopping patterns in the Hispanic world.

Outline

Estructura 1   The future tense
Estructura 2   The conditional tense
Estructura 3   The future and conditional used to express probability
Estructura 4   Future and conditional perfect (For recognition)

Where Can I Find It?

Allan Spaulding, a young businessman, has studied Spanish and knows how to speak it very well. That's why the American company he works for has sent him to several South American countries.

In Quito, Ecuador:

S.: Excuse me, sir. Could you tell me where the post office is? I need some stamps and postcards.

Man: Of course. Follow this avenue. You'll come to the López drugstore. Turn right there and you'll see the post office.

S.: I'd also like to know if there's a bookstore in this neighborhood. I have to buy books and magazines in Spanish.

Man: Well, I know one that's on Flores Street. It's next to a pastry shop. There's another one on the Avenue of the 10th of August, opposite the church.

S.: Thanks a lot. Goodbye.

Man: You're welcome. Goodbye.

In Lima, Peru, speaking with the secretary in his company's office:

S.: Please, Miss, I'd like to find a barbershop. Would you know a good one near the office?

Secretary: The Paris Barbershop is nearby, but I don't know whether it's good.

S.: I'll see. Also, would you know if there's a jewelry store around here?

Secretary: You probably want to buy some gifts, right? Well, there's a lovely one around the corner.

In Santiago, Chile, speaking with Miguel Rivera, a Chilean who works for the same company as Spaulding:

R.: What will you do this afternoon when we finish our work? You must have plans, right?

S.: Yes, first I'll take my car to the garage (=mechanic's) so they can repair the brakes. Then I'll go to the cleaner's.

R.: It won't be a very amusing afternoon. Wouldn't you like to go with me to a discotheque?

S.: I'd love to, but we won't be able to go until I finish with all this.

R.: Look, I'll go with you and afterwards I'll take you to the Mistral Discotheque. How about that?

S.: Terrific.

Presentación

¿Dónde lo encuentro?

Allan Spaulding, joven hombre de negocios, ha estudiado español y sabe hablarlo muy bien. Por eso, la compañía norteamericana para la cual trabaja lo ha mandado a varios países sudamericanos.

En Quito, Ecuador:

Spaulding	—Perdone, señor, ¿podría Ud. decirme dónde queda el correo? Me hacen falta unos sellos y unas tarjetas postales.
Un señor	—Cómo no. Siga Ud. por esta avenida. Llegará a la farmacia López. Allí doble a la derecha y verá el correo.
Spaulding	—También me gustaría saber si hay alguna librería en este barrio. Tengo que comprar libros y revistas en español.
Un señor	—Pues, conozco una que queda en la calle Flores. Está al lado de una pastelería. Hay otra en la avenida 10 de agosto,[1] en frente de la iglesia.
Spaulding	—Muchísimas gracias, señor. Hasta luego.
Un señor	—De nada. Hasta luego.

En Lima, Perú, hablando con la secretaria en la oficina de su compañía:

Spaulding	—Por favor, señorita, me gustaría encontrar una peluquería. ¿Conocería Ud. una buena cerca de la oficina?
Secretaria	—La peluquería París está cerca, pero no sé si será buena.
Spaulding	—Voy a ver. Otra cosa, ¿sabría Ud. si hay una joyería por aquí?
Secretaria	—Querrá Ud. comprar unos regalos, ¿no es cierto? Bueno, hay una preciosa a la vuelta de la esquina.

---

[1] Streets in Spanish-American cities are often named for famous dates in the country's history. August 10 is the date when Quito declared its independence from Spain.

*En Santiago, Chile, hablando con Miguel Rivera, un chileno que trabaja para
la misma compañía que Spaulding:*

Rivera —¿Qué hará Ud. esta tarde cuando terminemos el trabajo? Tendrá sus planes, ¿verdad?

Spaulding —Sí, primero llevaré mi coche al taller para que me reparen los
frenos. Después iré a la tintorería.

Rivera —Hombre, no será una tarde muy divertida. ¿No le gustaría ir
conmigo a una discoteca?

Spaulding —Me encantaría, pero no podremos ir hasta que yo termine con
todo esto.

Rivera —Mire, iré con Ud. y después lo llevaré a la discoteca Mistral.
¿Qué le parece?

Spaulding —Me parece estupendo.

Ampliación

—¿Conoces bien el país?	*Do you know the country well?*
—No tanto. Por eso llevo un mapa.	*Not really. That's why I'm carrying a map.*
—¿Necesita Ud. sobres?	*Do you need envelopes?*
—Sí, los compraré en la papelería.	*Yes, I'll buy them at the stationery store.*
—¿Tendrá Ud. que ir al correo?	*Will you have to go to the post office?*
—No creo. Echaré las cartas al buzón de la esquina.	*I don't think so. I'll mail the letters at the corner mailbox.*
—Servirás **pan** hoy, ¿verdad? (carne, pescado)	*You'll serve **bread** today, won't you? (meat, fish)*
—Claro. Por eso iré a **la panadería.**	*Of course. That's why I'll go to the **bakery.***
(la carnicería, la pescadería)	*(butcher shop, fish store)*
—Y ¿pondrás flores en la mesa?	*And will you put flowers on the table?*
—Sí, las compraré en la florería.	*Yes, I'll buy them at the flower shop.*
—¿Por qué tienes tanta prisa?	*Why are you in such a hurry?*
—Están esperándome en la peluquería.	*They're waiting for me at the barbershop.*
—¿Te vas a cortar el pelo?	*Are you going to get a haircut?*
—Sí, y me afeitaré también.	*Yes, and I'll get a shave too.*
—¿Esta ropa está limpia?	*Is this clothing clean?*
—No, está sucia. Tengo que llevarla a la lavandería.	*No, it's dirty. I have to take it to the laundry.*

—¿Vas de compras al supermercado?

Are you going shopping at the supermarket?

—No hace falta. Lo tienen todo en la bodega.²

It's not necessary. They have everything at the grocery store.

—¿Comprasteis **gasolina** en esta gasolinera?
(aceite)

*Did you buy **gasoline** at this gas station?*
(oil)

—¿Sí, y un mecánico nos reparó **la llanta.**
(la batería)

Yes, and a mechanic repaired our tire.
(battery)

—Necesito crema para la cara.

I need cream for my face.

—Vamos a la droguería. Yo necesito **maquillaje.**
(perfume, jabón)

Let's go to the drugstore. I need makeup.
(perfume, soap)

—¿Dónde queda la sinogoga?

Where's the synagogue?

—Está en la calle Pizarro, al lado de la zapatería Salazar.

It's on Pizarro Street, next to the Salazar shoe store.

—¿Cuánto valdrá la alfombra?

I wonder how much the rug costs.

—Valdrá cien dólares.

It might cost one hundred dollars.

NOTA CULTURAL

Traditionally in Hispanic countries, doing one's shopping means going to several specialty stores: **la carnicería** for meat, **la pescadería** for fish, etc. Even bread and pastries are not purchased in the same store: people buy bread in the **panadería** and pastries at the **pastelería**. All medical needs can be met by the **farmacia**, while the **droguería** is the place to purchase cosmetics, perfumes, soaps, etc. At present large stores such as supermarkets are encroaching on the traditional domain of the small stores.

Preguntas sobre la Presentación

1. ¿Por qué manda la compañía a Allan Spaulding a varios países sudamericanos?
2. ¿Qué busca Allan Spaulding en Quito?
3. ¿Cómo puede llegar Allan Spaulding al correo?
4. ¿Dónde se encuentra la joyería en Lima?

---

² Many different words for *grocery store* are used in Spanish America. In addition to **bodega** one also hears **tienda de abarrotes, abasto, colmado, pulpería, almacén.**

5. ¿Qué hará Allan Spaulding después que él y Rivera terminen su trabajo?
6. ¿Adónde llevará Miguel a Allan Spaulding?

Vocabulario activo

el **aceite** oil
  afeitarse to shave
la **avenida** avenue
el **barrio** neighborhood
la **batería** battery
la **bodega** grocery store
el **buzón** mailbox
la **carnicería** butcher shop
la **compañía** company
la **cara** face
el **correo** post office
la **crema** cream
la **discoteca** discotheque
  doblar to turn
la **droguería** drugstore (*for sundries*)
  echar to throw, to mail
la **esquina** (*street*) corner
la **farmacia** drugstore
la **flor** flower
la **florería** flower shop
el **freno** brake
la **gasolina** gasoline
la **gasolinera** gas station
la **iglesia** church
el **jabón** soap
la **joyería** jewelry store
la **lavandería** laundry
la **librería** bookstore
  limpio clean
la **llanta** tire
el **mapa** map

el **maquillaje** makeup
el **mecánico** mechanic
los **negocios** business
la **panadería** bakery (*for bread*)
la **papelería** stationery store
la **pastelería** pastry shop
el **pelo** hair
la **peluquería** barbershop, hair dresser's
el **perfume** perfume
la **pescadería** fish store
  precioso lovely
  reparar to fix, repair
la **revista** magazine
el **sello** stamp
la **sinagoga** synagogue
el **sobre** envelope
  sucio dirty
el **taller** garage (*where mechanics work*); shop
la **tarjeta postal** post card
la **tintorería** cleaner's
  valer to cost; to be worth
la **zapatería** shoe store

EXPRESIONES

a la vuelta de la esquina around the corner
en frente de opposite, facing
¡hombre! (*interj.*) come now!
ir de compras to go shopping

Estructura 1

The future tense

Análisis

▶ The future tense (English *will, shall, 'll*) is formed in Spanish by adding a special set of endings to the infinitive. The endings are the same for *-ar, -er,* and *-ir* verbs.

FUTURE TENSE

-é	Doblar**é** aquí.	*I'll turn here.*
-ás	Doblar**ás** aquí.	*You'll turn here.*
-á	Doblar**á** aquí.	*He'll turn here.*
-emos	Doblar**emos** aquí.	*We'll turn here.*
-éis	Doblar**éis** aquí.	*You'll turn here.*
-án	Doblar**án** aquí.	*They'll turn here.*

▶ For certain verbs the future tense endings are added to slightly modified versions of the infinitive:

1. Verbs having **-d-** in place of the class vowel:

   poner → **pondré**
   salir → **saldré**
   tener → **tendré**
   valer → **valdré**
   venir → **vendré**

2. Verbs losing the class vowel:

   haber → **habré**   querer → **querré**
   poder → **podré**   saber → **sabré**

3. Verbs contracting the infinitive to a single syllable:

   decir → **diré**   hacer → **haré**

▶ The future tense in Spanish is often replaced by the **ir a** + *infinitive* construction or by the simple present tense when another element of the sentence specifies that future time is meant.

   Voy a comprar sellos mañana. ⎫
   Compro sellos mañana.   ⎬ **Compraré** sellos mañana.
                                                         ⎭

▶ The *future progressive* consists of the future of **estar** + **-ndo** *form.*

   ¿Dónde **estarán esperando?**   *Where **will** they **be waiting?***

Práctica

A. Restate each of the following sentences changing the verb from the present to the future tense.

   MODELO: Juegan béisbol hoy.   → Jugarán béisbol hoy.

1. Vas a la farmacia.
2. Pongo la mesa antes de cenar.
3. Se casan en marzo.
4. Me dice dónde está el estadio.
5. No podéis encontrar esa bodega.
6. Les pido unas flores amarillas.
7. Venimos a las cinco y cuarto.
8. Te gusta la joyería nueva.

B. Tell about the chores you will do as you and your friend walk through your neighborhood streets this afternoon. You will have to change all verbs from present to future.

LEAD SENTENCE: Tendré que hacer muchas cosas esta tarde.

1. Salgo de casa a la una.
2. Mi amiga me acompaña a las tiendas.
3. Vamos a la Avenida Salazar.
4. Primero, busco camisas en un almacén.
5. Después echo algunas cartas en el correo.
6. Doblamos en la Calle Pizarro.
7. Mi amiga saca su abrigo de la tintorería.
8. También quiere comprar aspirinas en la farmacia.
9. Almorzamos en un restaurante.
10. Por fin tomamos el autobús y volvemos a casa.

C. Your friend wants to know if you and other people have already done certain things. Tell him that you haven't as yet but that you will in the future.

MODELO: —¿Has depositado la plata?
            No, pero la depositaré.

1. ¿Has visto esa obra de teatro?
2. ¿Eduardo ha escrito los cheques?
3. ¿Los jugadores se han puesto los zapatos?
4. ¿Te he dicho lo de la librería?
5. ¿Uds. han recibido la tarjeta verde?
6. ¿Paloma ha hecho el viaje a Lima?

D. Answer the following questions using the future tense.

1. ¿A qué hora se acostará Ud. esta noche?
2. ¿Qué harás después de la clase de español?
3. ¿Qué comerán Ud. y sus amigos hoy?
4. ¿Adónde irás este fin de semana?
5. ¿Te casarás algún día? ¿Tendrás hijos?

Estructura 2

The conditional

Análisis

▶ The conditional (English *would*) is formed in Spanish by adding the endings of the imperfect of **-er** and **-ir** verbs to the infinitive. In the conditional these endings are used for **-ar** verbs as well.

CONDITIONAL

-ía	Asistiría a ese concierto.	*I'd attend that concert.*
-ías	Asistirías a ese concierto.	*You'd attend that concert.*
-ía	Asistiría a ese concierto.	*He'd attend that concert.*
-íamos	Asistiríamos a ese concierto.	*We'd attend that concert.*
-íais	Asistiríais a ese concierto.	*You'd attend that concert.*
-ían	Asistirían a ese concierto.	*They'd attend that concert.*

▶ Verbs whose infinitives are modified in the future show the same change in the conditional: **vendría** (*I'd come*), **podrían** (*they'd be able to*), **diríamos** (*we'd say*).

▶ *The conditional progressive* consists of the conditional of **estar** (or **seguir**) + the **-ndo** form.

Sabía que **estarías visitándome.**   *I knew **you'd be visiting me.***

Práctica

A. Restate each of the following sentences changing the verb from the present to the conditional.

MODELO: Vive en aquel hotel.   → Viviría en aquel hotel.

1. Recogemos legumbres.
2. Me encanta ir al cine.
3. Se visten en el dormitorio.
4. Hay lápices en la gaveta.
5. ¿Qué se dice?
6. Reparan los frenos.
7. Les pides los mapas.
8. No sé jugar fútbol muy bien.

B. When asked what you would do if you had all the time in the world and nothing that *had* to be done, respond using each of the following sentences, changing its verb from present to conditional.

MODELO: Estudio diez idiomas.   → Estudiaría diez idiomas.

1. Aprendo a tocar el piano.
2. Voy al teatro todos los días.
3. Juego tenis 6 horas al día.
4. Salgo a lugares diferentes.
5. Leo libros todo el día.
6. Preparo comidas riquísimas.
7. Invito a mis amigos a mi casa.
8. Hago un viaje a Latinoamérica.

C. Answer the following questions using the conditional.

1. ¿Te gustaría vivir en el campo o quedarte en la ciudad?
2. ¿Le interesaría a Ud. viajar a otros países? ¿A cuáles?
3. ¿Te gustaría celebrar tu cumpleaños con una fiesta?
4. ¿Qué sueños y ambiciones esperaría Ud. realizar (en la vida)?
5. ¿Te gustaría cambiar tu vida? ¿Cómo?

Estructura 3

The future and conditional used to express probability

Análisis

▸ The future tense in Spanish is used to express probability in present time and the conditional is used to express probability in past time. Futures and conditionals of probability often have English equivalents in *I wonder, can, could.*

—¿Qué hora es?	*What time is it?*
—No tengo reloj. **Serán** las once.	*I don't have a watch.* ***It's probably*** *eleven o'clock.*
—¿Por qué va Roberto al correo?	*Why is Roberto going to the post office?*
—Bueno, **tendrá que** comprar sellos.	*Well, he* ***probably has to*** *buy stamps.*
—¿Qué hora era cuando llegaron?	*What time was it when they arrived?*
—**Serían** las siete.	***It was probably*** *seven o'clock.*
—¿Cuánto **valdrán** los plátanos?	***I wonder*** *how much the bananas* ***cost.***
—**Valen** un dólar.	***They cost*** *a dollar.*

Práctica

A. Restate each sentence eliminating **probablemente** and changing the verb from present to future.

MODELO: Probablemente vuelve pronto.   → Volverá pronto.

1. Probablemente sacas buenas notas.
2. Probablemente se ofenden fácilmente.
3. Probablemente trabajáis en una zapatería.
4. Probablemente consiguen un empleo en la fábrica.
5. Probablemente tiene veinte años.
6. Probablemente ganamos el partido.

B. Answer each of the following questions with a sentence containing a form of the conditional in order to express probability in the past.

MODELO: —¿Qué tiempo hacía cuando trabajaban?
          —No sé. Haría frío.   *I don't know. It was probably cold outside.*

1. ¿Cuántos años tenía Julia cuando se mudó a Quito?
2. ¿Qué hora era cuando los cajeros abrieron las taquillas?
3. ¿Cuántos empleados había en su compañía?
4. ¿Qué tiempo hacía cuando Ricardo andaba en bicicleta?
5. ¿Qué hora era cuando saliste de la peluquería?
6. ¿Cuántos años tenían esos niños cuando murió su papá?

Estructura 4

Future and conditional perfect (For recognition)

Análisis

▸ The future and conditional of **haber** + **-do** *form* of verbs form the future perfect and the conditional perfect tenses, respectively.

Future perfect

Habré salido.	*I'll have left.*
Habrás salido.	*You'll have left.*
Habrá salido.	*She'll have left.*
Habremos salido.	*We'll have left.*
Habréis salido.	*You'll have left.*
Habrán salido.	*They'll have left.*

Conditional perfect

Habría hecho eso.	*I'd have done that.*
Habrías hecho eso.	*You'd have done that.*
Habría hecho eso.	*She'd have done that.*
Habríamos hecho eso.	*We'd have done that.*
Habríais hecho eso.	*You'd have done that.*
Habrían hecho eso.	*They'd have done that.*

▸ The use of the future and conditional perfect is similar in Spanish and English. The future perfect designates an event that will be completed in the future before another event occurs. The conditional perfect is used when there is a real or implied condition.

Habremos salido antes del concierto.	***We'll have left*** *before the concert.*
Con unas ideas como las tuyas, **no habría tenido tanto éxito.**	*With ideas like yours **she wouldn't have been so successful.***

▸ The future perfect is commonly used to express probability in the past.

—¿Adónde **habrá ido** María?	*Where **could** María **have gone?***
—No sé. **Habrá salido** de compras.	*I don't know. She **probably went out** shopping.*

Práctica

Make sure you can translate the following sentences into English.

1. No habrán ido de compras antes de la cena.
2. Ud. habrá abierto la cuenta antes del primero del mes.
3. Yo no me habría cortado el pelo así.
4. Nos habrían interesado muchísimo sus tradiciones.
5. Nos habremos afeitado antes de vestirnos.

6. ¿Habríais preferido otro perfume?
7. Habré visto al profesor antes de la clase.
8. Habríamos guardado los cajones primero.

Comunicando

Preguntas personales

1. Cuando vas de compras, ¿a cuáles tiendas vas? ¿Qué compras en cada una de ellas?
2. ¿Para qué vas a una gasolinera o a un taller?
3. ¿A qué hora **se levantará** Ud. mañana? (desayunará, saldrá de casa, se acostará)
4. ¿Qué hará Ud. cuando vuelva a su casa?
5. ¿Qué te gustaría hacer este fin de semana?
6. ¿Te interesaría visitar Ecuador, Perú y Chile? ¿Por qué?

Charlas

1. —**Tendré que ir de compras hoy.**
   ¿A cuáles tiendas irás? ¿Qué comprarás? ¿Cuánto dinero gastarás? ¿Pagarás con dinero o con tarjeta de crédito?

2. **Me gustaría trabajar en *una droguería.*** (una papelería, una gasolinera)
   ¿Qué harías allí? ¿Qué venderías? ¿Habría muchos clientes? ¿Qué sueldo recibirías?

Situación

Talk about a shopping trip you went on recently. Tell when you went, what stores you went to, what you bought in each store, how much you spent, who went with you, etc.

Para escribir

A. Rewrite each of the following sentences changing the verb from present to future.

MODELO: Siguen por esta calle.   → Seguirán por esta calle.

1. Se oyen los autobuses en la esquina.
2. Hay una sinagoga en frente.
3. Doblamos a la izquierda.
4. ¿Les hacéis el arroz con pollo?

5. Viene a las ocho menos cuarto.
6. Quiero viajar al norte.
7. No escriben nada en los sobres.
8. Te vistes de azul.

B. Rewrite each of the following sentences changing the verb from preterit to conditional.

    MODELO: Compró crema en la droguería.

           → Compraría crema en la droguería.

1. Los mecánicos me repararon los frenos.
2. No pudo ir a la iglesia.
3. Saliste de la librería.
4. Estuvisteis de vacaciones en Córdoba.
5. No comprendió todas sus ideas.
6. Me dijo la fecha del partido.
7. No tuvimos razón.
8. ¿Cuándo echaste las cartas al buzón?

C. Translate the following sentences into Spanish. The sentences form a dialogue between Carlos and Mercedes about shopping.

1. *Carlos:* I'd like to go shopping. Is the bakery around the corner?
2. *Mercedes:* Yes, turn right and you'll see a drugstore. The bakery is opposite it, next to the post office.
3. *Carlos:* Would you like to go with me?
4. *Mercedes:* Good idea. I'll mail my letters at the post office when you go to the bakery.
5. *Carlos:* What time could it be? (*use probability construction*)
6. *Mercedes:* It's probably 12:30. Why? (*use probability construction*)
7. *Carlos:* I have to pick up my car. The mechanics said they would repair the brakes for me.
8. *Mercedes:* I wonder how much that costs? (*use probability construction*)
9. *Carlos:* It can cost ninety-five dollars. (*use probability construction*)
10. *Mercedes:* There were probably many cars at the garage. (*use probability construction*)
11. *Carlos:* Not too many. The mechanics said there would be more tomorrow.

lección 18

Objectives

Structure You will learn and practice the forms and use of the imperfect subjunctive, and you will learn how to express conditions in Spanish.

Vocabulary You will learn terms relating to the economy and industry, the environment, and the names of some animals.

Conversation By the end of the lesson you will be able to discuss environmental pollution and some aspects of the economy such as industry and employment. You will also be able to talk about earning a living in certain trades and in computer programming.

Culture You will be introduced to Mexican-Americans, the largest Spanish-speaking minority in the United States. You will become acquainted with three generations of Chicanos living in Texas and will discover their reasons for emigrating and their aspirations for the future.

Outline

Estructura 1 The imperfect subjunctive
Estructura 2 Conditional sentences
Estructura 3 The past perfect subjunctive (For recognition)
Estructura 4 More conditional sentences (For recognition)

A Young Chicano Prepares His Future

Javier Guerrero is speaking:

We're Chicanos. We've lived in Texas since my grandfather left Mexico 50 years ago. He came to look for work in the U.S. and he found it in agriculture. My father, on the other hand, didn't want to pick oranges like my grandfather. He needed a job that was more secure to support his family. He hoped that his children would have a better life than he. He became a carpenter. He always advised us to learn a trade, but neither my brother Ernesto nor I was interested in being a carpenter or a plumber. Ernesto graduated from the university last year and is now taking courses in computer programming at night. He'll have very good opportunities when he finishes the program. For now he's earning a living working in the immigration office. They need many bilingual people like us there to speak with the illegal Mexican aliens. Ernesto was looking for a job that was interesting until finally he found this one.

I still have two years left before I graduate. Dad asked me to work with him in the shop. This way I can pay for my courses. I can also help my family with the money I earn; we're seven people and the cost of living is very high. When I graduate, I hope to get a job with the government. What I'm most interested in is fighting environmental pollution here in Texas. I think the large industries don't understand the dangers of technology. It's important that they produce the goods that are needed because that creates work, but the air, the rivers, and the ocean are so dirty, so polluted now. I don't like to discuss this with Dad because all this political stuff bothers him, but I consider ecology a very important science in today's world.

Presentación

Un joven chicano prepara su futuro

Habla Javier Guerrero:

Somos chicanos. Vivimos en Tejas desde que mi abuelo salió de México hace 50 años. Vino a buscar trabajo en Estados Unidos y lo encontró en la agricultura. Mi papá, al contrario, no quería recoger naranjas como mi abuelo. Necesitaba un empleo que fuera más seguro para mantener a su familia. Esperaba que sus hijos tuvieran mejor vida que él. Se hizo carpintero. Siempre nos aconsejaba que aprendiéramos un oficio, pero ni a mi hermano Ernesto ni a mí nos interesaba ser carpintero o plomero. Ernesto se graduó en la universidad el año pasado y ahora toma cursos de computación por la noche. Tendrá muy buenas oportunidades cuando termine el programa. Por ahora se gana la vida trabajando en la oficina de inmigración. Allí hacen falta muchas personas bilingües como nosotros para hablar con los inmigrantes indocumentados mexicanos. Ernesto buscaba un empleo que fuera interesante hasta encontrar este por fin.

A mí me quedan dos años todavía para graduarme. Papá me pidió que trabajara con él en el taller. Así puedo pagar los cursos. También ayudo a mi familia con la plata que gano; somos siete personas y el costo de la vida es muy alto. Cuando me gradúe, espero conseguir un empleo con el gobierno. Lo que más me interesa es luchar contra la contaminación del ambiente aquí en Tejas. Me parece que las grandes industrias no entienden los peligros de la tecnología. Es importante que produzcan los bienes que se necesitan porque eso da trabajo, pero el aire, los ríos y el océano están tan sucios, tan contaminados ahora. No me gusta discutir esto con papá porque a él le molesta todo lo de política, pero yo considero que la ecología es una ciencia importantísima en el mundo actual.

Ampliación

—¿Se produce mucho petróleo?
—Sí, y el país exporta muchísimo.

Is a lot of oil produced?
Yes, and the country exports a great deal.

—¿Cómo controla la inflación el gobierno?	*How does the government control inflation?*
—Trata de importar menos bienes.	*It tries to import less goods.*
—¿Qué pasa? ¿Por qué hay tantos obreros sin empleo?	*What's the matter? Why are there so many unemployed workers?*
—Es que hay mucho desempleo en el pueblo.	*Because there's a lot of unemployment in the town.*
—¿Habrá una huelga?	*Will there be a strike?*
—Si los obreros del sindicato votan por ella.	*If the workers in the union vote for it.*
—No pude sacar las cosas de la maleta.	*I couldn't take the things out of the suitcase.*
—Dudaba que la pudieras abrir sin la llave.	*I doubted that you would be able to open it without the key.*
—¿Javier iba a preparar el informe?	*Was Javier going to prepare the paper?*
—Con tal que tuviera una máquina para escribir.	*Provided that he had a typewriter.*
—¿Qué animales tiene el campesino?	*What animals does the peasant have?*
—Tiene caballos, vacas, gallinas, un perro, y un gato.	*He has horses, cows, chickens, a dog, and a cat.*

Preguntas sobre la Presentación

1. ¿De qué origen es Javier Guerrero?
2. ¿Para qué vino el abuelo de Javier a Estados Unidos?
3. ¿Qué quería el papá de Javier que hicieran sus hijos?
4. ¿Cómo se gana la vida Ernesto?
5. ¿Qué ambiciones tiene Javier para cuando se gradúe?
6. ¿Por qué trabaja Javier con su papá en el taller?

NOTA CULTURAL

Chicano is a word of uncertain origin that refers to people of Mexican descent living in the United States. There is a very large Chicano population in most of the southwestern United States, an area which until the middle of the last century was Mexican territory.

Vocabulario activo

actual at present
la **agricultura** agriculture

el **aire** air
el **ambiente** atmosphere

el **animal**   animal
los **bienes**   goods
  bilingüe   bilingual
el **caballo**   horse
el **campesino**   peasant
el **carpintero**   carpenter
la **computación**   computer
  programming
  considerar   to consider
la **contaminación**   pollution
  contaminado   polluted
  controlar   to control
el **costo**   cost
el **curso**   course
  chicano   Mexican-American
el **desempleo**   unemployment
  discutir   to discuss
la **ecología**   ecology
  entender (e→ie)   to understand
  exportar   to export
la **gallina**   chicken
el **gato**   cat
  graduarse   to graduate
la **huelga**   strike (*work stoppage*)
  importar   to import
la **industria**   industry
la **inflación**   inflation
el **informe**   paper, report
  luchar   to fight

la **llave**   key
la **maleta**   suitcase
  mantener (*like* **tener**)   to support
la **máquina para escribir**   typewriter
  molestar   to bother
la **naranja**   orange
el **océano**   ocean
el **oficio**   trade (*job*)
el **peligro**   danger
el **perro**   dog
el **petróleo**   oil
el **plomero**   plumber
la **política**   politics
  producir (**yo produzco; produje**)   to
  produce
el **programa**   program
el **pueblo**   town
el **río**   river
  seguro   secure
el **sindicato**   union
la **tecnología**   technology
la **vaca**   cow

EXPRESIONES
ganarse la vida   to earn a living
hacerse (+ *occupation*)   to become
  a ____
¿qué pasa?   what's the matter?

Estructura 1

The imperfect subjunctive

Análisis

▶ The forms of the imperfect subjunctive are derived from the third person plural forms of the preterit: **estudiaron, comieron.** Any irregularity or vowel change in the preterit form occurs in all persons of the imperfect subjunctive: **sirvieron, trajeron.** The preterit ending **-ron** is replaced by the following endings in all verbs:

IMPERFECT SUBJUNCTIVE

-ra		estudiara	comiera	sirviera
-ras		estudiaras	comieras	sirvieras
-ra		estudiara	comiera	sirviera
-ramos	Quería que	estudiáramos	comiéramos	sirviéramos
-rais		estudiarais	comierais	sirvierais
-ran		estudiaran	comieran	sirvieran

▶ There is an alternate form of the imperfect subjunctive with endings characterized by **-se** rather than **-ra.** The two sets of forms are interchangeable in most contexts but the **-se** forms are less common in speech.

-se		estudiese	comiese	sirviese
-ses		estudieses	comieses	sirvieses
-se	Quería que	estudiese	comiese	sirviese
-semos		estudiésemos	comiésemos	sirviésemos
-seis		estudieseis	comieseis	sirvieseis
-sen		estudiesen	comiesen	sirviesen

▶ The imperfect subjunctive is used in dependent noun clauses when the verb in the main clause appears in the preterit, imperfect, past perfect, or conditional.

Quería (quise) que lo **consideraran.**	*I wanted them to consider it.*
Había querido que lo **consideraran.**	*I'd wanted them to consider it.*
Querría que lo **consideraran.**	*I'd want them to consider it.*

▶ The use of the imperfect subjunctive rather than the present subjunctive after **ojalá** shows that the speaker feels it is unlikely that the wish expressed will come true.

| Ojalá que **podamos** ir. | *I hope we can go.* |
| Ojalá que **pudiéramos** ir. | *I wish we could go.* |

▶ The imperfect subjunctive is used in adjective clauses modifying indefinite and negative antecedents when the verb of the main clause is in the preterit, imperfect, past perfect, or conditional.

| No **conocía** a nadie que **fuera** carpintero. | *I didn't know anyone who was a carpenter.* |
| **Harías** lo que te **dijeran,** ¿no? | *You'd do whatever they told you, wouldn't you?* |

▶ The imperfect subjunctive is used in adverb clauses when the main verb is in the preterit, imperfect, past perfect, or conditional.

| **Volvió** al pueblo sin que lo **supierais.** | *He came back to town without your knowing it.* |
| Se lo **explicaríamos** para que lo **entendiera.** | *We'd explain it to you so that you'd understand it.* |

▶ The imperfect subjunctive is required after **como si** (*as if*) no matter what the tense of the verb of the main clause is.

| Gasta dinero como si **fuera** rico. | *He spends money as if he were rich.* |

Práctica

A. Practice the forms of the imperfect subjunctive by changing the verb of the dependent clause according to the cues in each of the following sentences.

1. Esperaban que tomara cursos.
   (yo, nosotros, tú, ellos, Ud., Uds.)
2. Prefería que sirviéramos naranjas.
   (yo, ellas, tú, Uds., ella, vosotros)
3. Era posible que aprendieran un oficio.
   (ella, Uds., tú, yo, nosotros, vosotros)

B. Substitute the proper imperfect subjunctive form of the verbs in parentheses for the verb in the dependent clause.

MODELO: Dudaban que lo **compraras.**   *They doubted you'd buy it.*
           (vender)
         → Dudaban que lo vendieras.   *They doubted you'd sell it.*

1. Sentía que no llegáramos.   (salir, ir, esperar, volver)
2. Era necesario que lo dijeran.   (discutir, traer, exportar, producir)
3. Le pedimos que se quedara.   (acostarse, vestirse, peinarse, levantarse)
4. Ojalá que la conocieras.   (encontrar, hacer, lavar, escribir)

C. Answer each of the following questions with a complete sentence using the imperfect subjunctive in the dependent clause.

1. ¿Qué querían tus papás que estudiaras?
2. ¿De qué tenías miedo cuando eras chica (chico)?
3. ¿De qué se alegró Ud. hoy?
4. ¿Qué le pidieron sus amigos ayer?

D. Change the verb in the main clause from present to imperfect and the verb of the dependent clause from present subjunctive to imperfect subjunctive. The sentences form a connected narrative about a company's difficulties in finding qualified employees.

MODELO: Busco una secretaria que   *I'm looking for a secretary who*
           hable español.   *speaks Spanish.*
         → Buscaba una secretaria   *I was looking for a secretary who*
           que hablara español.   *spoke Spanish.*

1. En nuestra compañía buscan empleados que sean bilingües.
2. No hay ninguno aquí que sepa español.
3. Según el jefe, necesitamos gente que quiera trabajar.
4. No hay oficina que tenga un ambiente más simpático que el nuestro.
5. No tenemos empleados que se quejen de su trabajo.
6. Entonces, ¿por qué no hay nadie que solicite un empleo?

E. Complete each of the following statements with an adjective clause in the imperfect subjunctive.

1. Querían un gobierno que . . .
2. Buscabas campesinos que . . .
3. No había ningún programa que . . .
4. Necesitabais hombres de negocios que . . .
5. No conocía a nadie que . . .
6. Buscábamos una bodega que . . .

F. Change the verb in the main clause to the form provided by the cue in parentheses. The verb in the dependent clause will change from present subjunctive to imperfect subjunctive. The sentences form a connected narrative about a problem that came up in planning Mercedes's party.

MODELO: Haremos la torta con tal que   *We'll make the cake provided*
          tú quieras.   (haríamos)   *that you want (us to).*
                                                (we'd make)

      → Haríamos la torta con tal que   *We'd make the cake provided*
          tú quisieras.   *that you wanted (us to).*

1. Te llamo para que podamos hablar sobre tu fiesta, Mercedes.   (llamé)
2. Quiero hablarte antes que te llame María.   (quería)
3. Ella piensa hacer una torta aunque a nadie le gusta.   (pensaba)
4. La va a hacer sin que tú lo sepas.   (iba)
5. Pero la fiesta tiene que ser como tú mandes.   (tenía)
6. Entonces ella no hará su torta a menos que tú digas.   (haría)

Estructura 2

Conditional sentences

Análisis

▶ Conditional sentences in both Spanish and English consist of two clauses: a **si**-clause (*if*-clause) and a main clause. The tenses selected for the two clauses are similar in both languages.

si-clause	main clause	
present	**future**	
Si vienen,	**los veré.**	*If they come, I'll see them.*
imperfect subjunctive	**conditional**	
Si vinieran,	**los vería.**	*If they were coming, I'd see them.*

Práctica

A. Change the verb in both clauses according to each cue.

1. Si puedes, lo harás.
   (yo, él, nosotros, vosotros, Uds.)
2. Si pudieran, lucharían.
   (ella, tú, yo, vosotros, tú y yo)
3. Lo saludaríamos si lo viéramos.
   (Ud., tú, Ud. y yo, él y ella, vosotros)
4. Si tuvieran hambre, comerían más.
   (yo, Uds. y yo, Uds., tú, él, ellas)

B. In each of the following sentences change the verb in the **si**-clause to the imperfect subjunctive and the verb in the main clause to the conditional.

1. Si trabajan mejor, producirán más.
2. Si exportamos petróleo, ganaremos mucho.
3. Se quejarán si hace calor.
4. Se echará si se siente cansada.
5. Si puedo, vendré temprano.

C. Using a conditional sentence consisting of a **si**-clause in the imperfect subjunctive and a main clause in the conditional, point out that you would be doing many interesting things if María were doing them too.

> MODELO: María no va. *María's not going.*
>   → Pero si ella fuera, *But if she were going, I'd go too.*
>   yo iría también.

1. María no va a la fiesta.
2. María no hace el viaje.
3. María no escucha la radio.
4. María no lee la revista.
5. María no llama a sus amigas.
6. María no sale esta noche.

D. Discuss some of your future plans by adding to each main clause an appropriate **si**-clause in the imperfect subjunctive.

1. Haría muchos viajes si . . .
2. Yo no me casaría si . . .
3. Seguiría estudiando si . . .
4. Estudiaría para profesor(a) si . . .
5. Iría al extranjero a trabajar si . . .
6. Sacaría buenas notas si . . .

Estructura 3

The past perfect subjunctive (For recognition)

Análisis

▸ The past perfect subjunctive consists of the imperfect subjunctive of **haber** + the **-do** *form* (past participle).

PAST PERFECT SUBJUNCTIVE

Él esperaba que	yo lo **hubiera hecho.**	*He hoped I had done it.*
	tú lo **hubieras hecho.**	*He hoped you had done it.*
	ella lo **hubiera hecho.**	*He hoped she had done it.*
	nosotros lo **hubiéramos hecho.**	*He hoped we had done it.*
	vosotros lo **hubiérais hecho.**	*He hoped you had done it.*
	ellos lo **hubieran hecho.**	*He hoped they had done it.*

▸ The past perfect subjunctive labels the action of the dependent clause as occurring further back in the past than the action of the main clause. The verb of the main clause is usually in the preterit or the imperfect.

Práctica

Be sure you can translate the following pairs of contrasting sentences into English.

1. a. Dudábamos que aquellos campesinos produjeran naranjas.
   b. Dudábamos que aquellos campesinos hubieran producido naranjas.
2. a. Se alegró que llegaran los secretarios bilingües.
   b. Se alegró que hubieran llegado los secretarios bilingües.
3. a. Era probable que el plomero terminara su trabajo a tiempo.
   b. Era probable que el plomero hubiera terminado su trabajo a tiempo.
4. a. Sentían que el gobierno no controlara la inflación.
   b. Sentían que el gobierno no hubiera controlado la inflación.
5. a. No creía que se abriera la maleta.
   b. No creía que se hubiera abierto la maleta.

Estructura 4

More conditional sentences (*For recognition*)

Análisis

▸ Another common type of conditional sentence in Spanish has the past perfect subjunctive in the **si**-clause and the conditional perfect in the main clause. Corresponding English sentences have the past perfect in the *if*-clause and the conditional perfect in the main clause.

past perfect subjunctive	conditional perfect	
Si hubieran venido,	**los habría visto.**	*If they had come, I'd have seen them.*

past perfect	conditional	
subjunctive	perfect	
Si no hubieras llamado,	**habrían salido.**	*If you hadn't called, they would have gone out.*

Práctica

Translate the following sentences into English.

1. Si Ernesto hubiera estudiado computación, habría tenido muchas oportunidades.
2. Si Uds. me hubieran pedido las llaves, se las habría dado.
3. Si me hubieran hecho falta algunos sellos, los habría comprado.
4. Si hubiéramos sabido lo que pasó, habríamos vuelto lo más antes posible.
5. Si las industrias hubieran tenido más cuidado, el ambiente de nuestro país habría estado menos contaminado.

Comunicando

Preguntas personales

1. ¿Eres bilingüe? ¿Qué idiomas hablas?
2. ¿Cómo vas a ganarte la vida cuando te gradúes?
3. ¿Te interesaría estudiar ecología?
4. ¿Cuál debe controlar la contaminación, las industrias o el gobierno?
5. ¿Cómo se puede luchar contra **la inflación?** (el desempleo, el alto costo de la vida)
6. ¿Cómo se puede explicar el precio tan alto de la gasolina?

Charlas

1. **—Soy de familia chicana.**
   ¿Dónde viven Uds.? ¿Para qué vinieron tus abuelos a los Estados Unidos? ¿Eres bilingüe? ¿Cómo te ganas la vida?

2. **—Hay mucha industria donde vivo.**
   ¿Dónde vives? ¿Qué se produce? ¿Cómo se controla la contaminación del aire y del agua? ¿Qué tal el costo de la vida allí?

Situación

You are a worker in a factory that produces cars. Because your bosses have refused to give the workers a raise and because they have recently fired many workers, your union has decided to go out on strike. You support the union's decision, but you also need a salary to support your family. Discuss this problem explaining how inflation and the high cost of living are affecting you, what the government is doing to help, etc.

Para escribir

A. In the following sentences, supply the appropriate form of the imperfect subjunctive of the verb in parentheses.

1. Queríamos que ellos _____ (cobrar) los cheques.
2. No había ningún jugador que _____ (jugar) en más partidos que él.
3. Yo me iría del pueblo a menos que se _____ (hacer) algo para controlar la contaminación del aire.
4. Dudaba que el mozo _____ (acordarse) del arroz.
5. Llamé al mecánico para que me _____ (reparar) el coche.
6. Preferíais que nosotros _____ (poner) el estéreo.
7. Buscaban un secretario que _____ (ser) bilingüe.

B. Complete each of the following statements about your university career using a verb in the imperfect subjunctive in each answer.

1. Quería asistir a una universidad que . . .
2. Mis papás preferían que yo . . .
3. Yo buscaba profesores que . . .
4. No había ningún curso que . . .
5. Yo siempre estudiaba mucho a menos que . . .
6. Mis papás me mandaban dinero para que . . .

C. Translate the following sentences into Spanish.

1. Juan went to the United States so that his family would have a better life.
2. He wanted to live in a town where there were many Chicanos.
3. He preferred his children learn a trade.
4. But his wife insisted that the children attend the university.
5. Juan said "yes" (=*que sí*) provided that they would work on Saturdays.
6. The government is trying to control inflation by importing fewer goods.
7. If our country would produce a lot of oil, then the government would export it.
8. We would earn a lot of money if we would sell oil abroad.
9. Of course, if the country produces more oil there will be more environmental pollution.
10. I just wanted you (**Ud.**) to understand the dangers of technology.

repaso 6

A. María is telling about her cousins' birthday party. Rewrite the story in the future tense.

1. Mis primos celebran su cumpleaños la semana que viene.
2. Salen a comer en un restaurante.
3. Se ponen su mejor ropa.
4. Toda la familia va con ellos.
5. Después vuelven a su casa.
6. Se cambian de ropa.
7. Toman un taxi al estadio.
8. Ven un partido de fútbol, el deporte favorito de ellos.

B. Mrs. González is having a busy time at home this morning trying to get organized. Complete the following story about her problems by adding the appropriate present subjunctive forms of the verbs in parentheses.

1. Niños, me voy de compras tan pronto como se _____ (abrir) las tiendas.
2. Jaime, sigue estudiando hasta que yo _____ (volver).
3. Mercedes, apaga la tele para que tu hermano _____ (poder) estudiar.
4. Francisco, cierra bien la puerta cuando _____ (irte) a la escuela.
5. Ay, acabo de acordarme. No puedo salir hasta que me _____ (llamar) Consuelo.
6. Me pidió que le comprara algunas cosas, lo que no me importa, con tal que me _____ (decir) lo que necesita antes de las diez.
7. Después que nos _____ (hablar), me voy a ir.
8. No sé por qué nunca puedo salir de casa sin que todo _____ (ponerse) tan complicado (=*complicated*).

C. Supply **por** or **para,** as required, in the following sentences.

1. Pagarás mucha plata _____ esa máquina de escribir.
2. Necesitaba una crema _____ la cara.

3. Los obreros querrán trabajar _____ otro jefe.
4. Hay mucha contaminación del ambiente _____ todas partes.
5. Os gustaría viajar _____ tren, ¿verdad?
6. Traje comida _____ el perro.
7. _____ plomero, no sabe reparar muchas cosas.
8. Hemos trabajado en la florería _____ dos años.

D. Rewrite the following story about a picnic in past time changing the first verb of each sentence to the preterit or imperfect and the verb of the dependent clause to the imperfect subjunctive.

1. Quiero que todos vayamos al campo a comer.
2. Tú no quieres ir sin que invitemos a Elena.
3. Raúl insiste en que juguemos béisbol.
4. Tus primos prefieren que andemos en bicicleta.
5. Yo le aconsejo a todo el mundo que traiga su cerveza.
6. Alicia trae su guitarra para que cantemos.
7. ¿Conoces a alguien más que pueda ir con nosotros?
8. Quiero que haya más gente para que nos divirtamos más.

E. Form conditional sentences by filling in the correct form of the verbs in parentheses. Be careful to select the proper tense according to the nature of the clause: *if*-clause or main clause.

MODELO: Si ellos van, yo los *saludaré* (saludar).

Si ellos *fueran* (ir), yo los saludaría.

1. Si encuentras la raqueta, nosotros _____ (poder) jugar tenis.
2. Si _____ (haber) más desempleo, habría una huelga.
3. Si caminaran por este barrio, ellos _____ (ver) la joyería.
4. Si nosotros _____ (hacer) un viaje, nos harían falta una maletas.
5. Si se _____ (controlar) la inflación, el costo de la vida no será tan alto.
6. Irías a la discoteca si _____ (terminar) tu trabajo.
7. Vosotros _____ (entender) los peligros de la tecnología si estudiáis ecología.
8. Yo viviría bien si _____ (mudarse) a Tejas.

F. Translate the following narrative into Spanish.

1. It's probably 7:30 already (*use future of probability*) and we have so many things to do!
2. Ana wants to go to the bakery (that is) around the corner.
3. I would get a haircut if I could find a good beauty parlor.
4. Rosa would go out with us provided that we go to a bookstore.
5. And I would take the car to a garage if someone would tell me where there's a good mechanic.

G. Translate the following dialogue into English.

1. —¿Por qué no vamos a ver el partido de baloncesto?
2. —De acuerdo, con tal de que haya más boletos.
3. —No te preocupes. Ayer le pedí a mi hermano que me comprara dos boletos.
4. —Hiciste muy bien. Dicen que Armando Gómez se rompió el brazo y que no va a poder jugar.
5. —Sí, ¡qué mala noticia! Y no hay otro que juegue tan bien como él.
6. —¿Sabes? No sé si nuestro equipo podrá ganar el partido sin Gómez.

H. *Reading passage.* The following passage will introduce you to some important places in Puerto Rico as seen through the travel plans of an American businessman who is working there.

Cognates are marked with a raised degree sign (°). New words in the passage are listed below. Study them until you can give the English equivalent for each Spanish word or phrase. After reading the passage, do the comprehension exercise that follows it.

alquilar to rent	el **líder** leader
la **apertura** opening	la **pelea de gallos** cockfight
el **baile flamenco** Flamenco dancing	el **plan: en plan de** intending to, with X in mind
la **cordillera** mountain range	
cuyo whose	el **político** politician
defenderse to get along	**recorrer** to travel through
entero whole	**respirar** to breathe
la **fortaleza** fortress	**S.A.** (*Sociedad Anónima*) Inc.
gallístico pertaining to cock-fighting (**el gallo:** *rooster*)	la **vuelta: de vuelta** back
no hacer más que to do nothing but . . .	

Michael Crawford va a Puerto Rico a trabajar

Siempre quería que la compañía para la cual trabajo me mandara a un país de lengua española. Yo estudié español en el colegio y en la universidad y no había nada que me hubiera gustado más que practicarlo en un país de Hispanoamérica. Por fin se realizó mi sueño cuando el presidente de la Compañía Electrónica Smith, S.A., decidió abrir una oficina en Puerto Rico. Porque yo sabía algo de español me destinaron° a la Isla para que yo arreglara todos los asuntos de la apertura. Llegué aquí hace tres meses, pero mi español no ha mejorado mucho. Les voy a contar por qué.

Desde que llegué no he hecho más que hablar de negocios, de aparatos electrónicos° y de instrumentos° científicos. Y he hablado sólo con especialistas° en tecnología y en computación, con políticos y líderes de sindicatos. Aquí toda esta gente de la clase alta tiene que defenderse en inglés porque el inglés

El viejo San Juan es un lugar muy interesante.

en Puerto Rico es una lengua oficial.° Déjenme decirles que ahora me siento cansado y aburrido porque no he visto casi nada de Puerto Rico, ni he practicado mucho el español. Anoche decidí que las cosas no podían seguir así. ¡No me van a ver de vuelta en Washington, D.C. hasta que yo llegue a conocer esta isla! Saldré en plan de turismo en cuanto pueda. Empezaré por hacer una excursión por San Juan este fin de semana. El sábado caminaré por algunos de los barrios de esta hermosísima capital. Visitaré el Viejo San Juan, zona° histórica° cuya arquitectura° española y cuyo ambiente colonial° me interesan mucho. Mientras estoy allí entraré en una de esas discotecas o clubes de baile flamenco. Para el domingo compraré un boleto para el concierto de la Orquesta Sinfónica° de Puerto Rico y quizás vaya a ver también un museo de arte. Si no se presentan muchos problemas en mi trabajo durante la semana, trataré de ir a conocer las afueras de San Juan. A ver si tengo tiempo para conocer la Universidad de Puerto Rico en Río Piedras y conocer algún centro comercial como la Plaza Carolina. Para el otro fin de semana alquilaré un coche, me compraré un mapa y viajaré por el interior° de la Isla. Me encantaría respirar un poco de aire fresco en la Cordillera Central.° Me interesa ver cómo viven los **jíbaros** (los campesinos puertorriqueños) en el campo. La Isla no es tan grande para que en dos días no pueda recorrerla toda. Trataré de conocer Arecibo en el norte donde hay un observatorio° interesante. También iré a ver Ponce, una ciudad importante del sur de Puerto Rico. Me han hablado muy bien del Museo de Arte de Ponce y tengo muchas ganas de verlo.

Sería estupendo si pudiera quedarme en Puerto Rico un año entero. Pero sé que cuando termine mi trabajo aquí—yo calculo que en un mes, como máximo—, mi jefe querrá que yo vuelva a Washington. Pero me he resuelto a conocer a fondo San Juan antes de irme de aquí. Mi lista° de lugares interesantes es larga: la Fortaleza el Morro, los museos, el estadio Hiram Bithorn, el Coliseo° Roberto Clemente y el Coliseo Gallístico donde se pueden ver las peleas de gallos. Y no olvidemos las otras regiones de esta encantadora isla. A ver si con tantas visitas° volveré a Washington hablando español como un hispanoamericano.

COMPREHENSION CHECK

Answer each of the following questions in a complete Spanish sentence.

1. ¿Adónde quería Michael Crawford que su compañía lo mandara?
2. ¿Cómo es que llegó a Puerto Rico?
3. ¿Cuánto tiempo hace que está en Puerto Rico?
4. ¿Con quiénes ha hablado desde que llegó?
5. ¿Qué decide Michael que tiene que hacer antes de volver a Washington?
6. ¿Adónde piensa ir el sábado? ¿Qué verá allí?
7. ¿Qué le gustaría hacer el otro fin de semana?
8. ¿Qué le interesa ver en el campo?
9. ¿A cuáles ciudades tratará de ir? ¿Qué querrá ver en ellas?
10. ¿Qué lugares le gustaría visitar en San Juan?

Appendices ❧

Appendix A

Guide to Spanish Pronunciation and Spelling

Pronunciation

Learning to speak a foreign language requires changing most of the pronunciation habits formed in learning your own language. Because these habits are so ingrained, acquiring acceptable pronunciation of a foreign language requires not only intensive practice but also analysis of the individual sounds—how they are produced and how they compare to those of your own language.

To discuss Spanish sounds and their representation in Spanish spelling certain symbols are used: basic sounds of the language are written between slashes; variants of a sound in certain positions are written between square brackets; and letters used in spelling are in boldface. Note that symbols chosen to transcribe a sound may or may not be the letter that represents it in the Spanish spelling system.

This initial presentation will limit itself to "Standard Spanish" as spoken in Hispanic America, a dialect devoid of regional peculiarities. Important dialect variations will be mentioned in the pronunciation sections of the laboratory manual.

Vowels

Spanish has five simple vowel sounds represented by the letters **a, e, i, o, u.** Listen to your instructor pronounce the following syllables. Notice that the Spanish vowels are shorter and tenser than any stressed vowel in English.

ba	ka	fa	sa	ma
be	ke	fe	se	me
bi	ki	fi	si	mi
bo	ko	fo	so	mo
bu	ku	fu	su	mu

Now repeat each of the above syllables after your instructor. If you compare English *see* and Spanish **si** you will observe that the vowel sound in *see* really consists of two vowels pronounced as one syllable—the vowel of *sit* plus a glide similar to the *y* in *you*: /iy/. Diphthong is the technical term for two vowels pronounced together as a single syllable. The English vowels of the words *bay*, *bow*, *boo* are also diphthongs: /ey/, /ow/, /uw/, respectively. The similarity between Spanish and English diphthongs is limited, however; in Spanish, diphthongs are far less frequent than in English.

Unstressed vowels

In English most unstressed vowels are reduced to a neutral vowel transcribed as /ə/. This is not reflected in English spelling and many pairs of words that are pronounced alike such as *affect / effect* or *accept / except* are spelled differently. Any of the five written vowels may represent /ə/ in English spelling in an unstressed syllable. For example, the vowel of the first syllable of each of the following words is /ə/:

machine   semantic   mirage   corrode   supply

In Spanish the sound /ə/ does not exist. All unstressed syllables have one of the five vowels **a, e, i, o, u.** Differences in unstressed vowels in Spanish not only distinguish countless pairs of words but also signal some of the most fundamental grammatical functions of the language.

Correlated with the reduction of unstressed vowels to /ə/ in English is the shortening of unstressed syllables. In other words, stressed syllables in English take longer to say than unstressed syllables. In Spanish, however, stressed and unstressed syllables are of the same length.

The following Spanish two-syllable words are all stressed on the first syllable. They have the vowel /a/ in both syllables. Repeat each one after your instructor, making sure to pronounce the /a/'s of both syllables alike and to make both syllables of equal length:

mala   sala   saca   sana   fama   mapa   matas

The following Spanish two-syllable words have /e/ in both syllables and are stressed on the first syllable. To pronounce them correctly, concentrate on the following points:

1. Avoid an /ey/ diphthong as in English *pay*.
2. Pronounce the /e/'s of both syllables alike.
3. Make both syllables of equal length.

Repeat after your instructor:

nene   mece   queme   peles   seques   meces

The following two-syllable words have /o/ in both syllables and are stressed on the first syllable. To pronounce them correctly concentrate on the following points:

1. Avoid an /ow/ diphthong as in English *toe.*
2. Pronounce the /o/'s of both syllables alike.
3. Make both syllables of equal length.

Repeat after your instructor:

como   loco   polo   lomos   monos   bonos

Now practive the following pairs of words. The members of each pair are distinguished solely by differences in the unstressed vowels.

a:o	coma / como		a:e	santón / sentón
	famosas / famosos			facundo / fecundo
	meta / meto			andino / endino
a:o	manita / monita		e:i	pesó / pisó
	tantito / tontito			delatan / dilatan
	morena / moreno			case / casi
a:e	tómala / tómela		o:u	dorado / durado
	cómalo / cómelo			fondón / fundón
	métalos / mételos			goloso / guloso
a:e	toma / tome			
	caminas / camines			
	alemanas / alemanes			

Consonants

b, v, d, g   The Spanish letters **b, v (b / v** have the same sounds in Spanish), **d,** and **g** (spelled **gu** before **e** and **i**) sound different depending on their position in a word or sentence. After a pause and after **m** or **n,** Spanish **b, v, d,** and **g** represent sounds similar to those corresponding to English *b, d,* and *g* as in *boy, does,* and *go.*

NOTE: Spanish /d/, however, is produced with the tip of the tongue touching the back of the upper teeth rather than the gum ridge above them as in English.

Repeat the following words after your instructor:

base	bote	vaso	ambos	bomba	envase
dote	dones	dime	donde	anda	conde
gasto	goza	gala	hongo	ganga	tango

We can call these versions of Spanish /b/, /d/, /g/ the hard variants of the sounds and transcribe them in square brackets thus: [b], [d], [g]. Note that [d] is also used after / l /:

falda   molde   balde   caldo

In all other positions **b, v, g, d** represent the soft variants of [b], [d], [g], which are transcribed as [ƀ], [đ], [ǥ].

[ƀ] is produced by forcing air through slightly parted lips.

    coba   cavamos   lobo   sabes   lavas   levante

[đ] is pronounced similarly to the *th* in *rather, father, other* but with much less friction.

    lodo   mida   podemos   comida   nudo

[ǥ] is produced similarly to [g] except that air is forced through a very narrow opening between the back of the tongue and the soft palate (back of the roof of the mouth).

    pago   digo   sigamos   agua   laguna

The soft variants [ƀ], [đ], [ǥ] are used between vowels even when the vowels are in two different words:

    yo bato   yo doy   yo gasto
    la boca   la dama   la gota

r   The sound represented by **r** in Spanish spelling is completely different from the one represented by *r* in English spelling. It consists of a single flap made by a rapid tap of the tongue against the gum ridge above the upper teeth. A similar sound exists in English and is represented in English spelling by *t, d, tt, dd* between vowels (where the first vowel is stressed):

    later   spider   batter   ladder

Repeat the following words after your instructor being careful to use a flap similar to the one appearing in the above English words:

    cara   mero   poro   toro   cura   lira

The flap occurring after an unstressed vowel is harder for English speakers to produce:

    pirata   paré   morimos   directo

This single flap /r/ is also used after consonants (written **r**). English speakers should pronounce *d*, not *r*, in pronouncing these consonant groups:

    preso   traste   cromo   grande   bravo   drama   frota

Spanish also has a multiple flap consonant /rr/ represented at the beginning of words by **r** and between vowels as **rr.** This sound consists of two or more flaps of the tongue against the upper gum ridge and does not exist in English. Repeat the following words after your instructor:

    carro   forro   cerro   Pirro   amarramos
    ropa   ramo   reto   rico   ruso

Before another consonant or at the end of a word the letter **r** may be pronounced either /r/ or /rr/, depending on the speaker. Repeat the following words after your instructor:

| puerta | corto | carpa | tomar | meter | ser |

j   In Spanish spelling the letter **j** and the letter **g** before **e, i** (but not before **a, o, u** or a consonant), represents a sound that does not exist in English. It is produced by forcing air through a narrow opening between the arched back of the tongue and the soft palate. Repeat the following words after your instructor:

jota	jefe	gente	gime	jale
lijo	moja	ajo	teje	caja
lijar	mojar	ají	tejer	cajera

ll, y   For a majority of speakers of Spanish both **ll** and **y** represent the sound /y/. This sound is considerably tenser than the first sound in English *yes*. English speakers must pay special attention to /y/, especially when it occurs between vowels. Repeat the following words after your instructor:

| llamo | hallo | boya | sello | rayo | yeso |

l   Spanish **l** is pronounced very much like the /l/ sound in English *leak, less*. In contrast to English, Spanish /l/ is pronounced the same at the end of a word as at the beginning.

| lata | lema | liso | losa | luna |
| cal | hiel | Gil | col | tul |

p, t, k   The sounds /p/, /t/, /k/ before stressed vowels differ from their closest English counterparts by being unaspirated. This term refers to the absence of the puff of air that follows these sounds in English.

Note also that English /t/ is made by touching the gum ridge above the upper teeth; for Spanish /t/ the tip of the tongue touches the back of the upper teeth.

In Spanish /k/ is spelled **qu** before **e** and **i** but **c** elsewhere. Repeat the following words after your instructor:

panes	pozo	plano	pica	prado
tapa	teme	tripas	tiza	tope
cama	queso	quise	clase	creo

s   For all Spanish Americans and for Spaniards in southern Spain the letters **s, z** and **c** (before **e** and **i**) represent a sound similar to the one represented by *s* in English *sale, so, see*. Repeat the following words after your instructor:

| sala | posa | rosas | comes | cinco | cacería |
| mozo | luz | luces | haces | zapato | zurdo |

f, m, n, ch   These letters and combination of letters in Spanish represent sounds similar to their English counterparts. Some examples:

    feo   rifa   mono   lima   nariz   zona   chato   techo

ñ The mark above the **n** is called a **tilde.** This letter represents a sound similar to the one written *ni* in English *onion.* However, in English the /n/ and the /y/ are pronounced in different syllables; in Spanish the /ny/ goes with the following vowel. This letter is rare in initial position.

    uña   daño   mañas   riñcn   ñame

h In Spanish spelling **h** represents no sound—it is a "silent" letter as in English *honor.* Repeat the following words after your instructor:

    hablo   haber   han   historia   hombre   humano

Spelling

The Spanish Alphabet

a	a	**j**	jota	**r**	ere
b	be *or* be larga	**k**	ka	**rr**	erre
c	ce	**l**	ele	**s**	ese
ch	che	**ll**	elle	**t**	te
d	de	**m**	eme	**u**	u
e	e	**n**	ene	**v**	uve, ve, ve corta
f	efe	**ñ**	eñe	**w**	doble ve
g	ge	**o**	o	**x**	equis
h	hache	**p**	pe	**y**	i griega
i	i	**q**	cu	**z**	zeta

Note the **ch, ll, ñ** are separate letters of the alphabet and receive their own sections in dictionaries. In non-initial position they are also treated as separate letters.

Syllabification

A syllable in Spanish may consist of a single vowel, a diphthong or a vowel or diphthong plus preceding and following consonants.

  1. A single consonant between vowels goes with the following vowel:

    rei-na   a-mo   ma-tan   cau-sas   te-mi-do

  2. Groups of two consonants that can begin a word **(p, t, c, b, d, g, f + l** or **r)** go with the following vowel in syllabification:

    co-pla   ha-blo   sue-gra   pa-dre   co-fre

  3. Other groups of two consonants are divided:

him-no	es-ta	mun-do	fal-ta	sor-do

4. Groups of three consonants are divided according to rules 2 and 3. When the last two consonants of the three form one of the groups mentioned in rule 2 they both go with the following vowel:

ram-bla	ham-bre	con-tra	san-gre	as-tro

If the last two consonants of a three-consonant cluster do not form one of the groups in rule 2 the third consonant goes with the following vowel:

cons-ta	trans-ferir	trans-porte

Accentuation

1. Spanish words ending in a vowel, **-n** or **-s** are stressed on the next to last syllable:

tri**s**te	ha**b**lan	e**s**criben	señoritas	provin**c**ias

2. Spanish words ending in a consonant other than **-n** or **-s** (usually **-d, -l, -z, -r**) are stressed on the last syllable:

a**z**ul	Portugal	Brasil	hotel	terminar	señor	usted

3. When **i** or **u** precedes or follows **a, e** or **o,** the two vowels are pronounced as one syllable:

estud**io**	s**ie**te	cienc**ia**	limp**io**
s**ei**s	c**ua**ndo	esc**ue**la	resta**u**rante

NOTE: Combinations of **a, e** and **o** form two syllables, not one.

tarea	museo	maestro	preocupado	desea

4. A written accent mark is required in Spanish when the stress of a word violates one of the above rules.

alemán	inglés	Canadá	está	cafés	Sánchez
sábado	jóvenes	miércoles	exámenes	médico	Méndez

NOTE: In the following words the combination of **i** + **a** or **o** forms two syllables, not one as in rule 3. A written accent is therefore placed over the **i:**

día	tío	tía	filosofía	García	geografía

5. Words that are spelled the same but have different meanings are distinguished in writing by a written accent mark:

él	he, him	**tú**	you (*familiar*)	**más**	more
el	the	**tu**	your	**mas**	but
mí	me	**sí**	yes		
mi	my	**si**	if		

Punctuation and Capitalization

1. Spanish questions are written with an inverted question mark (¿) at the beginning and a regular question mark (?) at the end of the sentence:

   ¿Habla usted español?   *Do you speak Spanish?*

2. Exclamations in Spanish begin with an inverted exclamation point (¡) and end with a regular exclamation point (!):

   ¡Qué lata!   *What a bore!*

3. Interrogative words in Spanish are written with an accent mark:

   ¿Quién? *Who?*   ¿Qué? *What?*
   ¿Cuándo? *When?*   ¿Dónde? *Where?*

4. Languages, nationalities, days of the week and months of the year are written with a small letter in Spanish rather than with a capital as in English:

   italiano *Italian*   lunes *Monday*
   americano *American*   junio *June*

5. The Spanish subject pronoun **yo,** *I* is written with a small letter when not the first word in a sentence.

6. **Usted** and **ustedes** are often abbreviated in writing as **Ud.** and **Uds.**

Appendix B

Verbs

Regular Verbs

	-ar	-er	-ir
INFINITIVE	cantar	comer	recibir
PRESENT PARTICIPLE	cantando	comiendo	recibiendo
PAST PARTICIPLE	cantado	comido	recibido

Simple tenses

Indicative mood

PRESENT	canto	como	recibo
	cantas	comes	recibes
	canta	come	recibe
	cantamos	comemos	recibimos
	cantáis	coméis	recibís
	cantan	comen	reciben
IMPERFECT	cantaba	comía	recibía
	cantabas	comías	recibías
	cantaba	comía	recibía
	cantábamos	comíamos	recibíamos
	cantabais	comíais	recibíais
	cantaban	comían	recibían
PRETERIT	canté	comí	recibí
	cantaste	comiste	recibiste
	cantó	comió	recibió
	cantamos	comimos	recibimos
	cantasteis	comisteis	recibisteis
	cantaron	comieron	recibieron

FUTURE	cantaré	comeré	recibiré
	cantarás	comerás	recibirás
	cantará	comerá	recibirá
	cantaremos	comeremos	recibiremos
	cantaréis	comeréis	recibiréis
	cantarán	comerán	recibirán
CONDITIONAL	cantaría	comería	recibiría
	cantarías	comerías	recibirías
	cantaría	comería	recibiría
	cantaríamos	comeríamos	recibiríamos
	cantaríais	comeríais	recibiríais
	cantarían	comerían	recibirían

Subjunctive mood

PRESENT	cante	coma	reciba
	cantes	comas	recibas
	cante	coma	reciba
	cantemos	comamos	recibamos
	cantéis	comáis	recibáis
	canten	coman	reciban
IMPERFECT (**-ra**)	cantara	comiera	recibiera
	cantaras	comieras	recibieras
	cantara	comiera	recibiera
	cantáramos	comiéramos	recibiéramos
	cantarais	comierais	recibierais
	cantaran	comieran	recibieran
IMPERFECT (**-se**)	cantase	comiese	recibiese
	cantases	comieses	recibieses
	cantase	comiese	recibiese
	cantásemos	comiésemos	recibiésemos
	cantaseis	comieseis	recibieseis
	cantasen	comiesen	recibiesen

Imperative mood

(tú)	canta	come	recibe
(Ud.)	cante	coma	reciba
(nosotros)	cantemos	comamos	recibamos
(vosotros)	cantad	comed	recibid
(Uds.)	canten	coman	reciban

Compound tenses

Indicative mood

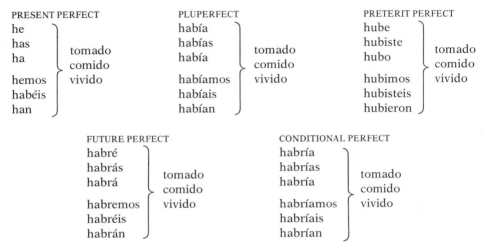

PRESENT PERFECT

he
has
ha
hemos
habéis
han

tomado
comido
vivido

PLUPERFECT

había
habías
había
habíamos
habíais
habían

tomado
comido
vivido

PRETERIT PERFECT

hube
hubiste
hubo
hubimos
hubisteis
hubieron

tomado
comido
vivido

FUTURE PERFECT

habré
habrás
habrá
habremos
habréis
habrán

tomado
comido
vivido

CONDITIONAL PERFECT

habría
habrías
habría
habríamos
habríais
habrían

tomado
comido
vivido

Subjunctive Mood

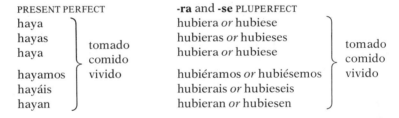

PRESENT PERFECT

haya
hayas
haya
hayamos
hayáis
hayan

tomado
comido
vivido

-ra and **-se** PLUPERFECT

hubiera *or* hubiese
hubieras *or* hubieses
hubiera *or* hubiese
hubiéramos *or* hubiésemos
hubierais *or* hubieseis
hubieran *or* hubiesen

tomado
comido
vivido

Verbs with Changes in the Vowel of the Stem

1. Stem-changing verbs of the **-a-** and **-e-** classes show changes in the vowel of the stem *only* in forms where the stress falls on the stem. The changes occur in the present indicative, present subjunctive and imperative (commands) in all persons except **nosotros** and **vosotros**. There are no changes in the vowel of the stem in any of the other tenses. The two types of stem-vowel modifications that occur in **-a-** and **-e-** class verbs are: **e → ie** and **o → ue.**

Sample conjugations:

pensar (e → ie)   *to think*
PRES. IND.:   pienso, piensas, piensa, pensamos, penséis, piensan
PRES. SUBJ.:   piense, pienses, piense, pensemos, penséis, piensen
IMPERATIVE: _____, piensa, piense, pensemos, pensad, piensen

Other tenses and forms present no changes in the vowel of the stem.

Like **pensar: comenzar, despertar(se), empezar, sentarse.**

entender (e → ie)   *to understand*
PRES. IND.:   entiendo, entiendes, entiende, entendemos, entendéis, entienden
PRES. SUBJ.:   entienda, entiendas, entienda, entendamos, entendáis, entiendan
IMPERATIVE: _____, entiende, entienda, entendamos, entended, entiendan

Other tenses and forms present no changes in the vowel of the stem.

Like **entender: perder, querer** (irreg. pret.).

recordar (o → ue)   *to remember*
PRES. IND.:   recuerdo, recuerdas, recuerda, recordamos, recordáis, recuerdan
PRES. SUBJ.:   recuerde, recuerdes, recuerde, recordemos, recordéis, recuerden
IMPERATIVE: _____, recuerda, recuerde, recordemos, recordad, recuerden

Other tenses and forms present no changes in the vowel of the stem.

Like **recordar: acordarse, acostar(se), almorzar, costar, encontrar, probar.**
Note: **jugar** changes **u → ue**

volver (o → ue)   *to go back*
PRES. IND.:   vuelvo, vuelves, vuelve, volvemos, volvéis, vuelven
PRES. SUBJ.:   vuelva, vuelvas, vuelva, volvamos, volváis, vuelvan
IMPERATIVE: _____, vuelve, vuelva, volvamos, volved, vuelvan

Other tenses and forms present no changes in the vowel of the stem.

Like **volver: doler, poder** (irreg. pret. and **-ndo** form).

2. Stem-changing verbs of the **-i-** class have three types of possible changes in the vowel of the stem: **e → ie, e → i, o → ue.** These verbs of the **-i-** class have the changes in the vowel of the stem in all persons of the present indicative (except **nosotros** and **vosotros**).

In addition to the expected changes in the present subjunctive and imperative, verbs having the change **e → ie** and **e → i** have **i** as the stem vowel and verbs having the change **o → ue** have **u** as the stem vowel in the following forms:

1. the **nosotros** and **vosotros** forms of the present subjunctive
2. the **nosotros** command and the negative **vosotros** command (taken from the present subjunctive)
3. the third person singular and third person plural forms of the preterit
4. all persons of the imperfect subjunctive—both **-ra** and **-se** versions—(based on the third person plural preterit form)
5. the **-ndo** form

Sample conjugations:

preferir (e → ie)   *to prefer*
PRES. IND.:   prefiero, prefieres, prefiere, preferimos, preferís, prefieren
PRES. SUBJ.:   prefiera, prefieras, prefiera, prefiramos, prefiráis, prefieran
IMPERATIVE: _____, prefiere, prefiera, prefiramos, preferid, prefieran
PRETERIT: preferí, preferiste, prefirió, preferimos, preferisteis, prefirieron

IMP. SUBJ.:   prefiriera (prefiriese), prefirieras, prefiriera, prefiriéramos, prefirierais, prefirieran
PRES. PART.:   (**-ndo** form) prefiriendo

Other tenses and forms present no changes in the vowel of the stem.

Like **preferir: convertir(se), divertirse, invertir, sentir.**

pedir (e → i)   *to ask for*
PRES. IND.:   pido, pides, pide, pedimos, pedís, piden
PRES. SUBJ.:   pida, pidas, pida, pidamos, pidáis, pidan
IMPERATIVE: _____, pide, pida, pidamos, pedid, pidan
PRETERIT: pedí, pediste, pidió, pedimos, pedísteis, pidieron
IMP. SUBJ.:   pidiera (pidiese), pidieras, pidiera, pidiéramos, pidierais, pidieran
PRES. PART.:   (**-ndo** form): pidiendo

Other tenses and forms present no changes in the vowel of the stem.

Like **pedir: conseguir, impedir, seguir, servir, vestir(se).**

dormir (o → ue)   *to sleep*
PRES. IND.:   duermo, duermes, duerme, dormimos, dormís, duermen
PRES. SUBJ.:   duerma, duermas, duerma, durmamos, durmáis, duerman
IMPERATIVE: _____, duerme, duerma, durmamos, dormid, duerman
PRETERIT: dormí, dormiste, durmió, dormimos, dormisteis, durmieron
IMP. SUBJ.:   durmiera (durmiese), durmieras, durmiera, durmiéramos, durmierais, durmieran
PRES. PART.:   (**-ndo** form): durmiendo

Other tenses and forms present no changes in the vowel of the stem.

Like **dormir: morir.**

Orthographic-Changing Verbs

Verbs that have stems ending in the letters *c, g, z* and *j* undergo spelling changes in certain tenses of the indicative and subjunctive moods (*indicative*: present and preterit; *subjunctive*: present, past) and in the imperative. These verbs are regular in the spoken language and the changes refer only to the written language.[1]

1. Verbs ending in **-car (c → qu** before **e)**
    The change occurs in the first-person singular in the preterit, in all persons in the present subjunctive and in command forms derived from the present subjunctive.

---

[1]See Lesson 7, Structure 8 and Lesson 11, Structure 6 for a complete discussion of spelling changes.

explicar   *to explain*
PRETERIT: expliqué, explicaste, explicó, explicamos, explicasteis, explicaron
PRES. SUBJ.:   explique, expliques, explique, expliquemos, expliquéis, expliquen

Other verbs with this change: **buscar, chocar, dedicarse, sacar, tocar.**

2. Verbs ending in **-gar (g → gu** before **e)**
The change occurs in the first-person singular in the preterit, in all persons in the present subjunctive and in command forms derived from the present subjunctive.

pagar   *to pay*
PRETERIT: pagué, pagaste, pagó, pagamos, pagasteis, pagaron
PRES. SUBJ.:   pague, pagues, pague, paguemos, paguéis, paguen

Other verbs with this change: **apagar, colgar, entregar, jugar, llegar.**

3. Verbs ending in **-zar (z → c** before **e)**
The change occurs in the first-person singular in the preterit, in all persons in the present subjunctive and in command forms derived from the present subjunctive.

realizar   *to achieve, attain*
PRETERIT: realicé, realizaste, realizó, realizamos, realizasteis, realizaron
PRES. SUBJ.:   realice, realices, realice, realicemos, realicéis, realicen

Other verbs with this change: **almorzar, comenzar, empezar.**

4. Verbs ending in **-ger** and **-gir (g → j** before **a** and **o)**
The change occurs in the first-person singular in the present indicative, in all persons in the present subjunctive and in command forms derived from the present subjunctive.

recoger   *to pick (crops)*
PRES. IND.:   recojo, recoges, recoge, recogemos, recogéis, recogen
PRES. SUBJ.:   recoja, recojas, recoja, recojamos, recojáis, recojan

exigir   *to demand*
PRES. IND.:   exijo, exiges, exige, exigimos, exigís, exigen
PRES. SUBJ.:   exija, exijas, exija, exijamos, exijáis, exijan

Other verbs with this change: **coger, escoger.**

5. Verbs ending in **-guir (gu → g** before **a** and **o)**
The change occurs in the first-person singular in the present indicative, in all persons in the present subjunctive and in command forms derived from the present subjunctive.

seguir   *to follow*
PRES. IND.:   sigo, sigues, sigue, seguimos, seguís, siguen
PRES. SUBJ.:   siga, sigas, siga, sigamos, sigáis, sigan

Conseguir also has this change.

6. Verbs ending in **e + er** (unstressed **i → y**)
The change occurs in the third-person singular and plural in the preterit, in all persons in the past subjunctive and in the present participle.

creer   *to believe*

PRET.:   créi, creíste, creyó, creímos, creísteis, creyeron
PAST SUBJ.:   creyera (creyese), creyeras, creyera, creyéramos, creyerais, creyeran
PRES. PART.:   creyendo

Leer also has this change.

Irregular Verbs

Note that verbs ending in a vowel + **cer** or **cir** have a change of **c** → **zc** before **a** and **o**. The change occurs in the first-person singular in the present indicative, in all persons in the present subjunctive and in command forms derived from the present subjunctive.

conocer   *to know*

PRES. IND.:   conozco, conoces, conoce, conocemos, conocéis, conocen
PRES. SUBJ.:   conozca, conozcas, conozca, conozcamos, conozcáis, conozcan

Ofrecer and **producir** also show this change.

Common Irregular Verbs[1]

andar   *to walk*

PRETERIT: anduve, anduviste, anduvo, anduvimos, anduvisteis, anduvieron
PAST SUBJ.:   anduviera (anduviese), anduvieras, anduviera, anduviéramos,
                      anduvierais, anduvieran

caer   *to fall*

PRES. IND.:   caigo, caes, cae, caemos, caéis, caen
PRETERIT.:   caí, caíste, cayó, caímos, caísteis, cayeron
IMPERATIVE: cae, caiga, caigamos, caed, caigan
PRES. SUBJ.:   caiga, caigas, caiga, caigamos, caigáis, caigan
PAST SUBJ.:   cayera (cayese), cayeras, cayera, cayéramos, cayerais, cayeran
PAST PART.:   caído

dar   *to give*

PRES. IND.:   doy, das, da, damos, dais, dan
PRETERIT: di, diste, dio, dimos, disteis, dieron
IMPERATIVE: da, dé, demos, dad, den
PRES. SUBJ.:   dé, des, dé, demos, deis, den
PAST SUBJ.:   diera (diese), dieras, diera, diéramos, dierais, dieran

decir   *to say, tell*

PRES. IND.:   digo, dices, dice, decimos, decís, dicen
PRETERIT: dije, dijiste, dijo, dijimos, dijisteis, dijeron
FUTURE: diré, dirás, dirá, diremos, diréis, dirán

---

[1]Only those tenses with irregularities will be indicated.

CONDITIONAL: diría, dirías, diría, diríamos, diríais, dirían
IMPERATIVE: di, diga, digamos, decid, digan
PRES. SUBJ.:   diga, digas, diga, digamos, digáis, digan
PAST SUBJ.:   dijera (dijese), dijeras, dijera, dijéramos, dijerais, dijeran
PRES. PART.:   diciendo
PAST PART.:   dicho

estar   *to be*

PRES. IND.   estoy, estás, está, estamos, estáis, están
PRETERIT: estuve, estuviste, estuvo, estuvimos, estuvisteis, estuvieron
IMPERATIVE: está, esté, estemos, estad, estén
PRES. SUBJ.:   esté, estés, esté, estemos, estéis, estén
PAST SUBJ.:   estuviera (estuviese), estuvieras, estuviera, estuviéramos, estuvierais, estuvieran

haber   *to have* (auxiliary)

PRES. IND.:   he, has, ha, hemos, habéis, han
PRETERIT: hube, hubiste, hubo, hubimos, hubisteis, hubieron
FUTURE: habré, habrás, habrá, habremos, habréis, habrán
CONDITIONAL: habría, habrías, habría, habríamos, habríais, habrían
IMPERATIVE: he, haya, hayamos, habed, hayan
PRES. SUBJ.:   haya, hayas, haya, hayamos, hayáis, hayan
PAST SUBJ.:   hubiera (hubiese), hubieras, hubiera, hubiéramos, hubierais, hubieran

hacer   *to do, make*

PRES. IND.:   hago, haces, hace, hacemos, hacéis, hacen
PRETERIT: hice, hiciste, hizo, hicimos, hicisteis, hicieron
FUTURE: haré, harás, hará, haremos, haréis, harán
CONDITIONAL: haría, harías, haría, haríamos, haríais, harían
IMPERATIVE: haz, haga, hagamos, haced, hagan
PRES. SUBJ.:   haga, hagas, haga, hagamos, hagáis, hagan
PAST SUBJ.:   hiciera (hiciese), hicieras, hiciera, hiciéramos, hicierais, hicieran
PAST PART.:   hecho

ir   *to go*

PRES. IND.:   voy, vas, va, vamos, vais, van
IMP. IND.:   iba, ibas, iba, íbamos, ibais, iban
PRETERIT: fui, fuiste, fue, fuimos, fuisteis, fueron
IMPERATIVE: ve, vaya, vayamos, id, vayan
PRES. SUBJ.:   vaya, vayas, vaya, vayamos, vayáis, vayan
PAST SUBJ.:   fuera (fuese), fueras, fuera, fuéramos, fuerais, fueran

oír   *to hear*

PRES. IND.:   oigo, oyes, oye, oímos, oís, oyen
PRETERIT: oí, oíste, oyó, oímos, oísteis, oyeron
IMPERATIVE: oye, oiga, oigamos, oíd, oigan

PRES. SUBJ.: oiga, oigas, oiga, oigamos, oigáis, oigan
PAST SUBJ.: oyera (oyese), oyeras, oyera, oyéramos, oyerais, oyeran
PRES. PART.: oyendo
PAST PART.: oído

poder   *to be able*

PRES. IND.: puedo, puedes, puede, podemos, podéis, pueden
PRETERIT: pude, pudiste, pudo, pudimos, pudisteis, pudieron
FUTURE: podré, podrás, podrá, podremos, podréis, podrán
CONDITIONAL: podría, podrías, podría, podríamos, podríais, podrían
IMPERATIVE: puede, pueda, podamos, poded, puedan
PRES. SUBJ.: pueda, puedas, pueda, podamos, podáis, puedan
PAST SUBJ.: pudiera (pudiese), pudieras, pudiera, pudiéramos, pudierais, pudieran
PRES. PART.: pudiendo

poner   *to put*

PRES. IND.: pongo, pones, pone, ponemos, ponéis, ponen
PRETERIT: puse, pusiste, puso, pusimos, pusisteis, pusieron
FUTURE: pondré, pondrás, pondrá, pondremos, pondréis, pondrán
CONDITIONAL: pondría, pondrías, pondría, pondríamos, pondríais, pondrían
IMPERATIVE: pon, ponga, pongamos, poned, pongan
PRES. SUBJ.: ponga, pongas, ponga, pongamos, pongáis, pongan
PAST SUBJ.: pusiera (pusiese), pusieras, pusiera, pusiéramos, pusierais, pusieran
PAST. PART.: puesto

producir   *to produce*

PRES. IND.: produzco, produces, produce, producimos, producís, producen
PRETERIT: produje, produjiste, produjo, produjimos, produjisteis, produjeron
IMPERATIVE: produce, produzca, produzcamos, producid, produzcan
PRES. SUBJ.: produzca, produzcas, produzca, produzcamos, produzcáis, produzcan
PAST SUBJ.: produjera (produjese), produjeras, produjera, produjéramos, produjerais, produjeran

querer   *to want, love*

PRES. IND.: quiero, quieres, quiere, queremos, queréis, quieren
PRETERIT: quise, quisiste, quiso, quisimos, quisisteis, quisieron
FUTURE: querré, querrás, querrá, querremos, querréis, querrán
CONDITIONAL: querría, querrías, querría, querríamos, querríais, querrían
IMPERATIVE: quiere, quiera, queramos, quered, quieran
PRES. SUBJ.: quiera, quieras, quiera, queramos, queráis, quieran
PAST SUBJ.: quisiera (quisiese), quisieras, quisiera, quisiéramos, quisierais, quisieran

saber   *to know*

PRES. IND.: sé, sabes, sabe, sabemos, sabéis, saben
PRETERIT: supe, supiste, supo, supimos, supisteis, supieron
FUTURE: sabré, sabrás, sabrá, sabremos, sabréis, sabrán

CONDITIONAL: sabría, sabrías, sabría, sabríamos, sabríais, sabrían
IMPERATIVE: sabe, sepa, sepamos, sabed, sepan
PRES. SUBJ.: sepa, sepas, sepa, sepamos, sepáis, sepan
PAST SUBJ.: supiera (supiese), supieras, supiera, supiéramos, supierais, supieran

salir   *to leave, go out*

PRES. IND.: salgo, sales, sale, salimos, salís, salen
FUTURE: saldré, saldrás, saldrá, saldremos, saldréis, saldrán
CONDITIONAL: saldría, saldrías, saldría, saldríamos, saldríais, saldrían
IMPERATIVE: sal, salga, salgamos, salid, salgan
PRES. SUBJ.: salga, salgas, salga, salgamos, salgáis, salgan

ser   *to be*

PRES. IND.: soy, eres, es, somos, sois, son
PRETERIT: fui, fuiste, fue, fuimos, fuisteis, fueron
IMPERFECT IND.: era, eras, era, éramos, erais, eran
IMPERATIVE: sé, sea, seamos, sed, sean
PRES. SUBJ.: sea, seas, sea, seamos, seáis, sean
PAST SUBJ.: fuera (fuese), fueras, fuera, fuéramos, fuerais, fueran

tener   *to have* (compounds like **mantener**, *to maintain, support,* are conjugated like **tener**)

PRES. IND.: tengo, tienes, tiene, tenemos, tenéis, tienen
PRETERIT: tuve, tuviste, tuvo, tuvimos, tuvisteis, tuvieron
FUTURE: tendré, tendrás, tendrá, tendremos, tendréis, tendrán
CONDITIONAL: tendría, tendrías, tendría, tendríamos, tendríais, tendrían
IMPERATIVE: ten, tenga, tengamos, tened, tengan
PRES. SUBJ.: tenga, tengas, tenga, tengamos, tengáis, tengan
PAST SUBJ.: tuviera (tuviese), tuvieras, tuviera, tuviéramos, tuvierais, tuvieran

traer   *to bring*

PRES. IND.: traigo, traes, trae, traemos, traéis, traen
PRETERIT: traje, trajiste, trajo, trajimos, trajisteis, trajeron
IMPERATIVE: trae, traiga, traigamos, traed, traigan
PRES. SUBJ.: traiga, traigas, traiga, traigamos, traigáis, traigan
PAST SUBJ.: trajera (trajese), trajeras, trajera, trajéramos, trajerais, trajeran
PRES. PART.: trayendo
PAST PART.: traído

valer   *to be worth*

PRES. IND.: valgo, vales, vale, valemos, valéis, valen
FUTURE: valdré, valdrás, valdrá, valdremos, valdréis, valdrán
CONDITIONAL: valdría, valdrías, valdría, valdríamos, valdríais, valdrían
IMPERATIVE: vale, valga, valgamos, valed, valgan
PRES. SUBJ.: valga, valgas, valga, valgamos, valgáis, valgan

venir *to come*

PRES. IND.:	vengo, vienes, viene, venimos, venís, vienen
PRETERIT:	vine, viniste, vino, vinimos, vinisteis, vinieron
FUTURE:	vendré, vendrás, vendrá, vendremos, vendréis, vendrán
CONDITIONAL:	vendría, vendrías, vendría, vendríamos, vendríais, vendrían
IMPERATIVE:	ven, venga, vengamos, venid, vengan
PRES. SUBJ.:	venga, vengas, venga, vengamos, vengáis, vengan
PAST SUBJ.:	viniera (viniese), vinieras, viniera, viniéramos, vinierais, vinieran
PRES. PART.:	viniendo

ver *to see*

PRES. IND.:	veo, ves, ve, vemos, veis, ven
PRETERIT:	vi, viste, vio, vimos, visteis, vieron
IMPERFECT IND.:	veía, veías, veía, veíamos, veíais, veían
IMPERATIVE:	ve, vea, veamos, ved, vean
PRES. SUBJ.:	vea, veas, vea, veamos, veáis, vean
PAST SUBJ.:	viera (viese), vieras, viera, viéramos, vierais, vieran
PAST PART.:	visto

Appendix C

Maps

La América del Sur

México

La América Central y las Antillas

España y Portugal

MAR CARIBE

OCÉANO ATLÁNTICO

Barranquilla
Cartagena
Maracaibo
Caracas
TRINIDAD
Puerto España

VENEZUELA
R. Orinoco
GUAYANA
Georgetown
SURINAM
Paramaribo
GUAYANA FRAN.
Cayenne

Medellín
Bogotá
COLOMBIA
Cali

Quito
ECUADOR
Guayaquil
Iquitos

Ecuador

Manaus
R. Amazonas
Belem

CORDILLERA DE LOS ANDES

R. Madeira

B R A S I L

Recife

PERÚ

Lima
Machu Picchu
Cuzco
L. Titicaca
BOLIVIA
La Paz
Sucre

Arequipa
Arica
Iquique

Salvador

Brasília

Belo Horizonte

PARAGUAY

Rio de Janeiro

Antofagasta
Asunción
São Paulo
Santos

Trópico de Capricornio

Tucumán

CHILE

OCÉANO PACÍFICO

Córdoba
R. Paraná
Rosario
Porto Alegre

Valparaíso
Mendoza
URUGUAY

Santiago
Buenos
Aires
Montevideo

A R G E N T I N A

La Plata
Río de la Plata

Concepción
Bahía Blanca

CORDILLERA DE LOS ANDES

Puerto Montt

0   1000 mi.
0   1600 km.

Islas
Malvinas

Punta Arenas
Estrecho de
Magallanes

Tierra del
Fuego
Cabo de
Hornos

La América del Sur

SANDERSON

314

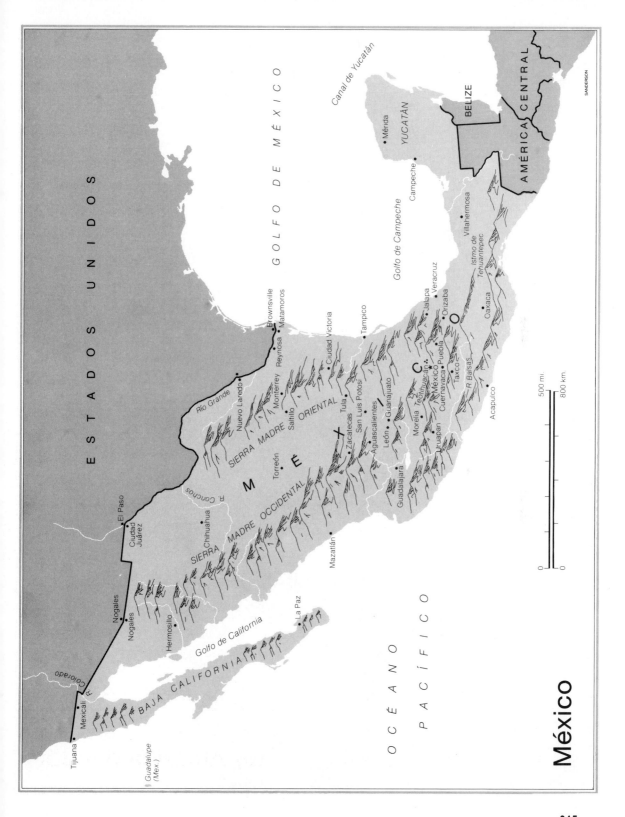

ESTADOS UNIDOS

Tijuana
Mexicali
R. Colorado
Nogales
Nogales
El Paso
Ciudad Juárez
R. Conchos
Chihuahua
Hermosillo
Guadalupe (Mex.)

BAJA CALIFORNIA

Golfo de California

La Paz

Mazatlán

SIERRA MADRE OCCIDENTAL

Torreón

SIERRA MADRE ORIENTAL

Saltillo
Monterrey
Nuevo Laredo
Río Grande

Reynosa
Matamoros
Brownsville

GOLFO DE MÉXICO

Ciudad Victoria
Tampico

San Luis Potosí
Zacatecas
Aguascalientes
Tula
León
Guanajuato
Guadalajara
Morelia
Uruapan
Teotihuacán
México
Cuernavaca
Puebla
Taxco
Acapulco
R. Balsas
Jalapa
Veracruz
Orizaba
Oaxaca
Villahermosa
Istmo de Tehuantepec
Golfo de Campeche
Campeche
Mérida
YUCATÁN
Canal de Yucatán

BELIZE

AMÉRICA CENTRAL

SANDERSON

MÉXICO

OCÉANO PACÍFICO

500 mi.
800 km.

México

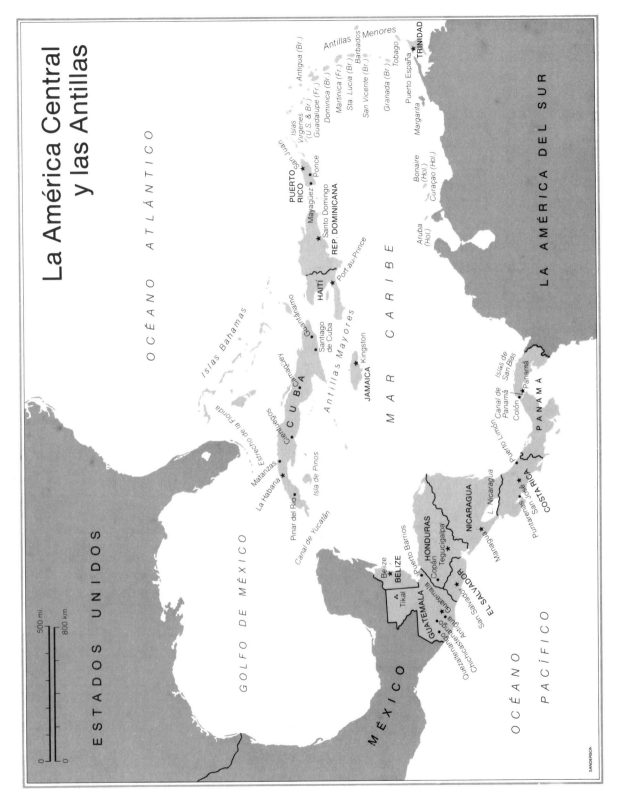

La América Central y las Antillas

ESTADOS UNIDOS

OCÉANO ATLÁNTICO

GOLFO DE MÉXICO

MÉXICO

500 mi.
800 km.

Estrecho de la Florida

Islas Bahamas

Pinar del Río
La Habana
Matanzas
Cienfuegos
CUBA
Isla de Pinos
Camagüey
Santiago de Cuba
Guantánamo

Canal de Yucatán

Antillas Mayores

JAMAICA Kingston

MAR CARIBE

HAITÍ
Port-au-Prince

REP. DOMINICANA
Santo Domingo

PUERTO RICO
Mayagüez
Ponce
San Juan

Islas Vírgenes (U.S. & Br.)
Guadalupe (Fr.)
Antigua (Br.)
Dominica (Br.)
Martinica (Fr.)
Sta. Lucía (Br.)
San Vicente (Br.)
Barbados
Granada (Br.)
Tobago
Puerto España
Margarita
TRINIDAD

Antillas Menores

Aruba (Hol.)
Curaçao (Hol.)
Bonaire (Hol.)

Belize
BELIZE
Puerto Barrios
Tikal
GUATEMALA
Guatemala
Quezaltenango
Chichicastenango
Antigua
San Salvador
EL SALVADOR
Copán
HONDURAS
Tegucigalpa
NICARAGUA
Managua
L. Nicaragua
L. Nicaragua
Puntarenas
San José
COSTA RICA
Puerto Limón
Canal de Panamá
Colón
Islas de San Blás
PANAMÁ
Panamá

OCÉANO PACÍFICO

LA AMÉRICA DEL SUR

SANDERSON

316

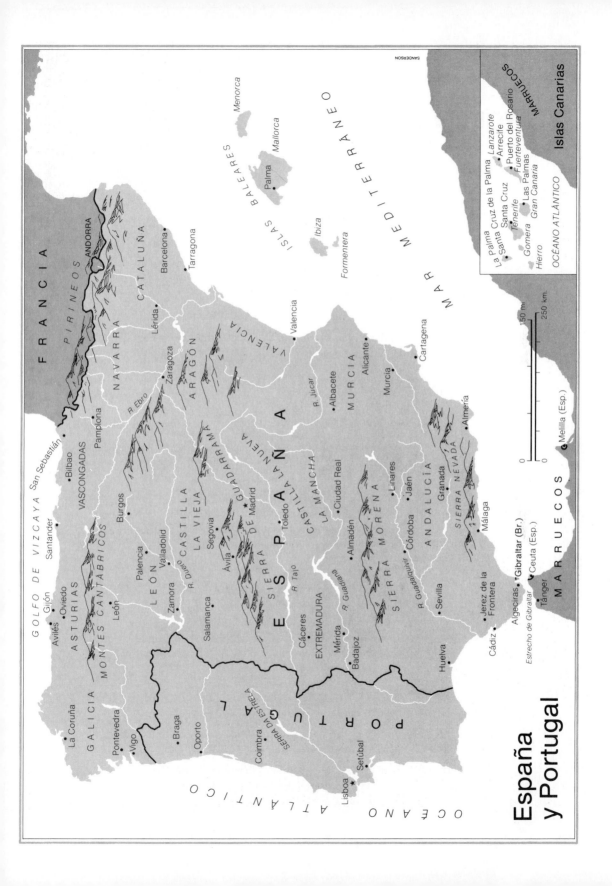

España
y Portugal

OCÉANO
ATLÁNTICO

MAR MEDITERRÁNEO

FRANCIA

ANDORRA

PIRINEOS

GOLFO DE VIZCAYA

San Sebastián
Bilbao
VASCONGADAS
Pamplona
NAVARRA
Santander
ASTURIAS
Oviedo
Gijón
Avilés
MONTES CANTÁBRICOS

CATALUÑA
Barcelona
Tarragona
Lérida
Zaragoza
ARAGÓN
R. Ebro

ISLAS BALEARES
Menorca
Mallorca
Palma
Ibiza
Formentera

La Coruña
GALICIA
Pontevedra
Vigo
Braga
Oporto
PORTUGAL
Coimbra
SERRA DA ESTRELA
Setúbal
Lisboa

Burgos
Palencia
Valladolid
LEÓN
León
Zamora
Salamanca
R. Duero
CASTILLA LA VIEJA
Segovia
Ávila
SIERRA DE GUADARRAMA
Madrid
ESPAÑA
CASTILLA LA NUEVA
VALENCIA
Valencia
R. Júcar
Albacete
MURCIA
Alicante
Murcia
Cartagena

Cáceres
EXTREMADURA
Mérida
Badajoz
R. Tajo
Toledo
Ciudad Real
LA MANCHA
Almadén
R. Guadiana
SIERRA MORENA
Córdoba
Linares
Jaén
Granada
ANDALUCÍA
SIERRA NEVADA
Almería
Málaga

Huelva
R. Guadalquivir
Sevilla
Jerez de la Frontera
Cádiz
Algeciras
Gibraltar (Br.)
Ceuta (Esp.)
Tánger
Estrecho de Gibraltar
MARRUECOS
Melilla (Esp.)

SANDERSON

OCÉANO ATLÁNTICO
MARRUECOS
Islas Canarias
La Palma
Santa Cruz de la Palma
Lanzarote
Arrecife
Santa Cruz
Tenerife
Puerto del Rosario
Fuerteventura
Gomera
Las Palmas
Gran Canaria
Hierro

150 mi.
250 km.
0

Answer Key for Review Lessons

Lessons 1–3

A. 1. entregas 2. debo 3. están 4. escribe 5. aprendemos 6. viven 7. trabajan

B. 1. Debemos llegar a la universidad a tiempo. 2. Los estudiantes desean leer seis libros. 3. Acabo de tomar el examen. 4. Necesito estar en casa los sábados.
5. ¿Tienes que sacar buenas notas en economía?

C. 1. abierto 2. tristes 3. cerradas 4. enferma 5. aburridos

D. 1. sus 2. su 3. nuestra 4. tus 5. mis 6. su

E. 1. I've just read so many history books! 2. His students are always bored in this class. 3. They have to work every day this week. 4. I'm taking a lot of subjects because I'm studying to be an engineer. 5. Who do you arrive at school with on Tuesdays?

F. *Comprehension check.* 1. This student studies history and political science. 2. She has to get very good grades because she wants to study law next year. 3. No, she doesn't spend much time with her friends in museums and cafes. 4. She works in the university library to pay for her studies. 5. She doesn't have to pay for the dormitory because she lives at home with her parents.

Lessons 4–6

A. 1. es 2. es 3. está 4. son estás es es es está es

B. 1. Sí, lo conozco. 2. Sí, los visito. 3. Sí, las encontramos. 4. Sí, puede (or puedes) llamarla. 5. Sí, pensamos (or piensan) buscarlos. 6. Sí, queremos venderla. 7. Sí, los tengo. (or Sí, los tiene.) 8. Sí, las comprendo.

C. 1. No 2. a 3. a 4. No 5. a 6. No

D. 1. conoces 2. sé 3. conoce 4. sabes 5. saben 6. conozco 7. sabemos

E. 1. Me dicen los precios. 2. Les doy veinte dólares. 3. Les enseñamos el Barrio.
4. Le pide las composiciones. 5. Le servimos un café. 6. Me venden unas blusas.

F. 1. Sí, me interesa la ingeniería. 2. Me gusta más la física. 3. Sí, me importa mucho si saco malas notas. 4. Todavía me faltan dos años. 5. Sí, me quedan cuatro exámenes. 6. Me parecen muy bien.

G. 1. Está sin empleo desde enero.   2. Les encanta comprar ropa en ese almacén.
3. ¿Cómo es tu hermano?   4. Voy a darle unos lápices.   5. Somos de España, pero estamos en Venezuela ahora.

H. 1. Do you know Mr. Durán?   2. I want to work as a secretary in his office, but I lack experience.   3. In his office all the employees have to know Spanish.   4. Unfortunately I don't speak it.   5. I have no choice.   6. I'm going to study Spanish so that I can get a job there.

I. *Comprehension check.* 1. b   2. c   3. c   4. a   5. a

Lessons 7–9

A. 1. Nos hacen falta unas vacaciones.   2. Pensamos hacer un viaje a Veracruz.   3. Les vamos a traer unos libros de México.   4. Salimos el jueves.   5. Volvemos de allí en dos semanas.

B. 1. Ya se lo sirvieron.   2. Ya te lo dije.   3. Ya nos la hicieron.   4. Ya se las trajo.
5. Ya vinimos con él.   6. Ya se la pidieron.   7. Ya se la di.   8. Ya lo vimos.

C. 1. me despierto   2. se levantan   3. me visto / me peino   4. me pongo   5. se quejan
6. nos vamos   7. se quedan   8. se sienten   9. nos echamos   10. sale / nos bañamos

D. 1. me desperté   2. se levantaron   3. me vestí / me peiné   4. me puse   5. se quejaron   6. nos fuimos   7. se quedaron   8. se sintieron   9. nos echamos
10. salió / nos bañamos

E. 1. Me acosté a las diez anoche.   2. Me pongo el abrigo cuando hace mucho frío.
3. Me quejo de los exámenes.   4. Esta mañana me duché.   5. Me enfada tener que esperar el autobús.   6. Sí, dormí la siesta ayer.

F. 1. que   2. quien   3. que   4. quienes   5. quien   6. que   7. que   8. que

G. 1. Son las dos menos cuarto ahora.   2. Almorcé con mis amigos hace una hora.
3. Pedimos pescado; estuvo rico.   4. Hoy hace frío y está nublado y va a nevar.
5. Cuando salimos del restaurante, volvimos a casa.   6. Nos quedamos en casa lo más posible en invierno.

H. 1. I don't remember that business about your neighbors.   2. Did you set the table before or after you got dressed?   3. They're always in a big hurry when they wake up late.   4. Jorge told us that Felipe insulted him.   5. You've been in the pool for a long time.   6. Don't you feel like tasting a spicy dish?

I. *Comprehension check.* 1. F   2. F   3. F   4. T   5. T   6. T   7. F   8. F   9. T   10. T
11. T   12. T

Lessons 10–12

A. 1. Pensaba en el futuro.   2. No veían las planillas.   3. Iba a dedicarme a mi profesión.   4. Era el médico que trabajaba allí.   5. Le dolía la garganta.   6. Te encontrabas con Antonio María.

B. 1. se despertó   2. tenía   3. dolía   4. dio   5. sufría   6. se levantó   7. fue   8. se lavó
9. se vistió   10. tomó   11. vio   12. tenía   13. volvió   14. decidió   15. creía   16. tenía
17. llamó   18. podía

C. 1. Dudo que a este paciente le duela la cabeza.   2. Sin embargo, es posible que tenga un poco de fiebre.   3. Es necesario que tome un antibiótico.   4. Le voy a aconsejar que pierda peso.   5. Me va a pedir que le dé una dieta.   6. Ojalá que la siga.   7. Tengo miedo de que se ponga peor si no sigue la dieta.   8. Yo siempre quiero que mis pacientes mejoren.

D. 1. tengo 2. necesito 3. espero 4. haya 5. prefiero 6. vaya 7. esté
8. deposite 9. creo 10. sea 11. podamos 12. tenemos 13. ganamos

E. 1. dé 2. sepan 3. tenga 4. trata 5. van 6. ayudan 7. se cuiden 8. den

F. 1. está 2. he 3. han 4. están 5. está 6. habéis 7. están 8. hemos

G. 1. Patricia y Pedro iban a casarse este verano.   2. Pedro conoció a Patricia en un banco. Ella era cajera.   3. Pero en junio Patricia se sintió enferma.   4. Los médicos le hicieron unos análisis y le dijeron que tenía que descansar por tres meses.   5. ¡Espero que mejore rápidamente!

H. 1. My cousin and his wife hadn't been getting along for four years when they decided to get a divorce.   2. My aunt got sick when she found out.   3. They had to take her to the hospital because her stomach and head hurt.   4. They gave her some pills and she improved quite a bit.   5. I hope she doesn't get sick again because of her children's problems.

I. *Comprehension check.* 1. Claudia vive con sus papás, sus tres hermanos, su abuela y la tía Rosalia.   2. Antes la abuela Eugenia vivía en un apartamento a dos cuadras de la casa de Claudia.   3. Los niños comían y jugaban con sus primos en casa de sus abuelos.
4. Los abuelos consentían a los niños.   5. El abuelo murió de una enfermedad del corazón.   6. Murió en el patio de su casa.   7. Leía el periódico cuando murió.   8. Les fue muy difícil aceptar su muerte.   9. Rosalia es la hija major de la abuela Eugenia.
10. No se casó nunca porque se dedicaba a sus papás y a sus sobrinos.   11. La abuela y la tía Rosalia fueron a vivir con la familia de Claudia. (El papá de Claudia era el hijo de la abuela Eugenia.)   12. Rosalia trabaja en un banco.   13. No quería dejar el trabajo porque quería ayudar a su hermano con los gastos de la casa.   14. A Claudia le parece que no hay nadie que sea tan bueno ni más generoso que su padre.   15. La abuela es la cabeza de la familia González. Todo el mundo le tiene mucho amor y respeto.

Lessons 13–15

A. 1. Se llevan los muebles al apartamento.   2. Se trajo la alfombra.   3. Se guardó la ropa en el armario.   4. ¿Dónde se va a poner la televisión?   5. Se debe dejar la televisión en la sala por ahora.   6. Se tiene que pintar la cocina.   7. Se tienen que colgar tres cuadros en la sala.   8. ¿Se ha traído todo?   9. ¿Se puede terminar la mudanza hoy?   10. Ahora se pone la televisión para que nos relajemos un poco.

B. 1. lee 2. escojas 3. dime 4. asistas 5. ven 6. escucha 7. vayas 8. diviértete

C. 1. arregle 2. vaya 3. explíqueselo 4. solicite 5. traiga 6. mándenos
7. llene 8. deme

D. 1. cuelguen 2. corran 3. pongan 4. siéntense 5. vengan 6. apaguen
7. relájense 8. guarden

E. 1. Yo vi más obras de teatro que mi amigo.   2. Nosotros miramos menos televisión que nuestros papás.   3. El tenía más documentos que yo.   4. Julia era mejor actriz que Blanca.   5. Pasan más películas dobladas en el cine Argentino que en el cine Colón. 6. Hay menos muebles arriba que abajo.

F. 1. Uds. están instalándose en su nuevo apartamento.   2. Tus hermanos están trayendo los cajones.   3. Tú estás colgando algunos cuadros en tu cuarto.   4. Todos están trabajando mucho.   5. Tu papá, muy cansado, se está durmiendo en el sofá. 6. Yo estoy preparándoles un café para que descansen un poco.

G. 1. los tuyos   2. la suya   3. las nuestras   4. la vuestra   5. la mía

H. 1. Sí, es la del dramaturgo alemán.   2. Sí, son los de doña Carmen.   3. Sí, son las de los niños.   4. Sí, es el del espectáculo que vimos.

I. 1. Sí, hablo del que compré ayer.   2. Sí, hablan de los que se escogen.   3. Sí, hablamos de las que hemos visto.   4. Sí, habla de la que se puso anoche.

J. 3. Se les olvidaron los anteojos.   4. Se nos olvidaron los anteojos.   5. Se nos cayeron los anteojos.   6. Se te cayeron los anteojos.   7. Se te rompieron los anteojos.   8. Se te rompió el plato.   9. Se me rompió el plato.   10. Se le rompió el plato.   11. Se le perdió el plato.   12. Se le perdieron los documentos.

K. 1. Vamos a pasar el día instalándonos en nuestro nuevo apartamento. 2. Ayúdanos. Corre la silla a la izquierda y deja el sofá delante de la ventana.   3. Pedro y Francisco, salgan a comprar café.   4. No podemos. Se nos olvidó la licencia de manejar en casa.   5. Yo puedo ir entonces. Pero me parece que prefieren que yo compre cerveza.   6. Buena idea. La cerveza es mejor que el café cuando estás instalándote.   7. El día de la mudanza es difícil, pero todos están divirtiéndose.

L. 1. The debut of a police film is being presented today.   2. Shut off that TV and come with me to see it.   3. If we don't leave now, the tickets are going to be sold out at the box office.   4. I think we should go by taxi.   5. Put on your coats while I look for my money.

M. *Comprehension check.* 1. a   2. b   3. b   4. c   5. c   6. a   7. b   8. c   9. a   10. c 11. b   12. a

Lessons 16–18

A. 1. Mis primos celebrarán su cumpleaños la semana que viene.   2. Saldrán a comer en un restaurante.   3. Se pondrán su mejor ropa.   4. Toda la familia irá con ellos. 5. Después volverán a su casa.   6. Se cambiarán de ropa.   7. Tomarán un taxi al estadio.   8. Verán un partido de fútbol, el deporte favorito de ellos.

B. 1. abran   2. vuelva   3. pueda   4. te vayas   5. llame   6. diga   7. hablemos   8. se ponga

C. 1. por   2. para   3. para   4. por   5. por   6. para   7. para   8. por

D. 1. Quería que todos fuéramos al campo a comer.   2. Tú no querías ir sin que invitáramos a Elena.   3. Raúl insistía en que jugáramos béisbol.   4. Tus primos preferían que anduviéramos en bicicleta.   5. Yo le aconsejé a todo el mundo que trajera su cerveza.   6. Alicia trajo su guitarra para que cantáramos.   7. ¿Conocías a alguien más que pudiera ir con nosotros?   8. Quería que hubiera más gente para que nos divirtiéramos más.

E. 1. podremos   2. hubiera   3. verían   4. hiciéramos   5. controla   6. terminaras   7. entenderéis   8. me mudara

F. 1. Ya serán las siete y media y tenemos tantas cosas que hacer.   2. Ana quiere ir a la panadería que está a la vuelta de la esquina.   3. Yo me cortaría el pelo si pudiera encontrar una buena peluquería.   4. Rosa saldría con nosotros con tal que fuéramos a una librería.   5. Y yo llevaría el coche a un taller si alguien me dijera donde hay un buen mecánico.

G. 1. Why don't we go to see the basketball game?   2. OK, provided that there are more tickets.   3. Don't worry. Yesterday I asked my brother to buy me two tickets.   4. That was a good thing (you did). They say that Armando Gómez broke his arm and that he's not going to be able to play.   5. Yes, what bad news! And there's nobody else who plays as well as he.   6. You know what? I don't know if our team will be able to win the game without Gómez.

H. *Comprehension check.* 1. Michael Crawford quería que su compañía lo mandara a un país de lengua española.   2. La compañía para la cual trabajaba lo destinó a Puerto Rico para que arreglara los asuntos de la nueva oficina.   3. Hace tres meses que está en Puerto Rico. 4. Ha hablado sólo con especialistas en tecnología y en computación, con políticos y líderes de sindicatos.   5. Michael decide que tiene que conocer Puerto Rico antes de volver a Washington.   6. El sábado piensa ir a ver algunos barrios de San Juan. Irá al Viejo San Juan donde verá la arquitectura española y un ambiente colonial.   7. El otro fin de semana le gustaría viajar por el interior de la Isla y respirar un poco de aire fresco.   8. Le interesa ver cómo viven los jíbaros en el campo. 9. Tratará de ir a Ponce donde visitará el Museo de Arte y a Arecibo donde verá el observatorio.   10. En San Juan le gustaría visitar la Fortaleza El Morro, los museos, el Estadio Hiram Bithorn, el Coliseo Roberto Clemente y el Coliseo Gallístico.

VOCABULARY

ABBREVIATIONS

adj. adjective
adv. adverb
Carib. Caribbean
coll. colloquial
conj. conjunction
dem. demonstrative
dim. diminutive
d.o. direct object
e.g. for example
fam. familiar
fem. feminine
fig. figuratively
i.o. indirect object

inf. infinitive
interj. interjection
intro. introductory note to
  the student
irreg. irregular verb
  (see verb charts)
Lat. Am. Latin American
lit. literally
masc. masculine
neg. negative
neut. neuter
pej. pejorative
pl. plural

poss. possessive
p.p. past participle
  (**-do** form)
P.R. Puerto Rico
prep. preposition
pret. preterit
R Repaso
rev. constr. reverse
  construction verb
  (see Lesson 6)
sing. singular
subj. subjunctive

Verbs marked *irreg.* have multiple irregularities and should be checked in the verb charts in the appendix. Verbs having an irregularity only in the **yo**-form of the present tense are marked as follows: **conocer (yo conozco).** Verbs with changes in the vowel of the stem are marked as follows: **poder (o → ue).**

Numbers after vocabulary entries refer to the lesson in which the item first appears.

Verbs with spelling changes are marked as follows:

seguir	**(gu → g/a,o)**	= *gu* changes to *g* before *a, o*.
coger	**(g → j/a,o)**	= *g* changes to *j* before *a, o*.
comenzar	**(z → c/e)**	= *z* changes to *c* before *e*.
llegar	**(g → gu/e)**	= *g* changes to *gu* before *e*.
buscar	**(c → qu/e)**	= *c* changes to *qu* before *e*.

Spanish–English

A

a to 2
abajo downstairs 14
abierto (*p.p.* **abrir**) open(ed) 3
el **abogado** lawyer 2
el **abrigo** overcoat 5
abril April 6
abrir to open 11
la **abuela** grandmother 3
el **abuelo** grandfather 3
los **abuelos** grandparents 3
aburrido bored 3; boring 16
acabar to end up, wind up; to finish 6
  acabar de (+ *inf.*) to have just done something 3
el **accidente** accident 12
el **aceite** oil 17
acompañar to accompany, go with 5
aconsejar to advise 11
acordarse (o → ue) to remember 9
acostarse (o → ue) to go to bed 9
el **actor** actor 15
la **actriz** actress 15
actual (*adj.*) present (*time*) 18
el **acuerdo** agreement 9
  de acuerdo OK, agreed 9
adaptarse (a) to adjust to 10
además besides 16
adiós good-bye 3
¿adónde? where (*with verbs of motion*) 6
el **aeropuerto** airport 7
afeitarse to shave 17
el **aficionado** fan, devotee 8

afirmar to strengthen R2
el **agente** agent 13
el **agua** (*fem.*) water 8
agosto August 6
la **agricultura** agriculture 18
ahí there (*near the person spoken to*) 3
ahora now 1
  ahora mismo right now 14
ahorrar to save 11
los **ahorros** savings 11
el **aire** air 18
alegrarse to be glad 11
alegre happy, cheerful 3
alemán German 1
Alemania Germany 4
la **alfombra** carpet 14
algo something 5
el **algodón** cotton 5
alguien someone 12
algún (alguno) some; (*pl.*) a few 3
  algún día some day 10
el **almacén** store 5
almorzar (o → ue) to have lunch 8
el **almuerzo** lunch 8
alquilar to rent R6
alto tall, high 4
allí there 3
amable kind, nice 16
amarillo yellow 5
la **ambición** ambition 10
el **ambiente** environment 18
la **amiga** friend (*fem.*) 3
el **amigo** friend (*masc.*) 3
el **amor** love
  mi amor dear, darling 14
el **análisis** (*medical*) test 12
anaranjado (*adj.*) orange (-colored) 5
andar to walk 16
  andar en bicicleta to ride a bike 16
el **animal** animal 18
anoche last night 7
los **anteojos** eyeglasses 13
antes (de) before 8
el **antibiótico** antibiotic 12
antipático unpleasant, not nice 16

la **antropología** anthropology 7
el **anuncio** ad 6
el **año** year 2
apagar to turn off (*appliance*) 14
el **aparato** appliance 14
el **apartamento** apartment 14
el **aperitivo** apéritif, predinner drink R3
la **apertura** opening R6
aprender to learn 2
apretado crowded R4
aquel, aquella that (*over there*) 2
  aquellos, aquellas those (*over there*) 2
aquí here 3
la **Argentina** Argentina 4
argentino Argentine 4
el **argumento** plot 15
el **armario** closet 14
arreglar to arrange, fix, fix up 13
arriba upstairs 14
el **arroz** rice 8
así like this, like that, thus 7
asistir (a) to attend 15
la **aspirina** aspirin 3
aumentar to increase 12
  aumentar de peso to gain weight 12
aunque although 10
el **autobús** bus 7
la **avenida** avenue 17
el **avión** airplane 7
ayer yesterday 7
ayudar to help 8
azul blue 5

B

bailar to dance 15
el **baile flamenco** Flamenco dancing 6
bajo low, short 5
el **baloncesto** basketball 16
el **banco** bank 1
bañarse to take a bath 9
el **baño** bathroom 9
barato cheap 5
el **barrio** neighborhood 17

bastante   enough; rather; quite a lot 1

la **batería**   battery 17

beber   to drink 8

el **béisbol**   baseball 16

la **biblioteca**   library 2

la **bicicleta**   bicycle 16

bien   well 1

los **bienes**   goods 18

bilingüe   bilingual 18

el **billete**   bill (*banknote*) 11

la **biología**   biology 2

blanco   white 5

la **blusa**   blouse 5

la **boca**   mouth 12

la **bodega**   grocery store 17

el **boleto**   ticket 15

el **bolívar**   monetary unit of Venezuela 5

el **bombero**   firefighter 13

bonito   pretty 4

el **Brasil**   Brazil 4

brasileño   Brazilian 4

el **brazo**   arm 12

bronceado   sunburned 7

bueno   well (*interj.*) 1; good 3

buscar   to look for 5

el **buzón**   mailbox 17

C

el **caballo**   horse 18

la **cabeza**   head 12

cada   each 3

caer (caigo)   to fall 13

el **café**   café 1

café (*adj.*)   brown 5

la **cajera** (*masc.*: el **cajero**) cashier 6; teller 11

el **cajón**   box 14

el **calcetín**   sock 5

calcular   to compute 11

el **calor**   heat 7

hacer calor   to be warm (*weather*) 7

tener calor   to be warm (*people*) 9

la **calle**   street 7

la **cama**   bed 3

guardar cama   to stay in bed 3

cambiar   to change 9

caminar   to walk 13

la **camisa**   shirt 5

el **campesino**   peasant 18

el **campo**   country, field 16

el **Canadá**   Canada 4

la **canción**   song 15

cansado   tired 3

cantar   to sing 15

la **capital**   capital city 7

la **cara**   face 17

¡caray!   gosh! 3

el **cargador**   mover, porter 14

el **cariño**   love, affection 7

cariños   love (*at the end of a letter*) 7

la **carne**   meat 8

la **carnicería**   butcher shop 17

caro   expensive 5

el **carpintero**   carpenter 18

la **carta**   letter 7; menu 8

la **cartelera**   entertainment listings 15

la **casa**   house 3

en casa   at home 3

casado   married 4

estar casado con   to be married to 4

casarse (con)   to get married (to) 9

casi   almost 10

la **casualidad**   coincidence 16

el **catarro**   cold (*illness*) 12

catorce   fourteen 3

la **cazuela**   stew, stew pot 8

celebrar   to celebrate 16

la **cena**   dinner 8

cenar   to have dinner 8

el **centro**   downtown 7

cerca (de)   near 7

cerrado   closed 3

cerrar (e → ie)   to close 11

el **certificado**   license, certificate 13

certificado de matrimonio marriage license 13

la **cerveza**   beer 8

la **ciencia**   science 2

ciencias políticas   political science 2

ciento   one hundred 9

cierto   true, certain 11

cinco   five 3

cincuenta   fifty 5

el **cine**   movies, movie theater 15

la **cita**   appointment, date 13

la **ciudad**   city 7

el **ciudadano**   citizen 13

claro   of course 4; light (*in color*) 5

la **clase**   class 2

el (la) **cliente**   customer, client 5

la **clínica**   clinic 12

cobrar   to cash 11

la **cocina**   kitchen 8

el **cocinero**   cook 8

el **coche**   car 7

la **cola**   line (*of people*) 11

el **colegio**   high school, school 2

colgar (o → ue)   to hang 14

Colombia   Colombia 4

colombiano   Colombian 4

el **color**   color 5

la **comedia**   comedy, play 15

el **comedor**   dining room 8

comenzar (e → ie; z → c/e)   to begin 10

comer   to eat 7

el **comerciante**   merchant, store owner R2

la **comida**   food, meal 7

como   like, as 2

¿cómo?   how? 2

cómo no   of course 9

la **cómoda**   chest of drawers 14

la **compañía**   company 17

la **composición**   composition 2

comprar   to buy 5

las **compras**   shopping 17

ir de compras   to go shopping 17

comprender   to understand 3

la **computación**   computer programming 18

la **comunidad**   community 4

con   with 1

con tal que (+ *subj.*) provided that 16

el **concierto**   concert 15

conjunto (*see* cuenta)

conocer (yo **conozco**)   to know 5

conseguir (e → ie; gu → g/a, o)   to get 6

consentir (e → ie)   to spoil (*a child*) R4
considerar   to consider 18
la **contaminación**   pollution 18
contaminado   polluted 18
contento   happy, content 3
contra   against 14
contrario: al —   on the contrary 10
controlar   to control 18
el **corazón**   heart 12
la **corbata**   necktie 5
la **cordillera**   mountain range R6
el **correo**   post office 17
correr   to run; to move something 14
cortar   to cut 16
la **cortina**   curtain 14
corto   short 9
la **cosa**   thing 7
costar (o → ue)   to cost 5
el **costo**   cost 18
la **costumbre**   custom 10
el **crédito** (*see* **tarjeta**)
creer   to think, believe 2
la **crema**   cream 17
la **criada**   servant R3
la **cuadra**   block (*city*) R4
el **cuadro**   painting (*picture*) 14
¿cuál(es)?   which? which one(s)? 2
¿cuándo?   when? 1
¿cuánto? (-a)   how much? 2
¿cuántos? (-as)   how many? 2
cuarenta   forty 5
el **cuarto**   room, bedroom 9
cuarto   fourth 13
cuatro   four 3
cuatrocientos   four hundred 9
Cuba   Cuba 4
cubano   Cuban 4
la **cuchara**   tablespoon 8
la **cucharita**   teaspoon 8
el **cuchillo**   knife 8
la **cuenta**   bill, check 8; account 11
cuenta corriente   checking account 11
cuenta de ahorros   savings account 11
cuenta de cheques   checking account 11

cuenta conjunta   joint account 11
el **cuerpo**   body 12
el **cuidado**   care, caution 10
tener cuidado   to be careful 10
cuidarse   to take care of oneself 12
el **cultivo**   culture (*in biology*) 12
la **cultura**   culture 10
el **cumpleaños**   birthday 16
cumplir   to become X years old 16
el **curandero**   native healer 12
el **curso**   course 18
cuyo   whose R6

CH

charlar   to chat R3
el **cheque**   check 11
chévere (*Carib.*)   great, terrific 13
la **chica**   girl 1
chicano   Mexican-American 18
el **chico**   boy 1
Chile   Chile 4
chileno   Chilean 4
chocar   to clash 10

D

dar (*irreg.*)   to give 6
darse cuenta de   to realize 10
de   of, from 2
deber   should, must, ought 2
débil   weak R4
decidir   to decide 10
décimo   tenth 13
decir (*irreg.*)   to say, tell 6
dedicarse (a)   to devote oneself to 10
defenderse (e → ie)   to get along, manage R6
dejar   to leave (*behind*) 8
delante (de)   in front of 14
delgado   thin 4
demasiado   too much; too 2
demasiados (-as)   too many 2
el (la) **dentista**   dentist 2
el (la) **dependiente**   salesperson, salesclerk 5

el **deporte**   sport 16
depositar   to deposit 11
el **depósito**   deposit 11
la **derecha**   the right side 14
a la derecha   to, on the right 14
el **derecho**   law (*field of study*) 2; right, privilege 13
desagradable   unpleasant 16
desayunar   to have breakfast 8
el **desayuno**   breakfast 8
descansar   to rest 3
desde   since 6
desear   to want 1
el **desempleo**   unemployment 18
despertarse (e → ie)   to wake up 9
después (de)   after, afterwards 8
detrás (de)   behind 14
de vuelta   back (*adv.*) R6
el **día**   day 1
todo el día   all day 1
todos los días   every day 1
el **diario**   diary 12
diciembre   December 6
diecinueve   nineteen 3
dieciocho   eighteen 3
dieciséis   sixteen 3
diecisiete   seventeen 3
la **dieta**   diet 12
diez   ten 3
diferente   different 10
difícil   difficult 4
el **dinero**   money 6
Dios   God
el **director**   director 15
el **disco**   record 15
la **discoteca**   discotheque 17
discutir   to discuss 18
divertido   amusing 15
divertirse (e → ie)   to have a good time, enjoy oneself 15
divorciarse   to get divorced 10
doblar   to dub (*film*) 15; to turn 17
doce   twelve 3
el **doctor**, la **doctora**   doctor 3
el **documento**   document; (*pl.*) papers 13
el **dólar**   dollar 6

doler (o → ue)   to hurt, ache 12
el **dolor**   ache, pain
el **domingo**   Sunday 1
 don   title of respect (*masc.*) 9
 doña   title of respect (*fem.*) 9
 ¿dónde?   where? 1
 dormir (o → ue; o → u)   to sleep 8
  dormirse   to fall asleep 12
  dormir la siesta   to take a nap 9
el **dormitorio**   bedroom 9
 dos   two 3
 doscientos   two hundred 4
el **drama**   drama 15
el **dramaturgo**   playwright 15
la **droguería**   drugstore (*for sundries*) 17
 ducharse   to take a shower 9
 dudar   to doubt 11
 durante   during 7

E

la **ecología**   ecology 18
la **economía**   economics 2
 echar   to throw; to mail 17
 echarse   to lie down 9
 efectivamente   exactly, indeed 11
 eficaz   efficient R2
el **ejercicio**   exercise 16
 el   the 1
 él   he, it 1
 eléctrico   electrical 14
 ella   she, it
 ellas   they (*fem.*) 1
 ellos   they (*masc.*) 1
el **embotellamiento**   traffic jam R3
 empeorar   to get worse 12
 emocionante   exciting 16
 empatar   to tie (*sports*) 16
 empezar (e → ie; z → c/e) (+a + inf.)   to begin (to) 6
el **empleado**   employee 6
el **empleo**   job 6
 en   in, at, on 1
  en cambio   on the other hand R5
  en seguida   immediately 10

 encantador   delightful 16
 encantar (*rev. constr.*)   to love (*things*) 6
 encontrar (o → ue)   to find 5
  encontrarse   to be (= **estar**) 9
  encontrarse con   to meet, run into someone 11
 enero   January 6
 enfadarse   to get angry 9
el **enfermero**, la **enfermera**   nurse 2
la **enfermedad**   sickness 12
 enfermo   sick 3
la **ensalada**   salad 8
 enseñar   to teach 2; to show 6
 entender (e → ie)   to understand 18
 entero   whole R6
 entonces   then 11
 entrar (en) (a)   to enter, go into 7
 entregar   to hand in 3
el **entusiasmo**   enthusiasm 12
el **equipo**   team 16
 equivocado   wrong 4
 escoger (g → j/a,o)   to choose 15
 escribir   to write 2
 escuchar   to listen 15
la **escuela**   school (*elementary*) 2
 ese, esa   that 2
 español   Spanish 1
el **espectáculo**   show 15
el **espejo**   mirror 14
 esperar   to wait 9; to hope 11
la **esposa**   wife 3
el **esposo**   husband 3
la **esquina**   corner (*street*) 17
la **estación**   season 10
el **estadio**   stadium 16
los **Estados Unidos**   United States 4
la **estancia**   stay, period of residence R3
 estar (*irreg.*)   to be 3
 este, esta   this 2
el **este**   east 13
el **estéreo**   stereo 14
el **estómago**   stomach 12
el **estreno**   debut 15
el (la) **estudiante**   student 3

 estudiar   to study 1
 estupendo   terrific 9
 Europa   Europe 4
 europeo   European 4
 evidente   evident 11
el **examen**   test, exam 2
 examinar   to examine 12
 excelente   excellent 15
 exigir (g → j/a, o)   to demand 11
el **exitazo**   hit (*success*) 15
el **éxito**   success 9
  tener éxito   to be successful 9
la **experiencia**   experience 6
 explicar   to explain 3
 exportar   to export 18
 extranjero   foreign 13
  ir al extranjero   to go abroad 13
 extrañar   to miss R4

F

la **fábrica**   factory 6
 fácil   easy 4
la **falda**   skirt 5
la **falta: hacer falta** (*rev. constr.*)   to need 7
 faltar (*rev. constr.*)   to be missing (lacking) something 6
la **familia**   family 3
 famoso   famous 15
 fantástico   great 16
la **farmacia**   drugstore 17
 favorito   favorite 16
 febrero   February 6
la **fecha**   date (*calendar*) 10
 feliz   happy 16
 feo   ugly 4
la **fiebre**   fever 12
la **fiesta**   party 16
el **fin**   end 2
  fin de semana   weekend 2
  por fin   finally 10
la **finca**   farm 13
 firmar   to sign 11
la **física**   physics 2
la **flor**   flower 17
la **florería**   florist, flower shop 17
 fondo: al fondo   in the back 14

los **fondos**   funds 11
el **formulario**   form (*paper*) 13
la **fortaleza**   fortress R6
la **fotografía**   photograph 15
  francés   French 1
  Francia   France 4
el **freno**   brake 17
  frente: en frente de   opposite, facing 17
  fresco: hace fresco   it's cool (*weather*) 7
el **frío**   cold (*weather*) 7
    hace frío   it's cold 7
    tener frío   to be cold (*people*) 9
  frito   (lit. *fried*)   washed up, done for 3
la **fruta**   fruit 8
  fuera (de)   outside (of), away from 10
la **función**   show 15
el **funcionario**   official, public employee 13
el **fútbol**   soccer 16
    fútbol americano   football 16
el **futuro**   future 10

G

la **gallina**   chicken, hen 18
  gallístico   pertaining to cockfighting R6
  gana: tener ganas de   (+ *inf.*) to feel like doing something 9
  ganar   to earn 1; to win 16
    ganarse la vida   to earn one's living 18
la **ganga**   bargain 5
la **garganta**   throat 12
la **gasolina**   gasoline 17
la **gasolinera**   gas station 17
  gastar   to spend 11
el **gasto**   expense R4
el **gato**   cat 18
la **gaveta**   drawer 14
la **gente**   people 8
el **gobierno**   government 13
  gordo   fat 4
  gracias   thank you 3
  gracioso   witty 16

el **grado**   degree (*temperature*) 7
  hace X grados   it's X degrees 7
  graduarse   to graduate 18
  grande   big 4
  grave   seriously ill 3
la **gripe**   flu 3
  gris   grey
el **grupo**   group 15
el **guante**   glove 5
  guapo   good-looking 4
  guardar   to keep; to put away 14
    guardar cama   to stay in bed 3
la **guía**   guidebook 7
la **guitarra**   guitar 15
  gustar   (*rev. constr.*)   to like (*something*) 6
el **gusto**   pleasure
    con mucho gusto   gladly 11

H

  hablar   to speak, talk 1
  hacer   (*irreg.*)   to do, make 7
    hacerse + *occupation*   to become a — 18
    hacerle caso   to pay attention to R4
  hacia   toward 10
  hasta   until 7
    hasta luego   see you later 11
  hay   there is, there are 4
    hay que + *inf.*   one must, has to — 12
el **helado**   ice cream 8
la **herida**   injury, wound 12
la **hermana**   sister 3
el **hermano**   brother 3
  hermoso   beautiful 5
la **hierba**   herb 12
la **hija**   daughter 3
el **hijo**   son 3
  hispano   Spanish-speaking 4
  Hispanoamérica   Spanish America 4
  hispanoamericano   Spanish American R2
la **historia**   history 2
  hola   hi, hello 2
el **hombre**   man 3
la **hora**   hour 3

  ¿qué hora es?   what time is it? 7
el **hospital**   hospital 3
el **hotel**   hotel 1
  hoy   today 1
la **huelga**   strike (*work stoppage*) 18
el **huevo**   egg 8

I

la **idea**   idea 10
la **identidad**   identity
    tarjeta de identidad   identification card 13
el **idioma**   language 2
la **iglesia**   church 17
  ilegalmente   illegally 13
  impedir   (e → i)   to prevent 11
el **impermeable**   raincoat 7
  importante   important 10
  importar   (*rev. constr.*)   to care about 6; to import 18
    no importa   never mind 3
  imposible   impossible 11
  improbable   improbable 11
  incluso   even 10
  indocumentado   without papers, illegal 13
    inmigrante indocumentado   illegal alien 13
la **industria**   industry 18
la **infección**   infection 3
la **inflación**   inflation 18
el **informe**   paper, report 18
la **información**   information 15
la **ingeniería**   engineering 2
el **ingeniero**   engineer 2
  Inglaterra   England 4
  inglés   English 1
  inmediatamente   immediately 11
la **inmigración**   immigration 13
el (la) **inmigrante**   immigrant 13
  inquieto   upset 14
  insistir (en)   to insist (on) 11
  insoportable   unbearable 13
  instalarse   to get settled in 14
  inteligente   intelligent 15
el **interés**   interest 11
  interesante   interesting 7

interesar (*rev. constr.*)   to be interested in 6
el **invierno**   winter 10
el **invitado**   guest 16
invitar   to invite 16
ir (*irreg.*)   to go 6
ir a + *inf.*   to be going to do something 6
irse   to go away 9
Irlanda   Ireland 4
irlandés   Irish 4
Italia   Italy 4
italiano   Italian 1
izquierda: a la izquierda   to (on) the left 14

J

el **jabón**   soap 17
el **jardín**   garden
jardín zoológico   zoo 16
el **jefe**   boss 6
el **jonrón**   homerun 16
joven   young 4
la **joyería**   jewelry store 17
el **jueves**   Thursday 1
el **jugador**   player 16
jugar (o → ue)   to play 16
el **jugo**   juice 8
julio   July 6
junio   June 6
juntos   together 15

K

el **kilómetro**   kilometer 9

L

el **lado**   side
al lado (de)   next door, next to 9
la **lámpara**   lamp 14
el **lápiz**   pencil 6
largo   long 9
la **lástima**   pity, shame 11
la **lata**   can, tin
¡qué lata!   what a bore! 1
Latinoamérica   Latin America 4
la **lavandería**   laundry 17
el **lavaplatos**   dishwasher 14

lavarse   to wash 9
la **leche**   milk 8
leer   to read 2
legalmente   legally 13
la **legumbre**   vegetable 8
lejos (de)   far (from) 7
lentamente   slowly 12
el **lente**   lens
lentes de contacto   contact lenses 13
levantarse   to get up 9
la **librería**   bookstore 17
la **libreta**   passbook (*bank*) 11
el **libro**   book 2
la **licencia**   license 13
licencia de manejar   driver's license 13
el **líder**   leader R6
limpio   clean 17
lindo   pretty, lovely 15
listo   ready 3
la **literatura**   literature 2
lo (*d.o.*)   him, you, it 5
lo siento   I'm sorry 1
lo (*neut.*)   the 9
loco   mad, crazy 2
la **locutora**   announcer (*female*) 15
luchar   to fight 18
luego   then, afterwards 6
el **lugar**   place 14
el **lunes**   Monday 1
la **luz**   light 14

LL

llamar   to call 5
llamarse   to call, be named Intro.
la **llanta**   tire (*car*) 17
la **llave**   key 18
llegar (g → gu/e)   to arrive 2
llenar   to fill 11
llevar   to wear, carry, take 5
llevarse bien (mal) con   to get along well (not get along well) with 10
llover (o → ue)   to rain 7

M

la **madre**   mother 3
magnífico   terrific,

magnificent 15
mal   badly 1; sick 3
la **maleta**   suitcase 18
la **mamá**   mother, mom 3
mandar   to order 11; to send 13
manejar   to drive 13
la **mano**   hand 12
mantener (*like* **tener**)   to support 18
la **manzana**   apple 8
mañana   tomorrow 1
la **mañana**   morning 7
el **mapa**   map 17
el **maquillaje**   makeup 17
la **máquina**   machine 14
máquina para escribir   typewriter 18
maravilloso   wonderful 10
el **marido**   husband 3
marrón   brown 5
el **martes**   Tuesday 1
marzo   March 6
más   more 1
las **matemáticas**   mathematics 2
la **materia**   subject (*school*) 2
el **matrimonio**   marriage 13
mayo   May 6
mayor   older, oldest 3
la mayor parte de   most of 4
el **mecánico**   mechanic 17
la **mecanógrafa** (el **mecanógrafo**)   typist 6
media   half 7
la **medicina**   medicine 2
el (la) **médico**   doctor 2
mejor   better, best 3
mejorar   to get better 12
el **membrillo**   quince jelly R3
menor   younger, youngest 3
menos   less 1
menos mal   fortunately 12
el **mercado**   market 7
la **mermelada**   jam R3
el **mes**   month 6
la **mesa**   table 8
mexicano   Mexican 4
México   Mexico 4
mi, mis   my 3
el **miedo**   fear 9
mientras   while 13
mientras tanto   meanwhile 13

el **miércoles**   Wednesday 1
mil   one thousand 9
la **milla**   mile 9
el **millón**   million 10
mirar   to look at 10
¡mira!   look!, hey! 6
mismo   same 10
el **modelo**   style 5
moderno   modern 10
molestar   to bother 18
la **moneda**   coin 11
moreno   dark-haired, dark-skinned 4
morir (o → ue; o → u)   to die 8
la **moza**   waitress 6
el **mozo**   waiter 6
la **muchacha**   girl 1
el **muchacho**   boy 1
mucho   a lot, much 1
muchos (-as)   many, a lot of 2
la **mudanza**   move, moving (*change of residence*) 14
mudarse   to move (*change residence*) 9
los **muebles**   furniture 14
la **muerte**   death R4
la **mujer**   woman, wife 3
el **mundo**   world 10
el **museo**   museum 1
la **música**   music 15
el **músico**   musician 15
muy   very 1

N

nacer (yo nazco)   to be born 10
el **nacimiento**   birth 13
nacional   national 15
la **nacionalidad**   nationality 4
nada   nothing 3
de nada   you're welcome 3
nadie   no one, nobody 12
la **naranja**   orange 18
la **nariz**   nose 12
la **náusea: tener náuseas**   to be nauseous 12
necesario   necessary 11
necesitar   to need; to have to 1
los **negocios**   business 17
negro   black 5
nevar (e → ie)   to snow 7

la **nevera**   refrigerator 14
ni   neither, nor 12
¡ni hablar!   nothing doing! 14
el **nieto**   grandchild R4
ningún, ninguno   no, none, not any 12
la **niña**   girl 4
el **niño**   boy 4
no   no, not 1
la **noche**   night 3
el **norte**   north 13
norteamericano   American (*from the U.S.*) 4
nosotros (-as)   we 1
la **nota**   grade, mark (*school*) 2
novecientos   nine hundred 9
noventa   ninety 5
noveno   ninth 13
la **novia**   girlfriend, fiancée 4
noviembre   November 6
el **novio**   boyfriend, fiancé 4
nublado   cloudy 7
nuestro (-a, -os, -as)   3
nueve   nine 3
nuevo   new 10
nunca   never 12

O

o   or 1
la **obra**   play 15
el **obrero**   worker 13
el **océano**   ocean 18
octavo   eighth 13
ochenta   eighty 5
ocho   eight 3
ochocientos   eight hundred 9
octubre   October 6
ocupado   busy 3
ocurrírsele   to dawn on someone 13
el **oeste**   west 13
ofenderse   to get insulted 9
la **oficina**   office 1
oficina de empleos   employment office 6
el **oficio**   trade (*line of work*) 18
el **oído**   ear (*inner*) 12
oír (*irreg.*)   to hear 9
ojalá   I hope 11
el **ojo**   eye 12
olvidarse   to forget 9

once   eleven 3
la **operaria** (*N.Y. Spanish*) garment worker 6
la **oportunidad**   opportunity 10
el **optimismo**   optimism 10
con optimismo   optimistically 10
la **oreja**   ear (*outer*) 12
el **origen**   origin, background 4
original   original 15
la **orquesta**   orchestra 15
oscuro   dark 5
el **otoño**   fall, autumn 10

P

el (la) **paciente**   patient 12
el **padre**   father 3
los **padres**   parents 3
pagar   to pay 1
el **país**   country (*nation*) 4
el **pan**   bread 8
pan tostado   toast R3
la **panadería**   bakery (*for bread*) 17
el **pantalón** (los **pantalones**) pants 5
el **papá**   father, dad 3
los **papás**   parents 3
el **papel**   paper 13
la **papelería**   stationery store 17
para   for, to 2
el **paraguas**   umbrella 7
parecer   to seem 1; (*rev. constr.*) to think, have an opinion of 6
la **pared**   wall 14
la **parte**   part 4
a todas partes   everywhere 9
la **partida de nacimiento**   birth certificate 13
el **partido**   match, game 16
pasado   past, last
pasado mañana   the day after tomorrow 1
el **pasado**   the past 10
el **pasaporte**   passport 13
pasar   to spend (*time*) 2; to show (*a film*) 15
¿Qué pasa?   What's the matter? 18
la **pastelería**   pastry shop 17

la **pastilla** pill 3
  patinar to skate 16
  pedir (e → i) to ask for, order 6
  peinarse to comb one's hair 9
la **pelea de gallos** cockfight R6
la **película** film 15
el **peligro** danger 18
el **pelo** hair 17
la **pelota** ball 16
la **peluquería** barber shop, hairdresser's 17
  pensar (e → ie) to think 5
    pensar (+ inf.) to intend to, expect to 5
  peor worse 3
  pequeño small, short, little 4
  perder (e → ie) to lose 9
  perdone excuse me 1
  perfectamente well, fine 3
el **perfume** perfume 17
el **periódico** newspaper 6
  permitir to permit, allow 11
  pero but 1
el **perro** dog 18
la **persona** person 12
  personal personal 10
  pesar: a pesar de in spite of 10
la **pescadería** fish store 17
el **pescado** fish 8
el (la) **pesimista** pessimist 2
el **peso** monetary unit 7; weight 12
el **petróleo** oil 18
el **piano** piano 15
  picante spicy 7
el **pie** foot 12
la **pierna** leg 12
la **piñata** paper receptacle that is filled with candies and toys and is broken with a stick at children's birthday parties 16
  pintar to paint 14
la **piscina** swimming pool 7
el **plan** plan 16
  en plan de intending to R6
la **planilla** form, slip 11
la **plata** money 11
el **plátano** banana 8
el **plato** plate, dish 8
la **playa** beach 7

la **plaza** square, plaza 7
el **plomero** plumber 18
la **pluma** pen 6
el **poblado** town R2
  pobre poor 11
  poco little (*not much*) 1
  pocos (-as) few 2
  poder (o → ue; irreg.) can, to be able to 5
el (la) **policía** policeman, policewoman 13
  policíaco (*adj.*) police 15
la **política** politics 18
el **político** politician R6
el **pollo** chicken 8
  poner (*irreg.*) to put 8; to turn on (*an appliance*) 14
    poner la mesa to set the table 8
    ponerse to put on (*clothing*) 9
    ponerse + adj. to become 12
  por for, by, through, around 1
    por desgracia unfortunately 1
    por Dios gosh 2
    por eso therefore, that's why 9
    por favor please 8
    por fin finally 10
    por primera vez for the first time 9
  ¿por qué? why? 2
  porque because 2
  portugués Portuguese 1
  posible possible 9
el **postre** dessert 8
el **precio** price 5
  precioso lovely 17
  precisamente exactly, for that reason 16
  preferir (e → ie) to prefer 5
  preguntar to ask 14
  preocupado worried 3
  preocuparse to worry 14
  preparar to prepare 8
  presentar to present 15
el **presente** present (*time*) 10
el **préstamo** loan 11
la **prima (el primo)** cousin 3
la **primavera** spring 10
  primero first 9
el **principio** beginning R4

la **prisa: tener prisa** to be in a hurry 9
  probable probable 11
  probar (o → ue) to taste, try 8
el **problema** problem 11
  producir (*irreg.*) to produce 18
la **profesión** profession 10
el **profesor (la profesora)** teacher, professor 2
el **programa** program 18
  prohibir to forbid 11
  pronto soon 7
la **propina** tip 8
el **pueblo** town 18
la **puerta** door 14
  Puerto Rico Puerto Rico 4
  puertorriqueño Puerto Rican 4
  pues (*interj.*) well 3
el **pulmón** lung 12

Q

  que that, which 2
  ¿qué? what? 1
    ¿qué tal? how are you? 2
    ¡qué va! are you kidding?, of course not 1
  quedar (*rev. constr.*) to have left 6; to be (*located*) 7
  quedarse to stay, remain 9
  quejarse to complain 9
  querer (e → ie; irreg.) to want; to love 5
  querido dear 7
el **queso** cheese 8
  ¿quién? (*pl.* **¿quiénes?**) who? 1
la **química** chemistry 2
  quince fifteen 3
  quinientos five hundred 9
  quinto fifth 13
  quitarse to take off (*clothing*) 9; to go away, get out of there R5
  quizás perhaps 5

R

el (la) **radio** 14
el (la) **radioyente** radio listener 15
  rápidamente rapidly, fast 12
la **raqueta** racket 16

raro strange R3
el **rato** while, period of time 9
la **razón** reason R5
  tener razón to be right 9
realizar to attain, achieve 10
realmente really 11
el (la) **recepcionista** receptionist 6
la **receta** prescription 12
  recibir to receive 7
  recoger (g → j/a, o) to pick (*crops*) 13
  recorrer to travel through R6
el **regalo** gift 5
  relajarse to relax 14
el **reloj** watch, clock 14
el **remedio** remedy, alternative 6
  no me queda más remedio I have no choice 6
  reparar to repair 17
la **república** republic 13
el **restaurante** restaurant 1
  retirar to withdraw 11
el **retiro** withdrawal 11
la **reunión** gathering R4
  reunirse to get together R4
la **revista** magazine 17
  rico delicious 8; rich 11
el **río** river 18
  rojo red 5
  romper to break, tear, rip 12
la **ropa** clothes 5
  rubio blond, fair-skinned 4
  Rusia Russia 4
  ruso Russian 1

S

el **sábado** Saturday 1
  saber (*irreg.*) to know 5
    saber (+ *inf.*) to know how to do something 16
  sacar to take out, get 9
    sacar buenas / malas notas to get good / bad grades 2
el **saco** jacket 5
la **sala** living room 9
  salir (*irreg.*) to go out, leave 7
la **salud** health 12
  saludar to greet, say hello 9
el **sandwich** sandwich 8
la **sangre** blood 12

la **secadora** dryer 14
la **sección** department (*in a store*) 5
el **secretario (la secretaria)** secretary 6
la **sed** thirst 9
  tener sed to be thirsty 9
  según according to 16
  segundo second 13
  seguro secure, sure 18
  seis six 3
  seiscientos six hundred 9
el **sello** stamp 17
la **semana** week 2
  la semana que viene next week 2
  sencillo simple 15
  sensible sensitive 15
  sentarse (e → ie) to sit down 14
  sentir (e → ie; e → i) to regret, be sorry 11
  sentirse to feel 9
el **señor** man, Mr., sir 1
la **señora** woman, Mrs., Madame 1
la **señorita** young woman, Miss 1
  septiembre September 6
  séptimo seventh 13
  ser to be (*irreg.*) 4
la **servilleta** napkin 8
  sesenta sixty 5
  setecientos seven hundred 9
  setenta seventy 5
  sexto sixth 13
  sí yes 1
  si if 5
la **sicología** psychology 2
  siempre always 3
la **siesta** nap 9
  siete seven 3
la **silla** chair 14
  simpático nice, likeable 16
  sin without 6
  sin embargo however 6
la **sinagoga** synagogue 17
el **sindicato** union 18
  sobre about 10
el **sobre** envelope 17
la **sobremesa** afterdinner conversation R3
el **sobrino** nephew 16

la **soda** soda 8
el **sofá** couch 14
el **sol** sun 7
  solamente only 13
  solicitar to apply for 6
  sólo only 5
  soltero unmarried R4
la **sopa** soup 8
  sorprender to surprise 11
  su(s) his, her, its, their, your 3
  sucio dirty 17
  Sudamérica South America 4
el **sueldo** salary 6
el **sueño** dream 10
la **suerte** luck 9
el **suéter** sweater 5
  suficiente enough 11
  sufrir (de) to suffer (with), have (*a disease*) 12
el **supermercado** supermarket 1
el **sur** south 13

T

  tal vez perhaps 11
el **talento** talent 15
el **taller** garage (*for car repair*) 17
  también also 5
  tampoco neither, not either 12
  tan so, as 4
  tanto (-a, -os, -as) so many 2
la **taquilla** box office, ticket office 15
  tarde late 2
la **tarde** afternoon, evening 3
la **tarjeta de crédito** credit card 11
la **tarjeta postal** post card 17
el **taxi** taxi 7
la **taza** cup 8
el **té** tea 8
el **teatro** theater 15
la **tecnología** technology 18
el **teléfono** telephone 15
la **televisión** television 14
la **temperatura** temperature 12
  temprano early 2
el **tenedor** fork 8
  tener (*irreg.*) to have 3
    tener X años to be X years old 10

tener calor   to be warm 10
tener cuidado   to be careful 10
tener la culpa   to be to blame 10
tener éxito   to be successful 9
tener frío   to be cold (*of people*) 9
tener ganas de (+ *inf.*)   to feel like doing something 9
tener hambre   to be hungry 9
tener miedo   to be afraid 9
tener prisa   to be in a hurry 9
tener que (+ *inf.*)   to have to 3
tener razón   to be right 9
tener sed   to be thirsty 9
tener sueño   to be sleepy 9
tener suerte   to be lucky 9
tener vergüenza   to be ashamed 10
el tenis   tennis 16
tercero   third 13
terminar   to finish, end 6
el terror   terror 15
el tiempo   time 2; weather 7
a tiempo   on time 2
la tienda   store 1
la tía   aunt 3
la tintorería   cleaner's 17
el tío   uncle 3
los tíos   aunt and uncle 3
tocar (c → qu/e)   to touch on, be the turn of 11; play an instrument 15
todavía   still, yet 3
todo   all, every 1
tomar   to take 2
tonto   stupid, silly 16
la torta   cake 8
la tortilla   omelette R3
trabajar   to work 1
el trabajo   work, job; term paper 3

la tradición   tradition 10
traer   to bring (*irreg.*) 7
el traje   suit 5
el traje de baño   bathing suit 7
tratar   to treat (*illness*) 12
tratar de (+ *inf.*)   to try to 14
trece   thirteen 3
treinta   thirty 5
tres   three 3
trescientos   three hundred 9
triste   sad 3
tú   you (*informal sing.*) 1
tu, tus   your 3
el turismo   tourism 13

U

último   last R3
la universidad   university 2
uno   one 3
usted (Ud.)   you (*formal sing.*) 1
ustedes (Uds.)   you (*pl.*) 1

V

la vaca   cow 18
las vacaciones   vacation 7
estar de vacaciones   to be on vacation 7
valer (*irreg.*)   to cost, be worth 17
el valor   value 10
varios   several 5
el vaso   glass (*drinking*) 8
el vecino   neighbor 4
veinte   twenty 3
vender   to sell 5
venezolano   Venezuelan 4
Venezuela   Venezuela 4
venir (*irreg.*)   to come 6
la ventana   window 14
la ventanilla   teller's or ticket window 11
ver (*irreg.*)   to see 5

el verano   summer 10
la verdad   truth 5
verde   green 5
la vergüenza   shame 10
el vestido   dress 5
vestirse (e → i)   to get dressed 9
la vez   time, occasion
otra vez   again 10
viajar   to travel 6
el viaje   trip 7
hacer un viaje   to take a trip 7
la vida   life 2
viejo   old 4
el viento   wind 7
el viernes   Friday 1
el vino   wine 8
el virus   virus 12
la visa   visa 13
visitar   to visit 1
vivir   to live 4
el volibol, el volleyball   volleyball 16
volver (o → ue)   to return, go back 7
volver a (+ *inf.*)   to do something again 10
vosotros (-as)   you (*informal pl. in Spain*) 1
votar   to vote 13
la vuelta: a la vuelta de la esquina   around the corner 17
vuestro   your (*informal pl. in Spain*) 3

Y

y   and 1
ya   already 1
ya no   no longer 10
yo   I 1

Z

la zapatería   shoe store 17
el zapato   shoe 5

English–Spanish

A

a   un(o), una
able: to be able   poder
about   sobre
accident   el accidente
accompany   acompañar
according to   según
account   la cuenta
ache   el dolor; doler
achieve   realizar
actor   el actor
actress   la actriz
ad   el anuncio
adjust to   adaptarse (a)
advise   aconsejar
afraid: to be —   tener miedo
after   después (de)
afternoon   la tarde
afterwards   después, luego
again   otra vez
against   contra
agent   el (la) agente
ago   hace + *time* + *pret*.
agree   estar de acuerdo
agreement   el acuerdo
agriculture   la agricultura
air   el aire
airplane   el avión
airport   el aeropuerto
all   todo (-a, -os, -as)
allow   permitir
almost   casi
already   ya
also   también

alternative   remedio
although   aunque
always   siempre
ambition   la ambición
American   norteamericano
amusing   divertido
an   un(o), una
and   y
angry: to get —   enfadarse
animal   el animal
announcer   la locutora
another   otro (-a)
anthropology   la antropología
antibiotic   el antibiótico
apartment   el apartamento
apple   la manzana
appliance   el aparato
apply (for)   solicitar
appointment   la cita
April   abril
Argentina   la Argentina
Argentine   argentino
arm   el brazo
around   por
   around the corner   a la vuelta
      de la esquina
arrange   arreglar
arrive   llegar
as   como, tan
ashamed: to be ashamed   tener
      vergüenza
ask   preguntar
   ask for   pedir
aspirin   la aspirina
at   en
attend   asistir a
August   agosto
aunt   la tía
autumn   el otoño
avenue   la avenida

B

back: in the —   al fondo
bad   malo
badly   mal
bakery   la panadería (*for bread*)
ball   la pelota
banana   el plátano
bank   el banco
barber shop   la peluquería

bargain   la ganga
baseball   el béisbol
basketball   el baloncesto
bathe   bañarse
bathing suit   el traje de baño
bathroom   el baño
battery   la batería
be   ser, estar
beach   la playa
beautiful   hermoso
because   porque
become   hacerse, ponerse
bed   la cama
   to go to bed   acostarse
   to stay in bed   guardar cama
bedroom   el dormitorio
beer   la cerveza
before   antes (de)
begin   comenzar, empezar
behind   detrás (de)
believe   creer
besides   además (de)
best   el (la) mejor
better   mejor
   to get better   mejorar
bicycle   la bicicleta
   to ride a bicycle   andar en
      bicicleta
big   grande
bilingual   bilingüe
bill   la cuenta, el billete (*currency*)
biology   la biología
birth   el nacimiento
   birth certificate   la partida de
      nacimiento
birthday   el cumpleaños
black   negro
blame   la culpa
   to be to blame   tener la culpa
blond   rubio
blood   la sangre
blouse   la blusa
blue   azul
body   el cuerpo
book   el libro
bookstore   la librería
bore: What a bore!   ¡Qué lata!
bored   aburrido (*with* estar)
boring   aburrido (*with* ser)
born: to be born   nacer
boss   el jefe

bother molestar
box el cajón
box office la taquilla
boy el chico, el muchacho, el niño
boyfriend el novio
brake el freno
Brazil el Brasil
Brazilian brasileño
bread el pan
break romper
breakfast el desayuno
  to have breakfast desayunar
bring traer
broken roto
brother el hermano
brown café, marrón
bus autobús
business los negocios
busy ocupado
but pero
butcher shop la carnicería
buy comprar
by por

C

cake la torta
call llamar
can poder
Canada el Canadá
capital la capital (*city*)
car el coche
card la tarjeta
care el cuidado
  to care about importar
  to take care of oneself cuidarse
careful: to be careful tener
    cuidado
carpenter el carpintero
carpet la alfombra
carry llevar
cash cobrar
cashier el cajero
cat el gato
celebrate celebrar
certain cierto
chair la silla
change cambiar
cheap barato
check la cuenta; el cheque
    (*payment order*)

cheese el queso
chemistry la química
chicken pollo, gallina
Chile Chile
Chilean chileno
choose escoger
church iglesia
citizen el ciudadano
city la ciudad
clash chocar
class la clase
clean limpio
cleaner's la tintorería
clinic la clínica
clock el reloj
close cerrar
closed cerrado
closet el armario
clothes la ropa
cloudy nublado
coffee el café
coin la moneda
coincidence la casualidad
 cold el frío (*temperature*); el
    catarro (*illness*)
  to be cold tener frío
Colombia Colombia
Colombian colombiano
color el color
comb: to comb one's hair
    peinarse
come venir
  to come back volver
comedy la comedia
community la comunidad
company la compañía
complain quejarse
composition la composición
compute calcular
computer programming la
    computación
concert el concierto
consider considerar
contrary: on the contrary al
    contrario
control controlar
cook el cocinero
cool: it's cool (*weather*) hace
    fresco
cost el costo; costar, valer
cotton el algodón

couch el sofá
country el país; el campo (*field*)
course el curso
cousin la prima, el primo
cow la vaca
crazy loco
cream la crema
credit card la tarjeta de crédito
Cuba Cuba
Cuban cubano
culture la cultura; el cultivo (*in
    biology*)
cup la taza
curtain la cortina
custom la costumbre
customer el (la) cliente
cut cortar

D

dad el papá
dance bailar
danger el peligro
dark oscuro
  dark-haired, dark-skinned
    moreno
darling mi amor
date la fecha (*calendar*); la cita
    (*appointment*)
daughter la hija
day el día
dear querido
debut el estreno
December diciembre
decide decidir
degree el grado (*temperature*)
delicious rico
delightful encantador
demand exigir
dentist el, (la) dentista
department (*in store*) la sección
deposit el depósito; depositar
dessert el postre
devote (*oneself to*) dedicarse a
diary el diario
die morir
diet la dieta
different diferente
difficult difícil
dining room el comedor
dinner la cena
  to have dinner cenar

director el director
dirty sucio
discotheque la discoteca
discuss discutir
dishwasher el lavaplatos
divorced: to get divorced
divorciarse
do hacer
doctor el doctor, la doctora; el
(la) médico
dog el perro
dollar el dólar
door la puerta
doubt dudar
downstairs abajo
downtown el centro
drama el drama
drawer la gaveta
dream el sueño
dress el vestido
to get dressed vestirse
dresser la cómoda
drink beber, tomar
drive manejar
driver's license la licencia de
manejar
drugstore la farmacia, la
droguería
dryer la secadora
dub (*a film*) doblar
during durante

E

each cada
ear el oído (*inner*); la oreja (*outer*)
early temprano
earn ganar
east el este
easy fácil
eat comer
ecology la ecología
economics la economía
egg el huevo
eight ocho
eighteen dieciocho
eighth octavo
eighty ochenta
electrical eléctrico
eleven once

employee el empleado
end el fin; terminar
engineer el ingeniero
engineering la ingeniería
England Inglaterra
English inglés
enjoy (*oneself*) divertirse
enough bastante, suficiente
enter entrar (en) (a)
enthusiasm el entusiasmo
envelope el sobre
environment el ambiente
Europe Europa
European europeo
even incluso
evening la tarde
everywhere a todas partes
evident evidente
exactly efectivamente,
precisamente
exam el examen
examine examinar
excellent excelente
exciting emocionante
exercise el ejercicio
expensive caro
experience la experiencia
explain explicar
export exportar
eye el ojo
eyeglasses los anteojos

F

face la cara
facing en frente de
factory la fábrica
fall (*season*) el otoño
fall caer
fall asleep dormirse
family la familia
famous famoso
fan (*devotee*) el aficionado
far (*from*) lejos (de)
farm la finca
fast rápidamente
fat gordo
father el padre, el papá
favorite favorito
fear el miedo

to be afraid tener miedo
February febrero
feel sentirse
**to feel like doing
something** tener ganas de
+ *inf.*
fever la fiebre
few pocos (-as)
fifteen quince
fifth quinto
fifty cincuenta
fight luchar
fill llenar
film la película
finally por fin
find encontrar
finish terminar, acabar
firefighter el bombero
first primero
fish el pescado
fishstore la pescadería
five cinco
fix arreglar
flower la flor
flower shop la florería
flu la gripe
food la comida
foot el pie
football el fútbol americano
for para, por
forbid prohibir
foreign extranjero
forget olvidarse
forgive perdonar
fork el tenedor
form (*paper*) el formulario, la
planilla
fortunately menos mal
four cuatro
fourteen catorce
fourth cuarto
France Francia
French francés
Friday el viernes
friend el amigo, la amiga
from de, desde
front: in front of delante de
fruit la fruta
funds los fondos
furniture los muebles
future el futuro

G

gain: to gain weight aumentar de peso
game el partido
garage el taller (*for car repair*)
garden el jardín
garment worker la operaria (*N.Y. Span.*)
gasoline la gasolina
gas station la gasolinera
German alemán
Germany Alemania
get conseguir, recibir, sacar (*a grade*)
   to get up levantarse
   to get along well / badly with llevarse bien / mal con
gift el regalo
girl la chica, la muchacha, la niña
girlfriend la novia
give dar
glass (*drinking*) el vaso
glove el guante
go ir
   to go away irse
   to go out salir
good bueno
good-bye adiós
good-looking guapo
goods los bienes
gosh! ¡caray!, ¡por Dios!
government el gobierno
grade (*mark*) la nota
graduate graduarse
grandfather el abuelo
grandmother la abuela
grandparents los abuelos
great fantástico
green verde
greet saludar
grey gris
grocery store la bodega
group el grupo
guest el invitado
guidebook la guía
guitar la guitarra

H

hair el pelo

hairdresser's la peluquería
half media
hand la mano
   on the other hand en cambio
hand in entregar
hang colgar
happen pasar
happy feliz, contento, alegre
   to be happy alegrarse
have tener
   to have to tener que + *inf.*, necesitar + *inf.*
he él
head la cabeza
   headache el dolor de cabeza
health la salud
hear oír
heart el corazón
heat el calor
hello hola
help ayudar
her su (*poss.*); la (*d.o.*); le (*i.o.*); ella (*after prep.*)
herb la hierba
here aquí
high alto
high school el colegio
him lo (*d.o.*); le (*i.o.*); él (*after prep.*)
his su
history la historia
hit (*success*) el exitazo
home la casa
   at home en casa
homerun el jonrón
hope esperar
   I hope ojalá
horse el caballo
hospital el hospital
hotel el hotel
hour la hora
house la casa
how? ¿cómo?
however sin embargo
how many? ¿cuántos (-as)?
how much? ¿cuánto (-a)?
hundred ciento, cien
hunger el hambre (*fem.*)
   to be hungry tener hambre
hurry: to be in a hurry tener prisa
hurt doler

husband el esposo, el marido

I

I yo
ice cream el helado
idea la idea
identification card la tarjeta de identidad
if si
illegally ilegalmente
immediately en seguida, inmediatamente
immigrant el (la) inmigrante
immigration la inmigración
import importar
important importante
impossible imposible
improbable improbable
in en
increase aumentar
indeed efectivamente
industry la industria
infection la infección
inflation la inflación
information la información
injury la herida
insist (on) insistir (en)
insulted: to get insulted ofenderse
intelligent inteligente
intend to pensar + *inf.*
interest el interés
interested: to be interested in interesar
interesting interesante
invite invitar
Ireland Irlanda
Irish irlandés
it él, ella (*subj. and after prep.*); lo, la (*d.o.*); le (*i.o.*)
Italian italiano
Italy Italia

J

jacket el saco
January enero
jewelry store la joyería
job el trabajo, el empleo
joint account (*bank*) cuenta conjunta

juice el jugo
July julio
June junio

K

keep guardar
key la llave
kilometer el kilómetro
kind (*adj.*) amable
kitchen la cocina
knife el cuchillo
know saber; conocer
 to know how to do something saber + *inf.*

L

lamp la lámpara
language el idioma
last (*adj.*) pasado; el pasado
 last night anoche
late tarde
Latin America Latinoamérica
laundry la lavandería
law (*subject*) el derecho
lawyer el (la) abogado
learn aprender
leave salir; dejar (+ *d.o.*)
left (*direction*) izquierda
 to, at, on the left a la izquierda
left: to have left quedar
leg la pierna
legally legalmente
lens el lente
 contact lenses los lentes de contacto
less menos
letter la carta
library la biblioteca
license la licencia
lie down echarse
life la vida
light la luz; claro (*in color*)
like (*something*) gustar
like como
 like this, like that así
line (*of people*) la cola
listen escuchar

little pequeño; poco (*quantity*)
literature la literatura
live vivir
living room la sala
loan el préstamo
long largo
look at mirar
 look for buscar
lose perder
lot: a lot of mucho (-a), muchos (-as)
love el amor, el cariño; encantar (*things*); querer (*people*)
lovely precioso, lindo
low bajo
lucky: to be lucky tener suerte
lunch el almuerzo
 to have lunch almorzar
lung el pulmón

M

machine la máquina
magazine la revista
magnificent magnífico
mail: to mail a letter echar una carta
 mailbox el buzón
make hacer
makeup el maquillaje
man el hombre, el señor
many muchos (-as)
map el mapa
March marzo
market el mercado
marriage license el certificado de matrimonio
married casado
 to get married casarse con
mathematics las matemáticas
May mayo
meal la comida
meanwhile mientras tanto
meat la carne
mechanic el mecánico
medicine la medicina
menu la carta
Mexican mexicano
Mexico México
mile la milla

milk la leche
million el millón
mirror el espejo
Miss la señorita
missing: to be missing (*lacking*) faltar
modern moderno
Monday el lunes
money el dinero, la plata
month el mes
more más
morning la mañana
most of la mayor parte de
mother la madre, la mamá
mouth la boca
move (*change residence*) la mudanza; mudarse
mover el cargador
movies el cine
movie house el cine
Mr. el señor
Mrs. la señora
much mucho
museum el museo
music la música
musician el músico
must deber
my mi

N

nap la siesta
napkin la servilleta
national nacional
nationality la nacionalidad
nauseous: to be nauseous tener náuseas
near cerca (de)
necessary necesario
need necesitar; hacer falta
neighbor el vecino
neighborhood el barrio
neither tampoco, ni
nephew el sobrino
never nunca
new nuevo
newspaper el periódico
next (to) al lado (de)
nice amable, simpático
night la noche

nine nueve
nineteen diecinueve
ninety noventa
ninth noveno
no no; ningún, ninguna
nobody nadie
no longer ya no
none ninguno, ninguna
nor ni
north el norte
nose la nariz
not no
nothing nada
nothing doing! ¡ni hablar!
November noviembre
now ahora
   right now ahora mismo
nurse el enfermero, la enfermera

O

ocean el océano
occur (*to someone*) ocurrírsele
October octubre
of de
of course claro
office la oficina
official el funcionario
oil el aceite, el petróleo
old viejo
older, oldest mayor
on en
one uno
only sólo, solamente
open abrir
opened abierto
opportunity la oportunidad
opposite (*location*) en frente de
optimism el optimismo
or o
orange la naranja
orange (-colored) anaranjado
orchestra la orquesta
order mandar; pedir (*in a restaurant*)
origin el origen
original original
ought deber
our nuestro
outside (of) fuera (de)

overcoat el abrigo

P

pain el dolor
paint pintar
painting (*picture*) el cuadro
pants el pantalón, los pantalones
paper el papel
papers (*official*) los documentos
parents los padres, los papás
part la parte
party la fiesta
passbook (*bank*) la libreta
passport el pasaporte
past el pasado
pastry shop la pastelería
patient el (la) paciente
pay pagar
pay attention to hacerle caso
peasant el campesino
pen la pluma
pencil el lápiz
people la gente
perfume el perfume
perhaps quizás
permit permitir
person la persona
personal personal
pessimist el, la pesimista
photograph la fotografía
physics la física
piano el piano
pick (*crops*) recoger
pill la pastilla
pity la lástima
place el lugar
plate el plato
play (*theater*) la comedia, la obra
play jugar, tocar
player el jugador
playwright el dramaturgo
please por favor
pleasure el gusto
plot (*story*) el argumento
plumber el plomero
police (*adj.*) policíaco
policeman, policewoman el, la policía
political science las ciencias

políticas
politics la política
polluted contaminado
pollution la contaminación
poor pobre
Portuguese portugués
possible posible
postcard la tarjeta postal
post office el correo
prefer preferir
prepare preparar
prescription la receta
present el presente (*time*); el regalo (*gift*)
present (*time*) (*adj.*) actual
present presentar
pretty bonito, lindo
prevent impedir
price el precio
probable probable
problem el problema
produce producir
profession la profesión
program el programa
provided that con tal que
psychology la sicología
Puerto Rican puertorriqueño
Puerto Rico Puerto Rico
put poner
   to put away (*things*) guardar
   to put on ponerse (*clothing*)

R

racket la raqueta
radio el (la) radio
rain llover
raincoat el impermeable
read leer
ready listo
realize darse cuenta de
really realmente
receive recibir
receptionist el (la) recepcionista
record el disco
refrigerator la nevera
red rojo
relax relajarse
remember acordarse (de)
repair reparar

report el informe
republic la república
rest descansar
restaurant el restaurante
return volver
rice el arroz
rich rico
right el derecho
  to be right tener razón
  to (on, at) the right a la derecha
river el río
room el cuarto
run correr
Russia Rusia
Russian ruso

S

sad triste
salad la ensalada
salary el sueldo
salesperson el (la) dependiente
same mismo
sandwich el sandwich
Saturday el sábado
save ahorrar
savings account la cuenta de
  ahorros
say decir
school la escuela; el colegio
science la ciencia
season la estación
second segundo
secretary el secretario
see ver
seem parecer
sell vender
send mandar
sensitive sensible
September septiembre
serious grave
settle: to get settled in instalarse
seven siete
seventeen diecisiete
seventh séptimo
seventy setenta
several varios
shame la lástima, la vergüenza
  to be ashamed tener vergüenza
shave afeitarse
she ella

shirt la camisa
shoe el zapato
shoe store la zapatería
shop: to go shopping ir de
  compras
short bajo, corto, pequeño
show el espectáculo, la función;
  enseñar
shower: to take a shower
  ducharse
sick mal, enfermo
sickness la enfermedad
side el lado
sign firmar
simple sencillo
since desde
sing cantar
sister la hermana
sit down sentarse
six seis
sixteen dieciséis
sixth sexto
sixty sesenta
skate patinar
skirt la falda
sleep dormir
  to be sleepy tener sueño
slowly lentamente
small pequeño
snow nevar
so tan
soap el jabón
soccer el fútbol
sock el calcetín
soda la soda
so many tantos (-as)
so much tanto (-a)
some unos, unas; alguno (-a),
  algunos (-as)
  some day algún día
someone alguien
something algo
son el hijo
song la canción
soon pronto
sorry: to be sorry sentir
  I'm sorry lo siento
soup la sopa
south el sur
South America Sudamérica
Spanish español

Spanish America
  Hispanoamérica
speak hablar
spend gastar; pasar (*time*)
spicy picante
spite: in spite of a pesar de
sport el deporte
spring la primavera
square la plaza
stadium el estadio
stamp el sello
stationery store la papelería
stay quedarse
stereo el estéreo
stew (*also stewpot*) la cazuela
still todavía
stomach el estómago
store el almacén, la tienda
street la calle
strike (*work stoppage*) la huelga
student el, la estudiante
study estudiar
stupid tonto
style el modelo
subject (*school*) la materia
successful: to be successful
  tener éxito
suffer sufrir
suit el traje
  bathing suit el traje de baño
suitcase la maleta
summer el verano
sun el sol
sunburned bronceado
Sunday el domingo
supermarket el supermercado
support mantener
sure seguro
surprise sorprender
sweater el suéter
swimming pool la piscina
synagogue la sinagoga

T

table la mesa
  to set the table poner la mesa
tablespoon la cuchara
take tomar, llevar
  take off (*clothing*) quitarse
talent el talento

tall alto

taste probar

taxi el taxi

tea el té

teach enseñar

teacher el profesor, la profesora

team el equipo

tear romper

teaspoon la cucharita

technology la tecnología

telephone el teléfono

television la televisión

tell decir

teller el cajero

temperature la temperatura

tennis el tenis

ten diez

tenth décimo

terrific magnífico, estupendo

terror el terror

test el examen; el análisis (*medical*)

thank you gracias

that que (*conj.*); ese, esa, aquel, aquella (*dem.*); eso, aquello (*neut.*)

theater el teatro

their su

then entonces, luego

there allí, ahí

there is, there are hay

therefore por eso

they ellos, ellas

thin delgado

thing la cosa

think pensar, creer

third tercero

thirsty: to be thirsty tener sed

thirteen trece

thirty treinta

this este, esta (*dem.*); esto (*neut.*)

three tres

throat la garganta

through por

throw echar

Thursday el jueves

ticket el boleto

tie (*score*) empatar; la corbata (*necktie*)

time el tiempo; la hora (*of the clock*); la vez (*occasion*)

on time a tiempo

tip la propina

tire (*car*) la llanta

tired cansado

to a

today hoy

together juntos

tomorrow mañana

day after tomorrow pasado mañana

too también

too many demasiados (-as)

too much demasiado (-a)

touch tocar

tourism el turismo

toward hacia

town el pueblo

trade (*line of work*) el oficio

tradition la tradición

travel viajar

treat (*an illness*) tratar

trip el viaje

to take a trip hacer un viaje

true cierto

truth la verdad

try tratar de + *inf.*

Tuesday el martes

turn doblar

turn off (*appliance*) apagar

turn on (*appliance*) poner

twelve doce

twenty veinte

two dos

typewriter la máquina para escribir

typist el mecanógrafo

U

ugly feo

umbrella el paraguas

unbearable insoportable

uncle el tío

understand comprender, entender

unemployment el desempleo

unfortunately por desgracia

union el sindicato

United States los Estados Unidos

university la universidad

unpleasant antipático,

desagradable

until hasta

upset inquieto

upstairs arriba

V

vacation las vacaciones

to be on vacation estar de vacaciones

value el valor

vegetable la legumbre

Venezuela Venezuela

Venezuelan venezolano

very muy

virus el virus

visa la visa

visit visitar

volleyball el volibol; el volleyball

vote votar

W

wait esperar

waiter el mozo

waitress la moza

wake up despertarse

walk caminar, andar

wall la pared

want querer, desear

warm: to be warm (*person*) tener calor; (*weather*) hacer calor

wash lavarse

watch el reloj

water el agua (*fem.*)

we nosotros (-as)

wear (*clothing*) llevar

weather el tiempo

Wednesday el miércoles

week la semana

next week la semana que viene

weekend el fin de semana

weight el peso

to gain weight aumentar de peso

welcome: you're welcome de nada

well bien, perfectamente; bueno (*interj.*), pues (*interj.*)

west el oeste

what? ¿qué?

when? ¿cuándo?

where? ¿dónde?; ¿adónde? (*with verbs of motion*)

which? ¿cuál?, ¿cuáles?

  which que (*conj.*)

while mientras tanto; un rato (*period of time*)

white blanco

who? ¿quién?, ¿quiénes?

why? ¿por qué?

wife la esposa, la mujer, la señora

win ganar

wind el viento

  it's windy hace viento

window la ventana; la ventanilla (*of a bank*)

wine el vino

winter el invierno

with con

withdraw retirar

withdrawal el retiro

without sin

witty gracioso

woman la mujer, la señora

wonderful maravilloso

work el trabajo; trabajar

  to work as a — trabajar de + *occupation*

worker el obrero

world el mundo

worried preocupado

worry preocuparse

worse peor

  to get worse empeorar

worth: to be worth valer

write escribir

wrong equivocado

Y

year el año

yellow amarillo

yes sí

yesterday ayer

you tú (*informal sing.*); Ud. (*formal sing.*); vosotros, vosotras (*informal pl.*); Uds. (*formal pl.*)

young joven

younger, youngest menor

your tu, su, vuestro; tuyo, suyo

Z

zoo el jardín zoológico

Index

1 2 3 4 5 6 7 8 9 0